The **ANU Indonesia Project**, a leading international centre of research and graduate training on the Indonesian economy and society, is housed in the **Crawford School of Public Policy's Arndt-Corden Department of Economics.** The Crawford School is part of **ANU College of Asia and the Pacific** at **The Australian National University (ANU).** Established in 1965 in response to profound changes in the Indonesian economic and political landscapes, the ANU Indonesia Project has grown from a small group of Indonesia-focused economists into an interdisciplinary research centre well known and respected across the world. Funded by ANU and the Australian Department of Foreign Affairs and Trade, the ANU Indonesia Project monitors and analyses recent developments in Indonesia; informs the Australian and Indonesian governments, business and the wider community about those developments and about future prospects; stimulates research on the Indonesian economy; and publishes the respected *Bulletin of Indonesian Economic Studies*.

ANU College of Asia and the Pacific's **Department of Political and Social Change** focuses on domestic politics, social processes and state–society relationships in Asia and the Pacific, and has a long-established interest in Indonesia.

Together with the Department of Political and Social Change, the ANU Indonesia Project holds the annual Indonesia Update conference, which offers an overview of recent economic and political developments and devotes attention to a significant theme in Indonesia's development. The *Bulletin of Indonesian Economic Studies* publishes the conference's economic and political overviews, while the edited papers related to the conference theme are published in the Indonesia Update Series.

The **ISEAS – Yusof Ishak Institute** (formerly Institute of Southeast Asian Studies) was established as an autonomous organization in 1968. It is a regional centre dedicated to the study of socio-political, security and economic trends and developments in Southeast Asia and its wider geostrategic and economic environment. The Institute's research programmes are the Regional Economic Studies (RES, including ASEAN and APEC), Regional Strategic and Political Studies (RSPS), and Regional Social and Cultural Studies (RSCS).

ISEAS Publishing, an established academic press, has issued more than 2,000 books and journals. It is the largest scholarly publisher of research about Southeast Asia from within the region. ISEAS Publishing works with many other academic and trade publishers and distributors to disseminate important research and analyses from and about Southeast Asia to the rest of the world.

DIGITAL
INDONESIA

Indonesia Update Series

DIGITAL INDONESIA

CONNECTIVITY AND DIVERGENCE

EDITED BY
EDWIN JURRIËNS
ROSS TAPSELL

First published in Singapore in 2017 by
ISEAS Publishing
30 Heng Mui Keng Terrace
Singapore 119614

E-mail: publish@iseas.edu.sg
Website: http://bookshop.iseas.edu.sg

ISEAS Library Cataloguing-in-Publication Data

Digital Indonesia : Connectivity and Divergence / Edited by Edwin Jurriëns and Ross Tapsell.
This book emanates from the Indonesia Update 2016 Conference presented by the Indonesia Project at Crawford School of Public Policy, The Australian National University and held on 18-19 September 2016.
1. Internet—Political aspects—Indonesia—Congresses.
2. Internet—Social aspects—Indonesia—Congresses.
3. Internet—Economic aspects—Indonesia—Congresses.
I. Jurriëns, Edwin, 1972-
II. Tapsell, Ross, 1981-
III. Australian National University. Indonesia Project.
IV. Indonesia Update Conference (34th : 2016 : Australian National University)

DS644.4 I41 2016 2017

ISBN 978-981-47-6298-4 (soft cover)
ISBN 978-981-47-6299-1 (hard cover)
ISBN 978-981-47-8600-3 (e-book, PDF)

Cover photo: Indonesian President Joko Widodo and Australian Prime Minister Malcolm Turnbull taking a 'selfie' at Tanah Abang market in Jakarta in November 2015.
Photo by Rusman Joni. Reproduced with permission from the Ministry of State Secretariat of the Republic of Indonesia.

Edited and typeset by Beth Thomson, Japan Online, Canberra
Indexed by Angela Grant, Sydney
Printed in Singapore by Markono Print Media Pte Ltd

Contents

Tables

Figures

Contributors

Kathleen Azali, Founder, C2O library & collabtive, Surabaya; and Research Officer, ISEAS - Yusof Ishak Institute, Singapore

Emma Baulch, Senior Research Fellow, Digital Media Research Centre, School of Communication, Queensland University of Technology, Brisbane

Grace Dewi, PhD Candidate, Department of Management and Global Business, Rutgers Business School, Newark and New Brunswick

Michele Ford, Professor of Southeast Asian Studies, Director, Sydney Southeast Asia Centre, and ARC Future Fellow, University of Sydney, Sydney

Usman Hamid, Indonesia Director, Amnesty International, Jakarta

Agung Hikmat, Advisor and Senior Official for Open Government, Executive Office of the President (Kantor Staf Presiden), Republic of Indonesia, Jakarta

Vivian Honan, Research Assistant, Sydney Southeast Asia Centre, University of Sydney, Sydney

Edwin Jurriëns, Lecturer in Indonesian Studies, Asia Institute, University of Melbourne, Melbourne; and Visiting Fellow, School of Humanities and Social Sciences, University of New South Wales, Canberra

Bede Moore, Co-founder and former Managing Director, Lazada Indonesia; Co-founder, Paraplou Group; and Founder and Chair, Conference for Australian and Indonesian Youth (CAUSINDY)

Yanuar Nugroho, Honorary Research Fellow, Manchester Institute of Innovation Research, University of Manchester, Manchester; and

Deputy Chief of Staff for Analysis and Oversight of Strategic Issues on Social, Cultural and Ecological Affairs, Executive Office of the President (Kantor Staf Presiden), Republic of Indonesia, Jakarta

Nava Nuraniyah, Analyst, Institute for Policy Analysis of Conflict (IPAC), Jakarta

Mari Pangestu, Former Minister of Trade (2004–11) and Former Minister of Tourism and Creative Economy (2011–14); currently Professor of International Economics, University of Indonesia, Jakarta

John Postill, Senior Lecturer, School of Media and Communication, RMIT University, Melbourne

Onno W. Purbo, Trainer, XECUREIT, Jakarta

Budi Rahardjo, Lecturer, School of Electrical Engineering and Informatics, Bandung Institute of Technology (Institut Teknologi Bandung), Bandung

Kurniawan Saputro, Lecturer, Indonesian Institute of the Arts Yogyakarta (Institut Seni Indonesia Yogyakarta), Yogyakarta

Martin Slama, Researcher, Institute for Social Anthropology, Austrian Academy of Sciences, Vienna

Ross Tapsell, Lecturer in Asian Studies, ANU College of Asia and the Pacific, Australian National University, Canberra

Acknowledgments

With the exception of the introductory chapter, all contributions to this volume are revised versions of papers that were presented at the thirty-fourth annual Indonesia Update conference held at the Australian National University (ANU), Canberra, on 16–17 September 2016. We would like to thank the authors for sharing their expertise—both at the conference and for this edited collection—on the impact of digital technologies across a wide array of disciplines and fields.

We are grateful to the institution that organises and hosts the conference, the Indonesia Project at the ANU. Special thanks to the Director of the Indonesia Project, Budy Resosudarmo, for his support and guidance throughout the entire process, from conceiving the idea for the conference through to publication and the plans for launching the book. Many thanks also to the staff members of the Indonesia Project, whose support was crucial in facilitating the conference and other activities related to this publication. We wish to specifically and gratefully acknowledge the tireless work of Kate McLinton, Nurkemala Muliani and Lolita Moorena.

Thanks to both Murdoch University's Asia Institute and the Lowy Institute for International Policy for supporting this research in the form of 'mini-updates' at their respective institutions, held immediately after the ANU conference.

The Department of Foreign Affairs and Trade has been a long-term supporter of the Indonesia Update through its grant to the Indonesia Project. We gratefully acknowledge that support, which has helped make the ANU a leading centre for the study of Indonesia's economy and society, and without which the conference and this book would not have been possible.

Special thanks to Beth Thomson, whose superb editorial work made this process a pleasure to be involved in. Her professionalism and efficiency were crucial to the thoroughness and swift publication of this book.

We are also very grateful for the ongoing support of the ISEAS - Yusof Ishak Institute in Singapore, which has been publishing the Indonesia Update series since 1994. Special thanks to Rahilah Yusuf and Ng Kok Kiong for their hard work during the production process.

Edwin Jurriëns and Ross Tapsell
Canberra, March 2017

Glossary

ACM-ICPC	Association of Computing Machinery International Collegiate Programming Contest
AFP	Australian Federal Police
Ahok	Basuki Tjahaja Purnama (Jakarta's governor)
APCERT	Asia Pacific Computer Emergency Response Team
APJII	Asosiasi Penyelenggara Jasa Internet Indonesia (Indonesian Internet Service Providers Association)
aqidah	theological teaching, creed
ARPANET	Advanced Research Projects Agency Network
ASEAN	Association of Southeast Asian Nations
bajaj	three-wheel vehicle
Bappenas	Badan Perencanaan Pembangunan Nasional (National Development Planning Agency)
BCN	Badan Cyber Nasional (National Cybersecurity Agency)
BIG	Badan Informasi Geospasial (Geospatial Information Agency)
BIN	Badan Intelijen Negara (State Intelligence Agency)
BKPM	Badan Koordinasi Penanaman Modal (Investment Coordinating Board)
BP3TI	Balai Penyedia dan Pengelola Pembiayaan Telekomunikasi dan Informatika (Telecommunications and Informatics Funding Provision and Management Agency)
BPS	Badan Pusat Statistik (Statistics Indonesia)
CCC	Chaos Computer Club
CDN	content delivery network
CERN	European Organisation for Nuclear Research
CERT	Computer Emergency Response Team
CISA	Certified Information Systems Auditor

CISSP	Certified Information Systems Security Professional
dakwah	proselytisation
DDoS	distributed denial of service (attack)
Desa Pinter	Desa Punya Internet (The Village Has Internet, or Smart Village, program)
DNS	domain name system
DoS	denial of service (attack)
DPR	Dewan Perwakilan Rakyat (People's Representative Council); the lower house of parliament
e-KTP	Kartu Tanda Penduduk Elektronik (Elektronic Resident Identity Card)
FDD	Forum Demokrasi Digital (Digital Democracy Forum)
fintech	financial technology
fiqh	Islamic law
Garuda	Garba Rujukan Digital
Gashibu	Gerakan Sehari Seribu (Thousand Rupiah a Day Movement)
GDL	Ganesha Digital Library
GDP	gross domestic product
Gerakan Nasional 1000 Startup Digital	National Movement for 1,000 Digital Start-ups
GFC	global financial crisis
GSM	Global System for Mobile Communications
GSRB	Gerakan Seni Rupa Baru (New Art Movement)
hadith	report or account of the words and deeds of the Prophet Muhammad transmitted through a chain of narrators
hajj	annual pilgrimage to Mecca
hijab	head covering worn by Muslim women
hijrah	'journey', migration'; refers to the migration or journey of the Prophet Muhammad and his followers from Mecca to Medina in 622 CE
HP	hand phone (mobile phone)
ICT	information and communication technology
ID-CERT	Indonesia Computer Emergency Response Team
ID-SIRTII	Indonesia Security Incident Response Team on Internet and Infrastructure
IDLN	Indonesian Digital Libraries Network (IndonesiaDLN)
IEC	International Electrotechnical Commission
InCU-VL	Indonesian Christian University Virtual Library
IndonesiaDLN	Indonesian Digital Libraries Network

InherentDL	Indonesia Higher Education Network
IP	Internet Protocol
IPI	Ikatan Pustakawan Indonesia (Indonesian Librarian Association)
ISAD	Indonesian Street Art Database
ISIPII	Ikatan Sarjana Ilmu Perpustakaan dan Informasi Indonesia (Indonesian Association of Library and Information Science Scholars)
ISIS	Islamic State in Iraq and Syria
ISJD	Indonesian Scientific Journal Database
ISO	International Organization for Standardization
ISP	internet service provider
IT	information technology
ITE Law	Undang-Undang No. 11 Tahun 2008 tentang Informasi dan Transaksi Elektronik (Law No. 11/2008 on Information and Electronic Transactions)
ITU	International Telecommunication Union
IVAA	Indonesian Visual Art Archive
JABN	Jaringan Arsip Budaya Nusantara (Indonesian Cultural Archive Network)
JDK	Junud Daulah Khilafah
JI	Jemaah Islamiyah
jihad	'to strive', 'to exert', 'to fight'; the meaning can range from a personal struggle against sinful tendencies to assisting the community in holy war
jihadi/jihadist	a Muslim who advocates or participates in militant jihad
Jokowi	Joko Widowo (current Indonesian president)
JTUB	Jasa Trans Usaha Bersama (Transport Service Cooperative)
Kalqulus	Kajian Al Quran Ala Ustadz (Examining the Qur'an à la Preachers)
kb/s	kilobit per second
kecamatan	subdistrict
kelurahan	village
KMK Online	Kreatif Media Karya Online (Creative Media Works Online)
KNPB	Komite Nasional Papua Barat (National Committee for West Papua)
Kominfo	Ministry of Communication and Informatics
Komisi I	Commission I of the Indonesian parliament (DPR)
Komnas HAM	Komisi Nasional Hak Asasi Manusia (National Commission for Human Rights)
korban	victim

KPI	Komisi Penyiaran Indonesia (Indonesian Broadcasting Commission)
KPK	Komisi Pemberantasan Korupsi (Corruption Eradication Commission)
KPU	Komisi Pemilihan Umum (General Election Commission)
KSP	Kantor Staf Presiden (Executive Office of the President)
KTP	Kartu Tanda Penduduk (Resident Identity Card)
kultwit	*kuliah Twitter* (Twitter lesson)
LAMs	libraries, archives and museums
LAPOR!	Layanan Aspirasi dan Pengaduan Online Rakyat (Online Service for People's Aspirations and Complaints)
LEKRA	Lembaga Kebudayaan Rakyat (Institute of People's Culture)
LIPI	Lembaga Ilmu Pengetahuan Indonesia (Indonesian Institute of Sciences)
LIS	library and information science
LKAAM	Lembaga Kerapatan Adat Alam Minangkabau (Consultative Body for Minangkabau Customary Law)
LSN	Lembaga Sandi Negara (State Cryptography Agency)
majelis taklim	religious study group
malware	malicious software posing as legitimate software
Mb/s	megabit per second
MIT	Mujahidin Indonesia Timur (Mujahidin of East Indonesia)
MITB	man in the browser (malware)
MPLIK	Mobil Pusat Layanan Internet Kecamatan (Mobile Subdistrict Internet Service Centre).
MUI	Majelis Ulama Indonesia (Indonesian Council of Islamic Scholars)
New Order	the Suharto era (1965–98)
ngaji	to recite (the Qu'ran)
NGAOS	Ngaji On The Street
OAI-PMH	Open Archives Initiative–Protocol for Metadata Harvesting
ODOJ	One Day One Juz
OECD	Organisation for Economic Co-operation and Development
ojek	motorcycle taxi
Organda	Organization of Land Transportation Owners

Pancasila	the five guiding principles of the Indonesian state (belief in God, humanitarianism, nationalism, democracy and social justice)
Pandham	Peduli Aset Dharmasraya Aman Makmur (Caring for the Assets of a Safe and Prosperous Dharmasraya)
pangkalan ojek	motorcycle taxi rank or stand
pasar	market, bazaar
PDS HB Jassin	Pusat Dokumentasi Sastra HB Jassin (HB Jassin Literature Documentation Centre)
Pemuda Pancasila	Pancasila Youth
pengajian	prayer session, study group
Perum PNRI	Perum Percetakan Negara Republik Indonesia (Indonesian Government Printing Office)
pesantren	Islamic boarding school
PISA	Programme for International Student Assessment
PKI	Partai Komunis Indonesia (Indonesian Communist Party)
PKS	Partai Keadilan Sejahtera (Prosperous Justice Party)
PLIK	Pusat Layanan Internet Kecamatan (Subdistrict Internet Service Centre)
PPRI	Persatuan Pengusaha Rental Indonesia (Indonesian Car Rental Entrepreneurs Association)
reformasi	the reform (post-Suharto) period
relawan	volunteer
riya	showing off one's religiousness; being pious with the intention of impressing others
RRI	Radio Republik Indonesia
SAFENET	Southeast Asia Freedom of Expression Network
Salafi	term for those who seek to return to the teachings and example of the early generations of Muslims
SIM	subscriber identity module
SLiMS	Senayan Library Management Systems
SMS	short messaging service
SNI	Standar Nasional Indonesia (Indonesian National Standard)
SP4N	Sistem Pengaduan Pelayanan Publik Nasional (National Public Service Complaint System)
suara	voice
Susenas	Survei Sosio-Ekonomi Nasional (National Socio-economic Survey)
tafsir	exegesis of the Qur'an
takfir	infidel, unbeliever
TFP	total factor productivity

tongsis	*tongkat narsis* (selfie stick, literally 'narcissist stick')
UCS	union catalogue server
UKP4	Unit Kerja Presiden untuk Pengawasan dan Pengendalian Pembangunan (President's Delivery Unit for Development Monitoring and Oversight)
umroh	pilgrimage to Mecca that is performed at any time other than the time specified for the *hajj*
USO	universal service obligation
ustadz	male preacher or teacher
ustadzah	female preacher or teacher
warnet	*warung internet* (internet cafe)
YBY	Yayasan Biennale Yogyakarta (Yogyakarta Biennale Foundation)
YLBHI	Yayasan Lembaga Bantuan Hukum Indonesia (Indonesian Legal Aid Foundation)
zikir	'remembrance'; prayer

Currencies

$	US dollar
HK$	Hong Kong dollar
Rp	Indonesian rupiah

© Australian National University
Base map CAP 12-215a
CAMBODIA
VIETNAM
THAILAND
South China Sea
PHILIPPINES
PACIFIC OCEAN
MALAYSIA
BRUNEI
SINGAPORE
Aceh
North Sumatra
Riau
Riau Is.
West Sumatra
Jambi
Banka Belitung
South Sumatra
Bengkulu
Lampung
Jakarta
Banten
West Java
Central Java
Yogyakarta
East Java
Bali
West Kalimantan
Central Kalimantan
North Kalimantan
East Kalimantan
South Kalimantan
Celebes Sea
Gorontalo
North Sulawesi
Central Sulawesi
West Sulawesi
South Sulawesi
South East Sulawesi
North Maluku
Maluku
West Papua
Papua
Java Sea
INDONESIA
Banda Sea
West Nusa Tenggara
East Nusa Tenggara
TIMOR LESTE
Arafura Sea
Timor Sea
INDIAN OCEAN
AUSTRALIA
International boundary
Province boundary
Jakarta Province name
0
1000
kilometres
10°N
0°
10°S
100°E
120°E
140°E

1 Challenges and opportunities of the digital 'revolution' in Indonesia

Edwin Jurriëns and Ross Tapsell

Digital technology is fast becoming the core of life, work, culture and identity in Indonesia. In a young nation with a median age of 28 and a rapidly growing urban middle class, Indonesians are using digital technologies in ways that have made the world take notice. In 2016 Indonesia had 76 million Facebook users, the fourth highest number in the world. Jakarta has been named the world's 'most active city on Twitter' (Lipman 2012), while other platforms such as Instagram, WhatsApp, LINE, Path and Telegram are all being used in unique and dynamic ways. It is now commonplace to walk into a cafe in one of Indonesia's cities and see a group of young Indonesians all sitting in silence, eyes fixed on their mobile phones. Even outside the cities, there is voracious demand for admittance into the digital world. In research exploring the 'improbability' of a nation with over 13,0000 islands, a coastline of 54,000 kilometres and a population of 250 million with dozens of ethnicities, journalist Elisabeth Pisani (2014: 3) observed villagers climbing trees in order to get 2G phone reception; 'Millions of Indonesians live on $2 a day *and* are on Facebook', she wrote.

Indonesia's digital economy is an area of great potential, as shown by the rise of Go-Jek and Grab, ride-sharing companies whose success has been propelled by the ubiquitous use of smartphones. In mid-2016 Go-Jek raised $550 million in new capital, giving it a value of $1.3 billion, an incredible result given it had launched its first mobile phone application only a year and a half earlier (Pratama 2016). On the back of Go-Jek and other e-commerce successes, President Joko Widodo (Jokowi) stated that Indonesia aimed to have '1,000 technopreneurs' and a digital economy worth $130 billion by 2020 (Tapsell 2015a; Wisnu 2016).

Politically, digital platforms are being used to organise mass rallies, assist with election monitoring and generally provide a space for greater freedom of opinion and expression on a variety of issues, contributing in no small way to the country's rambunctious democracy. Anyone running for political office must now consider how to engage with the world of online campaigning, in particular by nurturing a presence on social media. As this book explains, digital technologies have had a marked impact on the media industry, governance, commerce, informal sector employment, city planning, disaster relief, health, education, religion, artistic and cultural expression, and much more.

Yet this rapid advancement of online communication, predominantly in urban areas, is only part of the story. While the number of Indonesians using the internet has followed the upward global trend, increasing sevenfold from 8.1 million in 2005 to 56.6 million in 2015 (see Chapter 13 by Pangestu and Dewi), Indonesia's internet penetration rate remains at only 25 per cent,[1] with around four-fifths of the country's internet users located on the islands of Java and Sumatra. For communities in disadvantaged regions, the infrastructure and media for digital communication and information are underdeveloped or unavailable. This situation is gradually improving, but behind the glossy sell of social media-driven campaigns, tech start-ups and e-commerce growth, the disruption caused by digital technologies is presenting significant challenges.

One of Indonesia's biggest challenges is to make sure that the internet does not lead to a more divided and unequal society, as users in urban areas with better access to high-speed internet adapt to the digital world faster than their fellow citizens in rural areas. While enabling emancipation in some cases, in other cases digital technology maintains or even reinforces social class and status distinctions. Even among those who do have internet access, there are literally millions of Indonesians who use it only to access Facebook or WhatsApp on their mobile phones via 2G satellite technology. Given the low speeds, these people are unable to use even Google or Wikipedia effectively, let alone seize the opportunity to become one of Indonesia's '1,000 technopreneurs'. Bridging the 'digital divide' (van Dijk 2005; Tsatsou 2014: 116–32) remains a huge challenge for the Indonesian government but, if achieved, will have a profound impact on the country's economy, society and culture.

---

1 There are a number of conflicting reports on the level of internet penetration in Indonesia. Freedom House puts the penetration rate at 22 per cent but other sources claim that the figure is as high as 30 per cent, with rapid improvements in the year 2016. One of the difficulties in pinning the numbers down is that, when surveyed, many Indonesians answer 'yes' to using Facebook on their mobile phones, but 'no' to having internet access.

Other challenges brought about by digitalisation are equally stark. New technologies strengthen or produce political, commercial and socio-religious forms of surveillance, manipulation and suppression. The same digital mechanisms that give minorities and marginalised groups a voice are used to track, discredit and threaten them. Information and communication technology (ICT) helps hardline groups expand their networks and mobilises individuals to participate in violent online and offline behaviour and activities. The collapse of distinct demarcations between the private and public realms has opened gateways for cybercriminals to gain access to confidential information. While digital engagement gives rise to expanded and intensified forms of connectivity, it also leads to dramatic, and sometimes even fatal, forms of misinformation, miscommunication and socio-political divergence.

While there is clearly a high level of engagement with, and strong enthusiasm and talent for, digital technologies in Indonesia, framing a scholarly critique around 'digital Indonesia' is no simple task. How can we make sense of the rapidly changing arena of digitalisation in one of the world's most diverse, geographically vast nations? We argue that the first step is to put the very idea of a technological 'revolution' into critical perspective by positioning the realities of the digital world in a context of colliding socio-political, cultural and natural environments.

This book is intended to weigh arguments about the impact of digitalisation in Indonesia by explaining its opportunities, but at the same time defining its challenges. While staying clear of overt techno-optimism, we maintain that Indonesia is at the forefront of the global debate about the effect of digital technology. Indonesia can play a world-leading role in the development of ICT applications in areas as crucial as poverty reduction, education, health care, environmental sustainability and disaster relief, to name a few. Digital technologies offer significant and wide-ranging opportunities to make the world a better place, but realising those opportunities means evaluating the challenges the new technologies bring. We intend this book to be a place where this evaluation begins. In the rest of the chapter, we elucidate our argument and provide a guide to help readers navigate the remainder of the book.

FRAMING 'DIGITAL INDONESIA'

This book deals with the intersections between digital technology and a broad range of sectors of Indonesian life. By 'digital' we mean the translation of various aspects of life into digits for information and communication purposes. Digitalisation's simplified system of representation can enhance the speed, scope and efficiency of information and communication practices. Its potential to bridge or compress time, space and even entities has made it one of the driving forces behind globalisation or a globalised 'network society' (Castells 1996; Appadurai 1997; Tsatsou 2014: 58–9). One of the remarkable characteristics of the digital in contemporary life, including Indonesian culture and society, is its capacity to facilitate mobility, co-presence and interconnectivity (Hjorth 2009). The use of ICT enables unexpected social interventions and connections, signalling for some the possibility of shifting 'capitalist societies out of the era of the mass media and into a post-media age in which the media will be re-appropriated by a multitude of subject-groups' (Guattari 1989: 144). The post-media age has not been without its own difficulties, however, as the case studies in this book show.

Of course, digital technologies did not arrive in Indonesia in a vacuum. The origins of the internet are commonly identified with the Advanced Research Projects Agency Network (ARPANET), established in the United States in the 1960s. The word 'internet', short for 'internetworking', was introduced in 1974 (Tsatsou 2014: 14–15). While ARPANET was initially used by the military and computer scientists, the open-source movement of the 1980s worked on alternatives for the more open development and use of digital communication networks. The World Wide Web was released in 1989 by a research team from the European Organisation for Nuclear Research (CERN) in Geneva (Tsatsou 2014: 15).

The internet arrived in Indonesia in the second half of the 1990s, 'into a mediascape that was already stretching the Indonesian state's capacity to control' (Hill and Sen 2005: 28). Initially, internet cafes (*warung internet*, or *warnet*) constituted the main public venues for citizens to access the internet for private use (Hill and Sen 1997). The growth of the mobile phone market in the twenty-first century has enabled more flexible and individualised forms of internet use. David Hill and Krishna Sen (1997, 2005), Onno Purbo (2002), Merlyna Lim (2002) and Yanuar Nugroho (2007) have all published pioneering studies on the role of digital technologies in the archipelago. While the internet is a relatively young medium, after a few decades of impressive growth in Indonesia and worldwide, it has developed its own history, including a history of its studies (Tsatsou 2014: 15–19). This book maps and analyses the expansion and specific directions of digital technologies in Indonesia since the 1990s. In doing so it builds on existing academic work from the time when the internet was still a relatively limited and exclusive domain in Southeast Asia.

The smartphone has been a game changer in facilitating the adoption of the internet in Indonesia. In 2012, around 29 per cent of the 55 million Indonesians who connected to the internet did so via a mobile phone (Rao 2012: 6). By 2016 that share had increased to 70 per cent, largely because of the massive expansion of the smartphone market (Balea 2016). Despite the growth of both mobile phone and internet use, however, great disparities in access remain. Fewer than 40 per cent of Papuans own a mobile phone, compared with an estimated 97 per cent of Jakartans (Jurriëns and Tapsell 2016). A person's social or physical position in the geo-political landscape of Indonesia, with its highly uneven spread and quality of digital infrastructure, to a large extent determines whether, how fast, how long, with whom, and on what other terms and conditions one can have digital connectivity. Digital access, often misleadingly called 'free access', comes with various costs, ranging from the financial costs of technological infrastructure and individual consumer items to the environmental costs of e-consumption and e-waste, the 'flexploitation' of formal and informal internet-related labour (McRobbie 2005: 382–3) and the social costs of stigmatisation and intimidation. In the context of Indonesia's post-1998 reform movement, Hill and Sen (2005: 145) came to the rather pessimistic conclusion that 'the Internet may be at best yet another index of inequality, at worst yet another impediment to equal participation in an emerging democracy'.

We test this and other hypotheses by examining a diverse range of sectors and actors that have created, sustained, reinforced, resisted or undermined the various digital connectivities and divides in contemporary Indonesia. The complex and fluid nature of the topic has led us to an interdisciplinary approach that draws on media studies, cultural studies, sociology, anthropology, political science, economics and history, among others. As digital technology and Indonesian life in the twenty-first century are closely interwoven and mutually constitutive, we stay away from making firm predictions about the digital future. Instead, we have included studies that carefully describe, analyse and contextualise the digital realities of everyday life in the world's fourth most populous country. The empirically based and theoretically informed research in this book demonstrates that digital technology has triggered and shaped developments in society in interaction with other media, ideas and practices. The five sections in the book refer to closely interrelated aspects of digital Indonesia: connectivity (Part 1), divergence (Part 2), identity (Part 3), knowledge (Part 4) and commerce (Part 5).

CONNECTIVITY

Part 1 of the book focuses on the various types of connectivity that can be facilitated by digital technology. One of the most important benefits provided by digital technology is its ability to connect citizens with their governments in new and efficient ways. Indonesia's bureaucracy is notoriously slow and debilitating, in many ways still living in the shadow of the authoritarian practices of the New Order (1965–98). Digitalisation has the potential to make the public service more transparent, and therefore less corrupt (Huang, Ismiraldi and Thornley 2016). As governor of Jakarta, Jokowi attempted to reduce corruption among low- and middle-level bureaucrats, and generally to make the bureaucracy more efficient in its operations. During the 2014 presidential election, both Jokowi and his opponent, former army general Prabowo Subianto, promised to reform the bureaucracy. Prabowo traded on his image as a man of action to show that he would not tolerate long deliberations or excessive bureaucratic processes. Jokowi made unscheduled visits (*blusukan*) to government offices, where footage of him checking on the progress of infrastructure and other projects was uploaded to YouTube.

In Chapter 2, we hear a view on e-governance from inside the presidential palace: the authors, scholar and e-governance specialist Yanuar Nugroho and researcher Agung Hikmat, both hold positions in the Executive Office of the President (Kantor Staf Presiden, or KSP). They reiterate that Jokowi is determined to make e-governance a central part of his program, 'as a means not only to deliver better public services and facilitate collaboration, but also to bolster the credibility of his government' (p. 21). However, while e-governance may be a way to clean up corrupt official and unofficial bureaucratic practices, the authors recognise that it is not a magic bullet. Rather, it needs to be placed in the context of wider bureaucratic reform, 'away from the old, militaristic style of service delivery into a new era of more accountable and effective government' (p. 34).

Undoubtedly, public sector reform through e-governance will not happen easily. But in thinking about the implications of greater connectivity between citizens and government, Nugroho and Hikmat point out that the digital world is full of Indonesian citizens who are themselves innovating. For example, consumers can now order their favourite dinners delivered right to their doors through Go-Jek's new digital application, Go-Food. These improvements in efficiency in everyday aspects of life mean that citizens are increasingly expecting similar innovations and efficiencies from their governments. Moreover, the government can incorporate commercial and other technical innovations into its own processes, thereby improving e-governance. In other words, the breakthroughs in digital technology being made by the private sector should not necessarily be seen as separate from the goal of better governance.

From a consumer point of view, connectivity can also be found in the convergence of old media (television) and new media (the mobile phone). In Chapter 3, Emma Baulch demonstrates how consumers' engagement with digital technology is represented and shaped by the advertisements telecommunication network providers make for commercial television.

These ads promise freedom and innovation, and are central to 'the imagining of a digitally networked nation' (p. 45). They also confirm continuities, rather than breaks, between past and present forms of media use, and between past and present class-related distinctions. The telco ads focusing on smartphone and social media use confirm middle classness and social mobility, while those focusing on the cheaper SMS and voice call market confirm images and stereotypes of the lower economic classes or 'the masses'.

Nevertheless, even within a consumer regime shaped by television ads and controlled by media oligarchs, mobile phone and social media use, in combination with other cultural strategies, can offer opportunities to imagine new forms of self-identity, social connectivity and (lower-)class politics. For example, Baulch describes how the connectivity afforded by the mobile phone and social media has turned female concert goers in Bali from passive onlookers to active mediators between offline and online spaces. Music management and fans also use colloquial language and technologies associated with the lower class, such as text messaging, as cultural counterstrategies and as facilitators of alternative associational life.

One of the earliest and most prominent trends in digital connectivity in Indonesia has been the convergence of technologies and sectors in the media industry (Tapsell 2015b). In Chapter 4, Ross Tapsell describes the impact of media convergence on concentration of media ownership in Indonesia. Digital technology facilitates connections between information and communication formats and institutional forms that used to be relatively distinct from each other, such as the print media, radio and television (Jenkins 2006). The transformation of print, sound and vision into digital formats has given rise to new, multimedia ways of creating, transmitting and receiving media content. While this development promised to create greater diversity in news and entertainment, in practice the domination of a small number of politically powerful, Jakarta-based media companies with a national reach has reduced the level of diversity (Lim 2012; Nugroho, Putri and Laksmi 2012). Under oligopolistic circumstances, digitalisation contributes to the rationalisation of resources across media sectors and stages of the production process, strengthening the homogenisation of media content. Tapsell refers to a digital 'ecosystem' in which the media giants are aiming to incorporate more and more consumer services—beyond media services—into streamlined e-commerce packages. This is making it difficult for smaller, more specialised media companies to survive.

The chapters in Part 1 of this book go beyond the much-used and well-accepted concept of digital media convergence to highlight the centrality of new forms of connectivity to an understanding of power relations. Can bottom-up forces of the citizenry drive innovation and shape practices in the mainstream media, the advertising world and government? Or is the digital era simply allowing powerful media oligarchs and politicians to exert their power in new ways? The chapters in this section of the book identify a trend towards more centralised, homogenised forms of connectivity. This is not to deny or underestimate, however, the at times ingenious efforts of media activists, artists and ordinary citizens to overcome socio-technological divergence, as explored in the next section of the book.

DIVERGENCE

Part 2 of the book analyses real-life forms of social divergence and counter-strategies that shape the use of ICT. In Chapter 5, Onno W. Purbo, one of Indonesia's leading digital media activists (Barker 2015), argues that the digital divide is not only a matter of level of access to technology and material infrastructure, as the government seems to believe, but is also related to factors such as education, socio-economic status, age, income and location, all of which affect the ability to adopt digital media. Rather than technology access per se, adoption depends on people's awareness of the potential benefits of using the internet. In that sense, internet skills go beyond the acquisition of practical computer skills to require specific forms of digital literacy (Rheingold 2012). Various chapters in this book (Chapter 3 by Baulch, Chapter 9 by Slama, Chapter 10 by Nuraniyah, Chapter 11 by Azali, Chapter 12 by Jurriëns) demonstrate that the issues of digital adoption and digital divide are not only class related, but also have clear gender dimensions.

Especially in rural areas, a lack of internet affordability, skills, awareness and cultural acceptance, combined with a lack of content and services in local languages, constitutes a considerable hurdle to digital literacy. According to Purbo, top-down strategies by the government focusing on material infrastructure, such as the Smart Village program to connect all Indonesian villages to the internet, are insufficient. The sustainability of rural digital networks also relies on technical education, building infrastructure in response to local demand, keeping costs down and exploring the economic opportunities that can arise from the use of digital technology. As ICT is no longer a compulsory subject at school, the drive to increase digital literacy currently depends largely on the educational services and campaigns of NGOs, commercial media providers and independent electronic forums.

While the predicament of citizens with few digital literacy skills is often forgotten in the excitement around the digital 'revolution', so too is the plight of those unlucky citizens who have felt the wrath of the state for their online activities. In Chapter 6, human rights lawyer and researcher Usman Hamid reminds us of the role of digitalisation in enabling creeping state control. He highlights the cases of Alexander Aan, the moderator of a Facebook page for atheists who was jailed under the ITE Law for 'disseminating information aimed at inciting religious hatred or hostility' (Jurriëns and Tapsell 2016); and of the Papuan activists who have been subjected to online surveillance and crackdowns. For every techno-optimistic report of how Papuans film atrocities on their mobile phones and upload them to the internet for the world to see, there are numerous other reports showing how Papuan activists 'expose themselves to potentially fatal pushback from a state that can readily infiltrate social media, track down activists and impose severe sanctions' (p. 104).

Indonesia is ranked only 'partly' free in the latest Freedom on the Net report (Freedom House 2016), in part because of the rise in the number of online defamation cases brought under Law No. 11/2008 on Information and Electronic Transactions (the ITE Law). This contentious law is specifically tailored to control the online realm by making it easier to bring criminal online defamation cases; the number of prosecutions under the law rose from just two in 2009 to 41 in 2014 (SAFENET 2015). While the law is intended to protect the reputations of citizens who have been defamed online, in fact over a third of complainants are state officials, while the defendants include activists, lawyers, researchers and journalists, as well as ordinary citizens (Chapter 6 by Hamid).

The debate about freedom of expression on the internet can be linked to the turmoil surrounding 'hoax news' in Indonesia. Jokowi was reported as saying in early 2017 that while the 'Information Age is very open', information needs to be filtered 'or it will tear apart our unity' (Suherdjoko 2017). Budi Rahardjo (Chapter 7) tends to agree, writing that online hate speech and fake news is a 'destabilising force in Indonesian society' (p. 121). The Indonesian government has set up an agency inside the presidential palace to prevent the spread of slanderous and false news stories, and is asking the police to trace the perpetrators (Tapsell 2017).

Rahardjo also discusses cybercrime, in particular the balance between security and privacy. In 2014, Indonesia was ranked second (after China) among the countries from which cyberattacks were launched. Indonesian citizens who readily place information about themselves online are now vulnerable to identity theft and online fraud. Much like its solution to fake news, the Indonesian government is taking a centralised approach to the issue of internet security by creating a new national cybersecurity agency (Paskalis 2017). As Rahardjo observes, the government's use of website-blocking and content-filtering tools may reduce cybercrime, but it also runs the risk of being perceived as censorship, state overreach or an attempt to control society.

At the heart of these various issues of divergence lie the challenges of formulating internet policy. There are considerable differences in views both within government and in society about the role of government in narrowing the digital divide, identifying and limiting cybercrime, and managing citizen commentary online. These discussions are taking place globally, too, but they are being played out very openly in Indonesia's vibrant public sphere.

IDENTITY

Part 3 of the book focuses on the actual practices of digital technology users, and how these practices bring into being or further develop specific forms of individual and group identity. The chapters confirm that the digital mediascape is not determined solely by technologies and networks, but also by forms of human agency (Fuchs 2008; Tsatsou 2014: 38–41). Groups and individuals in the digital realm invite others to join their communities by offering subject positions that have broad appeal, in fields as diverse as social activism, religion and militant fundamentalism.

In Chapter 8, John Postill and Kurniawan Saputro examine how Indonesian activists have attempted to communicate key issues of the digital age to the broader public, by strategically using the common, personified categories of victim (*korban*), volunteer (*relawan*) and voice (*suara*). These three categories relate, respectively, to the fields of digital rights activism, data activism and media advocacy, each with its own specialist knowledge, use of media technology, and temporal and spatial scaling. Postill and Saputro elaborate their argument by providing an example of each.

Activists have used the victim (*korban*) category to mobilise public resistance against lawsuits brought by powerful individuals and organisations against ordinary citizens or minorities under the ITE Law's defamation clause (article 27(3)). In late 2014, the various digital victimhood movements formed an umbrella organisation, Digital Democracy Forum (Forum Demokrasi Digital, or FDD), to represent the digital rights and interests of civil society and negotiate with other stakeholders, including politicians and policy-makers. The volunteer (*relawan*) category is represented by the Election Guardians (Kawal Pemilu), an independent data activism movement that monitored the 2014 presidential elections in the public interest, by recruiting volunteers for the nationwide collection of polling station results. An example of the voice (*suara*) category is Papuan Voices, a video production and distribution program that enables Papuans to give expression to their oppression and marginalisation.

Digital technology is used not merely to present stories about Papua, but also to value the voices of local citizens themselves.

As one would expect in the country with the world's largest Muslim community, Indonesians also use digital social media to express religious piety and explore forms of religious practice and communality. The new media include Islam-related mobile phone applications, online study gatherings and social networking. In Chapter 9, Martin Slama demonstrates how these digital practices build on—but also deviate from—existing, offline forms of religious behaviour. For instance, discussions about religious and personal affairs that begin in offline prayer groups often continue through mobile phone messaging between individuals and their teachers. This typically involves female students requesting advice from, but sometimes also challenging the authority of, male teachers. Other groups use digital applications to read the Qur'an together, creating their own forms of social bonding, discipline and punishment. Some see posting religion-related status updates on Facebook as a form of proselytisation, even if the posts are not grounded in any form of theological expertise. At the same time, these social media users face the risk of being accused of the religiously objectionable act of seeking the admiration of others (*riya*).

Digital media applications are popular not only among the majority of moderate Muslims, but also among radical minorities. Some of these radical groups use encrypted mobile chat applications to sustain and strengthen their communities. Nava Nuraniyah argues in Chapter 10 that extremist chat groups facilitate more open and intimate discussion among members than more public social media such as Facebook and Twitter, in part because the chat groups are less subject to control by moderators. In general, the groups are about social bonding, cohesion and expansion, and are not directly aimed at planning and training for acts of terrorism. The fact that the recruitment of members often takes place through offline networks again confirms the strong interconnections and blurred lines between digital media and the 'real' world in Indonesia.

One of Nuraniyah's findings is that the majority of conversations in female chat groups are about mundane personal matters rather than radical religious affairs. Despite having a much smaller number of participants, the female chat group she studied was far more active in publishing messages than the male group. The members of both groups cherished the social dimensions of being part of a community of like-minded people in the digital world, often after becoming alienated from their families and friends in the offline world. In combination with offline practices, online socialisation can become a pathway to further radicalisation, including the plotting and execution of terrorism. As the online forums offer opportunities to monitor and possibly influence the behaviour of potential terrorists, Nuraniyah's advice for governments and their intelligence services is to engage with the digital communication technology rather than trying to ban it.

KNOWLEDGE

Apart from creating a sense of communal or individual identity, one of the primary functions of digital media use in contemporary society is to facilitate the sharing of knowledge. Part 4 of the book therefore focuses on the various ways of producing, collecting, transferring and receiving information that are facilitated by Indonesia's digital infrastructure. Key developments in recent years have been the digitisation of library and archive collections as well as the creation of digital resources for education, music and the visual arts. These initiatives have come with their own challenges.

As Kathleen Azali points out in Chapter 11, the politicisation of information in Indonesia since colonial times has not only made certain sources of knowledge inaccessible, but also created a general distrust of libraries and archives. The Indonesian library sector suffers from poor self-esteem and a negative public image as well as a lack of funds, material resources, staff, and professional knowledge and skills. Although the majority of staff in libraries are female, very few women are involved in digitising collections, thus confirming a serious gender divide in the development and application of digital technology in Indonesia.

Nevertheless, since the late 1990s a number of online educational, academic and creative initiatives have increased the availability of knowledge in the public domain. The most comprehensive of these systems is Indonesia OneSearch (http://onesearch.id/). Digitisation has made major collections of knowledge more accessible and affordable, and encouraged collaboration and convergence between libraries, archives and museums. At the same time, it has created new problems related to technological obsolescence, physical decay and failures in interoperability. At least as important as resolving such technological issues, Azali argues, is creating awareness about the social, legal, political, economic and cultural foundations and consequences of knowledge production through both offline and online repositories.

Another way of making knowledge and information available to the public, and avoiding or circumventing state crackdowns and surveillance, is to adopt hacking strategies. While hacking may disrupt services or infringe on intellectual copyright, normally it is not meant to create any permanent damage to information and communication systems

(Denning 2001: 241). Visual artists are one pioneering group using hacking as a means to access, generate and share data. In creative, imaginative and often unexpected ways, they are producing meaningful alliances between art, science and society, and between the virtual, material and natural environments (Jurriëns 2017).

In Indonesia, the Yogyakarta-based new media art collectives House of Natural Fiber (HONF), XXLab and Lifepatch are among the most active and adventurous communities (see Chapter 12 by Edwin Jurriëns). Some aspects of their work have materialised in art objects that have attracted the interest of art collectors and exhibition and festival organisers, but in general their art practices tend to be process rather than object oriented. These collectives have developed collaborative art projects with local communities to address problems related to agriculture, waste management and health, and to explore scenarios and solutions for a better, more sustainable future. Their projects and approaches are supported and facilitated by digital technology, but also build on longer, pre-digital traditions of social engagement in modern and contemporary art. XXLab, an all-female collective, is helping to close the gender gap in digital Indonesia by showcasing women's roles as active and innovative participants in art, science and society.

COMMERCE

While the production and sharing of digital knowledge is fundamental to Indonesia's long-term development, activities designed to generate an immediate financial benefit form a far more substantial part of the country's digital information and communication services. The commercial application of digital technology in Indonesia constitutes the main theme of Part 5 of the book.

In Chapter 13, former minister of trade (2004–11) and minister of tourism and creative economy (2011–14) Mari Pangestu and researcher Grace Dewi provide a comprehensive overview of the progress of Indonesia's digital economy. Although the contribution of the digital economy to GDP grew from just 2.5 per cent in 2005 to 7.2 per cent in 2015, Pangestu and Dewi argue that Indonesia 'is not extracting full economic value from the digital economy, including its potential to contribute to development and inclusion' (p. 248), and in fact lags behind its ASEAN peers. The authors chart policy solutions to address this situation, including both improving communications infrastructure and developing human resources. In analysing the potential for economic growth through the digital economy, Pangestu and Dewi find that the success stories are concentrated in two areas, retail sales and transport, due to the ability of tech companies in these industries to raise capital both domestically and abroad. The remaining chapters in Part 5 of the book provide specific case studies relating to these two industries.

In Chapter 14, Bede Moore, an Australian national and Harvard University graduate, provides an insider's account based on his role as a founding member of the e-commerce industry in Indonesia. He discusses the growth of the industry from 2011 to 2016, a period when Indonesia's digital economy was still in the 'relatively early stages of inception' (p. 256). One of his key findings concerns the role of large conglomerates in shaping, and in turn dominating, the industry. In 2015, for example, Cosseboom (2015) described how Indonesia's 10 largest conglomerates were investing in the start-up world, arguing that 'Indonesia's big families recognize they must be a part of the tech boom, or face certain redundancy in 10 years' time'. The concentration of capital in digital start-ups suggests that Indonesia's so-called '1,000 technopreneurs' may all be fishing from the same small pool. As Moore explains, changes to regulations in 2014 gave local conglomerates a significant advantage over foreign investors. This created the rather paradoxical situation in which the president was calling for more foreign investment in the digital economy, despite the government imposing restrictions that limited foreign business and capital.

One of the most prominent e-businesses in Indonesia is Go-Jek. Initially providing only motorcycle taxi services, by 2016 Go-Jek had expanded its services to 12 different app-supported businesses, ranging from various types of transport and courier services to food, entertainment and banking. In their analysis of the impact of the new technology on labour rights and opportunities for workers in the informal sector, Michele Ford and Vivian Honan (Chapter 15) ask a straightforward research question: is a Go-Jek driver better off than a traditional *ojek* driver? The answer is central to the debate on labour relations in the twenty-first century. As the authors explain, the app-based transport providers have faced fierce resistance from conventional transport providers in Indonesia, leading to protests and violence.

Until recently, conventional transport providers were subject to much stricter licensing and tax regulations than digital providers. The government introduced new tax and licensing regulations for app-based businesses in 2016 (Faisal 2016) but left the motorcycle taxi services largely untouched. Taxi drivers and informal workers who have made the switch to app-based transport companies have seen improvements in their working conditions and wages, but do not have control over ride pricing and still lack job security. Go-Jek drivers are also confronted with payment cuts and fines issued by the company's management, amidst rapidly increasing competition from other online transport companies and drivers. At the same time, Ford and Honan argue, Go-Jek's status as a pseudo-employer allows its drivers to organise themselves, stage demonstrations and partake in collective bargaining, in ways that are not available to truly self-employed workers in the informal sector.

The case studies in Part 5 of the book tap into global debates about the creative destruction and disruption to traditional business models caused by digitalisation (Christiansen 1997; Danneels 2004). But they also provide a fascinating and original insight into the burgeoning issue of what might be called 'digital resource nationalism'. Much of the debate about Indonesia's digital economy is framed in terms of making sure that Indonesia reaps most of the rewards. This manifests itself in a number of ways. For example, Indonesians commonly express concern that Indonesia's best and brightest young technopreneurs are being wooed away by foreign companies in Silicon Valley, creating a brain drain in the local tech industry. Second, the Indonesian government frequently claims that large foreign corporations are deliberately and regularly underpaying taxes, singling out Google on a number of occasions in this regard (Idris 2017). Third, the entry of foreign tech companies (such as Malaysian-born online transport company Grab) has led to calls to ensure the success of locally grown companies (such as Go-Jek). Central to future policy settings for the digital economy in Indonesia will be broader debates about the effectiveness of globalisation and free trade, and the role of nationalistic economic policy-making.

CONCLUSION

This book explores how a broad range of actors, including governments, businesses, journalists, activists, artists, educators, religious fundamentalists, rescue and security forces, and ordinary citizens, engage with digital technology and mediate connections with others. The case studies in the book demonstrate how the digital has blurred the boundaries between producers and consumers of technology, between the public and private spheres, between the virtual and the 'real', and between the global, the national and the local. Some manifestations of the digital bring a critical and refreshing perspective to the very idea of Indonesia as a geo-political entity, by enabling the mapping and imagining of alternative networks and communities.

Overall, the research presented in this volume confirms an expansion of opportunities provided by people's engagement with digital technology in the specific socio-political constellation of twenty-first-century Indonesia. The new technology has facilitated the exchange of information and communication at an unprecedented speed, scale and volume. The development of online data platforms has increased access to knowledge previously hidden in libraries, archives and museums, and has compensated for the limited availability of such resources in the first place. Through the convergence of old and new technologies, news media are able to channel the latest information in cost-effective, flexible and attractive formats. Fast and far-reaching digital networks are enabling governments and businesses to deliver services and products that are fine-tuned to the needs of citizens and consumers. Digital technology has given minorities and marginalised groups, including women, new opportunities to shape their identities and share them with the world. It has also opened up a spectrum of creative possibilities, including artist- and NGO-initiated projects aimed at community empowerment and environmental sustainability.

To realise the full potential of digitalisation, and create awareness about its darker side, Indonesia needs to harness the collaboration of all parties involved in or affected by the digital, including governments, businesses, civil society, academics, activists, artists, journalists and consumers. For its digital aspirations to bear fruit, the country needs to be able to draw on in-depth studies of the historical continuities and divergences between old and new media usages, as well as analyses of the complex interrelations between the virtual, material and natural environments. With this book, we attempt to present one cog in what needs to be a larger collaborative and interdisciplinary machine.

REFERENCES

Appadurai, A. (1997) *Modernity at Large: Cultural Dimensions of Globalization*, University of Minnesota Press, Minneapolis.

Balea, J. (2016) 'The latest stats in web and mobile in Indonesia (infographic)', *Tech in Asia*, 28 January. Available at https://www.techinasia.com/indonesia-web-mobile-statistics-we-are-social. Accessed 26 February 2017.

Barker, J. (2015) 'Guerilla engineers: the internet and the politics of freedom in Indonesia', in S. Jasanoff and S.-H. Kim (eds) *Dreamscapes of Modernity: Sociotechnical Imaginaries and the Fabrication of Power*, University of Chicago Press, Chicago: 199–218.

Castells, M. (1996) *The Rise of the Network Society*, The Information Age: Economy, Society and Culture, Volume 1, Blackwell, Oxford.

Christiansen, C.M. (1997) *The Innovator's Dilemma: When New Technologies Cause Great Firms to Fail*, Harvard Business School Press, Boston.

Cosseboom, L. (2015) 'Here's how 10 of Indonesia's richest families invest in tech start-ups', *Tech in Asia*, 27 November. Available at https://www.techinasia.com/indonesia-10-family-owned-conglomerates-tech-investments-lists. Accessed 26 February 2017.

Danneels, E. (2004), 'Disruptive technology reconsidered: a critique and research agenda', *Journal of Productive Innovation Management*, 21(4): 246–58.

Denning, D.E. (2001) 'Activism, hacktivism, and cyberterrorism: the internet as a tool for influencing foreign policy', in J. Arquilla and D. Ronfeldt (eds) *Networks and Netwars: The Future of Terror, Crime, and Militancy*, RAND Corporation, Santa Monica: 239–88.

Faisal, F. (2016) 'Indonesia sets new rules for ride-sharing companies', *The Conversation*, 10 May. Available at http://theconversation.com/indonesia-sets-new-rules-for-ride-sharing-companies-57187. Accessed 26 February 2017.

Freedom House (2016) 'Freedom on the Net 2016: Indonesia'. Available at https://freedomhouse.org/report/freedom-net/2016/indonesia. Accessed 26 February 2017.

Fuchs, C. (2008) *Internet and Society: Social Theory in the Information Age*, Routledge, New York.

Guattari, F. (1989) 'The three ecologies', translated by C. Turner, *New Formations*, 8(Summer): 131–47.

Hill, D.T., and K. Sen (1997) 'Wiring the *warung* to global gateways: the internet in Indonesia', *Indonesia*, 63(April): 67–89.

Hill, D.T., and K. Sen (2005) *The Internet in Indonesia's New Democracy*, Routledge, London and New York.

Hjorth, L. (2009) *Mobile Media in the Asia-Pacific: Gender and the Art of Being Mobile*, Routledge, London and New York.

Huang, A., Y. Ismiraldi and A. Thornley (2016) 'Digital governance in Indonesia: an on and offline battle', *In Asia: Weekly Insights and Analysis*, 18 May. Available at http://asiafoundation.org/2016/05/18/digital-governance-indonesia-offline-battle/. Accessed 5 March 2017.

Idris, M. (2017) 'Soal pajak Google, dirjen: kita tidak diam' [About the Google tax, director-general: we won't remain silent], *detikfinance*, 22 February. Available at https://finance.detik.com/berita-ekonomi-bisnis/d-3429237/soal-pajak-google-dirjen-kita-tidak-diam. Accessed 26 February 2017.

Jenkins, H. (2006) *Convergence Culture: Where Old and New Media Collide*, New York University Press, New York and London.

Jurriëns, E. (2017) *Visual Media in Indonesia: Video Vanguard*, Routledge, London and New York.

Jurriëns, E., and R. Tapsell (2016) 'New technology may bring Australia and Indonesia closer', *Canberra Times*, 8 September.

Lim, M. (2002) 'Cyber-civic space: from panopticon to pandemonium?' *International Development and Planning Review*, 24(4): 383–400.

Lim, M. (2012) 'The league of thirteen: media concentration in Indonesia', research report, Ford Foundation and Participatory Media Lab at Arizona State University, Tempe. Available at http://www.academia.edu/7282028/Lim_M._2012_The_League_of_Thirteen_Media_Concentration_in_Indonesia. Accessed 27 August 2014.

Lipman, V. (2012) 'The world's most active Twitter city? You won't guess it', *Forbes*, 30 December. Available at https://www.forbes.com/sites/victorlipman/2012/12/30/the-worlds-most-active-twitter-city-you-wont-guess-it/#5728c31755c6. Accessed 26 February 2017.

McRobbie, A. (2005) 'Clubs to companies', in J. Hartley (ed.) *Creative Industries*, Blackwell, Malden: 375–90.

Nugroho, Y. (2007) 'Does the internet transform civil society? The case of civil society organisations in Indonesia', PhD thesis, University of Manchester, Manchester.

Nugroho, Y., D.A. Putri and S. Laksmi (2012) 'Mapping the landscape of the media industry in contemporary Indonesia', research report, Center for Innovation Policy and Governance and HIVOS Regional Office Southeast Asia, Jakarta. Available at http://www.academia.edu/2608710/Mapping_the_landscape_of_the_media_industry_in_contemporary_Indonesia. Accessed 26 February 2017.

Paskalis, Y. (2017) 'Wiranto: anggota Badan Cyber Nasional tak sembarangan' [Wiranto: members of National Cybersecurity Agency are not just ordinary people], *Tempo.co*, 6 January. Available at https://m.tempo.co/read/news/2017/01/06/063833190/wiranto-anggota-badan-cyber-nasional-tak-sembarangan. Accessed 26 February 2017.

Pisani, E. (2014) *Indonesia etc.: Exploring the Improbable Nation,* Granta, London.

Pratama, A.H. (2016) 'Go-Jek: a unicorn's journey (infographic)', *Tech in Asia,* 13 August. Available at https://www.techinasia.com/how-go-jek-became-unicorn. Accessed 26 February 2017.

Purbo, O.W. (2002) 'Kekuatan komunitas Indonesia di dunia maya' [The strength of the Indonesian community in cyberspace], *Pantau*, 4 February. Available at http://www.pantau.or.id/?/=d/122. Accessed 29 November 2016.

Rao, M. (2012) 'Crossroads of innovation', Mobile Southeast Asia Report 2012, Momo. Available at http://www.mobilemonday.net/reports/SEA_Report_2012.pdf. Accessed 29 November 2016.

Rheingold, H. (2012) *Net Smart: How to Thrive Online*, MIT Press, Cambridge, MA.

SAFENET (Southeast Asia Freedom of Expression Network) (2015) 'Protecting freedom of expression and digital rights', Jakarta, 25 March.

Suherdjoko (2017) 'Main danger of Information Age are lies and slander, says Jokowi', *Jakarta Post,* 9 January. Available at http://www.thejakartapost.com/news/2017/01/09/main-danger-of-information-age-are-lies-and-slander-says-jokowi.html. Accessed 26 February 2017.

Tapsell, R. (2015a) 'When Turnbull came to town', *New Mandala,* 13 November. Available at http://www.newmandala.org/when-turnbull-came-to-town/. Accessed 26 February 2017.

Tapsell, R. (2015b) 'Platform convergence in Indonesia: challenges and opportunities for media freedom', *Convergence: The International Journal of Research into New Media Technologies*, 21(2): 182–97.

Tapsell, R. (2017) 'Post-truth politics in Southeast Asia', *Inside Story*, 17 February. Available at http://insidestory.org.au/post-truth-politics-in-southeast-asia. Accessed 26 February 2017.

Tsatsou, P. (2014) *Internet Studies: Past, Present and Future Directions*, Ashgate, Surrey and Burlington.

van Dijk, J.A.G.M (2005) *The Deepening Divide: Inequality in the Information Society,* Sage, Thousand Oaks.

Wisnu, A. (2016) 'Jokowi targets to produce 1,000 entrepreneurs', *Tempo.co,* 18 February. Available at https://en.tempo.co/read/news/2016/02/18/056746079/Jokowi-Targets-to-Produce-1000-Technopreneurs. Accessed 26 February 2017.

PART 1

Connectivity

2 An insider's view of e-governance under Jokowi: political promise or technocratic vision?

Yanuar Nugroho and Agung Hikmat

This chapter provides an insider's perspective on some aspects of the digital strategy of the Joko Widodo (Jokowi) administration—both authors hold positions in the Executive Office of the President (Kantor Staf Presiden, or KSP). Among the priorities Jokowi has continuously emphasised is the need to enhance the nation's competitiveness (Ministry of State Secretariat 2014). As he often said during his presidential campaign, one way to achieve this is to make all government services available and accessible online. Another motivation for promising to introduce a full range of electronic services, from e-planning and e-budgeting through to e-catalogue, e-procurement and even e-complaint handling, was to realise the benefits of e-governance for government administration. Jokowi anticipated that the roll-out of electronic government would help to reduce corruption and improve the transparency and accountability of the bureaucracy, in addition to widening the participation of citizens in policy-making (Ministry of State Secretariat 2014). That is, he saw putting government services online as a means not only to deliver better public services and facilitate collaboration, but also to bolster the credibility of his government (Raharjo 2015).

* We would like to thank Gibran Sesunan and Robertus Theodore for help in preparing material on One Map, One Data, LAPOR! and Smart City; Hellena Yoranita Souisa for transcribing the presentation on which this chapter is based; and participants at the 2016 Indonesia Update Conference in Canberra for helpful comments and input.

E-governance has transformed the way governments deliver services to citizens, increasing the convenience, efficiency and transparency of interactions (Carter and Belanger 2004). The core elements of e-governance are information and communication technology (ICT), organisational change and new skills (Pina, Torres and Acerete 2007). E-governance improves public services and democratic processes and strengthens public support for government programs by increasing the quantity and quality of government interactions with citizens and businesses (Denhardt and Denhardt 2000).

This chapter offers a critical perspective on the Jokowi administration's e-governance strategy. It aspires to draw out some of the lessons that have been learned so far: what has worked and what has not; which factors have enabled or constrained implementation; and the strengths and weaknesses in the overarching framework. This is important, because there are always consequences—both intended and unintended—that need to be taken into account when implementing any ambitious government program (Chen et al. 2006). Through an examination of how e-governance is being implemented by the Jokowi administration, we hope to reach an understanding of whether the president's vision is on track to be realised, or will remain in the realm of political promise.

This chapter focuses on four e-governance programs—One Map, One Data, LAPOR! and Smart City—to show how the Indonesian government is campaigning for e-governance 'by the governed, for the governed, and of the governed' (Yusuf 2013). The digital technology advocates in the administration believe that the use of ICT can boost the quality of service delivery, lead to reform of the bureaucracy and lift the level of engagement with citizens. But is the government's pledge to implement e-governance merely a populist political promise to win the hearts of the younger generation, or is it a well-thought-out technocratic vision? Following John (1998), Parsons (1995) and others, we argue that the successful application of e-governance requires at least three integrated frameworks: a regulatory framework to provide official directives to the bureaucracy, without which it would not be able to mobilise its resources; an institutional framework to govern the organisational arrangements across government institutions; and an accountability framework to ensure that progress is monitored, reported and measured in an open and transparent manner. All three elements are crucial to ensure that the government is able to provide citizen-centric services, convince businesses and the economy of the validity of its approach, and consolidate its political support. Only in this way can the government translate its political promise into an effective program that makes a real difference to people's lives.

E-GOVERNANCE, PUBLIC SERVICE DELIVERY AND DEVELOPMENT PRIORITIES

Indonesia has come a long way since the reform period began in 1998. Even before the arrival of the smartphone and Facebook, the country was moving away from authoritarian control and towards more open decision-making processes. Of course, the advent and adoption of the internet and other technologies have helped widen citizens' participation in every aspect of society (Lim 2002, 2003; Nugroho 2008, 2010, 2011a; Nugroho and Tampubolon 2008; Bertot, Jaeger and Grimes 2010). As a result, the voice of Indonesian citizens is heard more clearly and openly today than ever before (among many, see Nugroho 2011b).

The Indonesian government has moved from a centralised mode of service delivery with closed access to decision-making, to a more democratic, more decentralised decision-making system (Hadiz 2010). Faced with vocal public demand for better services, however, it has at times seemed confused about how to respond. Moreover, the civil service has remained somewhat militaristic and bureaucratic in style, despite reforms aimed at changing its culture. By strengthening Indonesia's digital platforms, Jokowi's administration believes that it can improve both the way in which the bureaucracy engages with Indonesian society and the quality of public services (Ministry of State Secretariat 2014). We now live in an era in which technological progress, particularly ICT innovation, affects not only the dynamics of society itself, but also how the government functions. That is why e-governance is central to Jokowi's development strategy.

Scholars define e-government and e-governance differently, with no consensus so far on the precise definitions of these terms (Estevez and Janowski 2013). Nevertheless, when describing the differences between the two concepts, academics tend to focus on five areas: government, technology, interaction, customers and society. The differences between e-governance and e-government often seem negligible, yet it is important to understand these notions because of their implications for both policy-making and public administration.

The difference between 'government' and 'governance' is explained by the type of relationship that exists between citizens and political structures. 'Government' is about how decisions are carried out, while 'governance' is more about the ways in which decisions are made. 'Government' deals with how to deliver public services, while 'governance' concerns whether or not to provide a particular service. Therefore, 'e-government' is 'the provision of routine government functions and transactions using electronic means', while 'e-governance' is the 'technology-mediated relationship between citizens and their governments

[...] over civic communication, over policy evolution, and in democratic expressions of citizen will' (Marche and McNiven 2003: 75).

Like Heeks (2001: 2), we believe that the key to e-governance is its ability to create 'a wealth of new digital connections'. These include:

- Connections within government—permitting 'joined-up thinking'.
- Connections between government and NGOs/citizens—strengthening accountability.
- Connections between government and business/citizens—transforming service delivery.
- Connections within and between NGOs—supporting learning and concerted action.
- Connections within and between communities—building social and economic development (Heeks 2001: 2).

'As a result', Heeks adds, 'the focus grows from just parts of e-administration to also encompass e-citizens, e-services and e-society'.

Spurred by the deployment of broadband infrastructure, affordable mobile devices and other online enablers, Indonesians are embracing a digital lifestyle. There are now more mobile SIM cards in Indonesia than there are people; 85 per cent of adults own a mobile phone and 43 per cent own a smartphone; and 34 per cent of Indonesians are active internet users, with internet use growing by 15 per cent in the year to January 2016 (Balea 2016). The shift in the way society is communicating and consuming media is evident in the statistics: Jakarta was declared the world's Twitter capital in 2013 (Lukman 2013) and Indonesia had 68 million Facebook users in 2015 (Loras 2016). The value of e-commerce transactions hit $2.6 billion in 2014 as Indonesians adopted new ways of performing commercial transactions (Demystify Asia 2016).

This rapid uptake of digital technology provides both opportunities and challenges for the government in the area of public service delivery. One promising opportunity is to leverage the breakthroughs made by the country's digital entrepreneurs to solve some of the 'wicked problems' in public service delivery. It may be possible, for example, to improve the daily commuting experience of the public by integrating Go-Jek's app-based ride-sharing service with the country's overloaded public transport system (Stead and Pojani 2017; see also Chapter 15 by Ford and Honan in this book). The government needs to be aware of, and seize, the opportunities arising from digital innovation. It also needs to recognise that this will mean accepting an unprecedented level of public participation in governance.[1] The Kawal Pemilu phenomenon, in which

---

1 See Nugroho (2011b) for an early study of the use of social media by civil society in Indonesia.

a group of tech-savvy 'election guardians' (*kawal pemilu*) succeeded in posting cross-checked results from every polling station during the 2014 presidential election, is a good example of how the Indonesian government could use technology to improve the functioning of the electoral system (Graft, Verhulst and Young 2016; see also Chapter 8 by Postill and Saputro).

In practice, e-governance is about facilitating two-way communication between citizens and service providers. More than just delivering services through the use of technology, it is about improving the *quality* of those services by using online platforms. This is a priority for the Jokowi government. It believes that e-governance can transform the way government delivers services, making them more convenient, efficient and transparent—although it also means that both bureaucrats and citizens will have to learn new skills. It is convinced that e-governance can strengthen democratic processes and increase public support for the government's development programs, by increasing the quantity and quality of interactions between government, citizens and businesses.

The main development focuses of the Jokowi government are food and agriculture, energy, maritime connectivity and infrastructure, particularly transport (Ministry of State Secretariat 2014). As well as fulfilling the constitutional requirement to provide health and education services and reduce poverty, the administration is committed to making further bureaucratic reforms. In the president's first plenary cabinet meeting, Jokowi added two more priorities: tourism and industry (Humas Sekneg 2015). While e-governance can certainly help the government to improve the quality of service delivery in these areas, we argue that this will only be possible if the policy is underpinned by a clear regulatory framework, a proper institutional setting within the government, and robust monitoring and evaluation. Without these essential elements, e-governance will remain a political promise, rather than becoming a well-designed technocratic policy that can change people's lives.

To support our argument, we now consider some key case studies that underline both the potential and the challenges of e-governance.

CASE STUDIES

Case study 1: One Map

The One Map policy was originally developed by Susilo Bambang Yudhoyono's government (2004–14) to address the absence of consistent geospatial information to inform government decision-making. For decades, government ministries and agencies had been producing their own maps, whose inconsistencies quickly became apparent when those maps were overlaid. The government identified three basic problems. First, there was no single, official geospatial map at an appropriate scale that all government bodies throughout Indonesia could rely on as an authoritative source of information. Second, the maps that ministries and agencies had produced to meet their own particular needs (known as thematic maps) were not accurate or reliable because they were not based on a single, official source. And third, the thematic maps were not easily usable or comparable because they used a variety of different scales.

Why does this matter? First, consistent geospatial information is essential for all government bodies, but especially those dealing with land-use, licensing and development-related matters. If the geospatial information they rely on to make decisions is not valid, then the result may be slow or—worse—misguided policy-making. Second, good geospatial information should help to reduce the incidence of corruption, especially illegal land activity involving natural resources, which is a big problem in Indonesia. Access to reliable data would assist the Corruption Eradication Commission (Komisi Pemberantasan Korupsi, or KPK) to gather evidence on illegal land-use activity, and help ministries and local governments to make better, evidence-based decisions on natural resources. Third, it would increase compliance with tax and non-tax revenue laws. Currently, around 70 per cent of the 11,000 natural resource firms operating in Indonesia do not contribute any non-tax revenue to state coffers, and the compliance of the other 30 per cent is questionable.[2] A single reference map would allow the government to understand exactly who owns what land in which areas, and tax them accordingly. Fourth, a single map would make local governments less likely to issue business permits over areas that overlap with forest and conservation areas. And finally, One Map would help the government to deliver on its flagship infrastructure projects, which have been prone to be delayed by spatial conflicts.

Given the importance of the One Map project and the degree of intergovernmental cooperation required, the president's office itself has been leading the project. The Yudhoyono government initiated the One Map policy in 2011. The project made some headway under the leadership of Kuntoro Mangkusubroto, the head of the President's Delivery Unit for Development Monitoring and Oversight (Unit Kerja Presiden untuk Pengawasan dan Pengendalian Pembangunan, or UKP4), working closely with the Geospatial Information Agency (Badan Informasi Geospasial, or BIG). Following the transition to the Jokowi administration, the Coordinating Ministry for Economic Affairs was given responsibility for coordinating the One Map project, under a new regulatory regime

---

2 Interview with KPK official, Jakarta, August 2016.

(Presidential Regulation No. 9/2016). The new regulatory framework establishes clear targets, milestones and institutional settings to speed up the delivery of the program. For the thematic maps, the target is to produce 85 thematic maps covering all 34 provinces, and integrate them into the official base map, by 2019. The thematic maps will provide geo-spatial information on forest coverage, spatial planning, land use, land tenure, natural resources and so on. Most of the maps will be produced at a scale of 1:50,000, the minimum necessary to support accurate decision-making. Given the large number of themes and the necessity to gather information from a wide variety of sources, at least 19 ministries and government agencies will need to be involved in the One Map initiative, as well as civil society organisations, development partners and other non-government bodies.

To manage this effort, Presidential Regulation No. 9/2016 establishes a robust institutional framework with several layers of governance. The head of BIG is responsible for policy execution, while the coordinating minister for economic affairs is responsible for accelerating implementation of the policy. Together, they oversee a secretariat that coordinates the work of two taskforces and 19 ministries. One taskforce is responsible for map compilation and integration, that is, collating thematic maps and integrating them into the official base map. The other is tasked with map synchronisation, that is, overlaying the thematic maps in order to identify and resolve conflicts. This process is expected to produce useful policy insights. For example, overlaying the forestry, conservation and land-use maps should reveal the existence of overlapping or illegal land-use permits. To ensure accountability, the Coordinating Ministry for Economic Affairs coordinates and monitors the activities of the ministries and government agencies, and reports every three months to the Executive Office of the President (KSP), which also acts as a channel for public input. All reports are submitted and monitored through an information system managed by KSP. This information system helps stakeholders understand the level of compliance with the goals set out in the action plan up until 2019. The routine technical meetings that are held to follow up on reports therefore also serve as forums to 'name and shame' any ministry that has not met the goals set for it.

These robust regulatory and institutional settings should help to speed up the implementation of the One Map policy, especially during the map compilation stage. Integrating the maps—especially making sure that they meet the required quality standards—has proved technically complex. Other challenges have included an unexpected directive from the president to prioritise the mapping of the Kalimantan provinces over other areas. While this resulted in a minor hiccup, the governance structure has proved sufficiently robust and flexible to accommodate the change in policy direction. The progress of the One Map initiative can be seen at http://tanahair.indonesia.go.id/home/.

Case study 2: One Data

One Data involves the implementation of the international Open Data Charter standard to ensure that all government agencies provide accurate, reliable, interchangeable and interoperable data for use in development policy-making (Open Data Charter 2015).[3] The problem in Indonesia is that datasets are scattered all over the place and do not correspond with each other because of a lack of institutional coordination in the way data are gathered and processed. At the moment, the ministries all produce their own datasets but do not communicate with each other. To give one example among many, the civil registration data held by the Ministry of Home Affairs are not correlated with the data on births generated by the Ministry of Health; as a result, those data are not standardised, exchangeable or interoperable. The fact that decision-makers cannot get reliable figures from government agencies and regions has grave implications for the quality of policy-making.

Another problem is that much of the data contained in ministry reports is still available only on paper, or in unsearchable pdf or jpg files if delivered 'electronically'. Not only does this make it difficult for other government agencies to access the data, it also creates insurmountable problems for data integration. For example, the poverty data from surveys conducted by Statistics Indonesia (Badan Pusat Statistik, or BPS) used to be distributed in an uneditable pdf file (or as an Excel file if the client was prepared to pay a fee). As a result, some social safety net programs, such as health and education subsidies for the poor, were not only inaccurately targeted but delivered late. It is these types of problems that the One Data initiative aims to resolve. The outcome should be more efficient public services, delivered in a more accountable and transparent manner. This can be achieved by gathering information into an online 'warehouse' where the data are cleaned, published in an open and interoperable format, and made accessible to all units of government.

While the benefits of One Data are clear, the system has not yet been implemented nationally, despite being started back in 2012, when it was promoted by UKP4 under Kuntoro Mangkusubroto's leadership. To date, there is still no regulatory framework making it compulsory for all government ministries and subnational governments to make their data

---

3 The program was originally known as Open Data (and is still generally referred to in this way). It was then officially named One Data to address the reservations of some government agencies about the notion of 'open' data.

freely available in an open data format. It is true that there is a growing collection of some 1,700 datasets, most of them conforming to the Open Data Charter standard, freely accessible through the One Data portal (www.data.go.id), but this is nowhere near enough.

Given the urgency of the need, KSP, the National Development Planning Agency (Badan Perencanaan Pembangunan Nasional, or Bappenas), BPS and BIG have put a three-track strategy in place to speed up the implementation of the One Data policy. First, Bappenas is leading the process of preparing the regulatory framework that will provide the legal basis for government agencies to implement One Data. Second, KSP is facilitating the piloting of One Data in a few 'champion' ministries—namely the ministries of health; education and culture; maritime affairs and fisheries; research, technology and higher education; energy and mineral resources; and environment and forestry—in addition to Bappenas itself. This should help to sharpen the content of the regulatory framework, in particular by helping to clarify the requirements for the institutional setting and the criteria for the accountability framework. At the technical level, the new regulations will need to take account of the ways in which government agencies actually share and use data. Finally, to make sure that implementation goes smoothly and all agencies are 'on board', KSP, Bappenas and BPS convene a forum every four to five weeks at which staff from government data and information units can discuss and provide feedback on the proposed changes. This forum will serve as an interim arrangement until the presidential regulation establishing a permanent regulatory framework is published. The target is to have the regulatory, institutional and accountability frameworks ready in 2017 and for all ministries to implement the One Data strategy in 2018.

It cannot be stressed enough that Indonesia's need for big data to inform development policy is imminent and urgent—in particular to help policy-makers identify problems in society more clearly. Open data protocols also provide a way for civil society and other non-government actors to interact with the government, not only by contributing thematic data (on, for example, poverty or health), but also by providing a mechanism for the public to verify and correct published, official data. At the moment, however, the potential of big data to inform and improve policy-making is only just beginning to be explored.

Given that some government bodies have already adopted the Open Data Charter standard, without waiting for national regulations to be drafted, it would be fair to say that the Indonesian government has been 'building the ship while sailing'. Central government agencies such as Bappenas, KSP and BPS have been supporting local governments that want to implement One Data in a number of ways: by helping them to set up regulatory, institutional and accountability frameworks; by fostering collaboration with civil society and other One Data advocates; by leveraging the open data commitments set out in the central government's Open Government Indonesia action plans (see, for example, Open Government Indonesia Secretariat 2016); and by providing an 'implementation toolkit' that allows local governments to share their experiences with record keeping and data sharing through a freely accessible platform.

Case study 3: LAPOR!

The Online Service for People's Aspirations and Complaints (Layanan Aspirasi dan Pengaduan Online Rakyat, or LAPOR!) is the national complaint-handling mechanism of the Indonesian government. At the moment, LAPOR! is able to handle complaints related to some 100 government agencies, 48 local governments, 90 state-owned enterprises and 130 embassies.

LAPOR! is accessible through a variety of different platforms: an SMS number, a website, Twitter and a smartphone app. It also provides a mechanism to allow whistleblowers to report secretly. Behind the screen, LAPOR! staff manually verify all complaints (currently running at around 600 per day) and channel them to the relevant ministries, agencies or governments for follow-up and action in line with agreed standards and criteria. Members of the public, including whistleblowers, can track the progress of their complaints online. To ensure accountability, LAPOR! regularly publishes statistics on the number of complaints received and how they were handled. As intended, LAPOR! has become a two-way mechanism for government to engage with citizens, for citizens to report deficiencies in public services and disclose fraud, and to empower and protect whistleblowers.

To give just one example, on 18 November 2015 a citizen of Solo called Fatkhul Imron complained to LAPOR! that the Surakarta Land Agency was holding on to his land deed for no good reason. The land agency notified LAPOR! three days later that it would check up on and respond to the complaint, and on 23 November the problem was resolved. The officer-in-charge explained the circumstances to LAPOR! and provided help to have the document returned. This case may sound minor, but in Indonesia there are very few checks and balances on the bureaucracy, so LAPOR! plays a valuable role in forcing civil servants to behave more professionally. It is hoped that this will lead to a 'trickle-down' effect where the bureaucracy wants to get it right first time, rather than having incompetent or unprofessional behaviour exposed by LAPOR!

The regulatory framework for LAPOR! sets strict service standards. All government agencies using LAPOR! must agree to verify complaints within three working days and to respond within five working days. The institutional setting provides a mechanism for verification and channelling of complaints and to ensure follow-up. The ability for the public to track complaints online is the key mechanism to ensure accountability. With LAPOR! picking up its mistakes, the bureaucracy is at least heading in the right direction for reforming government services.

The government wants to ensure that LAPOR! remains an effective, mainstream channel for the public to provide input into government well into the future. It has therefore changed its name to the National Public Service Complaint System (Sistem Pengaduan Pelayanan Publik Nasional, or SP4N) and is transferring its management from KSP (a non-structural agency) to the Ministry of Administrative and Bureaucratic Reform and the Ombudsman (structural or line agencies). To ensure a smooth transition, KSP remains responsible for overseeing the transition to these two agencies.

Case study 4: Smart City

The purpose of the Jokowi government's Smart City policy is to encourage subnational governments to make greater use of ICT to improve their governance and decision-making processes. In Jokowi's words, the goal is to foster 'citizen-centric' development through e-governance (Ministry of State Secretariat 2014). In practice, this means putting government services online where citizens can more easily access, make use of and benefit from them, and promoting greater interaction between citizens and key policy-makers. Smart City is widely acknowledged to offer the best opportunity for all levels of government, but especially subnational governments, to have a positive impact on Indonesian society.

The government promotes Smart City through the Open Government Indonesia initiative, launched in 2012 to help Indonesia meet its commitments under the international Open Government Partnership.[4] The idea of open government is to ensure high-quality public service delivery through the use of ICT across government, in order to facilitate and promote transparency, accountability, participation and innovation. As a founding member of the Open Government Partnership, Indonesia has formally committed to supporting its subnational governments to become 'smarter'.

Indonesia's Smart Cities now include Jakarta, Bandung, Semarang, Surabaya, Bojonegoro and Makassar. The case of Jakarta shows what a subnational government has to do to become a Smart City. The first

4 For more information, see the Open Government Indonesia website at http://www.opengovindonesia.org/ and the Open Government Partnership website at http://www.opengovpartnership.org/.

requirement is to ensure that governance and policy-making processes are evidence based. Hence, the government of Jakarta formed a Smart City Management Unit tasked with finding ways to use technology to deliver public services and run the bureaucracy more effectively. The unit is staffed by data scientists who gather and analyse vast amounts of data to inform decision-making. The city's decision to introduce new traffic policies, for example, was based on robust data from various sources, including leading local and global location-based application providers. All of the city's policies are to be decided in a similar manner: on the basis of evidence.

Given the importance of data in policy-making, it was natural that the government of Jakarta would commit to implementing the Open Data scheme. Government authorities now convert all data to a standard, machine-readable format, and make sure that their datasets include comprehensive meta-data. The data are then made available through a web portal that is freely accessible to the public. The city's leaders view the Smart City project as a 'co-creation' between the public and the government—ensuring that the public's views are not only captured by the government, but also reflected in policy-making. In addition, the city has introduced an accountability mechanism, a complaint-handling system called Qlue that was developed jointly with the private sector. It has rapidly gained in popularity and developed a reputation for its credibility in handling citizens' grievances.

The success of Smart City implementation in Jakarta can be attributed to strong leadership, vision and commitment; substantial regulatory change; and a well-designed institutional set-up. It is worth noting that the Smart City Management Unit reports directly to the Jakarta government, providing the proper chain of authority and accountability. Jakarta's civil service regime is also known to be effective in promoting meritocracy; by linking evidence-based service-delivery indicators to the incentive scheme for officials, the city has created a more agile bureaucracy. Wherever the citizens of Jakarta are, they can contact the city government through a public service point or service provider. This ensures that all citizens have the opportunity to participate in government. As a result, the number of complaints has fallen sharply, the number of high-quality datasets is increasing, and the economy has been improving.

Another case involves the lesser-known region of Bojonegoro in East Java, which has a population of 1.5 million. Bojonegoro was one of 15 subnational governments across the world to be selected by the Open Government Partnership to pioneer the open government model. After taking part in the pilot program in 2016, the Bojonegoro government reported that the implementation of open government had changed the district's culture from one of 'complain and complaints' to one in which people learned from each other and provided solutions, inspiration and ideas (Open Government Partnership 2016). The Bojonegoro government noted that it had become easier to construct paved roads because such projects were more scalable and less prone to corruption; that the district's oil and gas resources were better managed; that grants to high-school students were being targeted more effectively; and that civil society organisations' engagement with rural communities had become more meaningful.

As a result, the economic performance of the district improved dramatically. Between 2008 and 2015, the unemployment rate dropped from 5.9 per cent to 3.1 per cent, the poverty rate fell from 23.9 per cent to 14.0 per cent and, most impressively, the economic growth rate rocketed from 10.2 per cent to 19.9 per cent. While other factors of course contributed to this improvement, clearly the presence of a more open, determined government that was constantly looking for ways to collaborate and reform was one of the keys to success.

As in Jakarta, the district head of Bojonegoro was highly committed to the Smart City initiative, and never hesitated to issue laws, rules and regulations to guide the work of the local bureaucracy. His government put comprehensive institutional arrangements in place to promote collaboration between the government and academia, civil society, the media and the private sector—and made sure that all these relationships could be mediated online. Finally, by creating a direct communication channel between the government and the public that allowed citizens to complain openly about anything, Bojonegoro built not only an effective accountability framework, but also deeper, more meaningful, more trusting relationships with its citizens.

CONCLUDING REMARKS

We will conclude with some reflections on the state of e-governance in Indonesia. First, it is important to stress that Indonesians themselves are innovating—not just the government. Rather than being passive recipients of services, they have become engaged citizens who expect the government to deliver on its promises and to be more transparent and accountable. This is essential when we think of the impact that e-governance can have on society: engaged and innovative citizens are at the heart of any successful e-governance approach. The government *must* harness public participation. This is simply a must. It must be proactive in collecting ideas from a multitude of stakeholders, including civil society, the private sector and academics, and it must listen and respond to public grievances and aspirations through a multitude of channels. This is the basic framework that Indonesia is looking to adopt. Although it may sound simple, in many ways this is a new approach for the Indonesian government, given the country's emergence from authoritarian rule less than 20 years ago.

Second, a key factor in the success of e-governance will be the willingness of the bureaucracy to undertake reform. If we cannot convince bureaucrats that they need to move away from the old, militaristic style of service delivery into a new era of more accountable and effective government, then the promise of e-governance will remain a dream. E-governance should not be an end in itself; it should be part of wider civil service reform. Without such reform, the government will be wasting its time. To make the right kinds of reforms, we need to have a strong understanding of how the machinery of government works and how to improve it. Often this will mean tailoring reforms to specific sectors, as there is no 'one-size-fits-all' approach to e-governance that will work for every sector. Of course, an umbrella regulatory framework for e-governance is necessary, but sector-specific issues will still need to be taken into account.

The government is currently attempting to prepare a regulatory framework on e-government and e-governance that will be generally applicable across the bureaucracy and provide a foundation for the institutional set-up of the system. The aim is to provide a framework to assist the government agencies responsible for implementing the e-government policy—namely the Ministry of Administrative and Bureaucratic Reform, the Ministry of Communication and Informatics, and Bappenas—so that they can adjust their business processes and come up with an adequate coordination mechanism to deliver e-services. Without an effective coordination mechanism, the government will be running on a treadmill—that is, it will give the appearance of being busy with e-governance initiatives but it will not achieve anything substantial or lasting. E-governance requires a strong understanding of the machinery of government and how the 'centre' interacts with the periphery in each sector.

Third, it is of course necessary to invest in digital platforms and infrastructure, so money will have to be set aside in the budget to pay for this. The government must make clear, non-redundant investments in new technologies that support e-governance and data sharing. It must also convince the Indonesian people that the open data system has integrity, that is, that it is good for society rather than hindering citizens' autonomy. Put simply, Indonesians won't want to provide data if they think that the people they are giving it to lack integrity. It is therefore imperative to convince them that investments in digital platforms are smart, and help to improve society.

Fourth, e-governance needs a firm foundation in order to function well and deliver on its promises. Three integrated frameworks are necessary to ensure this: a regulatory framework to provide the legal basis for the bureaucracy to implement e-governance; an institutional framework to make sure that all actors and stakeholders are involved in a meaningful way; and an accountability framework to maintain public trust in the capacity of e-governance to deliver better public services. It is worth noting that permanent government agencies with the relevant mandate should be encouraged to take ownership of the initiative in order to ensure the sustainability of the system.

Finally, like any deep-seated government reform, the e-governance initiative requires strong vision and endorsement from the country's political leaders. Fundamental reform is difficult and needs to be encouraged. It is easy to promise reform, but translating it into an effective government program is an entirely different matter. Nevertheless, e-governance is essential for the government to provide citizen-centric services, convince the market and the economy of the validity of its approach, and consolidate its political support. Realising the political promise to deliver e-governance will not be easy, but it can be done.

REFERENCES

Balea, J. (2016) 'The latest stats in web and mobile in Indonesia (infographic)', *Tech in Asia*, 28 January. Available at https://www.techinasia.com/indonesia-web-mobile-statistics-we-are-social. Accessed 22 December 2016.

Bertot, J.C., P.T. Jaeger and J.M. Grimes (2010) 'Using ICTs to create a culture of transparency: e-government and social media as openness and anti-corruption tools for societies', *Government Information Quarterly*, 27(3): 264–71.

Carter, L., and F. Belanger (2004) 'Citizen adoption of electronic government initiatives', *Proceedings of the 37th Annual Hawaii International Conference on System Sciences*, IEEE.

Chen, Y., H. Chen, W. Huang and R.K. Ching (2006) 'E-government strategies in developed and developing countries: an implementation framework and case study', *Journal of Global Information Management*, 14(1): 23–46.

Demystify Asia (2016) 'E-commerce in Indonesia: what makes it so successful', *Demystify Asia*. Available at http://www.demystifyasia.com/e-commerce-indonesia-makes-successful/. Accessed 14 January 2017.

Denhardt, R.B., and J.V. Denhardt (2000) 'The new public service: serving rather than steering', *Public Administration Review*, 60(6): 549–59.

Estevez, E., and T. Janowski (2013) 'Electronic governance for sustainable development: conceptual framework and state of research', *Government Information Quarterly*, 30(Supplement 1): S94–S109.

Graft, A., S. Verhulst and A. Young (2016) 'Indonesia's Kawal Pemilu. Elections: free, fair and open data', GovLab and Omidyar Network, January. Available at http://odimpact.org/static/files/case-study-indonesia.pdf. Accessed 14 January 2017.

Hadiz, V.R. (2010) *Localising Power in Post-authoritarian Indonesia: A Southeast Asia Perspective*, Stanford University Press, Stanford.

Heeks, R. (2001) 'Understanding e-governance for development', i-Government Working Paper No. 11, Institute for Development Policy and Management, University of Manchester, Manchester. Available at http://unpan1.un.org/intradoc/groups/public/documents/NISPAcee/UNPAN015484.pdf. Accessed 14 January 2017.

Humas Sekneg (2015) 'Presiden Jokowi: potensi sektor pariwisata kita lebih dari negara lain' [President Jokowi: our tourism sector has more potential than any other country's], Ministry of State Secretariat of the Republic of Indonesia (Kementerian Sekretariat Negara Republik Indonesia), 16 February. Available at http://www.setneg.go.id/index.php?option=com_content&task=view&id=8726. Accessed 23 December 2016.

John, P. (1998) *Analysing Public Policy*, Continuum, London.

Lim, M. (2002) 'Cyber-civic space: from panopticon to pandemonium?', *International Development and Planning Review*, 24(4): 383–400.

Lim, M. (2003) 'The internet, social networks and reform in Indonesia', in N. Couldry and J. Curran (eds) *Contesting Media Power: Alternative Media in a Networked World*, Rowman & Littlefield, Oxford: 273–88.

Loras, S. (2016) 'Social media in Indonesia: big numbers with plenty of room to grow', *ClickZ*, 22 February. Available at https://www.clickz.com/social-media-in-indonesia-big-numbers-with-plenty-of-room-to-grow/94062/. Accessed 14 January 2017.

Lukman, E. (2013) 'Indonesia is social: 2.4 per cent of world's Twitter posts come from Jakarta (infographic)', *Tech in Asia*, 13 March. Available at https://www.techinasia.com/indonesia-social-jakarta-infographic. Accessed 22 December 2016.

Marche, S., and J.D. McNiven (2003) 'E-government and e-governance: the future isn't what it used to be', *Canadian Journal of Administrative Sciences*, 20(1): 74–86.

Ministry of State Secretariat (2014) *Nawacita* [Nine Aspirations], Kementerian Sekretariat Negara Republik Indonesia (Ministry of State Secretariat of the Republic of Indonesia). Available at http://indonesia.go.id/?page_id=7853. Accessed 22 December 2016.

Nugroho, Y. (2008) 'Adopting technology, transforming society: the internet and the reshaping of civil society activism in Indonesia', *International Journal of Emerging Technologies and Society*, 6(22): 77–105.

Nugroho, Y. (2010) 'NGOs, the internet and sustainable urban development: the case of Indonesia', *Information, Communication & Society*, 13(1): 88–120.

Nugroho, Y. (2011a) 'Opening the black box: the adoption of innovations in the voluntary sector', *Research Policy*, 40(5): 761–77.

Nugroho, Y. (2011b) 'Citizens in @ction: collaboration, participatory democracy and freedom of information', Manchester Institute of Innovation Research, University of Manchester, and HIVOS Regional Office Southeast Asia, Manchester and Jakarta, March.

Nugroho, Y., and G. Tampubolon (2008) 'Network dynamics in the transition to democracy: mapping global networks of contemporary Indonesian civil society', *Sociological Research Online*, 13(5). Available at http://www.socresonline.org.uk/13/5/3.html. Accessed 14 January 2017.

Open Data Charter (2015) 'International Open Data Charter', September. Available at http://opendatacharter.net/wp-content/uploads/2015/10/opendatacharter-charter_F.pdf. Accessed 22 December 2016.

Open Government Indonesia Secretariat (2016) 'Open Government Indonesia Action Plan 2016–2017', Jakarta, October. Available at http://www.opengovpartnership.org/sites/default/files/Indonesia_NAP_2016-2017_ENG.pdf.

Open Government Partnership (2016) 'Bojonegoro, Indonesia: OGP subnational pioneers', 24 February. Available at http://www.opengovpartnership.org/node/8968.

Parsons, W. (1995) *Public Policy: Introduction to the Theory and Practice of Policy Analysis*, Edward Elgar, Cheltenham.

Pina, V., L. Torres and B. Acerete (2007) 'Are ICTs promoting government accountability? A comparative analysis of e-governance developments in 19 OECD countries', *Critical Perspectives on Accounting*, 18(5): 583–602.

Raharjo, P. (2015) 'Developing administrative reform of the working cabinet', *International Journal of Advanced Research*, 3(11): 1,238–45.

Stead, D., and D. Pojani (2017) 'The urban transport crisis in emerging economies: a comparative overview', in D. Stead and D. Pojani (eds) *The Urban Transport Crisis in Emerging Economies*, Springer: 283–95.

Yusuf, M. (2013) 'Fenomena kepemimpinan politik Jokowi' [The phenomenon of Jokowi's political leadership], *GaneÇ Swara*, 7(1): 26–31.

3 Mobile phones: advertising, consumerism and class

Emma Baulch

One of the major challenges facing scholars seeking to investigate political and ideological developments in contemporary Indonesian public life is the coincidence of two significant phenomena with distinct historical roots: regime change in 1998, and changes to the media technologies by which public life is produced, circulated and sensed. For the most part, scholars of Indonesian politics have sought to negotiate this challenge by treating new media technologies as a neutral factor that has played no role in shaping political and ideological developments. Major studies of contemporary Indonesian politics sketch a continuum on which regime change in 1998 and decentralisation in 2001—but not technological developments—feature as major turning points shaping the contours of public life.

In this chapter, I develop an alternative historical framework for analysing the ideological implications of the spread of new media. I argue that we cannot hope to understand the role of technology by positioning the digital in a post-authoritarian frame—the predominant one for analysing political change in contemporary Indonesia. There is little doubt that post-authoritarianism is useful for studying the intricacies of the formal dimensions of Indonesian democracy in the twenty-first century, but it should not be accorded primacy in the study of digital change. When we hitch the study of digital Indonesia to an agenda that seeks to

* The author would like to thank the Australian Research Council for funding the project on which this paper is based: 'Mobile Indonesians: social differentiation and digital literacies in the 21st century'. Several paragraphs in this chapter will be published in *Cultural Politics* (Baulch, forthcoming).

understand emerging forms of political organisation by looking at society through the lens of elections, parties, social movements and states, we forgo the opportunity to use the lens of media technologies. In other words, we forgo the opportunity to understand political change through theories of media change.

This chapter draws on such theories to consider how changes in media technologies precipitate political change. It does so by focusing on an important part of digital Indonesia as we know it today: the mobile phone. The vernacular term for a mobile phone in Indonesia is 'HP'—short for 'hand phone'. In this chapter I discuss both the historical roots and the social and political implications of the rapid uptake of mobile phones in Indonesia over the last few years. I trace the rise in popularity of the HP to a set of post-Cold War media deregulation packages that opened up the telecommunications sector, and consider its place, not as a singularly revolutionary object, but as one that rode in the wake of cultural changes set in motion by the spread of other new media technologies, most notably advertising-funded television. I understand the HP, then, to inhabit a broader 'new technological paradigm' (Castells 2010) that was set in train by the economic reforms of the late 1980s—the social and cultural consequences of which unfolded over the next couple of decades—and that coincided with, and to some degree was shaped by, regime change in the late 1990s. I aim to examine the ideas about what it means to be digitally connected that emerge from this paradigm, and to analyse the nascent forms of social organisation it is generating.

A NEW TECHNOLOGICAL PARADIGM

Most people in Indonesia have a mobile phone, however basic. This only became true less than 10 years ago, when the number of people subscribing to a mobile service began to outstrip the number connected to a landline. Between 2000 and 2015, mobile phone subscriptions increased from 1.8 to 132.4 per 100 people. Over the same period, fixed-line connections increased from 3.2 to a mere 8.8 per 100 people.[1]

A number of developments have given rise to this astounding transformation of Indonesia's communication landscape. First, the costs associated with connecting to and using mobile networks fell dramatically because of increased competition between providers (Lee and Findlay 2005). As a result, cheap handsets began to appear on the market; the informal repair-and-recycle economy began to grow, making buying,

1 Based on International Telecommunication Union (ITU) data; see http://www.itu.int/en/ITU-D/Statistics/Pages/stat/default.aspx.

maintaining and upgrading a phone more affordable for ordinary people; and mobile telephony became a more visible, audible and influential part of public life throughout the archipelago. Second, from the late 1980s the Indonesian government embarked on a series of reforms that transformed the telecommunications sector, including the liberalisation of licensing and the divestiture of state-owned enterprises. This decade of policy reform was essential to create the conditions of increased competition and falling costs that supported the uptake of the HP.

From 1964 to 1989, under Law No. 5/1964 on Telecommunications, two bodies were responsible for infrastructure and services: PN Telekomunikasi and ITT. PN Telekomunikasi, which became Perumtel in 1974 and PT Telkom in 1991, was responsible for domestic telephony services, while ITT, which became Indosat in 1980, was responsible for international telephony services. Network expansion was funded directly from the state budget and through loans from donor organisations such as the Intergovernmental Group on Indonesia.

When the funding for network expansion began to dry up in the mid-1980s, the government was forced to consider other ways to fund telecommunications infrastructure. In 1989 it passed Law No. 3/1989 on Telecommunications, which allowed private operators to participate in the market for the first time (in partnership with state-owned enterprises). This led to a number of agreements between private investors and state-owned enterprises to supply basic telephony services. The 1989 law also liberalised the internet and paging markets, leading to public–private arrangements between Telkom and foreign companies such as France Cables et Radio, Telstra, Cable & Wireless Singapore and SingTel. The first 2G Global System for Mobile Communications (GSM) licences were issued between 1994 and 1996 to Excelcomindo (now known as XL Axiata), Satelindo and Telkomsel, all of which were joint ventures between private investors and incumbents (Lee and Findlay 2005; Rasyid 2005; Latipulhayat 2010).

After the Asian financial crisis in 1997–98, Indonesia agreed to reform its telecommunications sector further as part of a recovery package proposed by the International Monetary Fund (IMF); in particular, the IMF wanted the Indonesian government to annul the exclusive rights granted to Telkom in the fixed-line sector and to relax restrictions on foreign investment. Around the same time, Indonesia signed up to the World Trade Organization's General Telecommunications Agreement, which committed the government to providing fair competition in the telecommunications sector under the supervision of an independent regulator, and to eliminating fixed-line exclusivity in the local, long-distance and international telephony markets according to a fixed timetable (Lee and Findlay 2005: 355).

In 1999, the Indonesian government promulgated a new telecommunications law, Law No. 36/1999 on Telecommunications. This law introduced two important changes. First, it did away with the need for private operators to collaborate with state-owned incumbents in providing basic services for fixed-line and mobile telephony. Second, it relaxed restrictions on foreign investment. Controversially, Singapore Technologies Telemedia bought a 42 per cent stake in Indosat in 2002, effectively turning it into a private (rather than state-owned) company. GSM licences were issued to IM3, Mobile-8 Telecom, Lippo Telecom and Bakrie Telecom in 2002 and 2003 (Lee and Findlay 2005; Latipulhayat 2010). The deregulation of the telecommunications sector gave rise to the current state of affairs in mobile telephony, in which six providers compete for a market of 353.7 million mobile phone users (Business Monitor International, cited in Fast Market Research 2016). Telkom subsidiary Telkomsel is the dominant player in this market, followed by Indosat and XL Axiata. Together, they enjoy an 84 per cent market share (Latipulhayat 2010; BMI 2015).

It is important to note this policy background here, because it highlights the absence of any inherent links between post-authoritarianism and the process of telecommunications reform. This suggests that the proliferation of the HP in the twenty-first century was not a product of post-authoritarian reform, but rather of the earlier reform of Indonesian capitalism precipitated by a host of deregulation measures after the end of the Cold War.

While the telecommunications industry was being deregulated in the 1990s, other developments were also afoot. The most significant of these, in terms of its cultural effects, was the deregulation of television. In 1988, the government issued a decree that ended its monopoly over television. This led to the establishment of five new private television stations between 1988 and 1995 (Sen and Hill 2000) and a further five between 2000 and 2002 (Hollander, d'Haenans and Bardoel 2009).

As a consequence, the share of television in the overall media consumption of Indonesians grew considerably in the 1990s and 2000s (Hendriyani et al. 2011, 2012, 2016). The commercial television stations also began to deliver new kinds of programs, especially news programs (Sen and Hill 2000; Hollander, d'Haenens and Bardoel 2009). With the growth in TV stations and TV audiences, the advertising industry grew at a staggering rate. Sen and Hill (2000: 115–16) have estimated that the number of television sets grew sixfold in the 1980s, and that advertising expenditure grew at a commensurate rate in the early 1990s.

Sen and Hill (2000) argue that the first wave of commercial television expansion did not signal a paradigm shift in a political or economic sense; as they point out, the Suharto family retained firm control of the television industry. However, the deregulation of television did usher in important cultural shifts. The business model of the commercial stations relied on paid advertising, so viewers not only began to watch more television, they also began to watch more advertisements. As a result, consumerist ideology began to play a more prominent role in the formation of cultural tropes. In an earlier work (Baulch 2007), I have discussed how the new kinds of pop music programming on commercial television stations in the mid-1990s influenced notions of identity among young people, detaching them from the traditional one of the patriotic youth (*pemuda*) and moving them towards the more flexible, ephemeral narratives shaped by television.

Following Castells (2010: 5), I argue that the expansion of private television in the 1990s and 2000s laid the basis for a 'new technological paradigm' that encouraged consumerism and allowed the class distinctions established under the New Order to be articulated in new ways. Castells focuses on the 'informational economies' where post-Keynesian economics delivered economic stability and growth after the end of World War II, a category that obviously does not include Indonesia.[2] Nevertheless, by linking emerging social and cultural imaginings and modes of organisation to technological change, Castells' work opens a path for us to understand the HP as part of a broader scaffold of communication technologies, rather than as part of a post-authoritarian polity.

The beginnings of the new technological paradigm that is the setting for the HP can be traced to the late 1980s and the reforms set in train by falling oil prices and the end of the Cold War. Viewing the mobile phone in this context reveals a history in which regime change takes something of a back seat. The period preceding the reforms had been marked by the use of the press and state television to instil a strong sense of a society constituted by two social forces—the middle class and the masses.

The technological paradigm that is the subject of this chapter emerged after the end of the Cold War and featured the expansion of, first, commercial television advertising and, slightly later, digital technologies. During this period, the notion of consumer sovereignty began to play an increasingly influential role in how Indonesians saw themselves. The

2 For Indonesians, the decades from the end of World War II to the mid-1970s were a period of upheaval. Stability and economic growth were not delivered until the 1970s, a period of economic decline and restructuring in much of the Global North. The oil price rises that sparked rampant inflation and reform in the United States were a windfall to an Indonesian authoritarian state overseeing the consolidation, rather than fragmentation, of class formations. The Indonesian case provides a perspective on the processes and nature of changes leading up to the development of a digitally equipped capitalism that is distinct from that to be gained through a focus on the Global North.

sense of the middle class as exclusively secular and Western began to dissolve as a Muslim fashion and consumer culture developed, and as various forms of East Asian pop culture were enthusiastically consumed by urban middle-class youth. Conspicuous consumption and wealth became increasingly accepted features of the public culture, but more aggressively celebratory articulations of lower class-ness also emerged during this period (Heryanto 2009; Weintraub 2011).

Below, I explore how the HP both shapes and is shaped by the new technological paradigm, largely by focusing on changes and continuities in the articulation of class distinctions. I consider whether the acute user sensitivities associated with mobile phones afford the lower classes the opportunity to contest and manipulate this consumerist ideology, or only cause them to be enveloped by it (Dean 2014; Hinson 2014).

I address these questions from two angles. First, I consider the powerful understandings of what it means to be digitally networked that have emerged from the major centres of media production. By analysing the ads that telecommunications companies make for television, I hope to draw out some of the cultural implications of the concurrent expansion of televisual and telecommunications networks in the late twentieth and early twenty-first centuries. The telcos rely on television advertising to render their products and services into commodity form—that is, to make them marketable and desirable. This reliance pricks at the myth of the disruptive capacity of the digital, given that advertising-funded television (despite being relatively new) addresses audiences in ways that reinforce longstanding class distinctions. Second, I consider whether and how the HP has enhanced people's capacity to manipulate such powerful ideas about what it means to be digitally connected. On the one hand, consumerism has reinforced longstanding class distinctions, but on the other, it has given rise to new forms of civic engagement organised around notions of ethical consumption. Although not limited to the lower classes, these new forms of associational life have pried open opportunities for the articulation of an aggressive lower-class cultural politics.

ASPECTS OF THE INDONESIAN ADVERTISING MARKET

When the HP phenomenon began to gather momentum in the early twenty-first century, it did so in an environment in which advertising-funded television had only just become an important part of many Indonesians' everyday lives. Therefore, it rode in the wake of a rapidly evolving and dynamic media environment that was already precipitating the rise of a new consumerism. In this context, the advertisements made by telecommunications companies for television forcefully shaped dominant understandings of what it meant to be connected to a digital network.

Before examining some of these ads, I would like to flag a couple of features of the Indonesian market. First, unlike in countries such as the United Kingdom and Australia, where spending on digital ads is fast eclipsing spending on TV ads, in Indonesia, most advertising expenditure goes to television (about 55 per cent, compared with 28 per cent in Australia). Between 2008 and 2015, Indonesia's expenditure on television advertising increased more than fourfold, from $1,603 million to $6,508 million. In 2015, the TV spend was eight times more than the digital media spend ($809 million).[3] By comparison, advertising expenditure on digital media in Australia rose from $1.8 billion in 2008 to $4.8 billion in 2015, while ad spending on television remained steady over the same period, at around $3.5 billion.[4] The telecommunications sector is Indonesia's fifth-biggest spender on television advertisements, after personal care, food and beverages, the public sector and the pharmaceutical industry, and is on a par with the auto industry.[5]

The second feature of note concerns the size and nature of the Indonesian market for telecommunications products. Although the mobile phone market is huge, the majority of the market is made up of prepaid subscribers, almost all of whom use their phones to make voice calls or send text messages. On average, these subscribers spend only two or three dollars each per month to maintain their connections to their networks. There is intense competition between the dominant telcos—especially Telkomsel, Indosat and XL Axiata—to capture this market of SMSers and voice callers, because even though their monthly outlays may be tiny, their numbers are enormous (BMI 2015).

Although Indonesians spend more than twice as much time per day looking at their mobile devices as they spend watching television, expenditure on TV ads makes sense in view of low smartphone penetration (about 23 per cent), the predominance of 2G (rather than more advanced) mobile networks, and the fact that 97 per cent of the population watches television at least once each month.[6] In short, the telcos rely

3 See https://www.statista.com/statistics/386393/advertising-expenditures-by-medium-indonesia/, accessed 11 November 2016.

4 See http://www.statista.com/statistics/386360/advertising-expenditures-by-medium-australia/, accessed 3 October 2016.

5 See https://www.statista.com/statistics/466397/ad-spend-industry-indonesia/, accessed 12 November 2016.

6 See http://redwing-asia.com/market-data/market-data-media/, accessed 21 September 2016.

on television to reach a market largely made up of SMSers and voice callers. Television therefore remains central to the imagining of a digitally networked nation.

I focus on the ads produced by four providers: As, Simpati, Mentari and XL Axiata. As and Simpati are both subsidiaries of the partly state-owned Telkomsel group and have a combined market share of around 46 per cent; Mentari is owned by the partly state-owned Indosat group and has a market share of 21 per cent; and XL Axiata is a privately owned company with a market share of around 16 per cent. I conceive of telco ads as texts that imbue telecommunications products and services with social meaning by turning them into commodities that are capable of being marketed to a consuming public.

The ads I have selected mainly use celebrity endorsements, representations of social media and representations of SMSing and voice calling to address consumers.[7] My analysis of the content of these ads indicates that they contain mixed messages about the digitally networked consuming public and the novelty of digital technology. On the one hand, the ads using celebrity endorsers give a sense of a nation that is in flux and contested, suggesting that the new telecommunications products can be associated with new ways of being. On the other hand, the depictions of particular products—SMS and social media—restore old ways of being. Social media, used only by the web-connected, smartphone-owning few, is shown as increasing users' social capital, whereas SMS and voice calling, functions used primarily by the non-smartphone-owning, non-web-connected many, are depicted in ways that reinstate elitist notions of the masses as unruly crowds. Therefore, the ads propose that the new telecommunications infrastructure can be associated with a limited kind of change, in which the cultural ascendance of the middle class is retained.

DEPICTIONS OF SOCIETY THROUGH THE PRISM OF TELEVISION ADVERTISING

The use of celebrities to endorse telecommunications products and services began around 2012. The well-known faces associated with major brands included Agnes Monica, a Chinese Indonesian singer and actor (contracted to Simpati); the pop band Noah and its lead singer Ariel, who had just been released from prison after spending three years in jail for distributing pornographic material (XL Axiata); Anggun, a 'lady rocker'

7 All ads discussed in this chapter were retrieved from YouTube. Gde Putra and Roro Sawita undertook the research for this section of the article, published in Sawita, Putra and Baulch (2014).

who had achieved success in Europe in the 1990s and was rebooting her Indonesian career in the 2000s (Mentari); and Sule, a low-brow comedian who had risen to fame through his appearances on the prime-time slapstick show *Opera Van Java* (As). This cohort of celebrities intimates a national body politic that is fragile, contested, in motion and full of hybridity; it works to associate a digitally networked nation with change and novelty.

Simpati began to consistently showcase strong, independent women from around 2011—presumably as a metaphor for the network's strong signal—and placing Monica at the forefront of the brand drove this association home. Monica has attained fame despite her marginal status on several fronts—she is Christian, Chinese and single. One of the ads shows her celebrating her independence and confidence; dressed in a tight-fitting gym outfit, she commands a group of male dancers to 'speak their minds'.

XL Axiata's strategy has been to target school-age social media users by promoting cheap data packages. The company's contract with Noah, especially Ariel, has reinforced the brand as one designed for middle-class, social-media-savvy youth. In 2010, Ariel was sentenced to three and a half years in jail for distributing recordings of himself having sex with fellow celebrities. His story is entwined with the power and allure of social media: the video-recordings for which he was jailed were circulated widely on social media and could be viewed on YouTube. Ariel was convicted shortly after the parliament had passed a highly controversial bill that sought to eradicate pornography from the public sphere by regulating the way people, especially women, appeared in public. Ariel was charged under that law (Law No. 44/2008 on Pornography), and the high level of public support for him at the time was widely considered to be closely linked to the public opposition to the new law.

For Mentari, the contract with Anggun was part of a new branding strategy aimed at breaking into the high end of the market, especially the market for smartphones. Prior to 2012, the Mentari and As brands had not been well differentiated—both had targeted the lower end of the market comprising mainly SMS and voice calls. By contracting Sule, who plays on his persona as a villager with a thick provincial accent, As signalled its intention to remain associated with the lower end of the market.

Unlike Ariel, Anggun and Sule are not contentious figures, but they both could be called hybrid ones. Anggun has spent much of her adult life living in France and is married to a French national. Sule, meanwhile, is a nationally famous comedian who lives in Jakarta—not (or no longer) the uncouth villager he portrays in his comedy routines. The As campaign in which he stars also features other hybrid figures; in one of the ads, Sule appears alongside Eurasian actor Rianti Cartwright and the effeminate Smash boy band (https://www.youtube.com/watch?v=hv-tNCin2h8).

Although celebrity endorsers commonly evince hybridity, contestation and flux, that does not mean that the more stable, longstanding distinctions between social classes become indiscernible. On the one hand, the telecommunications networks are keen to associate their brands with people who stretch the boundaries of the nation, but on the other, those people also have socio-economic characteristics that suggest the endurance of class distinctions and their attendant high–low dimensions. Moreover, class-based distinctions are used to match celebrities with particular segments of the HP market, thereby reinforcing the portrayal of the digitally networked nation as a sharply hierarchical society. Thus Sule, the uncouth villager, is assigned responsibility for representing the market for SMS and voice calls, while Monica and Ariel, the sophisticated urban dwellers, are responsible for representing the market for smartphone-owning data users.

Similarly, an XL Axiata ad featuring Ariel shows how the telecommunications networks can function as an avenue for social capital and mobility (https://www.youtube.com/watch?v=dWWdkeZWSRU). In the ad, the car in which Ariel and his band members are travelling breaks down on a country road. A mechanic fixes the car and offers to forgo payment if Ariel agrees to pose with a group of onlooking fans. When the mechanic uploads the photo to Facebook, a bar appears on his screen showing a huge and rapidly increasing number of 'likes'.

This ad tells a story of mobility while reminding the viewer of the ever-present possibility of immobility, as represented by the broken-down car. As mentioned earlier, the majority of telecommunications users in Indonesia pre-pay for their connections, spending very small amounts (approximately $2–3 per month) (BMI 2015: 18). Therefore, many telco users face being disconnected from the network without warning if their credit runs out. The ad presents XL Axiata's affordable rates as a solution to this constant source of anxiety, while positioning social media as a crucial source of social capital needed to make it in consumer society. In the ad, the use of social media puts ordinary people on an upwardly mobile path towards celebrity.

In contrast to the portrayals of social media emphasising the emancipatory promise of social media platforms for ordinary people, the advertisements for the SMS and voice call market make no such promise. Most SMS ads use large banner text to alert viewers to bonuses and free SMS services, but a few use actors to situate their products in particular social settings. In doing so, they depict a realm that is quite distinct from that of the web-connected data users who star in the social media ads. Rather than linking the telcos' products to spectacular stories of upward mobility, the advertisements for the SMS and voice call market depict a realm of schoolyard micro-politics, the humdrum working lives of the lower classes or slapstick humour prioritising colour and movement over narrative.[8] A view of an acutely hierarchical tele-networked society emerges from this corpus of ads, in which web-connected users inhabit the tele-connected 'sublime', while SMSers and voice callers are relegated to the 'ridiculous'. We should not overstate the importance of social media in the Indonesian telecommunications landscape given that 75 per cent of telco users do not use social media, but nor should we underestimate its mythical force.

Telco ads constitute the 'undercoat' of the televisual canvas, but the HP affords telco users the ability to add their own 'topcoat'—that is, to manipulate the stereotypes proposed by the broadcast media. First, as Weiss (2014: 92) argues, social media spaces add a virtual (cyberspace) domain to the existing real-world topography, giving social media users the ability to alter the times and spaces in which they engage with the technology. Second, the HP gives people the capacity to edit images independently of the major centres of production, with little technical expertise or capital outlay. A growing body of work on selfies, for example, examines the extent to which people play with their own images to posit social alternatives (Senft and Baym 2015).

In the next section, I discuss the role the HP plays in emerging forms of associational life precipitated by the rise of consumerist ideology. Organisations such as the Hijabers Community and Indonesia Gardening (Indonesia Berkebun) focus on single issues such as food or the *hijab* while adhering to a moral code that positions them as separate from an imagined consumerist mainstream.[9] Many such organisations are decidedly urban and middle class, and employ Instagram, Facebook and Twitter. But new kinds of lower-class politics are also being articulated as variants of the emerging forms of associational life revolving around ethical consumption. The case I discuss next—that of the Balinese pop idol Nanoe Biroe and his fans—is one such variant.

---

8 For an example of each, see respectively https://www.youtube.com/watch?v=owjY99TYLsk (produced by AS); https://www.youtube.com/watch?v=pSKKRER7SQA (produced by XL Axiata); and https://www.youtube.com/watch?v=hv-tNCin2h8 (the XL Axiata ad featuring Ariel discussed earlier).

9 The Hijabers Community was established in Jakarta by a group of young Muslim women to discuss issues of interest to girls; see http://hijaberscommunity.blogspot.com.au/. Indonesia Berkebun is an urban farming movement dedicated to building environmental awareness and providing green spaces in the city; see http://indonesiaberkebun.org/about/.

A NEW ASSOCIATIONAL LIFE

In the early years of the twenty-first century, a strange new word erupted on the streets of Denpasar. The word, 'Baduda' (from *baduda* meaning 'dung beetle'), refers to the fans of the Balinese pop singer Nanoe Biroe, who is best known for his songs about social issues, sung in low Balinese. The Baduda are easily recognised by the clothing and other paraphernalia they wear while riding their motorbikes around the city. Belonging and acting like a Baduda holds a special political potency. The group emerged in the context of a revival of ethnic Balinese-ness, in which the pure and the high were formally privileged. The name 'Baduda', by contrast, suggested a fondness for dirt, the low and the impure.

Nanoe Biroe's rise to fame can be understood in the context of two developments. The first was the privatisation of the television industry, which gave rise to new patterns of relationships between pop musicians and their audiences, and prompted a proliferation of fan cultures, of which the Baduda serve as a good example (Baulch 2013). The second development was the transformation of popular conceptions of the value of regional languages (*bahasa daerah*) as a consequence of the implementation of decentralisation in 2001. Once viewed as markers of backwardness, regional languages have become not only indicators of local authenticity and pride in the context of local elections, but also ways of accommodating and expressing notions of advancement and modernity within youth culture.

In the face of significant change on a number of fronts, the HP has become one of a mix of tools people use to to stake a place for themselves among the changes taking place around them. Put another way, in order to grasp what the HP 'does' to the televisual canvas, we need to acknowledge that it is just one component of a broader assemblage. In the case of the Baduda, this mix includes selfies and SMS, but also t-shirts and language play. For example, when I asked the Baduda what appealed to them about being a Nanoe Biroe fan, they consistently replied '*menyama*'—solidarity or togetherness. 'Menyama' is also the title song from Nanoe Biroe's seventh album, *Timpal Sujati* [True Friend]; it speaks, broadly speaking, to the importance of loving your neighbour, working hard, being faithful to your friends and showing empathy to the downtrodden. The appeal of *menyama* as a key word for the Baduda, then, points to the power of Biroe's lyrics, seen as encapsulating the fans' communal identities and moral aspirations.

Like Biroe's songs, the t-shirts sold at U-Rock, the official Nanoe Biroe merchandise outlet, use low Balinese inflected with the rough Denpasar dialect to express a valorisation of the common people and a disdain for conspicuous shows of wealth. The messages printed on them include

'Lacur sugih patuh gen yen meju mengkep' [Whether you are poor or rich, your shit stinks just the same], *'Ajum ci'* [You're so up yourself], *'Med cang kene'* [I'm so bored] and *'Pang cang kene'* [Leave me alone].

The Baduda fans I interviewed listed t-shirt wearing (over buying CDs or attending concerts) as the most important way of participating in Nanoe Biroe fandom. The importance of t-shirts can be partly understood in the context of Biroe's art school background and his talent for composing eye-catching designs. But it also reflects a broader desire to use ordinary objects as anchors for the new moral codes emerging in contemporary, consumerist Indonesia.

When I asked the Baduda how they realised the key virtue of *menyama* to connect with other fans, they referred me to two types of gathering that allowed them to express their moral aspirations as Baduda. Both shed light on the vital role the HP plays in marking the Baduda's ethical code as something that is both contemporary and a product of the lower classes.

The first of these gatherings was a regular Saturday night get-together of the kind that has been a common part of Indonesian pop culture consumption for decades. However, the Baduda version, which fans refer to as a *'seminar'* (from *semeton minum arak*, or 'palm wine drinking community'), reveals a shifts in the usual ritual, suggested by the presence of women. I want to suggest that the feminisation of such gatherings results from the spatial complexity brought about by the introduction of mobile phones to such gatherings. The use of smartphones by female Baduda (Badudawati) opens these traditionally masculine gatherings to alternative modes of performance, particularly by women.

Conventionally, the Saturday night gatherings would showcase the talents of those with musical or rhetorical abilities, relegating others to a kind of onlooker status, referred to as *bengong*, or 'staring emptily into space'. Since the popularisation of smartphones, though, this has become a thing of the past; the onlookers (mainly women) at such gatherings are no longer silent and disengaged, but busy and preoccupied with their phones. When I asked the women what they were doing with their phones, they said they were issuing shout-outs to people who were not in attendance, or uploading photos of the gathering to Facebook. This suggests that the smartphone has altered the power dynamics of the Saturday night gathering by providing those on the periphery with a new social function: bridging the gap between the online and offline Baduda spaces, between presence and absence at a Baduda gathering.

The Badudawati's Facebook posts about their adventures at these gatherings indicate that the smartphone has increased the spatial and temporal complexity of the Saturday night *seminar*, opened it to various modes of performance and enabled those on the margins to create an alternative social space while still being present at the 'boys' party'. Indeed, when I hooked up with some of these women on Facebook, I discovered that they took their careers as Badudawati very seriously, adopting the word 'Baduda' or a Nanoe Biroe album title as their profile names, and clearly taking pride in their visibility as Baduda. A young woman called Gektu Sukma, for example, consistently appeared in the Baduda 'uniform' of a backward-facing baseball cap and black t-shirt. The fact that young women like Gektu link Facebook use to their presence at a *seminar* highlights the significance and degree of agency inferred by the selfies they post on their Facebook feeds. The Badudawati may be marginal to this core Baduda ritual, but on Facebook they appear front and centre, often wearing t-shirts bearing the word *'seminar'*, as if to reclaim this event as a feminine one. In one post, Putu Tomboyz leads a phalanx of Badudawati dressed in Nanoe Biroe designs, among which her own *seminar* t-shirt stands out. On Facebook, these women cannot be overlooked or silenced. They demand attention.

The second event fans referred me to when I asked them how they realised *menyama* was a concert that took place on 13 August 2012 on a stage erected on the filthy Badung river that runs through Denpasar. In later press interviews, Biroe said that the concert was a bid to focus authorities' attention on the need to clean up the river, but it was also clearly a publicity stunt to earn him a fourth listing in the Indonesian Museum of Records – this time for the first concert performed on a river. Previous listings were earned for having the longest (extendable) album cover, singing for 80 hours straight and signing the most CD covers ever signed (TrashstockBali 2015).

The fans I interviewed described the concert as a seminal experience for them in their careers as Baduda, saying that being in the river, getting wet and splashing around had changed them in fundamental ways. When asked how they came to know about the concert, they said they had received an SMS from Nanoe Biroe's management team telling them when and where it would take place. Biroe's store manager and brother, Man Danoe, later confirmed to me that this highly successful event had indeed been promoted entirely by SMS. He described how U-Rock staff diligently record customers' mobile phone numbers at the time of purchase, then transfer those numbers to a database. The database is then used to SMS consumers about sales promotions, or to invite them to spectacular events that may transform them as Baduda.

This mode of addressing consumers is not unique to Bali or to Nanoe Biroe, but what makes it significant for a study of the Baduda as a group with a distinct social identity are the particular meanings attributed to SMS in Indonesia, and, by extension, how the use of SMS positions people on the social hierarchy. When I asked Man Danoe why the management team preferred SMS over, say, Twitter or WhatsApp, he replied that Twitter was 'too confusing' and that SMS was simpler, more direct and easier to use. I contend that this sort of affinity for one media form, and antipathy towards others, is shaped not by the technical capacities of each application, but rather by the cultural discourses that surround them—discourses that have been accentuated by the advent of the smartphone.

In contemporary Indonesia, the SMS is infused with a decidedly low-class flavour—it occupies the realm of the rough, the vulgar, the direct. Thajib (2011) writes about how the lower classes use SMS to code their speech, causing the urban elites to relegate them, and the medium, to the realm of the uncivilised. SMS is a consistent theme in the lower-class genre of popular songs known as *dangdut*. Readers of the *Bali Post* send text messages to the editor for publication in a special section titled 'SMS', using the rough, critical tones reminiscent of Nanoe Biroe's speech. However, as Biroe's adept use of SMS to reach a lower-class public demonstrates, the medium does not just disempower people by tagging them with a low social status; it can also throw up resources for the production of counterpublics—a sociality that 'maintains at some level, conscious or not, an awareness of its subordinate status. The cultural horizon against which it marks itself off is not just a general or wider public, but a dominant one' (Warner 2002: 119).

CONCLUSION: MOBILE PHONES, CONSUMERISM AND CLASS

In Asian contexts, the increasingly visible presence of multinational corporations, in the form of media content, new technologies or food, has advanced 'projects of middle-class advancement and social distancing' (Doron 2012: 566; see also Liechty 2003; Mazzarella 2003; Wang 2008). Doron pays particular attention to how the perpetuation of class divisions lies at the heart of the global proliferation of digital technologies. He contends that, 'even when equipped with the liberating technology of mobile phones, and enhanced access to information, the underprivileged remain excluded and are alienated from spaces where the "wizardry of consumer seduction" is exercised' (Doron 2012: 566). He demonstrates this by showing how class distinctions are articulated through distinct mobile phone care-and-repair economies in India. The Nokia repair centres offer customers respite from the heat and dust of the Indian street. People queue in an orderly fashion, are served by a receptionist, watch television as they wait and provide feedback in the form of emojis when they leave. Beyond their cool, clean exteriors, however, such centres provide no more certainty of successful repair than their street-side counterparts—the *mistriis*. Doron describes the street-side repair shops in which the *mistriis* labour as 'places of disorder where the plans of global capitalist enterprises are fragmented and adapted to suit the needs of tens of millions of Indians' (Doron 2012: 566). Although disorderly, the streetside repair shops also operate according to rules and regulations that privilege certain kinds of customers over others. Having a personal connection with a *mistriis* can smooth the process and deliver speedier service (Doron 2012: 572).

Doron's article draws attention to the complexity of the digital cultures that have emerged from the expansion of consumer capitalism across the region. I have tried to evoke this complexity in the course of this chapter. The rapid spread of digital technologies has cultural and political implications that refuse to sit sweetly on a continuum of technological advancement stretching from enslavement to emancipation. They become subsumed by other processes that sometimes produce change and at other times ensure that old ways of doing things are upheld. My analysis of telco ads for television provides a good example of the dynamics of change and continuity associated with the development of the new telecommunications infrastructure. On the one hand, the networks assign meanings to their products that associate them with novelty and freedom, but on the other, they reiterate old, class-based distinctions by assigning a higher cultural status to some technologies than others.

But it is not just the confusing overlaps between continuity and change that make Indonesian digital cultures so complex. As I argued earlier, in the Indonesian case, the contextual terrain that subsumes and shapes the HP is especially perilous. This terrain was formed not only by the expansion of consumer capitalism, but also by a series of major political reforms, including both democratisation and decentralisation. The latter precipitated important shifts in attitudes towards regional languages that expanded the repertoire of linguistic resources for articulating modernity/ies.

The Baduda provide a good opportunity to understand how the HP is connected to these processes. As argued above, consumer capitalism has done more than just reinforce pre-existing class divisions in Indonesia; it has also generated new kinds of organisational life oriented primarily towards *ethical* modes of consumption. Decentralisation, in turn, has thrown up new linguistic resources for articulating these modes of ethical consumption. Nanoe Biroe and the Baduda reveal how these developments intersect; through the use of low Balinese they have created a consumerist identity ('consumerist', because buying t-shirts sits at the centre of it) that is both ethical and a form of counterpublicity—counter, that is, to dominant representations of Balinese-ness. As well as perpetuating class divisions, digitally equipped consumer capitalism throws up resources for the aggressive rearticulation of class distinctions, through the tactical use of digital technologies associated with the lower classes. The mobile phone has done much to open this lower-class counterculture to women. Through the HP, the marginalised are able to appropriate consumerism, and in doing so 'contest and reconfigure some of the premises of consumer capitalism, thereby transforming the social life of the technology' (Doron 2012: 564). The Badudawati use Facebook and selfies to emphasise their presence at key Baduda rituals. The dominant discourse about the HP may privilege middle-class uses, but the widespread availability of the mobile phone also gives rise to uses that the representatives of global capital neither foresaw nor intended.

REFERENCES

Baulch, E. (2007) 'Cosmopatriotism in Indonesian pop music imagings', in E. Jurriëns and J. de Kloet (eds) *Cosmopatriots: On Distant Belongings and Close Encounters*, Rodopi, Amsterdam: 177–204.

Baulch, E. (2013) 'Longing band play at Beautiful Hope', *International Journal of Cultural Studies*, 16(3): 289-302.

Baulch, E. (forthcoming) 'The everyman and the dung beetle: new media infrastructures for lower class cultural politics', *Cultural Politics*, 13(2).

BMI (Business Monitor International) (2015) 'Indonesia telecommunications report Q4 2015', London.

Castells, M. (2010) *The Rise of the Network Society*, second edition, Wiley-Blackwell, Chichester, UK, and Malden, MA.

Dean (2014) 'Communicative capitalism and class struggle', *Spheres: Journal for Digital Cultures*, 1(November). Available at http://spheres-journal.org/communicative-capitalism-and-class-struggle/.

Doron, A. (2012) 'Consumption, technology and adaptation: care and repair economies of mobile phones in North India', *Pacific Affairs*, 85(3): 563–85.

Fast Market Research (2016) 'Indonesia telecommunications report Q1 2017', 3 November. Available at http://www.fastmr.com/prod/1233189_indonesia_telecommunications.aspx?afid=301. Accessed 20 January 2017.

Hendriyani, E. Hollander, L. d'Haenens and J.W.J. Beentjes (2011) 'Children's television in Indonesia', *Journal of Children and Media*, 5(1): 86–101. Available at https://www.researchgate.net/publication/254249701_Children's_Television_in_Indonesia.

Hendriyani, E. Hollander, L. d'Haenens and J.W.J. Beentjes (2012) 'Children's media use in Indonesia', *Asian Journal of Communication*, 22(3): 304–19.

Hendriyani, E. Hollander, L. d'Haenens and J.W.J. Beentjes (2016) 'Changes in cultural representations on Indonesian children's television from the 1980s to the 2000s', *Asian Journal of Communication*, 26(4): 371–86.

Heryanto, A. (ed.) (2009) *Pop Culture in Indonesia: Fluid Identities in Post-authoritarian Politics*, Routledge, London.

Hinson, T. (2014) 'On signs and subjectivity: a response to Jodi Dean', *Spheres: Journal for Digital Cultures*, 1(November). Available at http://spheres-journal.org/on-signs-and-subjectivity-a-response-to-jodi-dean/.

Hollander, E., L. d'Haenens and J. Bardoel (2009) 'Television performance in Indonesia: steering between civil society, state and market', *Asian Journal of Communication*, 19(1): 39–58.

Latipulhayat, A. (2010) 'State control and the privatisation of the Indonesian telecommunications industry: from ownership to regulation', *Journal of International Commercial Law and Technology*, 5(2): 58–72.

Lee, R.C., and C. Findlay (2005) 'Telecommunications reform in Indonesia: achievements and challenges', *Bulletin of Indonesian Economic Studies*, 41(3): 341–65.

Liechty, M. (2003) *Suitably Modern: Making Middle-class Culture in a New Consumer Society*, Princeton University Press, Princeton.

Mazzarella, W. (2003) *Shoveling Smoke: Advertising and Globalisation in Contemporary India*, Duke University Press, Durham and London.

Rasyid, A. (2005) 'Indonesia: liberalization at the crossroad, impact on sector performance, teledensity and productivity', MPRA Paper No. 2452, Munich Personal RePEc Archive (MPRA), Munich. Available at http://mpra.ub.uni-muenchen.de/2452/.

Sawita, R.., G. Putra and E. Baulch (2014) 'Citra perempuan Indonesia dalam iklan produk provider' [Images of Indonesian women in the advertisements of product providers], *Jurnal Perempuan*, 19(2). Available at http://eprints.qut.edu.au/78970/.

Sen, K., and D. Hill (2000) *Media, Culture and Politics in Indonesia*, Oxford University Press, Melbourne.

Senft, T., and N. Baym (2015) 'What does the selfie say? Investigating a global phenomenon', *International Journal of Communication*, 9(2015): 1,588–606.

Thajib, F. (2011) 'Bhs Sgktn di SMS' [SMS abbreviations], *Kultur Cell*, 7 January. Available at http://kulturcell.kunci.or.id/?p=361.

TrashStockBali (2015) 'Nanoe Biroe: menginspirasi, bukan menggurui' [Nanoe Biroe: inspires without patronising], *Bale Bengong*, 14 June. Available at http://balebengong.net/kabar-anyar/2015/06/14/nanoe-biroe-bukan-menggurui-tapi-menginspirasi-2.html. Accessed 3 March 2016.

Wang, J. (2008) *Brand New China: Advertising, Media and Commercial Culture*, Harvard University Press, Cambridge MA.

Warner, M. (2002) *Publics and Counterpublics*, Zone Books, New York.

Weintraub, A.N. (2011) *Islam and Popular Culture in Indonesia and Malaysia*, Routledge, London.

Weiss, M.L. (2014) 'New media, new activism: trends and trajectories in Malaysia, Singapore and Indonesia', *International Development Planning Review*, 36(1): 91–109.

4 The political economy of digital media

Ross Tapsell

It is well known that the business models of the mainstream media industry have been thrown into disarray by the arrival of the internet, which has enabled widespread diversification of media content, mostly delivered for free. In fact, of all industries, digitalisation's impact has affected the media industries first, and most compellingly. Although Indonesia's official internet penetration rates remain low, Indonesians with internet access are living in a time of tremendous choice for online news, information and entertainment. Individual citizens can also maintain their own participatory media sites, including blogs, Facebook pages and YouTube channels. For the mainstream media companies, digitalisation is bringing enormous challenges, but also significant opportunities. This chapter explains how digitalisation has favoured the larger media companies, whose owners have become wealthier and more politically powerful, and has hindered smaller news sites, some of which are dying out. Despite the fragmentation of media content caused by the internet, digitalisation has enabled further concentration of the mainstream media. Industrial media remains a key avenue by which elites exert power in Indonesia.

In the early days of the internet, many scholars predicted that the 'new' online media platforms would replace the 'old' or 'traditional' media of print, radio and television. Rather, what occurred was that the platforms converged, and the distinct delineation between online and print or television media became largely redundant as old and new media began to 'collide' (Jenkins 2006). All major news companies in Indonesia began to acquire digital television and radio stations; online news and social media sites; citizen journalism ventures; and even new daily print publications as newspapers merged and converged.

The mainstream media companies believe that to survive financially in the digital era, they must swiftly morph into multiplatform news services. New digital technologies are allowing for a convergence of social media with print, television, radio, telecommunications, cable television, satellites, gaming, citizen journalism and much more. The previously traditional media companies are now branching out into other digital business ventures such as e-commerce, creating larger digital 'ecosystems'. This has led many in the media industry and those who study it to rightly ask: 'What exactly *is* a media company in the digital age?' (Economist 2006).

MAINSTREAM MEDIA CONCENTRATION

Mainstream media companies around the world have responded to digitalisation by making swift and often far-reaching adaptations. In Indonesia, levels of concentration in the industry have clearly increased. Media owners and executives in Indonesia believe that in the highly uncertain future of the digital era, it is better to expand your platforms, audience and readership reach than to remain specialised in one platform. Thus, companies have spent significant amounts to buy or create new platforms. The year 2011 saw the greatest number of mergers and acquisitions in the Indonesian media industry's history (Oxford Business Group 2012: 267). These mergers and acquisitions have created 'digital conglomerates': national, multiplatform companies whose business portfolios extend to investments in communications infrastructure. Indonesia's eight digital conglomerates are Chairul Tanjung's Trans Corp, Hary Tanoesoedibjo's Global Mediacom, the Sariaatmadja family's Emtek, the Bakrie family's Visi Media Asia, Surya Paloh's Media Group, the Riady family's BeritaSatu Media Holdings, Dahlan Iskan's Jawa Pos Group and Jacob Oetama's Kompas Gramedia Group. These eight companies dominate the Indonesian media landscape and are the most influential in the production and dissemination of news content, both online and through traditional media platforms such as television and radio.

The eight digital conglomerates are all based in Indonesia's capital, the sprawling metropolis of Jakarta. It is in Jakarta that the owners of these companies reside, and where the majority of business decisions are made. As a result, Indonesia's media has become increasingly Jakarta-centric, involving a highly centralised model of news production and ultimately reducing the potential for a wide variety of news from other regions (Lim 2011; Nugroho, Putri and Laksmi 2012). Television ratings in particular depend heavily on the demands of audiences in the capital, because 60 per cent of all viewers surveyed by ratings agency AC

Nielsen live in Jakarta. Of course, the trend to appeal to a Jakarta-based market is not confined to media companies, but it is particularly prevalent in the media industry because digitalisation has allowed for increasingly efficient models of newsgathering and distribution between larger digital conglomerates in Jakarta and smaller regional partners.

Of the eight digital conglomerates, some are larger and more financially successful than others. The companies that have emerged as market leaders in Indonesia are those that started out as television companies, in particular Chairul Tanjung's Trans Corp and Hary Tanoesoedibjo's Global Mediacom. The past decade has been a highly productive period for the large television companies. For most of this time, around 70 per cent of all media advertising in Indonesia was directed towards television, compared with only 20 per cent for print media. Media advertising expenditure increased from Rp 9 trillion in 2001 to Rp 60 trillion in 2010 (Rakhmani 2013: 45). Private television stations raked in around 80 per cent of this amount in 2004, making them the most financially viable medium, as free-to-air television was far and away the most highly consumed medium (Rakhmani 2013: 45). Television is still the medium with the most reach and popularity throughout the archipelago, with most of Indonesia's adult population watching the news on television at least once a week (Lim 2012: 3). Surveys show that the proportion of the adult population watching television in a given week went from 60 per cent (around 26 million adults) in the late 1990s to a staggering 90 per cent (nearly 150 million adults) in 2015 (SPS 2014: 20). A survey conducted by polling company Lembaga Survei Indonesia in September 2014 found that when asked 'Where do you get your news and information?', 79 per cent of respondents said 'television', 8 per cent said 'the internet' and only 2 per cent answered 'radio'. It is not surprising, then, that television remains the medium to which the greatest amounts of advertising revenue flow.

Meanwhile, professional print and radio companies are struggling financially. Although Indonesia's print landscape appears at first glance to be bountiful, with the country having around 634 daily printed news media in 2013 (SPS 2014: 22), the overall number of print publications has been decreasing. The Jakarta tabloids have experienced the biggest drop in both numbers and circulation, from 73 daily tabloids with a circulation of about 5 million in 2011, to 56 tabloids with a circulation of 3.65 million in 2013 (SPS 2014: 54–5). In Jakarta, as in major cities elsewhere in the world, the rule holds that where internet penetration rises, print media circulation declines.

As their revenues and circulations have fallen, many of Indonesia's print media have been forced to sell their assets to digital conglomerates. Some examples include *Suara Pembaruan* (which was bought by the

Lippo Group in 2006), the *Surabaya Post* (purchased by the Bakrie Group in 2008) and many independent regional newspapers. Other newspapers have been forced to close, including one of Indonesia's oldest dailies, the Jakarta-based *Sinar Harapan*, which was established in 1961. But in the digital era, *Sinar Harapan* did not join a digital conglomerate, nor did it have the capital to become one. Its inaugural editor, Aristides Katoppo, explained:

> A newspaper now, by itself, is insufficient and inadequate. You have to have electronic and digital media as well. All over the world newspapers are in difficulty. It's not just the demise of newspapers that makes me anxious; it is the crisis in journalism. How does journalism still maintain principles and values of the public good? (Aristides Katoppo, personal communication, November 2015).

Katoppo said that he was approached by some wealthy businessmen with offers to buy the newspaper. He felt he could not accept, explaining that: 'A lot of financiers believed in a certain kind of journalism which is not what I support. I could not guarantee the delivery of the quality I believe in'. *Sinar Harapan* closed on 1 January 2016. Its story is being replicated across Indonesia as independent print media publications are acquired by large conglomerates such as the Jawa Pos Group and Kompas Gramedia, which dominate the local print media industry around the archipelago. The Jawa Pos Group owns over 140 local print titles, most of them with '*Radar*' or '*Pos*' in the masthead.

Executives admit that the circulations and revenues of most of Indonesia's largest newspapers are declining. To compound their problems, the vast majority of newspaper revenue comes from government advertising and advertorials: Rp 5.3 trillion, or 73 per cent of all newspaper advertising, in 2015 (Nielsen Indonesia data, quoted in Jakarta Post 2016). To conclude, it is not outlandish to suggest that if provincial governments in Indonesia stopped advertising their initiatives and objectives in local newspapers, the majority of Indonesia's print media publications would collapse.

Radio, despite its wide spread, has waned in popularity, with household ownership of a radio falling since 2006 (Oxford Business Group 2012: 67). The size of radio audiences has steadily declined; in 2011, only 23.5 per cent of the population listened to the radio in any given week, compared with 50 per cent in 2003 (Lim 2011). Of the seemingly bountiful 1,178 radio stations in 2014, most were commercial stations devoted to playing music, rather than news and journalism. The number of commercial radio stations fell from 845 in 2008 to 774 in 2014 (Nugroho, Putri and Laksmi 2012: 46). Like the print media tabloids, independent commercial radio stations have been struggling to survive in the face of increased competition from other media, including television and the internet. Some of the smaller owners have sold their analogue radio frequency rights (which are in limited supply) to the highest bidders, generally the digital conglomerates. According to an official from the Indonesian Broadcasting Commission (Komisi Penyiaran Indonesia, or KPI), the conglomerates paid around Rp 3 billion ($227,530) for those rights in 2015 (KPI official, personal communication, 2015).

With significant capital behind them, the owners of television stations have been able to invest quickly in other media platforms. Sensing the trend towards multiplatform news, Indonesia's print media companies have also scrambled to purchase or create other broadcast-based platforms and communications infrastructure. In summarising where the industry appeared to be heading, the chief editor of the *Jakarta Post*, Meidyatama Suryodiningrat, wrote in 2012:

> The long-term outlook for the sector is for smaller, independent media companies to be acquired by larger groups, while few new players enter the business. While niche independent parties can pop up in the electoral landscape every five years or so, the smaller independent press is dying, as firms are amalgamated in giant corporations (Oxford Business Group 2012: 271).

By 2016, his analysis had proven to be correct. The new digital technologies have indeed favoured companies with significant capital and large market shares, rather than allowing a diverse array of innovative new media companies run by the new breed of entrepreneurs to flourish.

What does this mean for news quality? Indonesia's most respected print publication is *Tempo*, a weekly news magazine that is regarded as Indonesia's best example of quality investigative journalism. While its owner, the Tempo Group, views expansion to become a multiplatform operation as crucial to its survival, it has not been financially successful and it has failed to enter the ranks of the digital conglomerates. In 2001 it launched a new daily newspaper, *Koran Tempo*, which has persistently bled funds. The group also started *Tempo Interaktif*, which had ambitious plans to become the leading site for citizen journalism as mobile phone use expanded across Indonesia. Instead, the strategy had to be abandoned, and the site was relaunched (without the 'interactive' element) as *Tempo.co*; the rebranded site, rather than being a beacon of quality journalism, seems somewhat similar to every other online news site based in Jakarta. Like *Koran Tempo*, *Tempo.co* struggles to make money, so both the online medium and the daily newspaper are subsidised by the Tempo Group's more profitable weekly magazine.

In 2006, the Tempo Group ambitiously established TempoTV through a partnership with Kantor Berita Radio 68H owner Tosca Santoso. But Tempo did not have the funds to keep the operation going. In 2012 Tempo executive Toriq Hadad said:

> We can't let Tempo be history, and Tempo stands alone as independent media organisation for all platforms. We need to get investors on board who have the same vision of independence, because we need a voice for independence, especially in Indonesian TV. We have made proposals to investors explaining why [TempoTV] will make a better Indonesia (Toriq Hadad, personal communication, 2012).

The plan did not work, and other problems with digital television licensing meant that Tempo had no choice but to abandon its regular TV operation, reduce its staff to seven journalists and eight editors, and produce only specialist online video content, most of it not particularly influential. Tempo's shares were trading at Rp 81 in January 2011 and after some growth in 2012 and 2013 were down to Rp 68 in December 2015. In late 2015, Tempo built a new multiplatform newsroom modelled on the centralised 'one newsroom' structure of many other digital conglomerates.

Clearly, the difficulty for Tempo is that, despite its best attempts to become a multiplatform content provider, its online ventures have so far failed to bring in significant revenues. Furthermore, the group is minimally involved in the race to acquire communications infrastructure, which has become a crucial feature of a digital conglomerate. This is not to say that the group has no future in the digital era, but its executives are concerned about how digitalisation has benefited the larger media companies with wealthy owners, at the expense of majority shareholder-owned media that specialise in quality print journalism.

Surely eight digital conglomerates are enough to provide a reasonable amount of diversity? Considering that governments control much of the media in other countries (including the Southeast Asian region), are not eight independent, large, market-driven media conglomerates sufficient to give a perfectly reasonable amount of consumer choice? As I have argued elsewhere (Tapsell 2014), this might be the case if the business models of Indonesia's digital conglomerates did not look virtually the same: they are all attempting to become national, multiplatform companies, and to achieve this they have all set up centralised offices providing homogenised news content. The business plan of each company is also the same: to take as big a share of the mainstream Indonesian audience in as many platforms as possible, and to build an 'ecosystem' of linked media and online business and communications infrastructure. Unsurprisingly given their business models, the large conglomerates all tend to cover the same set of stories (Sudibyo 2004; Nugroho, Putri and Laksmi 2012). Thus, while subtle differences do exist, for the most part it is rather difficult to distinguish between the news content produced by each digital conglomerate. All are predominantly focused on the production of news from the capital, delivered to a national audience via multiple platforms, with very few deeply investigative stories.

In the early 2000s, many predicted that the rise of global Western media 'superoligarchs' would dominate the developing world's media landscapes. Scholars who looked at trends in media globalisation believed that large US-based conglomerates such as CNN and Time Warner would dominate the global media market, swallowing up local media companies and making media production more homogenised (Lau and Ang 1998). This did not happen, however: the global news companies do not dominate the Indonesian market and they are not the key drivers of the Indonesian media industry. Rather, it is the national media conglomerates that have gained in power and influence. The larger Western-based companies that have succeeded in gaining a foothold in the Indonesian media market are the ones that have entered into alliances with Indonesia's digital conglomerates. Recent examples include Chairul Tanjung's partnerships with CNN and CNBC. In fact, rather than being dwarfed by global companies, Indonesian media companies are themselves beginning to spread out to Southeast Asia and beyond, producing content in multiple languages for a variety of regional audiences. The rise of the global internet-based sites Facebook and Google is an emerging threat to these companies, as they are fast becoming central to the production of news and information for many Indonesians. But at present, it is Indonesia's digital conglomerates that remain the nation's key providers of news and information.

EMERGING DIGITAL MEDIA 'ECOSYSTEMS'

The arrival of detikcom, an online news site established in 1998 by four Jakartans, heralded the start of what is now a highly crowded online news space in Indonesia. Detikcom specialised in short, fast-breaking news stories and titbits of information. In this respect it was quite different from its namesake, the Suharto-era print publication *Detik*, which had a highly respected history of alternative investigative journalism. It was banned by the Indonesian government in 1994. If journalism is the 'what, why, where, when and how', detikcom's business model was to concentrate on 'who, when and where', and not bother so much about the 'why' or the 'how'. Nevertheless, it was highly successful financially.

In 2011, Chairul Tanjung's Trans Corp purchased the site, reportedly for $60 million, although the precise figure was never disclosed (Forbes Indonesia 2012). Detikcom has become even more popular in the digital era because its short, punchy articles are highly suitable for consumption via the mobile phone. Other online news outlets that have emulated its business model include Kompas.com (owned by Kompas Gramedia), Viva.co.id (Bakrie Group), Liputan6.com (Emtek), okezone.com (Media

Nusantara Citra, or MNC) and beritasatu.com (Lippo Group). As most media executives would admit, all these sites are similar in style and content, although the speed at which they produce content varies. In 2015, detikcom stood out in terms of its sheer number of reporters, at around 550 (compared with Kompas.com's 450 and Liputan6.com's 300), and was therefore able to publish more news items at a faster rate.

As elsewhere in the world, media companies in Indonesia have been reluctant to introduce paywalls to cover the costs of their digital news organisations. There are simply so many free options available that citizens prefer to go elsewhere for free news rather than pay for a particular online news service. Yet there is little doubt that younger Indonesians are increasingly accessing news online, which means that digital conglomerates need to adapt quickly to the changing patterns of media consumption in the country. The predicament for media companies is clear: the 'rivers of gold' from print classified advertising have dried up; online television streaming is making the PayTV market redundant; and so far there is little ad spend for online news. With the exception of detikcom, most of the online news sites in Indonesia run at a loss. Media companies are therefore seeking to find other ways to capture a share of the money Indonesian consumers spend online.

As we heard earlier in this book, Indonesia is a burgeoning market for social media platforms, with global sites Twitter and Facebook maintaining a strong presence, and even social media platforms that were unsuccessful elsewhere in the world, such as Path, proving highly successful in Indonesia. Because of this, Indonesian media oligarchs have looked to incorporate social media sites into their business portfolios.

In 2011 Hary Tanoesoedibjo's MNC group became the local partner for the WeChat messaging service owned by Chinese company Tencent (Forbes Indonesia 2012: 56). Tencent director Benny Ho said that partnering with MNC 'gives local insight, as MNC's media assets help us to get into the user market' (Benny Ho, personal communication, 2015). He said that WeChat Indonesia planned to become more than an online messaging service: it aimed to compete with Facebook and other sites to become the most popular 'social' application on Indonesians' mobile phones. A new interface would allow users to post photos and videos, find 'friends' and get the latest news. Ho described the strategy in this way:

> Every day, most people use only five to seven apps. You don't want a lot of apps because they use up a lot of storage. Most people have one messaging app, one or two social media apps, one entertainment or music app, and one news app or RSS feed. Beyond these it is hard to gain a presence on the mobile phone. Perhaps this will change, but for now you need to be one of them. You have to create a product that people find invaluable to use (Benny Ho, personal communication, 2015).

Hary Tanoesoedibjo explained that the investment in WeChat was again about the idea of being a multiplatform company in the digital age:

> The one media that MNC didn't have was social media. The option was to start our own, or to merge. Tencent proposed a joint venture as they were trying to get into the market here. All media of MNC will support this new company. Our programs will have official WeChat accounts and our programs will promote WeChat on them. For example, during Ramadan, if the traffic is bad, people can spread the news on WeChat and we can announce this on our news programs. This is user-generated content, and it is all just starting out (Tanoesoedibjo, personal communication, 2015).

In 2013, the Bakrie Group invested $25 million in the Path social media site. Path had around 23 million customers at the time of the purchase, most of them in Indonesia. Anindya Bakrie (son of the politician and businessman Aburizal Bakrie) said in early 2015: 'Path is an interesting approach because people ask: why can't Indonesia be the key for Southeast Asia and Southeast Asia be the key for our expansion?' (Anindya Bakrie, personal communication, 2015). He said the main reason for investing in Path was to 'leverage the success of Path to other assets' and to include social media in the group's media portfolio. There was some concern among netizens that the Bakrie Group would use the site to promote Aburizal's tilt for the Indonesian presidency in 2014, but this did not eventuate. However, by May 2015 the Bakrie Group was not investing any more money in the site, and Path was sold to Korean giant KakaoTalk.

The digital conglomerates have their sights set on e-commerce ventures as the next big way to generate significant amounts of revenue. Central to these ventures is the smooth integration of online payment systems and the companies' apps on mobile phones and other digital devices. In other words, the conglomerates have set their sights on developing digital 'ecosystems'. 'Ecosystem' is a word commonly uttered inside Indonesian newsrooms, generally to describe the increased linkages between media companies and other digital start-up and business ventures. Ultimately, the aim is to become the number one site to which Indonesians go when purchasing goods and services online. In 2016, for example, Emtek decided to invest in the fledgling BlackBerry messaging app, BBM, which it hoped would eventually rival WeChat. In announcing the deal, Emtek proclaimed:

> The deal will give BBM users access to Emtek content, and Emtek the opportunity to build an eco-system that combines messaging, social media, content, entertainment and—arguably the biggest prize—e-commerce, a sector that is growing as quickly in Indonesia as anywhere in Southeast Asia (Mumbrella 2016).

With intense competition between online news providers to capture the mobile phone audience, companies are looking to increase traffic to their sites by merging news, social and messaging apps into a single smartphone application. They aim to centralise everything people can do on their mobile devices through the one application—transport, banking, sports, shopping and much more.

Trans Corp executive Ishadi Soetopo Kartosapoetro explained the strategy for the company's detikcom news site in this way:

> We want to make detikcom the future highway for all business. Every business will go through there. They will all advertise on detik, do business through detik, find details on products or applications. Detik will not only be a news portal, it will also be a business portal (Ishadi Soetopo Kartosapoetro, personal communication, 2015).

In 2014, MNC established its own online shopping site, MNC Shop, and formed alliances with e-commerce site Alibaba.com; it is also looking to make WeChat a place where people can make bookings, which would allow it to receive commissions from the vendors on those sales. In 2012, Emtek set up a subsidiary company, Kreatif Media Karya Online (KMK Online), as a repository for its digital media assets, including news site Liputan6.com. Liputan6.com chief Manuel Irwanputera described the reasoning as follows:

> There are other reasons for people to visit the internet [beyond news]. We need to create lifestyle, travel, a portal that people go to for jobs and houses, and e-commerce. We want to introduce e-commerce and an e-ticketing company (Manuel Irwanputera, personal communication, 2015).

BeritaSatu director John Riady was quoted in early 2015 as saying that there was 'no money to be made in media' (Cosseboom 2015). He saw greater potential in e-commerce ventures such as MatahariMall, in which the Riady family's Lippo Group had just invested $500 million.

Despite the market dominance of the digital conglomerates, they still face serious challenges in the digital era in order to maintain their wealth and power. These challenges are unlikely to come from community-driven or independent organisations, but rather from the now ubiquitous global 'digital giants', Facebook and Google. In 2011, only four of the 15 most visited websites in Indonesia were locally owned (Lim 2011: 6). By 2015, locally owned e-commerce sites Bukalapak and Tokopedia were among the top 10, but global sites Google, Yahoo, Facebook and Twitter remained the most popular.[1] There is considerable concern among

---

1 This information was sourced from Amazon's Alexa web traffic site (www.alexa.com) in 2015.

media companies around the world that the global digital media companies (and Google and Facebook in particular) are completely dominating the online advertising market. Google's advertising revenue in the June quarter of 2016 was $19.14 billion (Taylor 2016). More than 1.7 billion people use Facebook each month, with 1.1 billion accessing the platform every day, and in the second quarter of 2016 Facebook reported advertising revenues of $6.4 billion (Mediaweek 2016). In a sign of where the industry is heading—and striking fear into the hearts of many Indonesian digital conglomerates—in 2016 Facebook (the parent company of both WhatsApp and Instagram) announced plans to develop its Messenger app into a commerce-oriented 'ecosystem' (Limongello 2016).

In 2016, the Indonesian tax office estimated that online content providers were making $830 million a year in advertising revenue, with Google and Facebook accounting for around 70 per cent of that (Suroyo and Danubrata 2016). Indonesian policy-makers and media owners argue that these global sites are hurting the country's economy by depriving local companies of media and advertising revenues and by failing to pay their fair share of tax. In 2016 the Indonesian tax office claimed that Google Indonesia had paid less than 0.1 per cent of the total income and value-added taxes it owed in 2015, and suggested that the company could face a bill of Rp 5.5 trillion ($418 million) in unpaid taxes for that year alone (Suroyo and Danubrata 2016).

Indonesia's digital conglomerates may have survived the threat that the global Western media 'superoligarchs' would dominate the country's media landscape, but whether they can hold their own against Facebook and Google remains to be seen. Restricting foreign media companies' satellite transmissions is far easier than limiting the spread of global social media sites. Unlike the Chinese government, the Indonesian government is unlikely to implement a protectionist approach towards the internet and the online media giants. Indonesians would be outraged if the government banned Facebook, Google and other global media giants in order to keep the national digital conglomerates afloat. What is more likely is that the national media conglomerates with the most power and influence will attempt to enter into alliances with the global digital giants. When he officially announced the opening of Twitter's Jakarta office in March 2015, then Twitter CEO Richard Costolo said he would be meeting with numerous Indonesian media companies to discuss the possibility of content sharing (press conference Jakarta, March 2015). Earlier that month, Facebook had announced a content-sharing arrangement with the *New York Times*, BuzzFeed and others that would allow these news sites to post articles directly to Facebook (Greenberg 2015). The transformative process of media convergence is unlikely to come to a sudden halt.

CONCLUSION

This chapter has argued that digitalisation has favoured the existing players in Indonesia's mainstream media, which have swiftly adapted to disruptive technologies to become larger, digital conglomerates. At the same time, many smaller professional media companies have faced the conundrum of either being forced into mergers with these digital conglomerates, or risk becoming defunct. In 2011, Merlyna Lim suggested that 12 large companies dominated the Indonesian media market (Lim 2011). I argue that, following further consolidation, there are now only eight large players in the mainstream media market. As a result, the market has become increasingly oligopolistic.

The intense competition between Indonesia's media oligarchs is reflected in the critical reports their news organisations run on each other. Thus, Dahlan Iskan's media outlets regularly covered the involvement of one of Aburizal Bakrie's companies in the East Java mudflow disaster; Bakrie's companies produced an exposé on the activities of Surya Paloh's companies in Africa and Paloh's connections with President Jokowi; Surya Paloh's media covered Dahlan Iskan's corruption trial; and so on. In other words, in an oligarchic media landscape, plenty of information is available in the public sphere for the concerned media consumer with access to a range of news outlets. Unlike in other countries in Southeast Asia where there is strong control from the government or political elites, in Indonesia most political topics are covered somewhere at some point by some organisation. Jeffrey Winters (2011: 184) has argued that in an environment in which the media companies are 'owned by oligarchs and used extensively in intra-oligarchic battles', party affiliation and being a contender for political office allow them to 'dismiss accusations as being purely political'. In short, it is in the media oligarchs' interest to own media companies, to attack each other through these companies but to support each other when there is a mutual benefit to be gained. This makes the media oligarchs a powerful force in Indonesian politics—far more powerful than they were in the early post-*reformasi* years of Indonesian democracy.

This chapter has shown that the business models of the digital conglomerates are virtually the same: they are all attempting to become national, multiplatform companies, and to achieve this they have all centralised their news production. The business plan of each company is also the same: to take as large a share of the mainstream Indonesian audience in as many platforms as possible, and to build an 'ecosystem' of linked media and online business and communications infrastructure. Studies conducted elsewhere have pointed to the general tendency of the large conglomerates to mimic each other in content production, resulting in very similar coverage of the same set of news stories (Sudibyo 2004).

While it is true that the media owners often compete with each other for political power, all are successful business leaders, and as such their media outlets tend to report in a pro-business direction (Kohli 2012). Any observer of Indonesian media can see regular stories attributing the successes of Indonesia's middle and upper classes to a pro-business mindset. In terms of media content, this pro-business mindset plays out in negative attitudes towards pro-poor government policies that affect profits (such as raising the minimum wage) and negative coverage of anti-establishment practices such as protests and labour union campaigns. For example, the mainstream media generally supported the new rules that prevent protesters from protesting outside the presidential palace on the grounds that it disrupts traffic and business efficiency in Jakarta. The mainstream media also makes it clear that it prefers 'technocratic' ministers who understand business interests over politicians who might question the role of big business in contributing to rising inequality.

At the same time, the mainstream media propagates positive images of successful businesspeople as 'self-made heroes', including regular coverage of media owners themselves, who are portrayed as pragmatic, non-ideological thinkers who have made their fortunes through hard work and tenacity. Those media owners who run for political office use their capacity to amass wealth as an example that pro-business attitudes towards democracy lead to improved prosperity for the common people.[2] Pro-business values are likely to become further entrenched among Indonesians as the digital conglomerates strengthen their stranglehold over the media and extend their reach into the digital economy.

We can also conclude that the Indonesian mainstream media, while operating in a democratic and free press environment, is more partisan than it was prior to the digital era. This was clearly exemplified in the coverage of the presidential elections in 2014, when most media companies overtly supported the campaigns of either Prabowo Subianto or Joko Widodo (Tapsell 2015). There are many reasons for this increased partisanship, but the heightened power of the media owners due to increased conglomeration and concentration of the industry has certainly exacerbated this trend. This has profound implications for a diverse, impartial and informative media landscape in one of the world's largest democracies. Owning a media company has allowed a select group of individuals to become more politically powerful: as their digital conglomerates have grown and become more centralised in Jakarta, they have been able

2 For an example of this type of content, see the article on Surya Paloh in *Men's Obsession* (Sahrudi 2015).

to exert more influence over Indonesian politics. A cursory reading of the 2016 *Forbes* rich list (http://www.forbes.com/billionaires/) suggests that national media owners are a powerful but perhaps understudied force around the world, a few examples being the Marinho family in Brazil, Subhash Chandra and others in India, Emilio Azcárraga Jean in Mexico and Surang Prempree in Thailand.

In Indonesia as elsewhere, the media industry was the first to be impacted by the communications technology of the World Wide Web. As Hardy (2014: 195) has argued, during the later decades of the twentieth century, there were vociferous and persistent calls for greater media diversity within media systems in order to break up corporate gains in oligopolistic markets. For a time, it seemed as though the new technologies of the internet would automatically allow for this—and in some ways they did indeed threaten the fortunes and power of media moguls, particularly those in the print newspaper industry. For a while, online news sites such as detikcom did pose a threat to the power and dominance of the mainstream media companies. The corporate media sector was aware that it needed to drastically change its business model in order to keep up with the changing patterns of audiences and advertising revenues, or risk becoming redundant as news sites flourished and audiences began to create their own content, challenging the dominance of traditional news media companies.

Indonesia's media owners have successfully adapted. The country's private media companies were still being reimagined in the unstable post-*reformasi* environment, but a select group of businesspeople quickly managed to dominate the traditional platforms of television and print, consolidating the industry. The Indonesian case shows that big media is getting bigger in the digital era. Media moguls are becoming more wealthy, powerful and dynastic, and the competitive nature of the oligarchic landscape is making the mainstream media landscape more partisan. In this regard, digitalisation has actually been a tool of the media elites because it has allowed for consolidation of the industry, thus reducing the potential for the arrival of the internet in the late 1990s to create a wider diversity of viewpoints. This conclusion is supported by Western political-economy scholars such as Robert McChesney (2013: 124), who argued that: 'The corporate media sector has spent much of the past fifteen years doing everything in its immense power to limit the openness and egalitarianism of the Internet'. The capitalist media in Indonesia has managed to do this by turning themselves into digital conglomerates, using digital technologies to build multiplatform businesses, becoming more efficient in the way they gather and disseminate news, while at the same time pushing out or buying up competitors. Industrial media remains the dominant space where elites exert their power.

REFERENCES

Cosseboom, L. (2015) 'This is MatahariMall's gameplan to beat Rocket Internet', *Tech in Asia,* 13 March. Available at https://www.techinasia.com/indonesia-ecommerce-mataharimall-rocket-internet#. Accessed 18 December 2016.

Economist (2006) 'The gazillion-dollar question: so what is a media company?', *The Economist,* 20 April. Available at http://www.economist.com/node/6794282. Accessed 5 January 2017.

Forbes Indonesia (2012) 'Indonesia's 40 richest', *Forbes Indonesia,* December.

Greenberg, J. (2015) 'BuzzFeed and *NY Times* will now publish stories on Facebook', *Wired,* 13 May. Available at http://www.wired.com/2015/05/big-publishers-will-now-post-stories-straight-facebook/. Accessed 3 August 2016.

Hardy, J. (2014) *The Political Economy of the Media: An Introduction,* Routledge, London.

Jakarta Post (2016) 'Ad spending in print media suffers decline last year', *Jakarta Post,* 11 February. Available at http://www.thejakartapost.com/news/2016/02/11/ad-spending-print-media-suffers-decline-last-year.html.

Jenkins, H. (2006) *Convergence Culture: Where Old and New Media Collide,* New York University Press, New York and London.

Kohli, A. (2012) *Poverty amid Plenty in the New India,* Cambridge University Press, Cambridge.

Lau T.Y., and P.H. Ang (1998) 'The Pacific Rim', in A.B. Albarran and S.M. Chan-Olmsted (eds) *Global Media Economics: Commercialization, Concentration and Integration of the World Media Markets,* Iowa State University Press, Ames: 310–27.

Lim, M. (2011) '@crossroads: democratization & corporatization of media in Indonesia', Ford Foundation and Participatory Media Lab at Arizona State University, Tempe. Available at http://studylib.net/download/8085771. Accessed 31 March 2016.

Lim, M. (2012) 'The league of thirteen: media concentration in Indonesia', research report, Ford Foundation and Participatory Media Lab at Arizona State University, Tempe. Available at https://www.academia.edu/7282028/Lim_M._2012_The_League_of_Thirteen_Media_Concentration_in_Indonesia. Accessed 6 January 2017.

Limongello, T. (2016) 'The future of Messenger', *TechCrunch,* 6 April. Available at https://techcrunch.com/2015/04/06/the-future-of-messenger/. Accessed 12 December 2016.

McChesney, R. (2013) *Digital Disconnect: How Corporate Media Is Turning the Internet against Democracy,* New Press, London and New York.

Mediaweek (2016) 'Facebook revenues increase to $6.4 billion in Q2 2016', *Mediaweek,* 28 July. Available at https://www.mediaweek.com.au/facebook-revenues-increase-to-6-4b-in-q2-2016/. Accessed 30 July 2016.

Mumbrella (2016) 'Indonesian media giant Emtek acquires licences for Blackberry social messaging app BBM', *Mumbrella,* 28 June. Available at http://www.mumbrella.asia/2016/06/indonesian-media-giant-emtek-acquires-bbm-consumer-business/. Accessed 12 December 2016.

Nugroho, Y., D.A. Putri and S. Laksmi (2012) 'Mapping the landscape of the media industry in contemporary Indonesia', research report, Center for Innovation Policy and Governance and HIVOS Regional Office Southeast Asia, Jakarta. Available at http://www.academia.edu/2608710/Mapping_the_landscape_of_the_media_industry_in_contemporary_Indonesia.

Oxford Business Group (ed.) (2012) *The Report: Indonesia 2012*. Available at https://www.oxfordbusinessgroup.com/indonesia-2012.

Rakhmani, I. (2013) 'Rethinking Indonesian nationalism in an age of commercial Islam: the television industry, religious soap operas, and a national audience', PhD thesis, Murdoch University, Perth.

Sahrudi (2015) 'Surya Dharma Paloh: lifetime achievement', *Men's Obsession*, 20 March. Available at http://www.mensobsession.com/article/detail/837/surya-dharma-paloh-lifetime-achievement. Accessed 2 January 2017.

SPS (Serikat Perusahaan Pers) (2014) *Media Directory 2013/2014*, Indonesian News Publishers Association (SPS), Jakarta.

Sudibyo, A. (2004) *Ekonomi Politik Media Penyiaran* [Political Economy of Broadcasting Media], Institute for Study of the Free Flow of Information (Institut Studi Arus Informasi, ISAI) and Institute for Islamic and Social Studies (Lembaga Kajian Islam dan Sosial, LKiS), Jakarta.

Suroyo, G., and E. Danubrata (2016) 'Google may face Indonesian tax bill of more than $US400 million for 2015', *Canberra Times*, 19 September.

Tapsell, R. (2014) 'Platform convergence in Indonesia: challenges and opportunities for media freedom', *Convergence: The International Journal of Research into New Media Technologies*, 21(2): 182–97.

Tapsell, R. (2015) 'Indonesia's media oligarchy and the "Jokowi phenomenon"', *Indonesia*, 99(April): 29–50.

Taylor, H. (2016) 'Google (and Facebook) are getting almost all digital ad money', *CNBC Online*, 28 July. Available at http://www.cnbc.com/2016/07/28/google-and-facebook-are-getting-almost-all-digital-ad-money.html. Accessed 3 August 2016.

Winters, J. (2011) *Oligarchy*, Cambridge University Press, Cambridge and New York.

PART 2

Divergence

5 Narrowing the digital divide

Onno W. Purbo

This chapter reviews both government and community efforts to provide better internet access to Indonesia's rural areas and villages. Increasing internet penetration, and narrowing the digital divide, has considerable potential to increase economic growth in Indonesia. In low- and middle-income countries, it has been estimated that each 10 per cent increase in high-speed broadband penetration delivers a 1.38 per cent increase in per capita GDP growth (World Bank 2009: 45; ITU 2012: 5). The availability of internet access in rural areas has been identified as a key factor in development (Puskakom UI 2015: 2).

The majority of internet users in Indonesia live in the western region of the country, especially Java, where internet penetration has reached 36.9 per cent of the population (Puskakom UI 2015: 8). About 83 per cent of internet users live in urban areas, but even within Indonesia's largest cities there is a digital divide between those who have regular access to the internet (less than 20 per cent of urban dwellers) and those who do not (over 80 per cent). Indonesia is a 'mobile-first' country, with almost 85 per cent of current internet users accessing the internet on a mobile device (Puskakom UI 2015: 24). The best cellular access is in the cities and the worst in rural areas and villages;[1] providing wireless mobile phone coverage in rural areas is difficult because of the necessity to design systems that can overcome physical obstacles such as mountainous terrain. Given that 46.7 per cent of Indonesians live in rural areas (BPS 2014a), increasing the country's internet penetration will require a greater focus on rural villages. However, building expensive infrastructure for small

1 This information was sourced from the OpenSignal app, which monitors the coverage and performance of mobile connections.

populations in isolated areas is not economically feasible from a commercial operator's point of view.

The Indonesian mobile market has exploded over the past half-decade. In a country with a population of 250 million, cellular subscriptions stand at 326.3 million, meaning that many people own more than one mobile phone. We Are Social claims that 85 per cent of Indonesians own a mobile phone and 43 per cent own a smartphone (Balea 2016). The internet is largely operated by the private sector, and does not rely on significant funds from government budgets. There are more than 300 commercial internet service providers (ISPs) in Indonesia. The legal framework forces ISPs to use the network infrastructure provided by telecommunications services companies, especially Telkom (which is 51 per cent government owned) and Indosat (less than 50 per cent government owned). The telcos are crucial to the quantity and quality of the country's internet services: if they do not provide the network, there is no internet.

The 'digital divide' refers to the gap between those individuals, households, businesses and geographic areas that have good access to information and communication technology (ICT) and those that do not, owing to differences in socio-economic level, demography, geography and so on (OECD 2001: 5). At the level of the individual, research has shown that the main factors inhibiting internet or broadband adoption are a low level of education (less than secondary school); age above 65; location in a rural area; membership of a disadvantaged socio-demographic group; and low income (Montagnier and Wirthmann 2011: 4; ITU 2012: 83–5). Although all these factors are relevant in the Indonesian context, the Indonesian government persists in viewing the country's digital divide as an access-related issue.

Presidential Decree No. 45/2016 on the Government Work Plan for 2017 sets three priorities for the construction of broadband and broadcasting infrastructure: improving infrastructure in areas that are not attractive to commercial operators; removing regulatory bottlenecks and synchronising the deployment of broadband and broadcasting infrastructure; and developing human resources and the ICT industry to support the roll-out of infrastructure. The plan also calls for the construction of 127 cellular towers in mobile blind spots in 2017, and the establishment of 800 internet cafes (*warung internet*, or *warnet*) in areas where there are no commercial operators; by 2019 it projects that internet cafes will be operating in an additional 4,000 locations.

In this chapter, I will argue that the simplest option to increase internet penetration in Indonesia is for the government to survey citizens about their needs and give them the knowledge and technical capacity to handle the technology before infrastructure is deployed. This is essential to ensure that future top-down policies to improve rural internet access do not follow the failed path of their predecessors.

IMPROVING DIGITAL LITERACY

Many developed countries provide almost universal internet access for their citizens. However, even in countries with high rates of internet access, levels of adoption and awareness in rural areas may be deficient. As a result, rural-dwelling citizens may not be able to gain maximum benefit from the internet, putting them at risk of falling behind the rest of the country. Such citizens may not have the opportunity to acquire the simple skills needed to gather reliable information online, let alone the more complex skills required to take advantage of the burgeoning digital economy of start-ups, e-commerce and other entrepreneurial online activities. This forces a redefinition of the digital divide beyond the issue of access itself, where overcoming differences in the ability and motivation to maximise the benefits of the internet has become the next frontier in the effort to bridge the digital divide (EIU 2013: 25).

Open access to knowledge (Witt 2016) and digital inclusion of the citizen (Warschauer 2004; van Deursen, Helsper and Eynon 2016) have become important topics of global debate. Researchers agree that a person must have a certain level of internet skills in order to gain maximum benefit from the internet (Cohron 2015: 82; IDA 2015: 10; ITU 2015: 93–4; MCMC 2015: 10; World Economic Forum 2016: 9). Internet skills should be considered distinct from computer skills, as a higher level of skills is required to use the internet than to use a computer. For example, the ability to search on Google for accurate and reliable information, the capacity to use online communication tools and the competence to create online content all require some form of digital literacy (Ilomäki et al. 2016; van Deursen, Helsper and Eynon 2016).

In Indonesia, a lack of basic literacy and numeracy skills limits what people with internet access can actually do with their time online. Even people who are literate, and live in an area with good infrastructure, face various barriers to getting connected. These include high connection costs, poor ICT skills and a lack of awareness or cultural acceptance of the new technology. In some parts of Indonesia, internet adoption may also be hampered by a lack of content and services in local languages. This is important in the context of Indonesia, where many citizens speak local dialects rather than the national language, Bahasa Indonesia.

Solving the contemporary digital divide involves far more than merely providing more computers and internet connections. Access to ICT is embedded in many factors beyond physical, digital, human and social resources and relationships; in addition, content and language, literacy and education, and community and institutional structures must all be taken into account if meaningful access to new technologies is to be provided (Warschauer 2004: 6–8).

TOP-DOWN STRATEGIES BY THE GOVERNMENT

To meet the universal service obligation (USO) to give all Indonesians access to telecommunications services, no matter where they live, telecommunications network operators contribute 1.25 per cent of their gross revenue to the government's USO fund (Government Regulation No. 7/2009 on Types and Tariffs of Non-tax State Revenue Applicable to the Ministry of Communication and Informatics). USO funds are normally used to provide internet access in areas that are not profitable for commercial operators, leaving private investors to concentrate on those where a profit can be made from installing infrastructure. Law No. 36/1999 on Telecommunications (the Telecommunications Law) states that only licensed operators may build and operate telecommunications infrastructure. This seems to leave little room for rural communities to participate in the design and construction of internet infrastructure for their own purposes, even if they have the financial and technical capacity to do so.

The Smart Village program

In 2012, the government established the Smart Village (Desa Pinter) program, with the goal of giving all Indonesian villages access to the internet. The idea was to establish a local WiFi hotspot in each village and install two computers and a printer for public use. The program was funded with USO funds and rolled out by Telkom subsidiary Telkomsel in about 4,700 villages.

The Smart Village program has been plagued by problems, including poor internet connections, villages located in WiFi blind spots and limited availability of electricity (Telkomsel 2012). Moreover, with very little technical capacity in Indonesian villages, the villagers are finding it difficult to maintain and operate the systems.

The internet cafe (PLIK) and mobile internet cafe (MPLIK) programs

The two largest programs funded by the USO are the Subdistrict Internet Service Centre (Pusat Layanan Internet Kecamatan, or PLIK) and the Mobile Subdistrict Internet Service Centre (Mobil Pusat Layanan Internet

Kecamatan, or MPLIK). The purpose of the former program is to increase the availability of internet cafes in villages, while that of the latter is to provide mobile internet services for more remote villages. The mobile service uses modified vans fitted out with several laptops and a rooftop satellite dish. In 2013, the People's Representative Council (Dewan Perwakilan Rakyat, or DPR) wanted to abolish the MPLIK project on the grounds that it was being misused (Asril 2013a), but the minister of communications, Tifatul Sembiring, opted to keep it. It was alleged that several MPLIK vehicles had been used as mobile registration booths for political parties, or as payment points for the government-owned electricity company PLN (Asril 2013b).

Santoso Serad, the head of the agency responsible for running the MPLIK program—the Telecommunications and Informatics Funding Provision and Management Agency (Balai Penyedia dan Pengelola Pembiayaan Telekomunikasi dan Informatika, or BP3TI)—blamed the failures of the program largely on a lack of bandwidth, electricity and open-source resources. However, DPR member Tantowi Yahya questioned the accountability of BP3TI's use of funds on the grounds that it had spent only Rp 800 billion of its Rp 2.4 trillion budget in 2010, banking the remaining Rp 1.6 billion (Majalah ICT 2013). In 2014, the parliamentary committee responsible for overseeing the telecommunications sector, Commission I (Komisi I), decided to put the budget for the PLIK and MPLIK programs on hold because of the questions about their record (Ministry of Communication and Informatics 2014). In articles accompanied by photos of run-down or underused internet vans in Aceh, West Sumatra, South Sumatra, West Kalimantan and other provinces, the Indonesian media reported widely that the MPLIK program had failed in its objective of improving internet access for rural areas and villages (Hasbi 2014; Irawan 2016; Murdaningsih 2016; Suryadhi 2016; Wibowo 2016).

The Palapa Ring Project

One of the largest investments currently being undertaken by the Indonesian government is the construction of a fibre optic internet backbone to provide high-speed internet access to all 34 provinces and over 440 districts. The Palapa Ring Project involves laying 35,280 kilometres of fibre optic cable under the sea and 21,807 kilometres along highways and railways. In 2014 the Ministry of Communication and Informatics accelerated the roll-out of the Palapa Ring Project, as required by Presidential Decree No. 96/2014 on the Indonesia Broadband Plan for 2014–2019.

The nature of the infrastructure means that it will probably be of most benefit to the big cities, especially in lowland and coastal regions, where accessing the network is expected to be easier and faster. It is predicted that the project will dramatically improve high-speed broadband penetration by 2019 (Iskandar 2008; Puskakom UI 2015: 2). However, villages in rural and mountainous areas will have to wait longer to be connected to the main fibre optic cable, relying in the meantime on less stable wireless solutions.

Internet cafes

Although many Indonesian internet users have switched to smartphones, internet cafes remain an important way for rural people to access the internet in areas with limited or no broadband or WiFi access, and for newcomers to the internet to access information. The internet cafe business boomed from around 1999 to 2006, and in 2014 Indonesia still had 17,640 privately owned internet cafes. However, areas with low internet penetration, such as North Kalimantan, West Sulawesi, Maluku, North Maluku, West Papua and Papua, had fewer internet cafes than the rest of the country—on average, only 80 per province (BPS 2014b: 104). Today, with the switch to smartphones, many internet cafes in the big cities have been transformed into game centres.

Wireless access

The overall picture for mobile access in rural Indonesia is not bright. Of 82,190 villages in Indonesia, 55,870 receive a strong cellular signal, 18,603 receive a weak signal and 7,717 have no signal at all. Of the villages with no signal, 4,876 are located in areas with low internet penetration, mostly in Papua and the Maluku islands (BPS 2014b: 105). Only 27,084 villages have a cellular tower in the village itself. Even if the government installs an additional 575 towers by 2019 as planned, this will not be enough to cover all of the villages with no signal.

Indonesia must also deal with the extreme difficulty of deploying wireless networks in mountainous areas. Of Indonesia's 82,190 villages, 16,043 are located on mountain peaks or slopes and 3,630 are located in valleys surrounded by mountains. Once again, many of these villages are situated in provinces with low internet penetration, such as Papua, West Papua, Maluku, Aceh and North Sumatra (BPS 2014b: 16). The challenge of penetrating the terrain in mountainous regions is exacerbated by the need to install extra relay points and equipment because of the line-of-sight nature of radio signals.

Local government funds are not always available for these types of projects. In rural areas and villages, telecommunications and the internet have to compete for funding with areas such as health and education.

Commercial operators are not able to fill the gap in areas where incomes are low and the cost of building infrastructure high. Casual employees in agriculture in rural areas and villages have the lowest net average monthly income of all Indonesian workers, earning just Rp 772,800 per month (BPS 2014c: 22, 118). This restricts their ability to purchase goods and services: in rural areas, the average expenditure on goods and services is Rp 72,524 (10.1 per cent of the average monthly income), compared with Rp 1.1 million (14.2 per cent of the average monthly income) in urban areas (BPS 2015: 27). In rural areas, per capita spending on internet use is a maximum of Rp 10,000 (less than $1) per month. Commercial operators cannot make a profit in such circumstances.

Targeting rural areas

In 2015, the Ministry of Communication and Informatics announced that it would redesign the USO program and adopt a more bottom-up approach that would be better suited to the needs of rural districts and villages. Henceforth, the USO program would concentrate not only on infrastructure, but also on developing ecosystems to support that infrastructure (ICT training for schools and communities, training in licensing procedures for rural ICT operators and so on) (Widiartanto 2015). The new approach confirmed the failure of top-down projects that were not based on surveys of local capacity and not accompanied by ICT training.

The members of the DPR's Commission I have urged the Ministry of Communication and Informatics to prioritise internet network expansion to remote rural areas (Noor 2016b), and the authors of a University of Indonesia report have stressed the importance of internet access in rural areas as a key development factor (Puskakom UI 2015: 2). It appears that the government has some reservations, however: in 2015, then finance minister Bambang Brodjonegoro said that the telecommunications sector had to be able to function and develop without having to rely on the national budget (Ministry of Communication and Informatics 2015) and, as noted above, the Telecommunications Law states that only licensed operators are allowed to build and manage telecommunications infrastructure.

There are three main options to finance telecommunications infrastructure in rural areas: USO funds; the funds villages receive under Law No. 6/2014 on Villages; and self-financing by village communities. The keys to sustainable infrastructure development are keeping costs down, building local expertise and prioritising projects that benefit the local economy (Hosman 2010: 57–8). To achieve these goals, the Indonesian government should adopt an open development approach that includes 'open participation in use, open licensing to provide services, open content, open source, and open government' (Smith, Elder and Emden 2011: iii).

The government's earlier attempts to provide village and mobile internet cafes without assessing local capacity or providing training led to the failure of these projects. The current plan to install 575 cellular towers in rural areas by 2019 is a good start, but it will not be enough to give the 7,717 villages that currently have no cellular signal access to the internet.

BOTTOM-UP STRATEGIES

So what are the best solutions to narrow the digital divide between urban and rural areas, and between the haves and have-nots, in Indonesia? The government has successfully implemented several technologies in the field, including long-distance wireless networks, neighbourhood networks and community-based cellular networks, in addition to its less successful mobile internet cafes and other Smart Village projects.

The government's first cyberproject, Nusantara 21, was established in 1997. The aim was to transform Indonesia's 'traditional society' into a 'knowledge-based society', using the internet as the main vehicle (Purbo et al. 1998: 4). Although Nusantara 21 received some government funding and was subject to government policies and regulations, the real impetus for the program came from local communities themselves. Perhaps the most important outcome of the Nusantara 21 program was not the expansion of technology per se, but rather the way it empowered Indonesian communities to direct and fund their own projects (Purbo et al. 1998: 9).

Much of Nusantara 21 was never implemented owing to the severe economic and political crises of the late 1990s. Nevertheless, it is important to understand this program, because the community-based approaches and knowledge-sharing activities it fostered would become a key component of the civil society networks of the *reformasi* period. The emergence of Indonesia's first 'geeks, hackers and techies' in the late 1990s (Chon 2016: appendix E), together with innovations such as the internet cafe, were also crucial during this time (Lim 2003).

The falling cost of equipment and the increase in funding to villages have expanded the opportunities for rural villages to provide their own internet infrastructure, should they see a benefit in doing so. Internet equipment is relatively inexpensive; a single off-the-shelf WiFi access point costs around $50–100, for example, and the cheaper smartphones and tablets cost around $100. Moreover, with the passage of Law No. 6/2014 on Villages, villages now have access to a funding pool of approximately Rp 56.3 trillion from the central government that they can use for a variety of different purposes. The amounts that villages receive differ widely: villages in Papua receive around Rp 1.1 million per year whereas those in Aceh receive Rp 240 million (Kompas 2015). The use of the funds depends on each village's internal politics and governance structures, but if there is a consensus within the village community, the money can be used to build or improve local internet infrastructure.

The process of adopting internet technology usually proceeds as follows. First, villagers become aware of the need for the internet through articles, discussions, seminars, workshops, the media, blogs and so on. Second, these villagers create demand for internet infrastructure. Third, infrastructure (such as a local area network) is built in response to demand, either by commercial operators or by the community itself. Finally, the domestic manufacturing ecosystem begins to manufacture the components (switches, cables, WiFi access points and so on) needed to operate the infrastructure so that equipment no longer needs to be sourced from abroad—although this is only just beginning to happen in Indonesia (Purbo and Walton 2010). The entire process can be self-financed using the community's resources, with government playing only a limited role.

Indonesia's community-based rural internet networks employ a range of technologies and infrastructure. These include long-distance WiFi-based networks, internet cafes, neighbourhood networks, the Voice over Internet Protocol (Purbo 2011) and local streaming servers (Andrean, Purbo and Johandri 2015). More advanced technologies suitable for rural and remote areas include wireless mesh networks (Li et al. 2008) and wireless networking using OpenBTS (Burgess 2010; Purbo 2013). A volume by Butler (2013) describes how to make best use of whatever resources are available to build affordable communication networks in developing countries. The author suggests using inexpensive off-the-shelf equipment to build high-speed data networks to connect remote areas, and providing broadband access in areas where there is no cellular phone access (Butler 2013: xviii). This model for connecting whole neighbourhoods to the internet could be adopted in Indonesia.

One example of successful development of community-driven infrastructure can be found in Manado, North Sulawesi, where a group of local IT specialists from PT Infotek Global Network has established a long-distance wireless network connecting many of the islands of North Manado and Maluku. A base station on Manado acts as a hub for the surrounding islands, with several relay stations extending the coverage as far as the Halmahera islands to the east of Manado and the Talaud islands to the north (close to the border with the Philippines). The network provides relatively fast speeds of up to 56 megabits per second at an affordable price. This has been made possible by the use of low-cost, high-performance infrastructure.

While the old-style internet cafes simply connect multiple computers in one room to the internet, neighbourhood networks such as the one just described connect computers in several houses in a neighbourhood. Technologically, these neighbourhood networks are similar to the campus networks in the developed world.

Estimating the number of neighbourhood networks in Indonesia is difficult because most networks run silently in order to avoid problems with the authorities. The records of wireless solutions provider MikroTik Indonesia indicate that 3,374 of its 87,000 users are running neighbourhood networks,[2] many of which would serve the villages. One such group, in Pemalang city in Central Java, is currently working to connect 211 villages in the northern part of the province.[3] Facebook currently hosts the largest MikroTik Indonesia discussion group for neighbourhood networks, RT RW Net Indonesia, which has more than 22,100 members.

Around 3,000 villages, or 3.6 per cent of all Indonesian villages, are currently connected to the internet through a wireless network. Businesses, schools, government institutions and ISPs would be heavy users of these networks. Using the conservative assumptions that villages account for 5 per cent of annual sales of wireless equipment and that each village installs, on average, 20 nodes, I estimate that around 200 additional villages are connected to the internet each year. Neighbourhood networks are normally financed by the communities themselves. Like internet cafes, they face closure by the police if it becomes known that they do not have an official ISP licence, have not contributed to a local tower construction fund or have illegally resold bandwidth. Telkom explicitly prohibits any bandwidth resale by neighbourhood networks.[4]

Traditional cellular networks are built by the large carriers either to make a profit or in response to political pressure from government. This often leaves areas that are less profitable, or lacking in powerful politicians, without communication services. Heimerl et al. (2014) attempted to address this problem by proposing an alternative model for small-scale cellular systems in rural areas; these systems would be based on OpenBTS technology, would be installed and operated by locals and would

---

2 Personal communication with Valens Riyadi, CEO of MikroTik Indonesia, 9 June 2016.

3 Personal communication with Andri Johandri, ICT Watch activist, 9 June 2016.

4 A copy of the PT Telkom letter banning the resale of bandwidth can be found at http://opensource.telkomspeedy.com/wiki/index.php/Image:Larangan-resale-akses-internet.jpg.

leverage local infrastructure where available. After 16 months, the first network, built in a rural village in Papua, had 349 subscribers and was generating nearly $1,000 per month for the operators. The authors argue that their bottom-up model is a cost-effective way of providing cellular connectivity to those without coverage, in ways that are both sustainable and profitable for local communities (Heimerl et al. 2014: 1–2).

On 6 January 2016, the minister of communications, Rudiantara, took part in an informal community discussion on the possibility of using OpenBTS more widely in rural areas (Noor 2016a). The discussion was held at the headquarters of ICT Watch, a civil society organisation established to support widespread, unfettered internet adoption throughout Indonesia. After much discussion, on 8 April 2016 Rudiantara signed Ministerial Decree No. 5/2016 on Technology Trials for Telecommunications, Informatics and Broadcasting, which supports non-commercial, short-term trials of rural technology applications.

NARROWING THE DIGITAL LITERACY DIVIDE

Empowering communities to improve their internet skills is important: it gives communities the ability to create and maintain local internet infrastructure; and it allows them to maximise the benefits of using the internet (Cohron 2015). The ability to use the internet properly and safely is particularly important for young internet users, and ideally, internet skills would be integrated into the school curriculum. However, in 2013 the then minister of education, Muhammad Nuh, removed ICT as a compulsory school subject, resulting in many public schools dropping the subject from their curriculums (Retaduari 2016). Indonesians have therefore had to rely on non-government organisations such as ICT Watch, Relawan TIK Indonesia and the Raihan Technology Foundation, as well as commercial wireless equipment distributors such as MikroTik Indonesia and Ubiquiti Networks, to gain the training and motivation they need to improve their ICT and internet skills. I will review some of these initiatives in this section.

On 29 April 2002, ICT Watch launched the Healthy Internet (Internet Sehat) website (http://internetsehat.org), which aims to promote freedom of expression through safe and wise use of the internet. Its approach has been to focus on the home and the school as the safest environments for internet use; to encourage the creation of positive, useful and interesting local content; and to empower civil society by facilitating the uptake of ICT. From 2009 to 2012, ICT Watch gave out Healthy Internet Blog & Content Awards to bloggers who offered outstanding content on their blog posts.

Another way to encourage young people to use the internet in innovative ways is to hold hacking marathons, or 'hackathons'. These have proved to be a good way to unearth bright young programmers and find the best ideas to solve problems. One of the most prestigious events for programmers is the Association of Computing Machinery's International Collegiate Programming Contest (ACM-ICPC), a multi-tier, team-based programming competition. The Indonesian winners tend to have computer programming as a hobby rather than being formally trained in ICT.[5] Some of the finalists have already made a substantial contribution to the development of internet applications in Indonesia.

E-commerce is a fast-growing application of the internet, with large Indonesian companies such as Lippo Group, as well as more recent start-ups, leading the Southeast Asian market. Some of the best programmers from ACM-ICPC have established successful start-ups, such as online shopping sites Bukalapak and Tokopedia. Bukalapak was founded in 2011 and now employs more than 200 people. Towards the end of 2015, it claimed to host 500,000 sellers with total average daily transactions of about Rp 8 billion (Ningrum 2015; Nurmayanti 2015). Tokopedia was founded in 2009 and has a staff of over 200. In 2015, it claimed to host 300,000 active sellers who sold a total of 6 million products each month (Prasetyo 2015).

The main avenues for Indonesia's 'techies' to keep up to date with technological developments are social media sites such as Facebook and Twitter, or discussion forums such as KASKUS, the largest Indonesian electronics forum with more than 6 million registered users. Some of the more knowledgeable contributors have compiled answers to the most frequently asked questions in blogs, websites and wikis, while publishers such as Elex Media Komputindo and AndiPublisher continue to publish books in print to reach a more traditional audience. For those who are interested in taking a structured online course, ICT enthusiasts have created free-access, Moodle-based e-learning sites such as eLearning Rakyat (http://lms.onnocenter.or.id/moodle/). These sites currently have more than 14,500 students, including teachers who want to create their own online ICT courses or help their schools make the switch to online exams.

Online exams are a very effective way to reduce education costs, as most schools spend Rp 6–20 million per semester on photocopying exam papers. A small server, on the other hand, would cost only Rp 10 million and could be used for at least five years. The Ministry of Education appears to encourage schools to offer online final exams but it provides only limited financial and technical support for them to do so. Since the end of 2015, a group of volunteer ICT teachers calling itself KOGTIK

---

5 Professor Teddy Mantoro, personal communication, 5 June 2016.

has conducted workshops on e-learning and online exams in 10 cities, with an average of 100 teachers participating in each city. Attendees were asked to pay about Rp 75,000–100,000 (about 2–5 per cent of a teacher's monthly salary) from their own pockets to participate in the event.

The Raihan Technology Foundation also organises ICT workshops, seminars and roadshows in many districts. Participation costs are low, at only Rp 25,000–35,000 ($2–3) per person. Since 2012, the foundation has held around 40 workshops in various districts, with an average of 500–600 people, most of them vocational high-school students, participating.[6]

MikroTik Indonesia and Ubiquiti Networks both provide short training courses for people who are interested in becoming professional wireless engineers. Together, they turn out about 1,500 engineers annually. The Ubiquiti courses are organised by Spectrumindo and documented on Facebook. They are offered at least four times a year, with each course attracting an average of 100 participants. In total, Ubiquiti trains about 500 wireless engineers per year.[7] The MikroTik training courses are organised by Citraweb. A minimum of 40 classes are held per year, each with about 24 participants. On average, MikroTik trains about 1,000 new wireless engineers per year. In addition, MikroTik Indonesia partners with 170 vocational schools and universities to develop their own MikroTik-certified training courses, and organises MikroTik user meetings. On 9–10 October 2015, the seventh Indonesian MikroTik user meeting, held in Yogyakarta, was attended by more than 2,500 participants, making it the largest such meeting in the world.[8]

Top-down strategies implemented by the government play only a minor role in improving digital literacy in Indonesia. As ICT has been removed from the formal school curriculum, communities themselves have had to take up the challenge of narrowing the digital literacy divide. To achieve this, they have turned to free online resources available through Facebook, Twitter, blogs and wikis, and paid for training courses out of their own pockets. Every year, these workshops and seminars are able to increase the digital literacy of about 1,000 schoolteachers, 5,000–6,000 students and 1,500 wireless engineers. It is bottom-up community activities such as these that are the driving force behind the digital literacy movement in Indonesia.

---

6 Personal communication with Dadang, CEO of the Raihan Technology Foundation, 9 June 2016.

7 Personal communication with Teguh Wijaya, CEO of Spectrumindo, 10 June 2016.

8 Personal communication with Valens Riyadi, CEO of Citraweb and Mikrotik Indonesia, 10 June 2016.

CONCLUSION

In this chapter, I have suggested that Indonesia's digital divide can be addressed through two major strategies: equipping people with better internet skills, and fixing infrastructure deficits.

Education is the key to equipping citizens with better internet skills. The simplest strategy to improve young Indonesians' internet competence would be for the minister of education to reinstate ICT in the school curriculum, re-employ ICT teachers and provide schools with better internet access. This would accelerate the process of upgrading internet skills and competence among young Indonesians, removing one barrier to internet adoption.

There are two main options that the government could consider to fix infrastructure deficits in rural areas: launching a full-scale government drive to improve internet infrastructure; and establishing combined public–private (people) partnerships for infrastructure improvement. To reduce the failure rate in the fully government-driven projects, the government must conduct broader surveys on local capacity, undertake more rigorous planning and improve the knowledge, technical capacity and level of engagement of citizens before infrastructure is deployed. This is essential to ensure that top-down policies to improve rural internet access do not follow the path of their failed predecessors.

Given the large number of neighbourhood networks, thousands of wireless engineers and many OpenBTS research groups in Indonesia, it would also be beneficial to strengthen public–private (people) partnerships in rural areas. The simplest strategy would be to create an ISP class licence for neighbourhood networks, similar to the licences for the WiFi frequency, although this would mean that the government would have to be ready to process ISP licences for neighbourhood networks in more than 80,000 villages.

Further research is needed to evaluate the best use of USO funds for communities, a sustainable level of network interconnection and other charges, and the optimal allocation of resources such as telephone area codes and cellular channels. The guiding principles for all infrastructure projects should be to keep costs down, to build local expertise and to select projects that benefit the local economy (Hosman 2010: 57–8).

REFERENCES

Andrean, J., O.W. Purbo and A. Johandri (2015) *Hacking Streaming*, Elex Media, Jakarta.

Asril, S. (2013a) 'Proyek internet ke desa kacau, Tifatul siap dilaporkan' [Following chaos in the village internet project, Tifatul should be prepared to be reported], *Kompas*, 19 March. Available at http://nasional.kompas.com/read/2013/03/19/00425254/%20Proyek.Internet.ke.Desa.Kacau.Tifatul.Siap.Dilaporkan. Accessed 20 June 2016.

Asril, S. (2013b) 'DPR: ada 4 temuan bobroknya proyek melek internet Kemenkominfo' [Parliament: 4 findings about the collapse of the Ministry of Communication and Informatics' internet literacy projects], *Kompas*, 24 July. Available at http://nasional.kompas.com/read/2013/07/24/1219472/DPR.Ada.4.Temuan.%20Bobroknya.Proyek.Melek.Internet.Kemenkominfo. Accessed 20 June 2016.

Balea, J. (2016) 'The latest stats in web and mobile in Indonesia (infographic)', *Tech in Asia*, 28 January. Available at https://www.techinasia.com/indonesia-web-mobile-statistics-we-are-social. Accessed 4 June 2016.

BPS (Badan Pusat Statistik) (2014a) 'Persentase penduduk daerah perkotaan menurut provinsi, 2010–2035' [Percentage of urban population by province, 2010–2035], Jakarta. Available at http://bps.go.id/linkTabelStatis/view/id/1276. Accessed 4 June 2016.

BPS (Badan Pusat Statistik) (2014b) *Village Potential Statistics of Indonesia*, Jakarta.

BPS (Badan Pusat Statistik) (2014c) *Income Statistics*, Jakarta.

BPS (Badan Pusat Statistik) (2015) *Expenditure for Consumption of Indonesia Based on September 2015 Susenas*, Jakarta.

Burgess, D. (2010) 'Low cost cellular networks with OpenBTS', *Open Source Business Resource*, March. Available at https://timreview.ca/article/332.

Butler, J. (ed.) (2013) *Wireless Networking in the Developing World*, third edition. Available at http://wndw.net/download/WNDW_Standard.pdf. Accessed 6 June 2016.

Chon, K. (ed.) (2016) *An Asia Internet History: Third Decade (2001–2010)*. Available at https://sites.google.com/site/annexcybercommonsnet/home/3book1605.pdf?attredirects=0&d=1. Accessed 4 June 2016.

Cohron, M. (2015) 'The continuing digital divide in the United States', *Serials Librarian*, 69(1): 77–86.

EIU (Economist Intelligence Unit) (2013) 'Redefining the digital divide', London. Available at http://www.huawei.com/ilink/en/download/HW_314193. Accessed 4 June 2016.

Hasbi (2014) 'Program MPLIK Aceh diduga gagal' [MPLIK program in Aceh alleged to have failed], *Sidak News*, 28 September. Available at https://www.sidaknews.com/program-mplik-aceh-diduga-gagal/. Accessed 5 June 2016.

Heimerl, K., S. Hasan, K. Ali, T. Parikh and E. Brewer (2014) 'A longitudinal study of local, sustainable, small-scale cellular networks', *Information Technologies & International Development*, 11(1): 1–19. Available at http://kurti.sh/pubs/vbts_itid_15.pdf. Accessed 6 June 2016.

Hosman, L. (2010) 'Policies, partnerships, and pragmatism: lessons from an ICT-in-education project in rural Uganda', *Information Technologies & International Development*, 6(1): 48–64.

IDA (Info-communications Development Authority of Singapore) (2015) 'Annual survey on InfoComm usage in households and by individuals for 2014', Singapore. Available at https://www.ida.gov.sg/~/media/Files/Infocomm

%20Landscape/Facts%20and%20Figures/SurveyReport/2014/2014%20 HH%20public %20report%20final.pdf. Accessed 11 June 2016.

Ilomäki, L. S. Paavola, M. Lakkala and A. Kantosalo (2016) 'Digital competence: an emergent boundary concept for policy and educational research', *Education and Information Technologies*, 21(3): 655–79.

Irawan, Y.K. (2016) 'Puluhan mobil internet kecamatan terbengkalai' [Vans used to provide internet are neglected in many subdistricts], *Kompas*, 23 May. Available at http://tekno.kompas.com/read/2016/05/23/08082247/puluhan.mobil.internet.kecamatan.terbengkalai. Accessed 20 June 2016.

Iskandar, B.Y. (2008) 'Prioritizing a national high capacity backbone network', presentation to the 8th annual Global Symposium for Regulators, Pattaya, 11–13 March. Available at https://www.itu.int/ITU-D/treg/Events/Seminars/GSR/GSR08/documents_presentations/Basuki_Yusuf_Iskandar.pdf. Accessed 4 June 2016.

ITU (International Telecommunication Union) (2012) 'Impact of broadband on the economy: research to date and policy issues', Geneva, April. Available at https://www.itu.int/ITU-D/treg/broadband/ITU-BB-Reports_Impact-of-Broadband-on-the-Economy.pdf. Accessed 12 June 2016.

ITU (International Telecommunication Union) (2015) 'Measuring the information society report', Geneva. Available at http://www.itu.int/en/ITU-D/Statistics/Documents/publications/misr2015/MISR2015-w5.pdf. Accessed 11 June 2016.

Kompas (2015) 'Dana Besar akan banjiri desa' [Village Fund will flood villages], *Kompas*, 27 February. Available at http://nasional.kompas.com/read/2015/02/27/15050061/Dana.Besar.Akan.Banjiri.Desa. Accessed 4 June 2016.

Li, F.Y, L. Vandonif, G. Ziccaf and S. Zanoli (2008) 'OLSR mesh networks for broadband access: enhancements, implementation and deployment', paper presented at the 4th IEEE International Conference on Circuits and Systems for Communications, Shanghai, 26–28 May.

Lim, M. (2003) 'The internet, social network and reform in Indonesia', in N. Couldry and J. Curran (eds) *Contesting Media Power: Alternative Media in a Networked World*, Rowan & Littlefield, Lanham: 273–88. Available at https://www.academia.edu/214239/Lim_M._2003_The_Internet_Social_Network_and_Reform_in_Indonesia_. Accessed 21 June 2016.

Majalah ICT (2013) 'Kepala BP3TI: PLIK–MPLIK tidak optimal karena sejumlah masalah' [Head of BP3TI: PLIK–MPLIK not optimal for various reasons], *Majalah ICT*, 21 July. Available at http://www.majalahict.com/kepala-bp3ti-plik-mplik-tidak-optimal-karena-sejumlah-masalah/. Accessed 5 June 2016.

MCMC (Malaysia Communication and Multimedia Commission) (2015) 'Internet users survey 2014', Cyberjaya. Available at http://www.skmm.gov.my/Resources/Statistics/Internet-users-survey.aspx. Accessed 11 June 2016.

Ministry of Communication and Informatics (2014) 'Komisi I DPR cabut blokir anggaran Kementerian Kominfo' [Parliament's Commission I revokes the freezing of the Ministry of Communication and Informatics' budget], Kemkominfo (Ministry of Communication and Informatics), Jakarta. Available at https://kominfo.go.id/index.php/content/detail/3766/Komisi+I+DPR+Cabut+Blokir+Anggaran+Kementerian+Kominfo/0/berita_satker. Accessed 6 June 2016.

Ministry of Communication and Informatics (2015) 'Bangun infrastruktur bisa cepat tanpa bergantung APBN)' [Infrastructure can be built fast without relying on the national budget], Kemkominfo (Ministry of Communication and Informatics), Jakarta. Available at http://palaparing.kominfo.go.id/?Flow=news&code=3. Accessed 5 June 2016.

Montagnier, P., and A. Wirthmann (2011) 'Digital divide: from computer access to online activities—a micro data analysis', OECD Digital Economy Papers No. 189, OECD Publishing, Paris. Available at http://www.oecd-ilibrary.org/science-and-technology/digital-divide-from-computer-access-to-online-activities-a-micro-data-analysis_5kg0lk60rr30-en. Accessed 12 June 2016.

Murdaningsih, D. (2016) 'Mobil penyedia internet kecamatan banyak terbengkalai' [Many of the vans used to provide internet in the subdistricts are neglected], *Republika*, 1 June. Available at http://www.republika.co.id/berita/dpr-ri/berita-dpr-ri/16/06/01/o82vpz368-mobil-penyedia-internet-kecamatan-banyak-terbengkalai. Accessed 5 June 2016.

Ningrum, D.W. (2015) 'CEO Bukalapak.com: 190 ribu seller, kami sar di Indonesia' [CEO of Bukalapak.com: 190,000 sellers, we are the largest in Indonesia], *Liputan6.com*, 25 April. Available at http://news.liputan6.com/read/2220240/ceo- bukalapakcom-190-ribu-seller-kami-terbesar-di-indonesia. Accessed 5 June 2016.

Noor, A.R. II (2016a) 'Diskusi sambil lesehan, menkominfo bahas Open BTS bareng Onno Cs' [Minister of communication has relaxed discussion on Open BTS with Onno Cs], *detik.com*, 7 January. Available at http://inet.detik.com/read/2016/01/07/185618/3113286/328/diskusi-sambil-lesehan-menkominfo-bahas-open-bts-bareng-onno-cs. Accessed 20 June 2016.

Noor, A.R. II (2016b) 'Pak Menteri, tolong lirik juga akses internet di desa terpencil' [Mr Minister, please check internet access in remote villages], *detik.com*, 10 June. Available at http://inet.detik.com/read/2016/06/10/085202/3229841/328/pak-menteri-tolong-lirik-juga-akses-internet-di-desa-terpencil. Accessed 20 June 2016.

Nurmayanti (2015) 'Bisnis toko online sangat menjanjikan' [Online shopping business is promising], *Liputan6.com*, 3 October. Available at http://bisnis.liputan6.com/read/2331904/bisnis-toko-online-sangat-menjanjikan. Accessed 5 June 2016.

OECD (Organisation for Economic Co-operation and Development) (2001) 'Understanding the digital divide', Paris. Available at https://www.oecd.org/sti/1888451.pdf. Accessed 22 June 2016.

Prasetyo, A.E. (2015) 'Debat komunitas: di mana kamu akan berjualan, Tokopedia atau Bukalapak?' [Community debate: where are you going to sell, Tokopedia or Bukalapak?], *Tech in Asia*, 19 October. Available at https://id.techinasia.com/talk/tokopedia-vs-bukalapak-di-mana-kamu-akan-berjualan. Accessed 20 June 2016.

Purbo, O.W. (2011) *VoIP Cookbook*, Internet Society Innovation Funds (SIF). Available at http://kambing.ui.ac.id/onnopurbo/ebook/ebook-voip/VoIP-Cookbook-20110211.pdf. Accessed 20 June 2016.

Purbo, O.W. (2013) *Bongkar Rahasia OpenBTS untuk Jaringan Operator Seluler* [Opening the Secrets of OpenBTS for Cellular Network Operators], Penerbit Andi, Yogyakarta.

Purbo, O.W., and M. Walton (2010) 'The foundation of cultural change in Indonesia', *Information Technologies & International Development*, Special Edition, 6: 45–8. Available at http://itidjournal.org/itid/article/view/621/261. Accessed 6 June 2016.

Purbo, O.W., G. Ramantoko, K. Pribadi and B. Nazief (1998) 'Nusantara 21: kerangka konseptual' [Nusantara 21: conceptual framework], Yayasan Litbang Telekomunikasi Informatika (YLTI), Jakarta. Available at http://digilib.

itb.ac.id/gdl.php?mod=browse&op=read&id=jbptitbpp-gdl-publ-1998-onno-795-nusantara. Accessed 4 June 2016.

Puskakom UI (Pusat Kajian Komunikasi, Universitas Indonesia) (2015) 'Profil pengguna internet Indonesia 2014' [Profile of internet users in Indonesia 2014], Asosiasi Penyelenggara Jasa Internet Indonesia (APJII), Jakarta.

Retaduari, E.A. (2016) 'Saat SBY dengarkan curhatan mantan staf ahli Jokowi' [When SBY listens to Jokowi's expert staff], *detik.com*, 14 March. Available at http://news.detik.com/berita/3164743/saat-sby-dengarkan-curhatan-mantan-staf-ahli-jokowi. Accessed 13 June 2016.

Smith, M.L., L. Elder and H. Emdon (2011) 'Open development: a new theory for ICT4D', *Information Technologies & International Development*, 7(1): iii–ix.

Suryadhi, A. (2016) 'Mobil internet kecamatan terbengkalai, Kominfo: itu milik swasta' [Vans used to provide internet are neglected in subdistricts, Ministry of Communication and Informatics: it belongs to the private sector], *detik.com*, 23 May. Available at http://inet.detik.com/read/2016/05/23/064357/3215131/328/mobil-internet-kecamatan-terbengkalai-kominfo-itu-milik-swasta. Accessed 20 June 2016.

Telkomsel (2012) '880 Desa Pinter gelaran Telkomsel untuk Indonesia' [Telkomsel rolls out 880 Smart Village packages in Indonesia], Jakarta. Available at http://www.telkomsel.com/about/news/865-880-Desa%20-PINTER-Gelaran-Telkomsel-Untuk-Indonesia.html. Accessed 20 June 2016.

van Deursen, A.J.A.M., E.J. Helsper and R. Eynon (2016) 'Development and validation of the Internet Skills Scale (ISS)', *Information, Communication & Society*, 19(6): 804–23.

Warschauer, M. (2004) *Technology and Social Inclusion: Rethinking the Digital Divide*, MIT Press, Cambridge, MA.

Wibowo, M.E.A. (2016) 'Mobil internet bantuan pusat tak beroperasi' [Internet vans donated by the central government are not operational], *Koran Sindo*, 2 June. Available at http://www.koran-sindo.com/news.php?r=5&n=148&date=2016-06-02. Accessed 5 June 2016.

Widiartanto, Y.H. (2015) 'Kemenkominfo hentikan sementara Desa Berdering [Ministry of Communication and Informatics temporarily stops Smart Village project], *Kompas*, 8 March. Available at http://tekno.kompas.com/read/2015/03/08/08090067/Kemenkominfo.Hentikan.Sementara.Desa.Berdering. Accessed 5 June 2016.

Witt, S.W. (2016) 'Access to knowledge at the heart of the profession and a key to sustainable development', *IFLA Journal*, 42(1): 3–4.

World Bank (2009) 'Information and communications for development 2009: extending reach and increasing impact', International Bank for Reconstruction and Development, World Bank, Washington DC. Available at https://openknowledge.worldbank.org/bitstream/handle/10986/2636/487910PUB0EPI1101Official0Use0Only1.pdf? sequence=1&isAllowed=y. Accessed 11 June 2016.

World Economic Forum (2016) 'Internet for all: a framework for accelerating internet access and adoption', white paper, April. Available at http://www3.weforum.org/docs/WEF_Internet_for_All_Framework_Accelerating_Internet_Access_Adoption_report_2016.pdf. Accessed 11 June 2016.

6 Laws, crackdowns and control mechanisms: digital platforms and the state

Usman Hamid

Indonesians have welcomed the emergence of new information and communication technologies such as the internet and social media platforms. Although internet use remains lower in Indonesia than in the advanced economies, the use of social media platforms has increased significantly. Scholars and observers of social media in Indonesia have pointed out that these platforms have had a positive impact on civil society activism, in particular by widening the civic space that facilitates citizens' freedom of expression. Nugroho (2011), for example, examined 'the patterns and processes of collaboration of civil society groups in Indonesia in promoting participatory democracy and freedom of information using new social media and ICTs' (p. 8), and concluded that 'the use of the Internet and social media in Indonesian civil society has brought significant implications not only to the organisation's internal managerial performance but more importantly to the external aspects of their work, particularly the dynamics of civic activism and socio-political engagement in the country' (p. 84).

Social media activism has become more prominent over the last few years due in no small part to the famous Prita Mulyasari case, in which a housewife was arrested for making critical comments in an email about her treatment at a private hospital (see Chapter 8 by Postill and Saputro). Based on an analysis of the types of social media campaigns that have attracted the most public support, Lim (2013: 636) suggests that 'social media activism is more likely to successfully mobilise mass support when its narratives are simple, associated with low risk actions and congruent with dominant meta-narratives, such as nationalism and religiosity'. Focusing on citizens' participation in the 2012 gubernatorial election in Jakarta, Priyono et al. (2014) argue that social media has become a powerful tool for civic engagement, by which citizens impart information, express opinions, participate in the political process and influence the agenda of the elected government in Jakarta. Tapsell (2014: 217) contends that, despite the big media companies still having the largest social media followings in Indonesia, 'the emancipatory ability of social media to highlight a significant issue [...] is a greater indicator of the power of social media to overcome mainstream media conglomerates'. Gazali (2014: 437) speculates that 'Should activists keep working [...] in the unique realms of social media, Indonesia may keep moving [...] towards a so-called "social media democracy"'. In this chapter, I will test social media use against the specific democratic principle of the free and safe participation in public debate by citizens, including minorities and marginalised groups.

While social media has undoubtedly had a positive impact on freedom of expression in Indonesia, the country has also seen a rise in the number of prosecutions against citizens who have expressed 'offensive' opinions online (ICT Watch 2014). Some of these prosecutions have taken place in the context of defamation suits, and others in the form of police and court actions against violations of Indonesia's anti-pornography and hacking laws. As a result of these and other developments, Indonesia's score on Freedom House's Freedom on the Net index deteriorated from 42 in 2015 to 44 in 2016 (Freedom House 2016a: 23).

The state and other conservative elites have used a number of legal and non-legal instruments to target social media users who are critical of public officials. In 2008, the government enacted a law that gave the state greater powers to crack down on online social media commentary: Law No. 11/2008 on Information and Electronic Transactions (the ITE Law). It includes a defamation clause (article 27(3)) that is similar to the one in the existing Criminal Code, but more specifically tailored to online posts and communications. A coalition of non-government organisations and prominent individuals asked the Constitutional Court to review the law, arguing that its defamation clause violated the fundamental right of a citizen to express his or her opinions, as enshrined in the constitution, and thus should be invalidated. The court rejected this view in 2009, stating that the defamation clause was necessary to protect the reputations of citizens who had been defamed online.

Since then, an increasing number of people have been prosecuted for making defamatory comments online, primarily statements critical of political or business leaders. Indonesian National Police documents show that the number of criminal online defamation cases brought by state and non-state actors rose sharply from five in both 2009 and 2010

Figure 6.1 Number of defamation cases, 2001–14

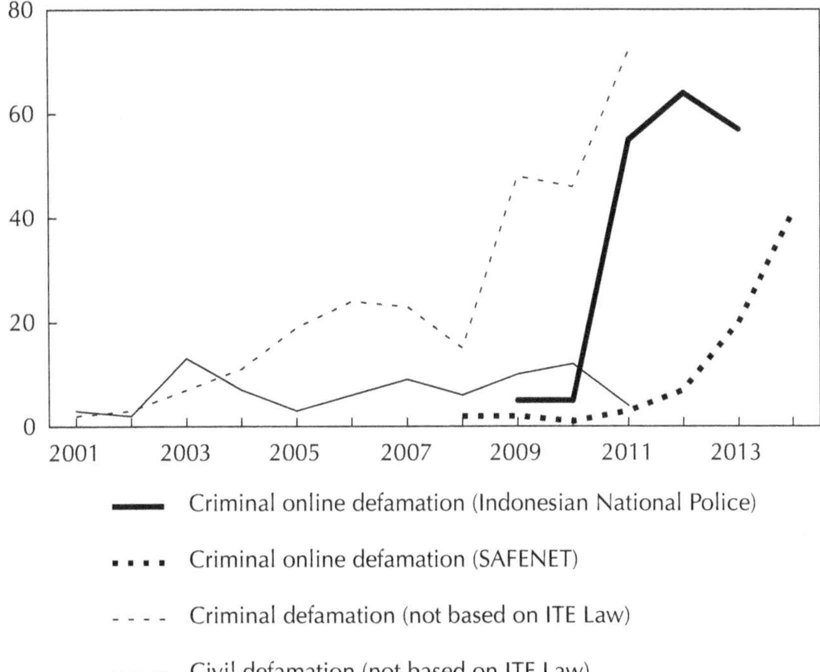

Note: Civil liability arises from publications likely to harm a person's reputation; penalties are usually monetary. Criminal liability arises from publications that affect the community; the proceedings are usually commenced by law enforcement authorities (rather than individuals) and the penalties may include imprisonment.

Source: Indonesian National Police; SAFENET (2015).

to 55 in 2011, 64 in 2012 and 57 in 2013 (Figure 6.1). The majority of these cases were based on either the ITE Law (44 cases, or 58.7 per cent) or the Criminal Code (24 cases, or 32.0 per cent). The Southeast Asia Freedom of Expression Network (SAFENET) documented a similar increase in the number of criminal online defamation cases using the ITE Law, from two in 2008 and 2009, and just one in 2010, to three in 2011, seven in 2012, 20 in 2013 and 41 in 2014 (SAFENET 2015).

While the numbers differ depending on which organisation has compiled the statistics, there can be no doubt that the number of criminal online defamation cases has increased significantly since 2010, when the law began to be applied in full (Figure 6.2). Thus, while more individuals may be expressing their opinions through social media, more legal cases are also being filed against these individuals. Between 2009 and 2013,

Figure 6.2 *Trends in the number of criminal online defamation cases, 2009–13*

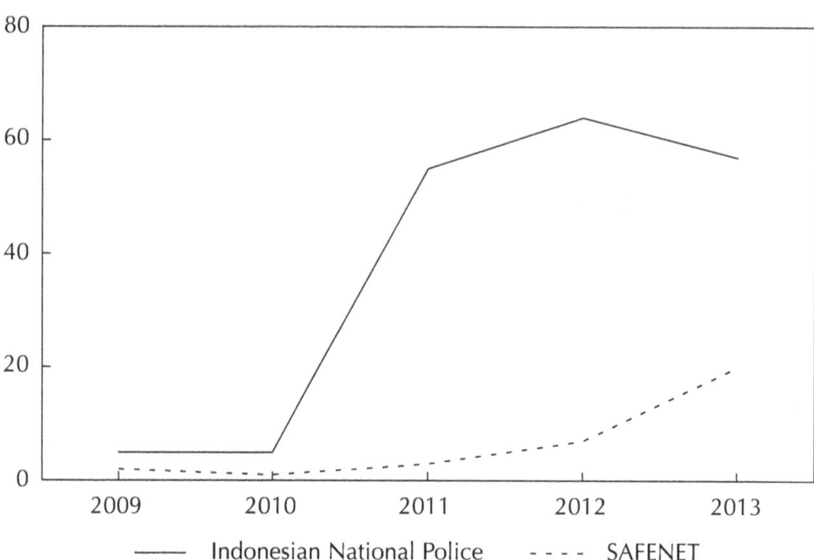

Source: Indonesian National Police; SAFENET (2015).

only 23 per cent of the lawsuits were criminal online defamation cases filed by individuals, while 77 per cent were criminal defamation cases initiated by groups (including Islamic and other socio-religious groups) who felt that they or their patrons had been defamed.

Moreover, according to SAFENET, state officials were one of the largest groups of complainants, mounting 36.5 per cent of cases. The defendants included activists, lawyers, researchers and journalists, as well as many 'ordinary' social media users. In almost all of these cases, the legal proceedings were accompanied by acts of physical intimidation against the defendants, carried out by the supporters of the government officials who had been criticised online. Thus, although the government likes to emphasise that the ITE Law is needed to crack down on computer hacking and the distribution of pornographic material through the internet, in fact it is mainly being used to prevent citizens from making critical comments on the internet (Figure 6.3).

SPECIFIC EXAMPLES OF STATE CRACKDOWNS

In 2015, I interviewed an Indonesian named Budiman who had posted negative comments on Facebook about the district head of Pangkep in

Figure 6.3 Number of criminal online defamation, pornography and hacking cases, 2009–13

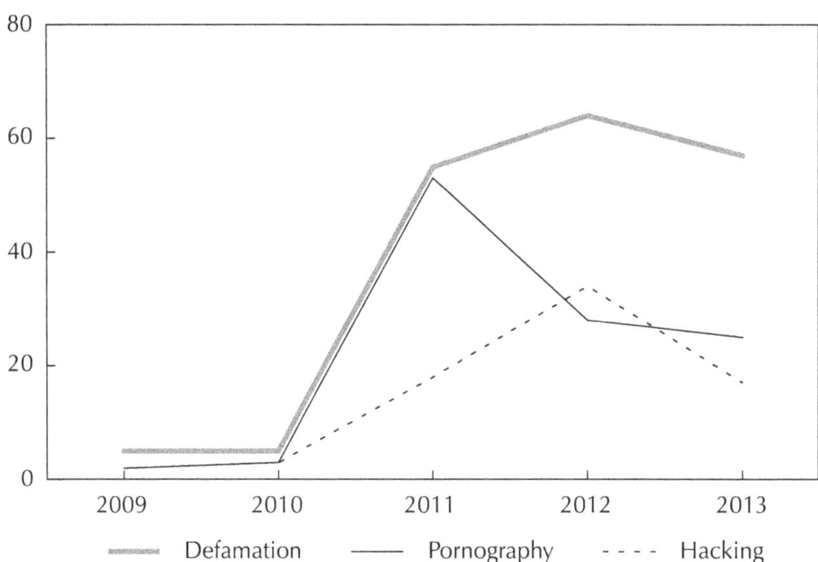

Source: Indonesian National Police.

South Sulawesi. This led to him being physically attacked by the district head's bodyguards and cadres of the Golkar Party. The mob also included dozens of members of Pancasila Youth (Pemuda Pancasila), a notorious gang of thugs groomed under Suharto's rule. Budiman was taken to the local police station for his own protection. When he felt it was safe enough to go home, he asked to be released and was told he could 'go home at his own risk'. The district head's staff then submitted a printout of the comments on Budiman's Facebook page to the police, who arrested him, told him he was 'up against a wall' and charged him with defamation under the ITE Law. However, the district head later announced publicly that he had 'forgiven' Budiman and declined to testify against him. Hence, the case did not make it to sentencing.

Others did not get away so 'lightly'. Fadhli Rahim was a resident of the district of Gowa in South Sulawesi who had worked as a civil servant since 2004, and for the local Tourism and Cultural Agency since 2013. He was a member of a LINE chatroom group called Ikasalis 99, consisting of eight friends from a senior secondary school in Sungguminasa, the capital of Gowa. The group was originally formed so that the friends could share their experiences of working in various parts of Indonesia, such as Papua, Kalimantan and Bali, but they soon began to discuss other topics. On 6 May 2014, a new member of the group, Yusuf, remarked that he had just returned from a nearby district and felt there was 'no progress in Gowa, unlike in districts such as Bantaeng, where the roads look nice'. This comment triggered a discussion in which most members supported Yusuf's opinion.

Rahim responded:

> I agree that Gowa is not innovative. […] The district head of Gowa is not up-to-date, and there is much corruption. Investors cannot be innovative in Gowa, and they do not invest in Gowa because there are so many levies.

He told the group that investors and contractors had shared their concerns about the district head with him, including an incident where a truck had been barred from entering an area because it was not affiliated with any of the business interests associated with the district head (*Tribun Timur*, 20 December 2014). Rahim went on to say:

> Investors have cancelled investment in Gowa because they couldn't reach a deal with the district head on the sharing of commissions and fees. I heard this directly from one of the investors.

Although Rahim had shared his views with only seven other people in a private chat group, in the opinion of the police and public prosecutor this was enough to make him subject to the ITE Law's defamation clause (article 27(3)) and he was duly charged with defamation. Before the trial, subordinates of the district head began to mobilise against Rahim. On 20 December 2014, for example, Arifuddin Saeni, the head of Gowa's public relations department, was quoted in *Tribun Timur* as saying: '[Rahim] accused the district head of receiving fees, and that's incorrect. It shows that he is an employee who is disloyal to his superior'. Rahim was found guilty of defaming the district head and was sentenced to eight months' imprisonment on 18 February 2015.

Before Rahim was sentenced, pro-democracy activists organised a demonstration in support of him and his mother, Rukmini Usman, an English teacher at a local secondary school who had taken a very public role in defending her son. However, dozens of thugs disrupted the demonstration, using iron and wooden sticks, broken glass bottles and stones to damage the protestors' vehicle. The police took no action to stop this violent attack (*Tribun Timur*, 20 February 2015). Rahim also claimed that security and prison officials had abused him after his detention on 24 November 2014, saying: 'My upper arms were badly scratched […] by the prison wardens, I was forced to pay for food and I was jailed in a small dirty cell' (author's interview with Fadhli Rahim, 3 March 2015). Finally, both Rahim and his mother were demoted from their respective positions in the bureaucracy. Rahim's rank was lowered, while his mother was moved from the school where she had worked for many years to one situated some 30 kilometres away from the city. Once more, a mixture of legal prosecution, social marginalisation, intimidation and abuse had been directed against a social media activist considered hostile by a member of the elite—in this case, as in many others, a local government head.

Perhaps the best-known example of a state crackdown on social media commentary involves atheist Alexander Aan. Born in Jakarta in 1981, Aan later moved to the district of Dharmasraya in West Sumatra, a province known for its high levels of Islamic piety and, in particular, for the local regulations issued in 2008 and 2011 discriminating against members of the Ahmadiyya Islamic sect.[1] In 2008, while studying statistics at Padjadjaran University in Bandung, Aan had become interested in atheism after discovering an online discussion forum called Faith Freedom Indonesia. In 2009, he joined Ateis Minang, a Facebook group for atheists primarily targeting the dominant ethnic group in West Sumatra, the Minangkabau (or Minang). Ateis Minang was founded by Jusfiq Hadjar, who was originally from West Sumatra but had been a lecturer at a university in France and had lived in the Netherlands for several decades. Aan recalls: 'At first I was just curious, [wondering] are there other people like me? When I typed "atheist" on the internet, there were international atheists, there were Indonesian atheists. Then I typed "Minang atheist" [*ateis Minang*], and it was there too'.

Aan became a critic of religion—and gradually shifted to atheism—despite being an employee of the same state that in 2010 had declined to extend constitutional protection from blasphemy legislation to atheists and others holding minority religious beliefs. By the end of 2011, he had adopted a highly Islam-critical and substantively atheistic position. His postings included criticisms of Islam under headings such as 'Muhammad is attracted by his own daughter-in-law' (18 October 2011), 'Scientific errors in Islam' (13 October 2011) and 'Answering Muslims' argument twisting' (18 November 2011). Due to his active role in stimulating discussion among group members, he was appointed administrator of Ateis Minang in August 2011 and became responsible for selecting the material uploaded to its Facebook page. By January 2012, Aan had approximately 500 Facebook friends, a relatively large number for a local civil servant, and his fan page had over 1,200 'likes'.

On the morning of 18 January 2012, Aan was attacked at his office by an angry mob who had heard about his beliefs. The attack was organised

---

1 The two regulations are Letter No. 03.02/14/PW.01/2008 of the Religious Office of the Subdistrict of Danau Kembar, dated 9 July 2008, requiring Ahmadi couples to abandon the sect before a marriage certificate can be issued; and Regulation No. 17/2011 of the Governor of West Sumatra on the Banning of Ahmadiyya Activities in West Sumatra.

by Mulyadi, the leader of a conservative local NGO called Caring for the Assets of a Safe and Prosperous Dharmasraya (Peduli Aset Dharmasraya Aman Makmur, or Pandham), who ordered youth gangs affiliated with his organisation to meet him at Aan's office. Aan recalled that around 2.30 pm:

> They came in droves, around 40 people, and beat me up. They came into my workspace. Some colleagues tried to protect me, but it was not enough to hold back the mob. They shouted, 'Infidel!', 'Burn!' and so on (author's interview with Alexander Aan, Jakarta, 18 January 2015).

The police arrived an hour later and eventually took Aan to the Dharmasraya police station, where he was placed in protective custody until the following day.

While the police initially seemed unsure about what to do with Aan, the head of the Indonesian Council of Islamic Scholars (Majelis Ulama Indonesia, or MUI) and customary leaders of the Minangkabau people urged the police to take legal action against him. The chair of the West Sumatra branch of MUI, Syamsul Bahri Khatib, stated that Aan had hurt the whole Minang community and damaged the basic structure of religion: 'This is contrary to the Pancasila',[2] he said, 'because atheism has no place in Indonesia' (Amri, Huda and Naldi 2012). On 20 January 2012, two days after the attack, Aan was charged with 'disseminating information aimed at inciting religious hatred or hostility' under article 28(2) of the ITE Law, 'religious blasphemy' under article 156(a) of the Criminal Code and 'calling for others to embrace atheism' under article 156(b) of the same code (American Humanist Association et al. 2012: 23; Amnesty International 2012). Article 156 of the Criminal Code is based on Law No. 1/PNPS/1965, originally issued in the form of a presidential decree in 1965. In other words, Aan was charged under laws dating from both the authoritarian and democratic periods.

On 14 February 2012, Aan wrote a letter of apology to the district head of Dharmasraya, the chair of the West Sumatra branch of MUI and the head of the Consultative Body for Minangkabau Customary Law (Lembaga Kerapatan Adat Alam Minangkabau, or LKAAM). Nevertheless, on 27 February 2012, the prosecutor's office decided to continue its investigation, and the first court hearing was held on 2 April.[3]

According to the indictment, the local community had captured Aan and handed him over to the Dharmasraya police because of the state-

---

2 The Pancasila are the five guiding principles of the Indonesian state: belief in God, in humanitarianism, in nationalism, in democracy and in social justice.

3 This section draws on the official record of the case: Decision of the Negeri Muaro District Court No. 45/PID.B/2012/PN.MR.

ments he had posted on the Ateis Minang Facebook page while working for the district government. The judges noted that 'the facts presented in court showed that Aan's task was to be a civil servant [...], not a journalist' and that his actions in posting or providing links to controversial information on the internet while using the computer facilities of the Dharmasraya district government were not in line with his main tasks and functions as a civil servant. Moreover, he did not have 'permission from the authorised officials, in this instance the minister of communication and information technology' to use office facilities for a non-work-related task (Decision of the Negeri Muaro District Court: 42).

Thus, the court dismissed the defence that Aan was a 'citizen journalist' and drew on a variety of administrative and legal provisions to convict him. The judges noted that Aan 'did not delete the content that is being debated', despite being warned to do so on 29 November 2011 by a group set up to oppose Ateis Minang's activities (Decision of the Negeri Muaro District Court: 44).[4] One of the judges differentiated between the right to hold an opinion and the right to express that opinion, stating that 'Aan holds an atheistic belief based on his right to freedom of belief, but he should not be allowed to openly declare this publicly on the internet, because the State of the Republic of Indonesia is based on One God as stipulated in the Pancasila and the 1945 Constitution' (Decision of the Negeri Muaro District Court: 44). On 14 June 2012, the district court of Negeri Muaro found Aan guilty of spreading religious hatred under the ITE Law and sentenced him to two years and six months in prison. The Padang High Court upheld the district court's ruling on 12 August 2012 and a further appeal to the Supreme Court was rejected in January 2013. This was the first time that an Indonesian citizen had been jailed for declaring that he was an atheist and sharing his views on atheism in a public forum. The actions of the state against Aan not only cost him his freedom, they also took away his livelihood. Aan lost his job and now lives in another province to avoid harassment (Amnesty International 2014: 21–2).

Aan's case sent shockwaves across Indonesia, discouraging anyone with similar beliefs from publicising their views. Thus, the Aan case has to be measured not by its singularity, but by its effect on freedom of expression. Moreover, while Aan's case stands out for its rareness, many other Indonesians have been prosecuted, socially sanctioned, intimidated or otherwise disadvantaged because they have expressed views that the state or mainstream religious leaders classify as heretical (Human Rights Watch 2013). With regard to atheism at least, the threat of severe sanc-

4 This group was Gerakan 10.000 Urang Minang Memblokir Ateis Minang (Movement of 10,000 Minang People Resisting Ateis Minang).

tions on the exercise of freedom of expression has effectively nullified the new opportunities that have opened up in the area of social media to express one's views, except for those Indonesians who operate on an international rather than domestic level.

The prosecution, intimidation, social sanctioning and career-related punishment of social media users who post critical comments online constitutes a heavy counterweight to the expanding space for freedom of expression offered by Indonesia's democratic opening and the availability of new online resources. Users are often indicted on vague charges, usually following pressure from influential politicians and their supporters. While the Suharto regime was clearly more systematic in its criminalisation of critics of the state, the failure of the democratic, post-1998 state to restrain the thuggery of gangs affiliated with local strongmen has had a similar silencing effect on critics. In many cases in which the state has indicted an activist but failed to secure a conviction, gangs have made sure that an alternative form of punishment is carried out. In addition, activists have been subjected to other non-formal sanctions, ranging from professional demotion to the shaming of their families. Hence, the limits on freedom of expression remain considerable in Indonesia, despite the rapid and major post-1998 reforms.

A PROACTIVE STATE

In addition to the threat of legal action, the state and its affiliated actors have used other methods to suppress hostile websites and encourage self-censorship. One popular tactic has been to create a new website with the same name as the targeted site and fill it with pro-government news. Another has been to attempt to destroy the reputation of the original account holder by posting incriminating material about that person on the web. Both of these tactics were used in late 2014 against a local news site in the district of Pangkep.

In 2014, *KORAN Pangkep* published several reports exposing budget mismanagement by the district government. In an online post dated 25 December 2014, it reported that a group of local parliamentarians were enjoying a stay at a luxury hotel in Jakarta, and showed a photo of them in the hotel's pool. Suddenly, however, a new *KORAN Pangkep* emerged with a new online address, running positive news about the district government and especially its deputy district head, Abdul Rahman Assegaf. While the 'real' *KORAN Pangkep* had been highly critical of Assegaf, the dummy news site strongly supported the deputy district head, and his candidacy for the position of district head in the upcoming December 2015 elections. Then, on 30 December 2014, someone created a fake account using the profile of the founder of *KORAN Pangkep*, Tata Syahrul Syaf. According to Syahrul: 'They created an account with exactly the same name, posting photos and posts attacking a candidate for the position of district head, and also openly propositioning a woman in a discussion group'.

Thus, while the state has refrained from officially blocking websites that are critical of state officials—despite having the legal means to do so—bureaucrats and other elites have found a variety of other ways to retaliate against social media users who expose them online. Their tactics range from active manipulation of content to cutting off career development opportunities, social isolation and intimidation. The frequent application of these instruments has seriously limited the freedom of expression Indonesians thought they would enjoy after democratisation and the rise of social media.

Prosecution and other sanctions, whether official or executed by state-affiliated groups, are an effective way for Indonesia's ruling elites to push back against the new freedoms created by the widespread availability of social media. In Papua, for example, no one has been prosecuted specifically for opinions expressed in online forums, but many pro-separatist activists and groups have been prosecuted for offline activities in which online mobilisation has played a significant role. The rise of social media has actually made it easier for the authorities to conduct surveillance of separatists. By monitoring online platforms, authorities gain a good understanding of when activities are planned and who is participating. In other words, 'the very technologies that many heralded as "tools of liberation" four years ago are now being used to stifle dissent and squeeze civil society' (Deibert 2015: 64). West Papuan journalist Oktovianus Pogau, for instance, discovered that the military was one of the most frequent visitors to his news website, *Suara Papua*. In an email interview with the author, he stated:

> I have just monitored the statistics of *Suara Papua*, and found that 83.61 per cent of visitors used the server provided by the Defence Ministry's Data and Information Centre. [This means that] most visitors seem to be security personnel. Meanwhile, only 3.23 per cent of visitors were using Telkom Indonesia's server.

The depth of surveillance activities by Indonesian security forces in Papua is well known and has been widely reported. In August 2011, Human Rights Watch revealed that the Indonesian military had been conducting surveillance of pro-independence activists, local politicians, religious and customary leaders, civil society organisations and foreigners, and urged the Indonesian government to cease its 'unlawful spying' (Human Rights Watch 2011). Papuan internet activists are under constant surveillance. Both online and offline surveillance has been used to track down separatists and arrest or even, in some cases, kill those who 'resist'. In the case of the murder of Martinus Yohame, the head of the Sorong branch of the National Committee for West Papua (Komite Nasional Papua Barat, or KNPB), the connection between the victim's online presence and the events that led to his death is particularly strong.

On 26 August 2014, just a few days after he had protested publicly against an upcoming visit by President Yudhoyono, Yohame's body was found floating in a sack in the sea near the city of Sorong. On 20 August, he had responded to a message sent to KNPB Sorong's Facebook page from someone claiming to be from Indonesia's highly respected National Commission for Human Rights (Komisi Nasional Hak Asasi Manusia, or Komnas HAM), although Fritz Ramandey of Komnas HAM later denied that anyone from the commission had approached Yohame. The chair of KNPB, Victor Yeimo, recalled:

> Yohame was active on Facebook. The beginning of his communication [with the perpetrator] started through the organisation's Facebook page, KNPB Sorong Raya. The day he was kidnapped, he told me: 'I have been in touch with people from Komnas HAM and a journalist through Facebook, and they've asked for an interview in a restaurant'. I replied, 'Yes, no problem. You can continue to communicate with them. Just let me know how it goes'. But I think he was tricked into the interview, then kidnapped and executed (author's interview, Jakarta, 20 May 2015).

Papua police spokesperson Sulistyo Pudjo said that it was difficult to determine the identity of the perpetrator and the cause of death because the family had refused an autopsy (*Tabloid Jubi*, 28 August 2014). For the police, this was the end of the matter. Three weeks before Yohame's abduction and murder, two French journalists had interviewed him about human rights issues in Papua, including the arrests that had occurred during recent KNPB rallies in Sorong. Shortly afterwards, they themselves were arrested for 'visa violations', and were released only in October 2015.

The Yohame case clearly demonstrates that while social media does create opportunities for dissidents in Papua to publicise their views and activities, it also carries huge risks, as the dissidents expose themselves to potentially fatal pushback from a state that can readily infiltrate social media, track down activists and impose severe sanctions.

ONLINE FREEDOM OF EXPRESSION IN INDONESIA: AN ASSESSMENT

Social media has given ordinary Indonesian citizens unparalleled opportunities to engage in public debate, shape the political agenda and achieve concrete change through concerted online campaigns. But at the same time, the state and affiliated actors have blocked the websites of certain groups and individuals, criminalised citizens for expressing critical opinions, tolerated physical attacks on users and used social media to track down opponents of the state. In other words, while many Indonesians have experienced the benefits of social media, a small group has experienced an onslaught of punishments.

The detention, physical intimidation and alleged murders of some social media users must weigh at least as heavily as the expansion of opportunities for freedom of expression for millions of Indonesian netizens. It would therefore be an exaggeration to ascribe a 'liberating' effect to social media in Indonesia. While it has provided citizens with new opportunities to express their views, it has not fundamentally reshaped the way Indonesian politics and society work. It is fair to say that it may give an opening to the so-called 'political opportunity structures' in democratisation (Gamson and Meyer 1996; Tarrow 1998; Meyer and Minkoff 2004) or provide ways for people to participate in the 'soft structures of feeling' that help them feel that their views matter (Papacharissi 2015: 116). However, it has not changed the elite-centred characteristics of the political and economic decision-making processes, and it has had little impact on the politico-ideological outlook of the state and its key actors. The reasons that the effects of social media have been so limited are related to the continuing deficiencies of Indonesian democracy, which this chapter has highlighted and which social media has been unable to overcome.

This context has constrained the potentially positive effects of social media and prevented it from bringing about more wide-ranging social and political change, or at least widening the political opportunity structures. At the same time, the limits that poor democratisation has placed on social media highlight and reinforce the key areas of democratic weakness in Indonesia. Activists and ordinary citizens have had websites disrupted and blocked; thugs have been hired to intimidate critics; fake websites have been developed; and social media content has been manipulated. To some extent, democratisation and decentralisation have strengthened these trends, by concentrating power in the hands of local district heads, who have pursued critics with impunity. As this chapter has shown, district heads have been particularly ruthless in using thugs, local security forces and monetary resources to silence critics on social media.

Democratisation has arguably allowed religious conservatism to flourish, with militant Islamic activists free to advance their agenda after decades of repression by the New Order. Indeed, social media has actually helped to cement these conservative ideologies in democratic Indonesia, with the state, the military, conservative forces and Islamic organisations making extensive use of social media to fight for their causes. The state has made it clear that ideological transgressions such as the propagation of territorial separation, atheism or non-mainstream Islamic ideas will attract either legal proceedings or intimidation by affected groups. These anti-democratic parameters set strict limits for social media use in Indonesia and place formidable hurdles in the way of the more progressive elements of social media.

One of the most serious flaws of post-Suharto democracy has been the continuously weak rule of law (Pompe 2005). Riddled by corruption and mismanagement, the weak legal sector has been instrumental in allowing the powerful and the wealthy to confront their social media critics. As we have seen, many activists have been pursued by law enforcement agencies keen to impress their political superiors or their corporate sponsors. Because of this manipulation of legal agencies by vested political and economic interests, critics who express their views on social media lack the protection they need to exercise their constitutional rights without fear of punishment. In fact, the punishments meted out to social media critics have increased in severity over the years. The current Jokowi government has proposed reducing the sentences for criminal defamation, particularly in online cases, but given the corrupt relationships between political power holders and law enforcement agencies at the local level, it seems almost certain that governors, district heads and other local strongmen will continue to find loopholes through which to pursue their critics in the courts.

In combination, oligarchic influence, ideological immobility and weak rule of law have kept Indonesian democracy from truly becoming institutionalised and moving to the next level of qualitative development. This setback has been recognised by several international democracy indexes, which have recorded a decline in democratic quality since the beginning of the second term of President Yudhoyono (2009–14). Not only have progressive elements in social media been unable to overcome these deficiencies, but they have been the victims of such democratic shortcomings. As demonstrated in this chapter, pro-democracy activists have pushed social media to its limits, but those limits have been strongly defended by anti-democratic forces nestling in the state and the economy. These forces continue to determine how and where such limits are drawn, with social media activists celebrating small victories but falling behind in the overall battle for democracy.

The Indonesian case seems to suggest that rather than social media being a powerful driver of democracy, it is democracy that is necessary for social media to flourish. Social media can boost democratic quality further in societies with sound democratic foundations, as citizens can use the new technologies without fear of punishment. But in weak democracies such as Indonesia, the limitations that conservative elites impose on the use of social media—with sanctions ranging from criminalisation and physical violence to (possibly) killings—balance out the benefits users may obtain from this innovation. Of course, social media gives voice to critics even in deficient democracies, as it has done in Indonesia. But to claim that it has resulted in large-scale social transformations and leaps in democratic quality would be an overstatement. International democracy indexers recorded a significant boost in Indonesian democracy between 1999 and 2006, when social media was still in its early stages; they registered a stagnation between 2006 and 2013, when its use rose sharply; and they diagnosed a decline after 2013 when social media use in Indonesia exploded (Freedom House 2012, 2013). Hence, for all of the positive effects on the ability to communicate and engage, the overall quality of democracy has been unaffected at best, and negatively affected at worst, by the rise of social media.

The Indonesian case also feeds into the global debate on the stagnation of democracy. If indeed, as the optimists suggest, social media provides unprecedented opportunities for democratic advancement, the statistics would bear this trend out. But on the contrary, Freedom House's evaluations show that in the last 10 years, the number of countries that experienced a decline in freedom has outnumbered the number that registered an increase (Freedom House 2016b: 3). In other words, the development of freedom around the world has recorded a net loss over the last decade. Similarly, there has been no increase in the percentage of electoral democracies, meaning that overall the number of democracies has remained stagnant for a decade. And all of this occurred during a time of escalating social media activity. As shown in this chapter, Indonesia itself fits this pattern perfectly: while social media expanded, Indonesia's overall democratic quality stagnated and ultimately declined. What is illustrated here is a seemingly paradoxical development that is playing out in Indonesia as well as in many other countries: namely that social media is opening up previously closed space for public communication and information exchange, but is doing little to lift significantly the overall quality of freedom of expression and democracy.

REFERENCES

American Humanist Association et al. (2012) '2012 report on discrimination against atheists, humanists, and the non-religious', American Humanist Association, Center for Inquiry, International Humanist and Ethical Union, Richard Dawkins Foundation for Reason and Science and Secular Coalition for America, Washington DC. Available at http://americanhumanist.org/news/details/2012-09-2012-report-on-discrimination-against-atheists-human.

Amnesty International (2012) 'Indonesia: atheist imprisonment a setback for freedom of expression', ASA 21/021/2012, 14 June.

Amnesty International (2014) 'Prosecuting beliefs: Indonesia's blasphemy laws', ASA 21/018/2014, November.

Amri, A.B., E. Huda and E. Naldi (2012) 'Alexander, ateis di negeri bersendi syarak' [Alexander, an atheist in a sharia-based state], *Viva.co.id*, 22 January. Available at http://fokus.news.viva.co.id/news/read/282106-alexander-ateis-di-negeri-bersendi-syarak.

Deibert, R. (2015) 'Authoritarianism goes global: cyberspace under siege', *Journal of Democracy*, 26(3): 64–78.

Freedom House (2012) 'Freedom in the World 2012: the Arab uprisings and their global repercussions'. Available at https://freedomhouse.org/sites/default/files/inline_images/FIW%202012%20Booklet--Final.pdf.

Freedom House (2013) 'Freedom in the World 2013: democratic breakthroughs in the balance'. Available at https://www.freedomhouse.org/sites/default/files/FIW%202013%20Booklet.pdf.

Freedom House (2016a) 'Freedom on the Net 2016: silencing the messenger'. Available at https://freedomhouse.org/sites/default/files/FOTN_2016_BOOKLET_FINAL.pdf.

Freedom House (2016b) 'Freedom in the World 2016: anxious dictators, wavering democracies'. Available at https://freedomhouse.org/sites/default/files/FH_FITW_Report_2016.pdf.

Gamson, W.A., and D.S. Meyer (1996) 'Framing political opportunity', in D. McAdam, J.D. McCarthy and M.N. Zald (eds) *Comparative Perspectives on Social Movements*, Cambridge University Press, Cambridge: 275–90.

Gazali, E. (2014) 'Learning by clicking: an experiment with social media democracy in Indonesia', *International Communication Gazette*, 76(4–5): 425–39.

Human Rights Watch (2011) 'Indonesia: military documents reveal unlawful spying in Papua', 14 August. Available at https://www.hrw.org/news/2011/08/14/indonesia-military-documents-reveal-unlawful-spying-papua.

Human Rights Watch (2013) 'In religion's name: abuses against religious minorities in Indonesia', 28 February. Available at https://www.hrw.org/report/2013/02/28/religions-name/abuses-against-religious-minorities-indonesia.

ICT Watch (Information and Communication Technology Watch) (2014) 'Indonesia internet landscape', Jakarta.

Lim, M. (2013) 'Many clicks but little sticks: social media activism in Indonesia', *Journal of Contemporary Asia*, 43(4): 636–57.

Meyer, D., and D. Minkoff (2004) 'Conceptualizing political opportunity', *Social Forces*, 82(4): 1,457–92.

Nugroho, Y. (2011) 'Citizens in @ction. Collaboration, participatory democracy and freedom of information: mapping contemporary civic activism and the use of new social media in Indonesia', Manchester Institute of Innovation Research, University of Manchester, and HIVOS Regional Office Southeast Asia, Manchester and Jakarta, March.

Papacharissi, Z. (2015) *Affective Publics: Sentiment, Technology, and Politics*, Oxford University Press, New York.

Pompe, S. (2005) *The Indonesian Supreme Court: A Study of Institutional Collapse*, Cornell University Southeast Asia Program Publications, Ithaca.

Priyono, et al. (2014) 'Media sosial: tool of the civil movement', Asia Foundation and HIVOS Regional Office Southeast Asia, Jakarta. {I changed "Public Virtue" to "HIVOS"]

SAFENET (Southeast Asia Freedom of Expression Network) (2015) 'Protecting freedom of expression and digital rights', Jakarta, 25 March.

Tapsell, R. (2014) 'Digital media in Indonesia and Malaysia: convergence and conglomeration', *Asiascape: Digital Asia*, 3(2014): 201–22.

Tarrow, S. (1998) *Power in Movement: Social Movements and Contentious Politics*, second edition, Cambridge University Press, Cambridge.

7 The state of cybersecurity in Indonesia

Budi Rahardjo

Indonesia has one of the largest populations of internet users in the world: 50 million in 2015 according to the Indonesian Internet Service Providers Association (Asosiasi Penyelenggara Jasa Internet Indonesia, or APJII).[1] The number is continuing to grow because most Indonesians are not yet on the internet. Indonesia also has one of the world's largest internet exchanges, OpenIXP. An internet exchange is the physical meeting point 'at which the networks of Internet Service Providers (ISPs), telecommunications carriers, content providers, webhosters and the like, meet to exchange IP traffic with one another'; the purpose of an internet exchange is 'to decrease network costs, to improve network performance and to make [networks] more redundant' (https://ams-ix.net/about/about-ams-ix). Indonesia's exchange connects more than 700 ISPs, content delivery networks (CDNs), government agencies and other service providers and has a peak throughput of 277 gigabits per second.

Indonesians are very active mobile phone users. The country has more mobile phones (270 million) than it has people (250 million) because some Indonesians own more than one mobile phone. Indonesians choose their providers on the basis of coverage, or to take advantage of the pro-

1 The exact number of internet users is difficult to calculate because of the different interpretations of what it means to be 'on the internet'. For example, some people say they are not on the internet but they also say that they use Facebook. Are they internet users? Another definition confines the number of internet users to those who pay for their internet connection. This would exclude, for example, students who connect to the internet at school, unless they had a personal internet account at home.

motions that are available from time to time. The large number of mobile phone users in Indonesia makes security problems inevitable.

Even before the country had developed a high degree of IT expertise, Indonesians were enthusiastically embracing information technology to solve national problems. To create more transparency around elections, for example, the government began to use the internet to relay real-time vote tallies during the presidential elections of 1999. Then, in the 2014 election, a group calling itself Kawal Pemilu (Election Guardians) mobilised large numbers of young, IT-savvy Indonesians to electronically count the results from every polling station in the country, making it more difficult to (for want of a better word) 'hack' the election results. The electoral system still relies on paper-based voting, but a bill to allow electronic voting is being considered by parliament.

Reports in the media about the state of Indonesia's cybersecurity tend to exaggerate the extent of the country's problems; an article in the *Jakarta Post* published in June 2016, for example, talks about a national 'emergency' and says that the number of cyberattacks is growing at an 'alarming' rate (Jakarta Post 2016). The Indonesia Computer Emergency Response Team (ID-CERT) provides more balanced coverage of the status of Indonesia's cybersecurity through the regular updates it posts on its website (http://www.cert.or.id). A report issued by this NGO in 2016, for example, provides a detailed analysis of the numbers and types of security incidents (spam, intellectual property theft, network incidents, spoofing/phishing and so on) that occurred in July and August of that year (ID-CERT 2016).

It is clear that cybersecurity has become a matter of increasing concern for citizens, the private sector and the Indonesian government. In 2014, Indonesia was ranked second among the countries from which cyberattacks were launched (after China), and is itself very vulnerable to cyberattack. The Indonesian government is taking a centralised, structured approach to improve internet security, to be coordinated by a new national cybersecurity agency. It is also collaborating with other security organisations and agencies in the region, including the Australian Federal Police (AFP). This chapter documents the status of Indonesia's cybersecurity regime, describing, in turn, the main types of cybersecurity incidents in Indonesia, the root causes of those incidents and the measures the country is taking to deal with them.

MAIN TYPES OF CYBERSECURITY INCIDENTS

Far from remaining constant, the popularity of particular types of cybersecurity incidents tends to rise and fall over time. Indonesia may experience widespread e-commerce-related fraud cases and very few website defacements in one year, for example, but mass defacements of government websites and very few e-commerce-related cases in the next. Changes in technology also affect the types of cybersecurity incidents experienced, with faster internet speeds and wider availability of internet banking leading to an increase in internet banking fraud, for example. These days, the hot topics among technology enthusiasts are the internet of things, e-government, and 'smart cities' connected by networks of CCTV cameras. Although security concerns have been taking a back seat to the exciting possibilities created by these technologies, I anticipate that we will witness problems in these areas in the near future.

Another area that is generating a lot of interest is financial technology, known as fintech. Indonesians are using online banking services in ever-increasing numbers. This has created opportunities for fintech start-ups to establish online businesses offering a wide array of payment, loan, insurance and other types of financial services. As this is a relatively new development, we do not yet know what types of security problems are likely to arise. We do know, however, that the financial services sector is particularly vulnerable to cybercrime, so it will be important to accelerate measures to entrench higher standards of cybersecurity in the fintech sector (Rahardjo 2017).

Like other countries, Indonesia must deal with the online security problems caused by hackers (or, more correctly, crackers) who break into computer systems, crack the protection on software programs, change or steal data and commit other malicious acts. It is common throughout the Asia Pacific region, but especially in Indonesia, Thailand and the Philippines, for hackers to break into and deface government websites. The main motivation seems to be to gain kudos within the hacking community, although politically slanted 'hacktivism' also occurs. During the unrest leading up to the fall of Suharto in 1998, for example, hackers changed the appearance of many government websites, and in 1999, when the looming independence of East Timor was a hot-button issue, Portuguese and Indonesian hackers both used website defacement to promote their differing political positions.

Most of the hackers involved in government website defacement are young people operating from within the country. Once they grow up, they usually drop their hacking activities. Some might stay in the security area by becoming cybersecurity consultants, but most simply disappear from the security scene. Online hacking groups also come and go, with only a few remaining active for extended periods of time. One example of the latter is Echo (http://wiz.echo.or.id/).

Most of the cyberattack cases recorded by ID-CERT are attacks that originate in Indonesia but target sites outside Indonesia; the reverse is

Table 7.1 Country of origin of internet attacks by source IP address, Q2 2014 (% of attack traffic)

No.	Country	Q2 2014	Q1 2014
1	China	43.0	41.0
2	Indonesia	15.0	6.8
3	United States	13.0	11.0
4	Taiwan	3.7	3.4
5	India	2.1	2.6
6	Russia	2.0	2.9
7	Brazil	1.7	3.2
8	South Korea	1.4	1.6
9	Turkey	1.2	1.7
10	Romania	1.2	1.6
	Other	16.0	25.0

Source: Akamai (2014b).

rarely the case. It is suspected that many of these attacks are a result of computers in Indonesia being compromised by Trojan horse malware (malicious software posing as legitimate software). Those computers are then taken over by the attackers and used as zombies or (ro)bots to send spam email, to infect other computers with malware or to attack computers outside Indonesia.

There have also been cases of illegal visitors to Indonesia using ransomware to infect the computers of companies outside Indonesia until a 'ransom' has been paid, and a suspected case of a child pornography site operating from inside Indonesia (informal discussion with AFP officer, 2016). Indonesia must clamp down quickly on any such activities in order to avoid being viewed as a safe haven by international cybercriminals.

Akamai, the owner and operator of the world's largest content delivery network (CDN), produces regular reports on the state of the internet/connectivity based on the huge volumes of traffic passing through its network (www.akamai.com). In 2014, Akamai released a report listing Indonesia as the third-largest source of internet attacks in the first quarter of 2014 (after China and the United States) and the second-largest source in the second quarter of 2014 (after China) (Table 7.1). In the third quarter, however, the number of attacks originating in Indonesia dropped to 1.9 per cent.

These statistics need some qualification. A closer look at the Akamai data shows that the number of computers (that is, the number of unique

Table 7.2 Number of computers (unique IP addresses) involved in internet attacks and average connection speed of attacks, Q1 2014

No.	Country	Share of attack traffic originating in country (%)	No. of unique IP addresses involved in attacks	Average connection speed (Mb/s)
1	China	41.0	123,526,069	3.2
2	United States	11.0	162,676,451	10.5
3	Indonesia	6.8	7,760,456	2.4

Source: Akamai (2014a).

IP addresses) involved in the attacks originating in Indonesia in the first quarter of 2014 was smaller than the number involved in the attacks originating in other countries, and that the average connection speed of the Indonesian attacks was also lower (Table 7.2). How, then, did Indonesia make it into the list of the top 10 countries from which internet attacks originate? A plausible answer would be that the attacks from Indonesia were sustained for longer periods of time. Internet security for home computers is quite lax in Indonesia, so it is feasible that attackers would be able to take over large numbers of home computers without the users or their ISPs detecting this for quite some time. This could prolong the length of attacks from Indonesia, compared with other countries where home computers are more secure.

Because online security is lax, transaction fraud in Indonesia is widespread. Transaction fraud is when a fake online seller offers to sell a product over the internet, collects the electronic payment and disappears without delivering the goods. One solution offered by some online marketplaces is to provide a protected bank account where buyers' payments are held until the goods have been delivered. Such solutions are important to overcome the problem of lack of trust in electronic commerce in Indonesia.

The three objectives of computer security are to preserve the confidentiality, integrity and availability of information system resources (Stallings 2011: 4–5). Confidentiality means preserving the secrecy of data to prevent its unauthorised disclosure. Integrity means guarding against improper modification or destruction of information. Availability means making sure that systems are available promptly when needed. In the next three subsections, I discuss cybersecurity incidents with reference to these three categories.

Confidentiality attacks

The release of the Pokémon Go application in 2016 was greeted enthusiastically by Indonesians. However, it was not welcomed by Indonesian government and military officials, who believed that it could pose a threat to national security (Margareth et al. 2016). They feared that people posing as Pokémon Go users might take photos of military sites or that the large amount of personal and location data collected on users could lead to the disclosure of confidential information. Some even suspected that the game was part of a US government intelligence-gathering operation. Thus, the use of the application was banned in several government offices. It should be noted, however, that many government entities continue to use free public email services such as Gmail (Kompas 2011), which poses a far greater security concern than the Pokémon Go application.

Local Indonesian start-ups have developed many popular applications for mobile devices, including Go-Jek (originally a motorbike taxi application but now offering a huge array of 'Go' services), Tokopedia and Bukalapak (both online marketplaces for clothing, electronics and other consumer goods). Some of these applications lack privacy protection, allowing users to see, for example, the transaction history of other users. Since there is no direct financial loss, most Indonesians feel that this lack of privacy is not a big problem. From a security point of view, however, it is a serious confidentiality issue.

The data obtained so easily from various sources make Indonesia a hotspot for identity theft and, consequently, fraud using stolen identities. The most common scam is for a thief to ask the friends of a person whose identity has been stolen to top up that person's (but actually the thief's) pre-paid mobile phone account. This scam was originally confined to SMS users but is now being used to target social media users as well.

The fact that many Indonesians use the same passwords and pin numbers for all their computer and mobile applications creates a major problem for cybersecurity. It means that if attackers can identify a hole in the security of one online service provider—one that reveals user credentials, for example—then they may be able to exploit that gap to gain access to the accounts users have with other online service providers. Hackers have in fact used this approach to attempt to crack passwords in Indonesia, testing pairs of identities and passwords on one site after another. Clearly there is a need to educate Indonesians about the need to use different passwords for different sites. At the same time, it is not surprising that many Indonesians baulk at the prospect of memorising a large number of different passwords for different applications and sites.

In general, Indonesians tend to be quite blasé about privacy. On their public Facebook pages, for example, they are happy to display their birthdates (so they can get birthday greetings), the schools they attended (so they can get invited to reunions), information about their families, photos of family and friends, and so on. Privacy concerns simply do not cross their minds. This is also the case in the real world; most Indonesians gladly give away private information about themselves to almost anyone who asks for it. Debates about online privacy are therefore less likely to gain traction in Indonesia than in other parts of the world. However, as more Indonesians become targets of identity fraud or even social media profile replication, issues of privacy and security can be expected to garner more attention.

Integrity attacks

Integrity attacks are often difficult to detect and can cause serious damage. An example of an integrity attack that is still causing problems in Indonesia is the so-called 'man in the browser' (MITB) attack. MITB is Trojan horse malware that infects web browsers. It does nothing (remains dormant) until the computer user visits a certain website, such as a bank's website. When this happens, the malware becomes active and tries to steal the user's credentials. For example, the malware might be programmed to display a pop-up window on the screen asking the user to enter a pin number in order not to be locked out of their bank account. This information can then be used to make illegal transactions on the account, such as transferring money to a bank account set up to receive stolen funds. The perpetrators of MITB attacks often use 'money mules' to receive stolen money and transfer it to other accounts; these 'mules' are generally unaware that the money has been obtained illegally. Fraud involving hundreds of millions of rupiah has been perpetrated through MITB attacks.

The problem for bank security personnel is that this type of attack targets customers' computers, not the banks' servers. The banks have done their part, securing their servers and applications, but ensuring the security of their customers' computers is out of their control. On the other hand, many customers believe that if an attack happens while they are on a bank's website, then the bank should take responsibility for it. Educating users about online security is the obvious solution to this type of stand-off. The Indonesian Financial Services Authority (Otoritas Jasa Keuangan, or OJK) has published a booklet about 'wise' e-banking in an effort to educate computer users about security when using online banking services (OJK 2015).

Computer viruses are the most common type of malware compromising the integrity of computers in Indonesia. These viruses range from malware that destroys computer files to ransomware that locks people out of their files until a certain amount of money has been paid. In Indonesia, the problem is exacerbated by the widespread use of illegally obtained software that is not updated regularly to address known security risks. Moreover, many computer users in Indonesia still do not install proper anti-virus programs or update their anti-malware software regularly.

Availability attacks

Attacks on availability are usually called 'denial of service' (DoS) attacks or, if they involve large numbers of computers, 'distributed denial of service' (DDoS) attacks. The goal of a DoS or DDoS attack is to render a service unavailable. This can be done by flooding the network and servers of a service provider with so many requests that the system is overwhelmed and cannot respond to them. The websites of several Indonesian service providers, including online marketplaces, have crashed when attackers flooded their domain name system (DNS) servers with fake traffic.[2] The bandwidth of such attacks can be in the order of hundreds of gigabits per second.

A DoS or DDoS attack is usually done through bots or zombies, that is, through computers or mobile devices that have been compromised and taken over. In most cases, malware in the form of a Trojan horse is installed on these 'host' computers, allowing them to be controlled remotely. The number of bots involved in a DDoS attack can be very large. The attack directed at the website of renowned cybersecurity journalist Brian Krebs on 20 September 2016, for example, involved an unprecedented number and variety of hacked devices (Krebs 2016).

As noted earlier, many Indonesians do not know that their computers have been compromised and are being used as bots. They therefore do not respond promptly, allowing an attack to be sustained for a long time. It is only when their computer or internet access becomes very slow that they suspect a problem and finally take action to fix it.

Protection against availability attacks can be achieved by creating redundancy (duplication or extra capacity) in IT systems and by conducting 'what if' capacity planning. However, this does increase costs. For companies whose operations are critical to the smooth running of the economy, such as banks, protection is nevertheless a must. Each bank must have a disaster recovery centre in addition to its data centre to protect it from availability attacks. A government regulation stipulates

2 For an example of how a DDoS attack can be amplified using DNS servers, see Evil Security (2015).

that all government disaster recovery centres and data centres must be located physically in Indonesia (Government Regulation No. 82/2012 on the Operation of Electronic Systems and Transactions, article 17). However, Indonesia's location on the Pacific Ring of Fire limits the areas where such centres can be situated, safe from the risk of earthquake.

ROOT CAUSES OF CYBERSECURITY INCIDENTS

A lack of secure methods of identity verification is one of the root causes of fraud in Indonesia's cyberspace. Since the mobile phone is the main platform to access the internet and perform electronic transactions, verification of the identity of mobile phone users is critical. Regulation No. 12/2016 of the Ministry of Communication and Informatics on the Registration of Telecommunications Service Users requires service providers to check the identity of anyone who obtains a mobile phone number. Despite this, it is easy to get a SIM card for a mobile phone without providing proper identification. The stalls that sell SIM cards simply enter random credentials without conducting any proper checking at all.

In early 2011, the government launched a biometrically enabled electronic identity card (Kartu Tanda Penduduk Elektronik, or e-KTP) that Indonesians could use to obtain passports and driving licences, make tax payments, apply for social assistance, verify financial transactions and so on. Although the e-KTP was theoretically more secure than the previous paper-based KTP, the project was suspended in 2014 after senior public officials, politicians and businesspeople were accused of taking kickbacks in connection with the project (Tempo 2016). With the e-KTP project in disarray, there is currently no mechanism to check the identities of mobile phone users.

Without access to the e-KTP database, Indonesia's popular online marketplaces are having difficulty confirming the identities of the sellers and buyers using their sites. The approach of some businesses is to assume that if a user has a bank account, then the identity of that person must have been verified by the bank. This means that those companies' security procedures are dependent on the security of the banks' procedures—an invitation to fraud.

The lax attitude of senior management towards online security is another problem. Security is often an afterthought and security breaches tend to be handled in an ad hoc manner. Many companies make only minimal investments in human and technical cybersecurity resources and some make no provision for security in their company structures at all.

INITIATIVES TO IMPROVE CYBERSECURITY

The national government, educational institutions and non-government organisations have established a variety of organisations to monitor and address cybersecurity concerns. One of the earliest was the non-governmental Indonesia Computer Emergency Response Team (ID-CERT), founded in 1998. The mission of ID-CERT is to coordinate security incident handling, increase security awareness, collect security statistics and assist research in the field of security (http://www.cert.or.id/tentang-kami/en/). It cooperates with other security organisations within Indonesia through information exchange, coordination of activities and training, and it collaborates with other CERTs in the region through its membership of the Asia Pacific Computer Emergency Response Team (APCERT). ID-CERT is one of several Indonesian agencies involved in the cybersecurity training sessions organised by the AFP.

In 2007, the Ministry of Communication and Informatics set up the Indonesia Security Incident Response Team on Internet and Infrastructure (ID-SIRTII) to monitor security incidents, provide training on internet security and support law enforcement. Unfortunately, however, ID-SIRTII ceased to operate at the end of 2016. A draft regulation by the ministry requires government agencies in charge of critical national infrastructure or critical systems to establish emergency response teams (CERTs) to handle online security incidents. The definition of 'critical national infrastructure' is still being debated, but the new regulation will certainly increase the number of CERTs in Indonesia. The existing ones include sector-specific CERTs such as Gov-CERT and Academic CERT, as well as various informal CERTs. ID-CERT is currently compiling a list of all known CERTs in Indonesia.

In Indonesia, as in many other countries, government initiatives in the area of cybersecurity tend to be uncoordinated and contained in silos. To bring all such activities under one roof, the Indonesian government plans to establish a national cybersecurity agency (Badan Cyber Nasional, or BCN), either as an independent entity or under an existing agency. Because it would be expensive to create a new structure, the government is currently leaning towards the latter option. The agencies that are being considered to host the national cybersecurity agency include the State Cryptography Agency (Lembaga Sandi Negara, or LSN), the State Intelligence Agency (Badan Intelijen Negara, or BIN), the Ministry of Communication and Informatics and the Coordinating Ministry for Political, Legal and Security Affairs. It could be expected that the Ministry of Defence would continue to strengthen its own cyberwarfare and cyberdefence capabilities, separately from BCN, but initiatives in this area are not widely publicised.

Despite the need for more cybersecurity experts in Indonesia, only the Padang Institute of Technology (Institut Teknologi Padang), the University of Indonesia, Gunadarma University and a few other tertiary institutions offer dedicated information security courses or post-graduate research opportunities. Compared with neighbouring countries, Indonesia also has very few IT specialists with professional cybersecurity certification—for example, certification as a Certified Information Systems Security Professional (CISSP) or as a Certified Information Systems Auditor (CISA). At present, certification is expensive, and it is not mandatory. Over time, the number of cybersecurity experts in Indonesia should increase as the number of educational institutions offering formal training expands and as local institutions offering more affordable certification are established.

The need to comply with government regulation is a key driver for businesses to implement cybersecurity measures. In the banking area, for example, a Bank Indonesia regulation requires banks (and other financial institutions) to perform periodical security audits of their systems and of the vendors that provide services to them (Regulation No. 9/15/PBI/2007 of Bank Indonesia on the Implementation of Risk Management in the Use of Information Technology by Commercial Banks). A similar regulation has been implemented in the energy sector. Further regulations covering other sectors are needed to ensure that other types of businesses also strengthen their cybersecurity capabilities.

The Ministry of Communication and Informatics has developed an application to evaluate the strength of government agencies' cybersecurity measures: the Information Security Index (Indeks Keamanan Informasi, or Indeks KAMI), which is based on the SNI ISO/IEC 27001:2009 standard (BSN 2009; Ministry of Communication and Informatics 2013). This index can be used to assess and compare the security status of various government entities. However, it is not compulsory for all government entities to use the application so the results are not comprehensive. The application needs to be used more widely to help identify and fix gaps in government agencies' security procedures.

The main law governing the regulation of cyberspace in Indonesia is Law No. 11/2008 on Information and Electronic Transactions (the ITE Law), issued on 21 April 2008. Some argue that this law tries to do too much, and that it should be broken down into several laws—one focusing on electronic transactions and another focusing on cybercrime, for example.

The most contentious part of the ITE Law is article 27(3), which makes it a criminal offense to defame people online. The potential for this article to be misused by influential individuals and organisations was highlighted by the case of Prita Mulyasari, a mother of two who was prosecuted under the law after complaining in a private email about her misdiagnosis at a private hospital. When the email became public and went viral, the hospital took her to court. Prita Mulyasari was jailed while awaiting trial, until public indignation about her case led to her release. After a series of court battles that went all the way to the Supreme Court, the hospital eventually dropped the case (see Chapter 8 by Postill and Saputro). Another well-known case is that of the Jakarta governor, Basuki Tjahaja Purnama (better known as Ahok). In November 2016 he was charged with inciting religious hatred under article 28(2) of the ITE Law, after a statement he had made about a verse in the Qur'an was uploaded to social media (Wijaya 2016).[3] To prevent further abuses of the ITE Law, the relevant clauses in articles 27 and 28 should be amended.

Some people are concerned that the ITE Law could be used by the government to silence critics, making it a tool of repression (see Chapter 6 by Hamid). That was not the intention of the law when it was created, and it should never be used for that purpose.

CONCLUDING REMARKS

In general, Indonesia faces similar problems to other countries in ensuring the security of cyberspace. However, the large number of internet users in the country and the relative naivety of Indonesian computer users do pose particular problems for internet security. Indonesia has more than its fair share of security incidents, ranging from spam emails, website defacement, malware distribution and DoS attacks to identity theft and financial fraud.

The lack of effective methods of identity verification is a root cause of cyberfraud and makes it difficult to catch the perpetrators. With the e-KTP project currently the subject of a corruption investigation, the effort to provide more secure means of proving one's identity remains a work in progress.

Indonesia is facing an epidemic of hate and hoax messages on social media and other online forums. The distribution of these types of messages creates problems in both cyberspace and the real world and is a destabilising force in Indonesian society. Some non-government organisations have taken steps to address the problem by creating forums and tools to identify and remove fake or defamatory messages. The government has also been taking measures to reduce the extent of the problem, by filtering online content and blocking certain websites. This approach

3 This charge was later dropped but Ahok still faces a blasphemy charge (Guardian 2016).

should be taken with caution because it can lead to censorship or be perceived as an attempt to control society.

In addition to the technical, legal and regulatory aspects of cybersecurity, education is a key factor in strengthening the security of Indonesian cyberspace. Senior managers in both the public and private sectors need to be convinced of the value of cybersecurity and the numbers of trained cybersecurity staff must be expanded. Collaboration between security agencies within and outside Indonesia is another important way of securing Indonesia's cybersecurity future.

REFERENCES

Akamai (2014a) 'Akamai's state of the internet connectivity report: Q1 2014'. Available at https://www.akamai.com/us/en/our-thinking/state-of-the-internet-report/global-state-of-the-internet-connectivity-reports.jsp.

Akamai (2014b) 'Akamai's state of the internet connectivity report: Q2 2014'. Available at https://www.akamai.com/us/en/our-thinking/state-of-the-internet-report/global-state-of-the-internet-connectivity-reports.jsp.

BSN (Badan Standarisasi Nasional) (2009) 'SNI ISO 27001:2009: teknologi informasi—teknik keamanan—sistem manajemen keamanan informasi—persyaratan' [Information technology—security techniques—information security management systems—requirements], National Standardization Agency (BSN), Jakarta. Available at http://sisni.bsn.go.id/index.php/sni_main/sni/detail_sni/10233.

Evil Security (2015) 'DRDoS—denial of service on steroids', *Evil Security*, 5 April. Available at http://www.evilsec.net/2015/04/drdos-denial-of-service-on-steroids/.

Guardian (2016) 'Indonesian court gives go-ahead to blasphemy trial of Jakarta governor Ahok', *The Guardian*, 27 December. Available at https://www.theguardian.com/world/2016/dec/27/indonesia-court-blasphemy-trial-ahok-jakarta-governor.

ID-CERT (Indonesia Computer Emergency Response Team) (2016) 'Laporan dwi bulanan IV 2016' [Incident monitoring report 2016], August. Available at http://www.cert.or.id/media/files/04-UMUM_Dwi_Bln_IV_2016.pdf.

Jakarta Post (2016) 'Cyber attacks in Indonesia rising at alarming rate: officials', *Jakarta Post*, 3 June. Available at http://www.thejakartapost.com/news/2016/06/03/cyberattacks-in-indonesia-rising-at-alarming-rate-officials.html.

Kompas (2011) 'Anggota DPR tak punya akun "dpr.go.id"' [People's Representative Council members do not have dpr.go.id accounts], *Kompas*, 5 May. Available at http://nasional.kompas.com/read/2011/05/05/17593665/Anggota.DPR.Tak.Punya.Akun.dpr.go.id.

Krebs, B. (2016) 'KrebsOnSecurity hit with record DDoS', *KrebsOnSecurity*, 16 September. Available at https://krebsonsecurity.com/2016/09/krebsonsecurity-hit-with-record-ddos/.

Margareth, A.D., S. Aritonang, H. Halim and Suherdjoko (2016) 'Pokémon Go poses threat to national security: TNI', *Jakarta Post*, 20 July. Available at http://www.thejakartapost.com/news/2016/07/20/pok-mon-go-poses-threat-national-security-tni.html.

Ministry of Communication and Informatics (2013) 'Indeks Keamanan Informasi (KAMI)' [Information Security Index], Jakarta, October. Available at https://kominfo.go.id/index.php/content/detail/3326/Indeks+Keamanan+Informasi+(KAMI)/0/kemanan_informasi.

OJK (Otoritas Jasa Keuangan) (2015) 'Bijak ber-ebanking' [Wise e-banking], Financial Services Authority (OJK), Jakarta, May. Available at http://www.ojk.go.id/id/kanal/perbankan/berita-dan-kegiatan/info-terkini/Documents/Pages/Buku-eBanking/BukuBijakBereBanking_1441890913.pdf.

Rahardjo, B. (2017) 'Fintech talk: dealing with vicious threats in fast-growing fintech services', *Jakarta Post*, 17 January. Available at http://www.thejakartapost.com/news/2017/01/17/fintech-talk-dealing-with-vicious-threats-in-fast-growing-fintech-services.html.

Stallings, W. (2011) *Network Security Essentials: Applications and Standards*, fourth edition, Prentice Hall.

Tempo (2016) 'Why the slow inquiry into the e-KTP corruption case?', *Tempo.co*, 13 October. Available at https://en.tempo.co/read/news/2016/10/13/314811937/Why-the-Slow-Inquiry-into-the-e-KTP-Corruption-Case.

Wijaya, C.A. (2016) 'Police drop charges of spreading hatred in Ahok case', *Jakarta Post*, 25 November. Available at http://www.thejakartapost.com/news/2016/11/25/police-drop-charges-of-spreading-hatred-in-ahok-case.html.

PART 3

Identity

8 Digital activism in contemporary Indonesia: victims, volunteers and voices

John Postill and Kurniawan Saputro

In early 2015 the British comedian John Oliver travelled to Moscow to interview the exiled NSA whistleblower Edward Snowden for a TV show. In the interview, which soon went viral, Oliver reacted to Snowden's laborious attempts to explain the privacy implications of the US government's mass surveillance programs by exclaiming: 'This is the whole problem. I glaze over. It's like the IT guy comes into your office and you go, "Oh shit—don't teach me anything. I don't want to learn. You smell like canned soup!"' The comedian then proceeded to ask Snowden a series of questions about the hypothetical fate of shared pictures of his—Oliver's—penis under the NSA's digital surveillance regime. By using his own privates to explain privacy, he succeeded in bringing Snowden's dry discourse to life (whilst extracting comedic value from it).

This hilarious exchange raises three intriguing questions. First, Oliver correctly identifies a fundamental problem at the heart of today's increasingly digitalised power struggles: digital activism 'nerds' such as Snowden are often not the best translators of key technical issues for the general public. For this reason, they frequently rely on intermediaries such as journalists, film-makers and even comedians to communicate their political views (Chadwick and Collister 2014). Second, and more problematically, Oliver's gag relies on the lazy popular stereotype of digital activists as young, white, male, Western 'geeks' (or hackers). In reality, this is a highly diverse constituency made up of women and men of all ages, races, nationalities and technical abilities, including people with no knowledge of coding or hacking (Postill 2014). Finally, it follows that the expanding transnational space of digital activism epitomised by

WikiLeaks, Anonymous, the Electronic Frontier Foundation or Global Voices is itself highly heterogeneous. Therefore, we must differentiate between its various subspaces, or fields, of political action—between digital rights, data activism, social protest or institutional politics, for example (Postill, forthcoming).

In this chapter we take these three observations as our guiding lines. Drawing from recent ethnographic and archival research in Indonesia, we explore how digital activists in that country translate or 'modulate' (Kelty 2008) key digital issues—which are sometimes highly technical and abstract—to reach diverse publics, often with remarkable success. We argue that Indonesia's digital activists have developed an effective pedagogical folksonomy in which three particular digital personas stand out, namely victims (*korban*), volunteers (*relawan*) and voices (*suara*) of the digital age. Each of these complexly mediated personas is endowed with unique attributes and located within a specific corner of Indonesia's digital activism space, and each is integral to efforts to educate diverse publics about the digital issues at stake. These three 'digital keywords' (Peters 2016) may seem both familiar and mundane, but we suggest that the work of personification that they enable has significant consequences for the framing of ongoing civil society struggles in post-Suharto Indonesia. We conclude that whether a certain individual or group is labelled a digital 'victim', 'voice' or 'volunteer' makes a difference to the evolution and eventual outcome of a given techno-political contention.

The chapter is organised as follows. We first discuss the personification of a key digital rights issue in Indonesia—the struggle over online freedom of expression—through the case of Law No. 11/2008 on Information and Electronic Transactions (the ITE Law) and the successful creation of a new category of digital personhood (ITE Law victims) to oppose it. We then consider a second process of digital personification at the time of the 2014 Indonesian presidential election, in which a small team of technologists strategically employed the notion of 'volunteers' (*relawan*) to mobilise over 700 fellow Indonesians to data-monitor the vote count so as to prevent electoral fraud. Our third case study is the transnational Papuan Voices project, whose aim is to empower ordinary citizens from Indonesia's most marginalised and oppressed provinces through video production and distribution. We then compare all three forms of digital personification by means of a set of variables, including their location within Indonesia's digital activism space, the main forms of knowledge they draw on (IT, media, law, project management and so on), their 'media ensembles' and their timescales (short term versus long term). We end with a recapitulation of the main argument and some suggestions for further comparative research.

VICTIMS OF A NOTORIOUS CYBERLAW

The social construction of victimhood never takes place in a historical or cultural vacuum. Different societies at specific historical conjunctures will identify and institutionalise certain categories of victim in distinct ways. The digital realm is no exception. Thus, in recent years a new social category and group of victims (*korban*) has been added to Indonesia's political and media lexicon: ITE Law victims (*korban UU ITE*). This neologism refers to those citizens (or 'netizens') deemed to have been negatively affected by the country's controversial ITE Law. It is increasingly common in Indonesia to find powerful individuals and organisations filing lawsuits against ordinary citizens for allegedly defaming them on social media, or even through private communications such as email or messaging. As a consequence, the number of charges filed under the ITE Law's defamation clause (article 27(3)) increased from 10 in 2012 to 78 in 2014. According to a recent report by Freedom House (2016):

> Prosecutions under the ITE Law, often to intimidate and to silence critics, continued [in 2016] with high profile cases drawing widespread public outrage. People frequently use the law for their own agenda, misguidedly mixing public and private digital space. A promised revision to the ITE Law had yet to materialize in mid-2016. Without proper training for Indonesian law enforcement and the judiciary, prosecutions are likely to continue to serve as retaliation for online speech.

Compared to the penalties established by the Criminal Code for *offline* defamation, the ITE Law's penalties for online hate speech, criminal defamation and inciting violence are draconian. Thus, article 45 of this law contemplates prison sentences of up to six years, whereas the maximum sentence under the Criminal Code is four years, and even then it is applied only in special cases. The discrepancy is even greater when it comes to financial penalties. For instance, while the Criminal Code fines are paltry for both spoken and written libel ($0.37), those under the ITE Law can reach the equivalent of $80,000 (Freedom House 2016).

But how did the new persona of 'ITE Law victims' come about? The making of this social category and group unfolded in two phases. First, there was a spectacularly effective online campaign in support of an early victim of the law, Prita Mulyasari. Then came the more routine, sustained work by digital activists and victims, including Prita herself, to recruit and mobilise further victims while consolidating the new category of 'ITE Law victims' through a series of public and private interventions. Let us consider each phase in turn.

Phase 1: the 'Coins for Prita' movement

In August 2008, the Tangerang housewife Prita Mulyasari, a mother of two, complained in a private email about the treatment she had received at Omni International Hospital in Jakarta. She claimed to have been misdiagnosed without being given an adequate explanation or monetary compensation. Her email found its way into numerous mailing lists and inboxes and eventually reached the private hospital's management. On 8 September 2008, the hospital put out a half-page advertisement responding to Prita's email. It also sued her for defamation, claiming Rp 500 million ($37,000) in damages (Hadin 2013). In May 2009, Prita was arrested and detained for three weeks, until public pressure secured her release. The hospital's lawyers successfully argued that Prita had violated Indonesia's ITE Law, and on 2 December 2009 the Tangerang District Court ordered her to pay Rp 204 million ($15,000).

Although an older demographic of social and political bloggers had begun posting about this case in May 2009 (Eliswati 2010), it only caught the attention of younger Indonesians when it spread to Facebook and other social media sites. This was when the Coins for Prita movement really took off:

> Once the Facebook support page was setup with the idea of contributing 500 rupiahs (~ US5 cents) to the fine—the 'Coins for Prita'—the movement took off and many more Facebook pages emerged. Posters were created and disseminated online and many Facebookers made the poster their profile picture. Some YouTube videos showcasing sentimental ballads for Prita also emerged (Lim 2013: 641).

Although the movement was born online, the legacy media, particularly commercial TV networks, played a crucial amplifying role. By 14 December 2009 organisers had gathered some $90,000, an amount that far exceeded the fine. When the Supreme Court acquitted Prita of all charges on 29 December 2009, the funds were transferred to a charity with the aim of helping other 'Pritas' (Lim 2013: 641). The saga did not end there, though, for on that same day the Tangerang prosecutors' office filed an appeal against the acquittal on the grounds that Prita had violated the country's ITE Law by writing and sending defamatory emails. Eventually, on 7 May 2013, Prita was cleared of all charges by Indonesia's Supreme Court (Hadin 2013).

How can we explain the remarkable success of a mass campaign related to a topic as seemingly arid as a new cyberlaw? First, for most Indonesians this was not really about the ITE Law at all. Instead, Prita represented an ordinary woman, a mother of two, taking on a much stronger adversary who had wronged her: the private hospital. As someone who described herself as a housewife put it: 'She is just like us. If this

Figure 8.1 One of numerous campaign images calling for the release of Prita Mulyasari and help with paying her Rp 204 million fine

Source: Kementerian Desain Republik Indonesia (KDRI), http://menteridesainindonesia.blogspot.com.au/2009/12/konser-koin-untuk-keadilan.html.

could happen to her, it could happen to me, to any one of us' (quoted in Lim 2013: 644–5).

This perception was sustained by the most commonly shared image around the case, showing Prita in a headscarf—a symbol of religious piety—with two young children on her lap (Lim 2013: 645). The case inspired a prodigious amount of digital artwork in the form of cartoons, songs, videos, posters and so on, with the most iconic image being a headshot of Prita in countless variations (Figure 8.1). This familiar David versus Goliath 'victimisation frame' (Lim 2013; cf. Sell 2013) came with Indonesian strings attached. As Hadin (2013) notes, middle-class hopes that the post-Suharto era would bring about a fair society had been dashed, with health and education becoming increasingly costly, consumer rights being routinely ignored and corruption becoming more rampant than ever.

The Prita case was a transmedia cocktail in which the digital and non-digital ingredients were thoroughly admixed. By simplifying the problem and allowing the public to show their support through 'low-risk activism', the Coins for Prita campaign transformed ordinary citizens into problem fixers who could make a difference merely by contributing a coin to the cause (Lim 2013: 646). The success of this campaign stood in stark contrast to the failure of many others to capture Indonesians' imaginations. For example, neither the Lapindo case (involving a mudflow disaster in East Java) nor the Ahmadiyya case (concerning a brutal attack on the Ahmadiyya religious minority) managed to attract much mainstream media coverage or popular mobilisation, partly because they did not lend themselves to simple explanations (Lim 2013: 648).

The same was true for other ITE Law victims who were not as culturally appealing as Prita. For instance, in 2012 a Sumatran public servant named Alexander Aan started a Facebook page for Indonesian atheists (see Chapter 6 by Hamid). He was then assaulted by an irate mob of religious conservatives and given a two-and-a-half-year jail sentence under the ITE Law for 'disseminating information aimed at inciting religious hatred or hostility' (Jurriëns and Tapsell 2016). In a country where it is compulsory to officially declare one's religious affiliation, atheism is not a legal option, nor is it a popular ideology with most Indonesians. As a result, and despite the case drawing the attention of the international media and secularist activists, as well as Jakarta's digital freedom activists, Aan's plight garnered little popular support in Indonesia.

Phase 2: making a social category and group

On 27 June 2013, just a few weeks after Prita Mulyasari was finally cleared of all charges, a group of 15 activists, bloggers and lawyers launched the Jakarta-based Southeast Asia Freedom of Expression Network (SAFENET) in Bali. SAFENET's stated goal is to monitor freedom-of-expression violations across the Southeast Asian region and advocate for those in need of help. By 2014, SAFENET had identified 78 victims of Indonesia's ITE Law, most of them charged with defamation (92 per cent), and the rest charged with religious blasphemy (5 per cent) or intimidation (1 per cent) (Juniarto 2014).

Although Prita Mulyasari was not Indonesia's first ITE Law victim, she was undoubtedly the most popular and 'iconic' (Muhajir 2014). Far from disappearing from the scene after her case was resolved, Prita became a vocal champion of other existing and potential victims. She started a petition on Change.org calling for the repeal of article 27(3) of the ITE Law. She also co-founded a support group for victims (*paguyuban para korban*), explaining that 'victims need the support of friends, especially from people who have had the same experience and understand the law' (Muhajir 2014).

In late 2014 the minister of communications, Rudiantara, announced a three-pronged approach to resolve the issues raised by the ITE Law: reducing the sentences served for those convicted; appointing specialist law enforcers; and educating law enforcers in how to assess such cases (Cosseboom 2014). This drew a sharp response from digital rights activists such as SAFENET coordinator Damar Juniarto, who argued that victims wanted article 27(3) to be repealed, not reduced sentences (Widiartanto 2015).

Upon its creation, SAFENET singled out the fight against the ITE Law as its focal point for Indonesia. Indeed, this law has become a galvanising issue for netizens across the country's digital activism space. Thus, when SAFENET, ICT Watch, Change.org and other groups established the Digital Democracy Forum (Forum Demokrasi Digital, or FDD) in December 2014, the plight of ITE Law victims took pride of place on the agenda. At an FDD event in February 2015 devoted to revising the law, and attended by one of the authors of this chapter, Prita's newly formed victims' association was one of four key stakeholders (*pemangku kepentingan*) present on the day, alongside policy-makers, digital democracy observers and civil society organisations (FDD 2015).

This process of institutionalisation of victimhood was reinforced through a savvy media strategy involving sympathetic media actors and organisations. For instance, following the event just mentioned, Juniarto and three victims were interviewed on the award-winning Metro TV show Mata Najwa. Juniarto repeatedly made the point that the government was using the ITE Law to criminalise internet users merely for sharing information, including private exchanges. The show's famous presenter, Najwa Shihab, faithfully reproduced the activists' framing of the problem around the category of 'ITE Law victims'.

The sustained efforts by SAFENET and other FDD members to construct and promote the collective category of ITE Law victims are reminiscent of those of a much older hackers' association from Europe: Germany's Chaos Computer Club (CCC). Kubitschko (2015a: 399) describes the interactions between CCC's hackers and other stakeholders in Germany (politicians, policy-makers, judges, journalists) as 'interlocking arrangements' leading over time to 'a virtuous circle':

> Politicians, legislators and judges learn about the organization's activities and expertise through the Club's multilayered media practices related to diverse media environments—self-mediation across alternative media and popular platforms, coverage by and different styles and modes of access to mainstream media.

Like the CCC, Indonesia's FDD is directed both 'inward to civil society by supporting emancipatory practices related to communicative infrastructures [and] outward to institutionalized politics' (Kubitschko

2015b). In the case of FDD, the civil society actors include LGBT activists whose websites have been shut down for being 'pornographic', while its institutional engagement to date has focused on the Ministry of Communication and Informatics. Similarly, FDD 'politicizes issues that otherwise might be understood as solely technological and are part of defining the predominant conception of what is understood as political' (Kubitschko 2015b). In the Indonesian case, the key to successful politicisation was *personification*, that is, a collective process whereby a small number of persons came to epitomise the deleterious effects of a specific piece of internet legislation.

VOLUNTEERS FOR DIGITAL DEMOCRACY

The financial crisis of 1997–98 triggered massive social unrest and political turmoil across much of Asia. In Indonesia, the student-led *reformasi* movement put an end to Suharto's authoritarian regime, ushering in an ongoing—and uneven—process of democratisation. One important strand of this process has been the continuing civil society struggle against corruption and electoral fraud. Although Indonesian citizens' efforts to monitor elections were already in evidence during the country's first post-Suharto democratic elections in 1999 (Hill 2003), the internet became fully integrated into 'monitory democracy' (Keane 2009) only during the 2014 presidential elections. Those elections pitted a 'clean', grassroots candidate, Joko Widodo (commonly known as Jokowi), against former army general Prabowo Subianto, who had served under Suharto. In 2014, a range of digital initiatives sprang up to monitor the voting process, all part of a wider narrative of *reformasi* and open governance.

Immediately after the ballot closed, the quick count results created tension because of their discrepancies. While seven pollsters declared a Jokowi victory, four declared exactly the opposite: a Prabowo win. The blatantly partisan TV channels did not help to clarify the confusion, merely supporting their favoured candidates' claims to victory. The confusion stoked rumours of vote rigging and fraud.

The most successful electoral monitoring initiative to emerge out of this chaos was Election Guardians (Kawal Pemilu). Set up by three Indonesian technologists living abroad, Kawal Pemilu swiftly recruited around 700 volunteers who entered the results from every polling station and successfully cross-checked most of the votes within one week. Given the atmosphere of generalised distrust, it was critical for Kawal Pemilu to be perceived by the public as being motivated by public interest (a clean and fair election), rather than personal interests (the victory of a particular candidate). Our interviews and observations confirmed that Kawal Pemilu volunteers were aware of the need to demonstrate an impartial stance through their words and deeds. The volunteers were keen to reassure the Indonesian public through media interviews and their own Facebook and Twitter stories that they were not being paid for their work and were in fact self-funding.

The problem was that virtually all of the volunteers were Jokowi supporters, which could have conflicted with the non-partisan requirements of their work. To manage this dissonance, they strictly separated their public communication channels (Facebook and Twitter) from the private communications (on WhatsApp) in which they revealed their preference for Jokowi. They also removed any visual markers on their social media accounts that could identify them as Jokowi voters. To further display their non-partisan stance, they celebrated their volunteerism by exchanging, and publishing, personal stories about how they had selflessly sacrificed their personal time and comforts for the sake of their data activism.

The success of the use of volunteer personas during the electoral campaign suggests that the election was perceived, at least on one level, as an abuse of ordinary people by powerful political players rather than as a fair competition between electoral platforms. Therefore, no one candidate was regarded as being free from hidden motives and self-interest. Accordingly, volunteers sought to connect the voters with the political elites through a moral framework rather than through formal political processes or contracts. Under a moral framework, the intrinsic virtue of a candidate is what makes the candidate's message effective and persuades the public to join his or her campaign. The public, on the other hand, can only rely on their own moral evaluation to guide their decision. They cannot establish an organisational apparatus to ensure that their candidate honours their trust, because organisations will inevitably be caught in political dealings and manoeuvres that can never be fully moral. Volunteers in Indonesian electoral politics essentially adopt a moral position, a position worth defending amid bitter competition. However, the involvement of volunteers will last only as long as the campaign itself. Kawal Pemilu's choice of social persona was crucial to the task of avoiding the charge of self-promotion, or of being political operatives, thus earning public trust.

DIGITAL VOICES FROM AFAR

In 1992, the musician Peter Gabriel joined forces with the Lawyers' Committee for Human Rights to found a non-government organisation called Witness. The new NGO distributed video cameras to human rights activists around the globe in the rather naive hope that they would record abuses 'and demonstrate to the world the validity of their claims against their government' (McLagan 2006: 192). The idea was premised on the inherently problematic assumption that 'seeing is believing'—problematic in that visual evidence 'can hold a deceptive immediacy and tends to overwhelm purely verbal arguments' (McLagan 2006: 192). Over time, video activists began to suspect that their repeated 'mobilisation of shame' was contributing to 'compassion fatigue', a malaise reportedly afflicting audiences in the Global North (Moeller 1999; Gregory 2006).

Eventually, Witness and similar organisations developed more sophisticated forms of video activism. The earlier appeals to an undifferentiated global audience were replaced by 'smart narrowcasting' to carefully targeted publics (Gregory 2006). Video activism was now part of a transnational 'circulatory matrix' with its own 'dedicated communications infrastructure' and circuits of events organised around human rights violations (McLagan 2006: 192). This audiovisual media practice was now inseparable from an increasingly savvy global 'reprioritization of local voices in local contexts' (Gregory 2006: 202).

In June 2012, Witness partnered with non-profit organisation EngageMedia to create Video4Change—a worldwide alliance of video activism organisations. Launched in March 2005, EngageMedia has its main offices in Australia and Indonesia and a lighter presence in other Southeast Asian countries. Its mission statement is to 'work with independent film-makers, video activists, technologists and campaigners to generate wider audiences for their work'. As this description suggests, EngageMedia specialises in brokering civil society partnerships involving digital media. Thus, in 2006–08, it brought together software developers and video activists through a series of events across Europe and Indonesia in order to develop 'online video distribution tools for social justice and media democracy' (Wikipedia 2016). More recently, in March 2015, it co-convened RightsCon, a large gathering of digital rights activists and other civil society actors from across the Asia-Pacific region (Postill 2015).

One of EngageMedia's flagship projects is Papuan Voices, funded by the Ford Foundation and organised in collaboration with Catholic Church groups in West Papua, Indonesia. The aim is to enable Papuans to 'tell their own stories' by training them in the production and distribution of short videos, thereby empowering them to understand their human rights and how to defend them. The objective is not to tackle head-on the issue of Papua's protracted struggle for independence from Indonesia, but rather to give Papuans the means to tell the stories 'behind the conflict' in their own words and images. For Alexandra Crosby and other members of Papuan Voices, this form of 'citizen journalism' is indispensable in places like Papua where foreign journalists are barred from entering and the domestic media fail to report the actualities on the ground (McDonnell 2012).

For the Papuan Voices film-maker and workshop trainer Enrico Aditjondro, it is crucial that these stories reach audiences beyond the world of activism: 'We don't want activists from NGOs making films for fellow activists' (Noviello 2014). Similarly, the local video-maker Wensi Fatubun (2015) argues that media activists often make the mistake of 'telling the issue, and not a life story'. For this reason, he wants his films to establish an 'emotional connection' with the viewer and regards his video-making as merely one aspect of a broader human rights strategy developed jointly with the villagers. The intended outcome is always 'a story about human rights'.

Wensi's life trajectory helps to explain his political stance and his commitment to Papuan Voices. At the age of 12, he witnessed the arrival of a South Korean lumber company in his West Papuan village. Unlike other youngsters his age, he was more interested in the Koreans' cameras—which he had never seen before—than in their bulldozers. He was particularly fascinated by the delighted reactions of fellow local people on seeing the photos taken of them. After some years spent studying philosophy in Sulawesi, Wensi returned to Papua to take up a post at the Office for Justice and Peace in the archdiocese of Merauke:

> I began to write reports and use a camera to speak out on the rights of native peoples and environmental issues. This is how the project Papuan Voices started. [...] I wanted this to be an advocacy and cultural project to permit the people of Papua to tell their own stories in films. So other people could learn about them together with them (Fatubun 2015).

Like Wensi, Asrida Elisabeth, originally from the island of Flores, found her way to Papuan Voices through a local church. In 2011, she joined a politically minded pastor in undertaking human rights work in Papua. She soon noticed that video 'resonated strongly' with local people, even though most videos were produced outside Papua. She wondered whether it would be possible for them to make their own videos and show them locally. After hearing about Papuan Voices, she acquired basic film-making skills from the organisation and went on to produce two videos independently. She then gained funding to make a documentary on the lives of women living in poor communities. The result was the critically and popularly acclaimed *Tanah Mama* (2015), which won the prestigious best documentary award at the 2015 Yogyakarta Documentary Film Festival (Wits 2016).

Since its inception, Papuan Voices has organised numerous film screenings in Papua, in other Indonesian provinces and overseas. These public events help to promote the organisation and raise awareness about life in Papua among diverse audiences. In January 2015, one of the authors of this chapter attended a screening in Yogyakarta, a major cultural centre and university town in Java with a sizeable student population from Papua. Over 300 people attended, about a third of them non-Papuans—a larger proportion than expected by the organisers. Eight short documentaries were shown, followed by a lively Q&A discussion. The opportunities to mingle with other attendees gave many non-Papuans their first chance to converse with Papuans.

Overseas events such as film festivals and academic meetings extend the reach of the project and are integral to its 'circulatory matrix' (McLagan 2006: 192). For instance, on 27 November 2015, a seminar devoted to Papuan Voices was held at Leiden University in the Netherlands. One of the films screened was *Love Letter to a Soldier*, winner of the best documentary award at the 2012 South to South Festival. The film is a video letter to Samsul, an Indonesian soldier stationed in the village of Bupul, near the border with Papua New Guinea, by a woman named Maria 'Eti' Goreti. The two had an intimate relationship but Samsul left the area when Eti was five months pregnant and never contacted her again. Eti begs him to come back for the sake of their now three-year-old daughter, Yani. For the director Wenda Tokomonowir, Eti is but one of a growing number of local women 'courted, impregnated and abandoned', or in some cases raped, by Indonesian soldiers. For Wenda, the plight of these 'victims of the border control soldiers' deserves to be known so that the issue can be addressed (Aditjondro 2012).

Despite this mention of victims, the focus of Papuan Voices is not on victimhood but rather on empowerment through the voicing (*menyuarakan*) of local issues. Audience reactions to another short film shown in Leiden, *Pearl in the Noken*, demonstrate this point. This documentary follows the Papuan doctor Maria Rumateray as she travels to remote areas by helicopter. As one audience member remarked, the film 'is unique and interesting as it does not focus on a "victim", as most advocacy films do'. Another participant, of Papuan origin, was 'impressed' that it showed 'an example of a Papuan success story' (Pratiwi 2016). Even in the case of *Love Letter to a Soldier*, the audience noted that although it had 'a strong political message', this was conveyed subtly (Pratiwi 2016).

The media theorist Nick Couldry (2010) has highlighted the political importance of voice in a neoliberal age. More than merely giving people a voice, he argues, we must find ways of *valuing* voice as a process that matters in its own right. In other words, we should privilege 'the act of valuing, and choosing to value, those frameworks for organizing human life and resources that themselves value voice (as a process)' (quoted in Tacchi 2012: 228). Papuan Voices is a clear example of precisely such a processual approach to valuing voice. Thus, for Egbert Wits of EngageMedia:

> Human rights activists or organizations will achieve greater impact if they can go beyond *letting* people tell their own stories and move towards actually *enabling* people to tell their own stories. [This is a] much more long-term and process orientated approach, acknowledging not all outputs can be predicted

> from the start. [...] Only then will more Asridas be given the opportunity to surface and address the world in more meaningful and impactful ways than any human rights organization can (Wits 2016, emphasis in original).

Speaking during a November 2012 video workshop in Sorong, West Papua, program manager Ade was tearful as she recounted how much she had learned from the experience. For Ade, video is 'the most effective medium for voicing an issue'. However, this faith in the empowering potential of video as a medium does not mean that the Papuan Voices team are believers in the naive 'technological solutionism' (Morozov 2013) routinely denounced by critics of digital activism, or that they subscribe to the overoptimistic video advocacy of the 1990s. Instead, as we can see from the above quote, they emphasise that their chosen approach is long term, messy and challenging—'a slow and tricky process' (Alexandra Crosby, quoted in McDonnell 2012).

As the media anthropologist Jo Tacchi (2012: 229) has noted, citing Appadurai (2004), the world's poor 'lack resources to voice their concerns'. In the field of information and communication technology for development, adds Tacchi, voice entails access, but this is more than a physical or technological challenge, for it includes 'cognitive, affective, political, economic and cultural domains [of action]'. Aware of this complexity, Papuan Voices states that its ambition is to overcome 'political, geographical and financial barriers—as well as lack of technology—to bring important Papuan stories to the world'. Again, there are no signs here of technological determinism (or solutionism), for technology is seen as just one of several interlinked barriers to be overcome.

Like sister initiatives around the globe, Papuan Voices seeks to 'circumvent governments, armies, corporations, or other entities that are violating rights and to connect with supporters abroad' (McLagan 2006: 191). For both scholars and activists, case studies of Papuan Voices and similar organisations offer valuable insights into 'the processes through which human rights categories are constructed through [digital] media' (Gregory 2006: 192)—in this case, the personification of political issues via the metonymic notion of voice. As we have just seen, in contrast to the anti-ITE Law campaign reviewed above, Papuan Voices regards the digital as a means to an end (human rights) rather than as an end in itself (digital rights).

NARRATING DIGITAL PERSONAS: FIELDS, SKILLS, MEDIA AND SCALES

Having reviewed three rather different cases of digital personification (ITE Law victims, Kawal Pemilu and Papuan Voices), we are now in an ideal position to sketch a multidimensional model of such processes in the context of contemporary Indonesia. The political personas analysed above did not materialise *ex nihilo*. Instead, four key variables shaped the concrete ways in which they were *narrated into being*: activist fields, specialist knowledge, media ensembles and time–space scales.

By 'activist fields', we mean the specific subspaces within Indonesia's overall space of digital activism in which each personification is located. Thus, the ITE Law victims inhabit the subspace (or field) of *digital rights activism*. This domain has experienced rapid growth in Southeast Asia in the current decade, with the digital rights conference RightsCon, held in Manila in March 2015, being a recent milestone (Postill 2015). The Kawal Pemilu volunteers, meanwhile, belong to the neighbouring subspace of *data activism*. In this dynamic field, whose most famous global representatives are WikiLeaks and Anonymous, agents speak data to power through actions such as whistleblowing, hacking or data monitoring—the latter being Kawal Pemilu's modus operandi. Papuan Voices exists in yet another corner of Indonesia's digital activism space: the field of *media advocacy*. This domain occupies a rather ambiguous position in relation to the other two subspaces in that it seeks to draw attention *away* from the digital so as to disintermediate the relationship between Papuans and non-Papuans through the assumed immediacy of storytelling. This is a paradoxical strategy, analogous to that of religious practitioners in many parts of the world who are driven by 'desires for immediacy' (Eisenlohr 2009: 278); an example would be the ritual healers who seek to connect directly with supernatural agents through electronic media such as PA systems or mobile phones (Eisenlohr 2009: 278).

The dominant forms of specialist knowledge that went into constructing the various personas also differed in substantial ways. Not surprisingly, the ITE Law victimisation project enjoyed considerable input from legal experts, particularly from Indonesia's small but active community of (often self-taught) internet law specialists. It also benefited from the journalistic know-how of influential media personalities such as Najwa Shihab of Metro TV. In contrast, Kawal Pemilu was first and foremost an IT project, but it would not have succeeded had it not recruited media-savvy volunteers from across the social media/legacy media divide. Finally, Papuan Voices relied not only on video-making and distribution expertise; it also depended on the advanced project management and pedagogical skills of both its Papuan and non-Papuan team members.

As for the particular sets of media technologies, or 'media ensembles' (Bausinger 1984; Monterde and Postill 2014), employed in each personification project, here we find once again significant contrasts as well as some parallels. All three initiatives combined online technologies with offline practices (meetings, screenings, workshops), yet under very different circumstances. Thus, while the anti-ITE Law activists astutely exploited the viral publicity generated by the plight of Prita Mulyasari, Kawal Pemilu's volunteers had no choice but to keep a tight rein on their media use in order to protect their crucial private communications from potential cyberattacks. Meanwhile, Papuan Voices opted for more gradual, non-viral, sustained growth through a combination of online videos, physical DVDs, public screenings and word of mouth.

This leads us to the fourth and final variable: temporal and spatial scaling. Here, a clear distinction must be made between Kawal Pemilu and the other two endeavours. Whereas Kawal Pemilu was an ephemeral, time-bound intervention that responded swiftly to what its participants perceived to be a national emergency, both Papuan Voices and the ITE Law campaign are long-term, open-ended ventures. In terms of spatiality, all three are multi-sited and transnational, though that is where the similarities end. Kawal Pemilu was the brainchild of a small group of Indonesian technologists, young 'rooted cosmopolitans' (Tarrow 2005) living abroad who recruited more than 700 volunteers over the internet. It was a textbook demonstration of 'the strength of weak ties' (Granovetter 1973) via telematic media. The ITE Law and Papuan Voices initiatives, by contrast, are more firmly anchored to domestic geographical locations in that their lead organisations are headquartered in Jakarta (SAFENET) and Yogyakarta (EngageMedia) respectively. Both Kawal Pemilu and the Prita campaign experienced robust expansion during the early stages of their life courses, only to decline almost as rapidly in their terminal phases. In contrast, Papuan Voices, as just noted, grew more slowly and over a longer period of time.

THE DEVIL IN THE DIGITAL

Effective collective agents such as the Indonesian digital activist groups reviewed in this chapter make strategic use of their chosen personas. These digital personas are identified and brought to life through the groups' master narratives and supporting stories. They can be thought of as actors on a public stage, yet the stages featured in our examples are not physical settings but rather social issues directly or indirectly linked to the digital realm.

One core task in any social struggle is to gain supporters and solidify the movement's group identity (Gerbaudo and Treré 2015). Personas can help to define the boundaries between insiders and outsiders—between the victims and the abusers in the case of the ITE Law, for example. Victims are the offspring of perceived injustices. They may be different from non-victims in many respects, but they are still an integral part of our shared moral universe. As members of the public, we are expected to side with the victims and challenge the perpetrators. When presented before a public, victims' identities are inseparable from the injustices perpetrated against them. The victims' persona developed by ITE Law activists shaped how they argued their legal case to the public, the focus being on how real people were personally affected by this controversial law. However, not all victims struck a chord with the general population, as shown by the case of the Sumatran atheist assaulted by a religious mob after publicly declaring his atheism on Facebook.

Volunteers are partly us, but they are not exactly us; for example, they can actively help a candidate win an election so that he or she can serve the public (us). The Kawal Pemilu volunteers entered Indonesia's national stage at a time of acute need, when the republic's hard-earned democratic order seemed under threat. Their collective persona was able to insert itself into public discourse because of the strong desire among a vast swathe of the Indonesian population, and especially its urban middle classes, for a transparent election. This desire was rooted in the fear of the country regressing to authoritarianism (as seen, for instance, in nearby Thailand). The volunteers' hastily crafted persona managed to focus society's attention not only on what they did, but also on who they were, namely selfless volunteers.

Meanwhile, the metonymic persona of Papuan Voices was created through a complex, open-ended series of interventions to break the domestic and international silence enveloping Papuans' stories. What makes giving voice to the unvoiced a worthwhile enterprise is precisely this deafening silence. The voiced persona is not one of us, since it connects us (the public) with them (the historically voiceless). Without a voice to relay the stories of Papuans, we denizens of other areas of Indonesia and overseas could not even begin to confront those who prevent the voiceless from speaking. This shared premise drives the voicing efforts of Papuan Voices' team members and local participants.

To return to the exchange between John Oliver and Edward Snowden that opened this chapter, it should be amply evident by now that popular Western representations of digital activists as white male 'IT guys' with poor communication skills are in need of urgent revision. As the Indonesian materials presented above testify, digital activism and its personifications can take myriad forms. These initiatives are often imaginative, sophisticated and courageous, and they are by no means confined to famed activists in the Global North. More detailed research in Indonesia and elsewhere is required to take these preliminary observations and ideas further. After all, the devil is in the digital.

REFERENCES

Aditjondro, E. (2012) 'EngageMedia video wins STOS Festival 2012 best documentary', *EngageMedia*, 27 February. Available at https://www.engagemedia.org/Members/ricoloco/news/engagemedia-video-wins-stos-festival-2012-best-documentary/view.

Appadurai, A. (2004) 'The capacity to aspire: culture and the terms of recognition', in V. Rao and M. Walton (eds) *Culture and Public Action*, Stanford University Press, Palo Alto: 59–84.

Bausinger, H. (1984) 'Media, technology and daily life', *Media, Culture & Society*, 6(4): 343–51.

Chadwick, A., and S. Collister (2014) 'Boundary-drawing power and the renewal of professional news organizations: the case of *The Guardian* and the Edward Snowden NSA leak', *International Journal of Communication*, 8(2014): 2,420–41.

Cosseboom, L. (2014) 'Indonesia's ICT minister in talks with Vimeo about restoring the nation's access', *Tech in Asia*, 27 November. Available at https://www.techinasia.com/indonesia-rudiantara-ict-minister-startup-asia-jakarta-2014.

Couldry, N. (2010) *Why Voice Matters: Culture and Politics after Neoliberalism*, Sage, London.

Eisenlohr, P. (2009) 'Technologies of the spirit: devotional Islam, sound reproduction and the dialectics of mediation and immediacy in Mauritius', *Anthropological Theory*, 9(3): 273–96.

Eliswati, V. (2010) *Setahun Koin Keadilan: Sebuah Kenangan dan Penghargaan untuk Orang-orang yang Berkehendak Baik* [One Year of Coins for Justice: Memories and Tributes to People of Goodwill], Rumah Langsat, Jakarta.

Fatubun, W. (2015) 'The eyes of the Papuans: a video advocacy process', *Tapol*, 23 April. Available at http://www.tapol.org/news/eyes-papuans-video-advocacy-process.

FDD (Forum Demokrasi Digital) (2015) 'Undangan "Dialog Kemerdekaan Berekspresi di Internet Indonesia: Menuju Revisi UU ITE"' [Invitation to 'Dialogue on Freedom of Expression on Indonesia's Internet: Towards a Revised ITE Law'], 26 January. Available at http://demokrasidigital.net/blog/undangan-dialog-kemerdekaan-berekspresi-di-internet-indonesia-menuju-revisi-uu-ite/.

Freedom House (2016) 'Freedom on the Net 2016: Indonesia'. Available at https://freedomhouse.org/report/freedom-net/2016/indonesia.

Gerbaudo, P., and E. Treré (2015) 'In search of the "we" of social media activism: introduction to the Special Issue on Social Media and Protest Identities', *Information, Communication & Society*, 18(8): 865–71.

Granovetter, M.S. (1973) 'The strength of weak ties', *American Journal of Sociology*, 78(6): 1,360–80.

Gregory, S. (2006) 'Transnational storytelling: human rights, Witness, and video advocacy', *American Anthropologist*, 108(1): 195–204.

Hadin, A.D. (2013) 'Social media and social movement: a review of "Coins for Justice"', Master 1 LEA Cultures, Affaires Internationales Asie-Pacifique, Universite de La Rochelle, La Rochelle. Available at https://www.academia.edu/6383855/Social_Media_and_Social_Movement_A_Review_of_Coins_for_Justice_by_Aryati_Dewi_Hadin_Master_1_LEA_Cultures_Affaires_Internationales_Asie-Pacifique.

Hill, D. (2003) 'Communication for a new democracy: Indonesia's first online elections', *Pacific Review*, 16(4): 525–47.

Juniarto, D. (2014) 'Presentasi kasus UU ITE 2008–2014' [Presentation on ITE Law cases, 2008–2014]. Available at http://www.slideshare.net/damarjuniarto/presentasi-kasus-uu-ite-20082014.

Jurriëns, E., and R. Tapsell (2016) 'New technology may bring Australia and Indonesia closer', *Sydney Morning Herald*, 8 September. Available at http://www.smh.com.au/comment/new-technology-may-bring-australia-and-indonesia-closer-20160908-grboq5.html.

Keane, J. (2009) 'Monitory democracy and media-saturated societies', *Griffith Review*, 24: 47–69.

Kelty, C.M. (2008) *Two Bits: The Cultural Significance of Free Software*, Duke University Press, Durham.

Kubitschko, S. (2015a) 'Hackers' media practices: demonstrating and articulating expertise as interlocking arrangements', *Convergence*, 21(3): 388–402.

Kubitschko, S. (2015b) 'Hacking politics: civic struggles to politicize technologies', *Civic Media Project*, 17 March. Available at http://civicmediaproject.org/works/civic-media-project/chaos-computer-club.

Lim, M. (2013) 'Many clicks but little sticks: social media activism in Indonesia', *Journal of Contemporary Asia*, 43(4): 636–57.

McDonnell, F. (2012) 'Raising voices', *UTS Newsroom*, 5 November. Available at http://newsroom.uts.edu.au/news/2012/11/raising-voices.

McLagan, M. (2006) 'Introduction: making human rights claims public', *American Anthropologist*, 108(1): 191–5.

Moeller, S.D. (1999) *Compassion Fatigue: How the Media Sell Disease, Famine, War and Death*, Routledge, New York and London.

Monterde, A., and J. Postill (2014) 'Mobile ensembles: the uses of mobile phones for social protest by Spain's indignados', in G. Goggin and L. Hjorth (eds) *Routledge Companion to Mobile Media*, Routledge, London: 429–38.

Morozov, E. (2013) *To Save Everything, Click Here: Technology, Solutionism, and the Urge to Fix Problems That Don't Exist*, Penguin UK, London.

Muhajir, A. (2014) 'Menggagas solidaritas korban UU ITE' [Building solidarity with ITE Law victims], *Tempo.co*, 16 April. Available at http://indonesiana.tempo.co/read/13621/2014/04/16/antonemus/menggagas-solidaritas-korban-uu-ite.

Noviello, A. (2014) 'Papuan Voices: a documentary', *YouTube*, 10 March. Available at https://www.youtube.com/watch?v=UwAjRvBmVmI.

Peters, B. (ed.) (2016) *Digital Keywords: A Vocabulary of Information Society and Culture*, Princeton University Press, Princeton.

Postill, J. (2014) 'Freedom technologists and the new protest movements: a theory of protest formulas', *Convergence*, 20(4): 402–18.

Postill, J. (2015) 'Internet struggles in Southeast Asia: an ethnographic account of RightsCon 2015, Manila', keynote address to the first Internet in Southeast Asia conference, Monash University Malaysia, Bandar Sunway, 3–4 December.

Postill, J. (forthcoming) *The Rise of Nerd Politics*, Pluto, London.

Pratiwi, K. (2016) 'Discussing Papuan Voices in the Netherlands', *Papuan Voices*, 21 March. Available at http://papuanvoices.net/2016/03/21/discussing-papuan-voices-in-the-netherlands.html.

Sell, S.K. (2013) 'Revenge of the "nerds": collective action against intellectual property maximalism in the global information age', *International Studies Review*, 15(1): 67–85.

Tacchi, J. (2012) 'Digital engagement: voice and participation in development', in H. Horst and D. Miller (eds) *Digital Anthropology*, Berg, Oxford: 225–41.

Tarrow, S. (2005) *The New Transnational Activism*, Cambridge University Press, Cambridge.

Widiartanto, Y.H. (2015) 'Lima korban "pasal karet" UU ITE' [Five victims of the ITE Law's 'rubber article'], *Kompas*, 30 January. Available at http://tekno.kompas.com/read/2015/01/30/16170037/Lima.Korban.Pasal.Karet.UU.ITE.

Wikipedia (2016) 'EngageMedia'. Available at https://en.wikipedia.org/wiki/EngageMedia.

Wits, E. (2016) 'Enabling storytelling: video for human rights advocacy', *EngageMedia*, 16 May. Available at https://www.engagemedia.org/blog/enabling-storytelling.

9 Social media and Islamic practice: Indonesian ways of being digitally pious

Martin Slama

Like 'non-digital Indonesia', 'digital Indonesia' is a realm of diverse religious expressions and practices. This is true in particular of those digital spaces that are inhabited by Indonesian Muslims. Today, we can observe myriad ways in which the internet and social media are turned into platforms of Islamic mediation. As I will show in detail in this chapter, the popularity of online Islamic practices has increased hugely in Indonesia due to the growth of 'smart' communication technologies and social media. The latter provide ample opportunities for Muslims to exhibit both visual and textual material, including people's expressions of piety, and to explore new forms of religious practice and sociality. Social networking sites in particular have become a focal point for displaying Indonesia's many 'Islamic faces'. Appearing pious on social media has evolved into a major 'cultural genre of content'—to borrow the phrase used by Daniel Miller (2011: 212) to designate the prevalent forms of online presence in particular (national) contexts. My own inter-

* This chapter is based on results of the research project 'Islamic (inter)faces of the internet: emerging socialities and forms of piety in Indonesia', funded by the Austrian Science Fund (FWF). The research team consists of Fatimah Husein (State Islamic University Sunan Kalijaga), Eva Nisa (Victoria University of Wellington), and Dayana Lengauer, Johann Heiss and myself (Institute for Social Anthropology, Austrian Academy of Sciences). I would like to express my gratitude to the Freiburg Institute of Advanced Studies (FRIAS) for giving me time, as a guest researcher in May and June 2015, to analyse data presented in this chapter.

est is in Indonesian ways of being digitally pious as these are reflected in both online and offline Islamic practices. I also attempt to tackle a bigger question, namely what the consequences of these digitalisations of Islamic practices might be for Indonesian Islam at large. My conclusions are necessarily preliminary, since the changes taking place in Indonesia today are being driven not just by religious verve, but also by new social formations, cultural ambiguity and rapid technological change.

Even the naive observer of religious life in Indonesia today would quickly realise that Indonesian Muslims have embraced social media in their daily religious lives, where we find great creativity and variety in the use of smartphones and apps (Barendregt 2012: 215). A devout Muslim I interviewed in Yogyakarta told me, for example, that when picking up her children from school, she likes to wait in her car where she can recite the Qur'an undisturbed thanks to a digitised version of the Qur'an she has saved on her smartphone. In addition to digital versions of the Qur'an, a variety of apps offer access to treatises on Islamic law (*fiqh*), exegesis of the Qur'an (*tafsir*) and other religious texts. Some Muslims even use their smartphones to assist them with their prayers (*zikir*), using an app to keep count of the number of recitations. This app was first developed by Indonesian programmers for the BlackBerry mobile phone, until recently the most popular smartphone among the Indonesian middle classes. Another development that would certainly not escape the attention of the naive observer and trained anthropologist alike is the widespread use of the selfie stick—called *tongkat narsis*, or *tongsis*, literally meaning 'narcissist stick'—to document one's religious life. Brought out before and after Islamic study gatherings, during pilgrimages in Indonesia or abroad, when meeting prominent Islamic preachers and so on, the *tongsis* seems to have become indispensable for those who want to keep a digital record of their religious devotions.

Although it is difficult to do justice to the variety and dynamics of Islamic practices in today's social media age, in this chapter I will seek to give an insight into how Indonesian Muslims are using social media for religious purposes. First, I will discuss how online interactions are shaping Islamic study groups (*majelis taklim*) and preacher-follower relationships, paying particular attention to the temporal and emotional aspects of these online exchanges. Next, I will examine Islamic practices such as regular reading of the Qur'an, to show how the new social media platforms have given rise to new ways of organising time and instilling self-discipline. I will then discuss what I call 'posting Islam', that is, the increasingly popular practice of posting messages with a religious theme on social networking sites with the intention of making a personal contribution to Islamic proselytisation. This is a contested field in Indonesia, generating competing discourses about the 'right' way of being pious and benevolent, especially among urban and mobile middle-class Muslims.

The chapter attempts to draw a picture of the many ways in which Indonesian Muslims are using social media in their religious lives. At the same time, it seeks to avoid portraying social media as the sole driving force behind current Islamic developments in Indonesia. Aware of the pitfalls of technological determinism, I try to develop a more nuanced argument of the ways in which social media have become entangled in Islamic lifestyles and in the field of Islam in Indonesia more generally. My approach pays heed to the many intertwining processes that have led to the contemporary—and it would seem lasting—tendency for Muslims to express their piety digitally.

Since the late 1970s, Indonesia has seen a surge in Islamic awareness and activities on an unprecedented scale. Over the last few decades, numerous new Islamic organisations, movements and networks, many of them originating in other parts of the Islamic world, have established themselves in Indonesia (van Bruinessen 2012; Kersten 2015). In many cases, it was Indonesia's expanding Muslim middle class that explored and sustained these novel ways of organising Islam, and introduced Islam into various spheres of consumption (Fealy 2008; Hasan 2009; Jones 2010). Urbanites (re)discovered the wisdom of Sufism, relocating it from rural Islamic boarding schools (*pesantren*) to the political and economic centres of Indonesia, where it has been embraced by white-collar workers, businesspeople and politicians (Zamhari and Howell 2012; Howell 2015). Similarly, but in the opposite direction, the reformist interpretations of Islam that had their strongholds in urban Indonesia gained a foothold in rural areas (Hefner 2009; Wildan 2013; Chaplin 2015). These developments were accompanied by the introduction of Islamic ways of dealing with economic issues, giving rise to a new generation of Islamic entrepreneurs, bankers and motivators to serve as role models for the Islamic community (Hefner 1996; Sakai 2008; Rudnyckyj 2010). A new group of Muslim celebrities who knew how to exploit the power of the mass media also emerged, with the Islamic TV preacher featuring as the most prominent example (Watson 2005; Hoesterey 2008, 2016). Pilgrimages to holy sites both within and outside Indonesia became increasingly popular, creating lucrative business opportunities (Darmadi 2013; Slama 2014; Alatas 2016). Moreover, a state that until the late 1980s was hostile to overt expressions of Islamic identity became, in many parts of Indonesia, a vehicle through which Islam was conveyed, leading to new entanglements between bureaucratic and Islamic procedures, interests and alliances (Bush 2008; Bowen 2013; Feener 2015).

I allude to these developments not only to give a sense of the 'analogue pre-history' of being digitally pious in Indonesia, but also to make visible a broader trend in which religious uses of social media are embedded. I am referring here to the rise of various forms of Islamic sociality and piety that have evolved relatively independently of Indonesia's well-established Islamic organisations and movements.[1] Compared with two or three decades ago, Indonesia now offers many more ways of practising and comprehending Islam and of being collectively pious, as the empirical examples presented in this chapter will attest. A major argument of this chapter is that, rather than precipitating the rise of a clear-cut phenomenon called 'digital Islam', the growing popularity of social media has accelerated and intensified an existing trend towards the diversification of Islamic ideas and practices. In many cases, social media have added new ways of practising Islam to existing ones, allowing both to develop alongside each other, rather than provoking breaks in how piety is perceived and performed. This chapter therefore seeks to give consideration to the continuities between the pre-digital and digital eras while attempting to identify genuine changes where this is justified.

SOCIALITY AND AUTHORITY

In Indonesia, the rise of new communication technologies has coincided with the emergence and spread of collective forms of piety. These range from the meetings at which *zikir* are recited (*majelis zikir*) and the Prophet Muhammad is praised in prayer and song (*majelis salawat*) (Zamhari and Howell 2012) to Islamic study groups (*majelis taklim*) and prayer sessions (*pengajian*) (Abaza 2004; Millie 2011; Nisa 2012; Winn 2012). Given the popularity of study groups and prayer meetings, a new market has opened up for both male and female preachers (*ustadz* and *ustadzah*) to deliver their services to Indonesians of all social backgrounds. Islamic study groups and prayer meetings are based on a variety of social formations and can differ considerably in size. Lower-class Indonesians usually meet in local mosques and form a large part of the audiences at the public events held by prominent preachers, which can attract huge crowds (Woodward et al. 2012). Perhaps because they can afford to engage a preacher, middle- and upper-class Indonesians seem to prefer smaller, private prayer sessions involving family members, neighbours, friends and colleagues. Such gatherings are usually held in homes or

---

1 The research presented here demonstrates that the interplay and intersections between the online and offline realms are giving rise to new social formations in Indonesia, thus confirming the centrality of the concept of sociality in anthropological research on online phenomena (Postill 2011; Boellstorff 2012).

office buildings, or in campus mosques or the mosques of middle-class neighbourhoods (Slama 2017).

Although the study group or prayer meeting continues to be a significant form of offline Islamic religiosity, in today's Indonesia, it usually includes an online element as well. Middle- and upper-class Muslims now expect to be able to contact their preachers between meetings through messaging apps such as WhatsApp, LINE, Telegram and BlackBerry Messenger (BBM). During my field research, I even encountered a case of a preacher from a lower-middle-class background in Jakarta who was given an iPad by his upper-class followers, who obviously thought that he was not sufficiently technologically connected. Indonesian Muslims use the private communication channels available through messaging apps to ask questions not only about proper Islamic practice, but also about personal matters. The prayer group, and the preacher–follower relationship, has thus ceased to be a strictly offline affair. The regular face-to-face meetings with an *ustadz* or *ustadzah* are now supplemented by frequent online exchanges, and posing questions to the preacher has become as uncomplicated as sending a message on WhatsApp. This means that the Islamic prayer group and the preacher have increasingly become part of the everyday lives of Indonesian Muslims.

This expansion of Islamic sociality into the realm of messaging apps has temporal, economic and emotional ramifications. When they send their questions to a preacher, middle- and upper-class Muslims expect to receive a quick answer, especially if the matter concerns a personal or family problem (*masalah keluarga*) such as an affair or a divorce. As I have argued elsewhere in more detail (Slama 2017), the 'subtle economy of time' surrounding the online exchanges between preachers and their followers inform the extent to which preachers are able to cater to the needs of their followers. In fact, many of the preachers I met complained about the number of messages they were receiving every day and about the complicated cases they were being confronted with. Nevertheless, these online exchanges have become crucial for what I call the Islamic preacher economy: because many preachers depend on their followers for a considerable part of their incomes, they have to put an effort into becoming and remaining popular through any means available to them, including social media. Today, this entails finding the right words at the right time in private online exchanges. One can observe a situation now in which those preachers who are not attentive to the emotional ups and downs of middle- and upper-class Indonesians—that is, preachers who are having difficulty with their new role as online consultants—risk not being able to gain or keep a share of Indonesia's Islamic preacher economy. Only celebrity preachers with their own TV shows or huge personal followings would appear to be exempt from this logic. However, even they generally employ social media teams to respond to personal messages, in an effort to project an image of someone who cares about their individual followers.[2]

As well as introducing a new dynamic into the preacher–follower relationship (and therefore the Islamic preacher economy), social media platforms have provided an outlet for a practice that first appeared before the rise of social media: the practice of 'pouring one's heart out' (*curahan hati*, or *curhat*). This phenomenon was first observed among urban teenagers and young adults in offline contexts, before becoming a major motivation in the early 2000s for young Indonesians to join internet chat rooms and other online forums. It must also be seen in connection with the complex cultures of shame (*malu*) that can be found in many parts of Indonesia. In these cultural settings, where exhibiting one's emotions is strongly discouraged, internet chat rooms provided the necessary privacy and anonymity to talk about one's personal problems openly and to seek emotional support (Slama 2010).

Interestingly, the *curhat* that took place in the chat rooms of the past seems to have migrated to the private communication channels of today's messaging apps, with the people who used to have heart-to-heart talks with their peers in chat rooms now seeking similar experiences with Islamic preachers on WhatsApp. There are differences in the way men and women have negotiated these changes, however. Whereas both young women and young men used to take part in the heart-to-heart chat room discussions of the past, today it is mainly the female followers of male preachers who pour their hearts out (*curhat*) on social media. When it comes to sharing personal issues, in the Islamic preacher economy the roles are clearly divided into female-follower-as-first-person-narrator and male-preacher-as listener-and-adviser. This reflects the general gender division in *majelis taklim*, which are much more popular among women than among men. It also reflects the proportions of male and female preachers in the Islamic preacher economy, with male preachers forming the clear majority. Thus, the most common model is for a female *majelis taklim* group to invite a male preacher to its gatherings. This is mirrored in the online activities of the group's members, who approach the preacher on social media after obtaining his mobile

---

2 Celebrity preachers prefer to use social media platforms that allow them (and their media teams) to address all their followers at once, such as Facebook or Twitter, rather than those that require them to engage in private exchanges. One popular way of spreading one's message is the 'Twitter lesson' (*kultwit*, an abbreviation of *kuliah Twitter*); for example, preachers might explain a saying of the Prophet Muhammad (*hadith*) by first tweeting the *hadith*, then tweeting their interpretation of it in subsequent tweets.

phone number, Facebook name or pin code (in the case of BBM) during an offline meeting.

Given this asymmetrical gender pattern of Islamic online consultation, one might expect social media to be a key factor in enhancing the authority of preachers. This is not necessarily the case, however, as followers are increasingly likely to question the authority of an *ustadz*. For example, Ustadz Quddus, a preacher who lives in Yogyakarta, told me that women like to ask him for advice concerning their unfaithful husbands and related problems. The *ustadz* would usually tell the women to be 'patient' (*sabar*). 'But sometimes', he told me, 'when I tell women they should be patient, they answer back and ask me whether I don't have any better advice than just being patient'.[3] Other preachers described similar experiences, including critical questioning of the primary textual basis of their advice. A remark by a preacher in Jakarta was particularly illuminating: he distinguished between his lower-class followers, who were fairly compliant, and his middle- and upper-class followers, who demanded what he called 'two-way communication' (*komunikasi dua arah*). The middle- and upper-class followers liked to involve him in discussions online, and could be critical of what he said.[4]

To reach the position of an online consultant in the first place, a preacher must demonstrate a talent for preaching offline, be well received by a largely female audience and, as discussed above, show that he can respond to online messages with empathy and without much delay. In this regard, one should not underestimate the role of the women who run Indonesia's *majelis taklim*, because it is they who determine who will be invited to preach at their meetings, and it is they who judge the content of the sermons and who exchange views on the preachers' online behaviour. They have what James Hoesterey (2016: 19) has called 'a new form of consumer power'. He was referring to the relationship between TV preachers and their audiences, but I argue that the women who dominate local Islamic study groups and those groups' online extensions have even more consumer power than the followers of popular TV preachers, because TV preachers are abandoned only in the most extreme cases, when their behaviour strongly alienates their fans. This happened to Aa Gym, the most popular TV preacher in Indonesia until 2006, when he made the unpopular decision to take a second wife (Hoesterey 2008).

Early studies of the Islamic online presence saw the internet as a sphere in which the authority of established Islamic scholars was being

---

3 Interview with Ustadz Quddus Zoher, Yogyakarta, 30 June 2014. The interview was conducted by the author and Fatimah Husein.

4 Interview with Ustadz Hasanuddin, Jakarta, 10 July 2014. I am grateful to Faried Saenong for putting me in contact with Ustdaz Hasanuddin.

undermined. For example, based on an analysis of Islamic websites, Jon Anderson (1999: 53) asserted that the internet had become 'an arena for alternative expressions of Islam both to popular and to traditional elite views' (see also Anderson 2005; Barker 2005). Contemporary uses of social media in Indonesia suggest a more complex picture. What we encounter in Indonesia today is a novel constellation of interfaces, that is, a mix of online and offline relationships and exchanges facilitated by social media. This provides opportunities for both the assertion and the questioning of authority by a variety of actors.[5] What we are currently witnessing is the rise of preachers who are not affiliated with the well-established Islamic organisations and movements. Not only are these new players obliged to compete with their more established colleagues (and each other), but they must also regularly demonstrate their Islamic expertise and social skills in online and offline settings. As a result, the question of who can be regarded as an Islamic authority is no longer decided solely by learned elites in Islamic and state institutions, but also by the mainly female organisers of Islamic study groups and followers of Islamic preachers. In these realms of Islamic sociality with their close online–offline connections, Islamic authority is more frequently constructed dialogically, with women in particular taking the opportunity to 'talk back'.

(SELF-)DISCIPLINE AND PUNISHMENT

Qur'an reading groups are another area where piety and everyday life meet in the online and offline realms in contemporary Indonesia. As in other parts of the Islamic world, reciting the Qur'an has long been a widespread practice in Indonesia (Gade 2004; van Doorn-Harder 2006). However, it has received additional impetus from the rise of social media, as reflected in the increasing popularity of the One Day One Juz (ODOJ) method of reading the Qur'an, where 'Juz' refers to one chapter of the Qur'an. Using messaging apps such as WhatsApp and Telegram, Muslims who want to practise ODOJ form groups of 30 people, with each member obliged to read a different chapter of the Qur'an every day for 30 days. As the Qur'an has 30 chapters, each group collectively reads the whole Qur'an every day. Over the course of 30 days, the group collectively reads the Qur'an 30 times, and each member personally completes the Qur'an once.

The WhatsApp Qur'an reading groups may be organised by preachers, by the women who run *majelis taklim*, by members of Islamic political

5 For a similar argument based on other contexts, see Cheong (2013).

parties such as the Prosperous Justice Party (Partai Keadilan Sejahtera, PKS) or by the organisers of the new OneDayOneJuz movement. The latter has more than 100,000 active members, and has its own website (www.onedayonejuz.org), Twitter account and Facebook page. People who are interested in participating in an online reading group register online and are then assigned to a group without consideration of their place of residence.

In addition to its strong online presence, OneDayOneJuz organises various offline activities. These include meetings at mosques to hear eminent preachers give sermons (known as Kajian Al Quran Ala Ustadz, or Kalqulus), and gatherings in public places to recite (*ngaji*) the Qur'an (known as Ngaji On The Street, or NGAOS).[6] For its offline activities, OneDayOneJuz has developed a hierarchical structure that resembles the political organisation of Indonesia, with representatives of the movement at the district, provincial and national levels organising events. To facilitate its online activities, OneDayOneJuz appoints an administrator to each WhatsApp group to supervise group members and report their recitation activities to a higher level of the organisation's structure.

My field research indicated that the WhatsApp Qur'an reading groups run by preachers have a similar structure to the groups run by OneDayOneJuz. Every group has an administrator or coordinator to run the group and liaise with the preacher. In addition to distributing the chapters of the Qur'an that have to be read, the coordinators have to make sure that members adhere to the rules on which the groups are based. The central rule is that every reader must report to the administrator every day at a given time—whether the person has actually read their chapter of the Qur'an or not. The coordinators then report daily to the preacher.

Some preachers insist on strict observance of the rules, as the following excerpt from a conversation between an *ustadz* in Jakarta and the coordinator of one of his WhatsApp groups shows. On 23 September 2014, the coordinator (a woman I have called 'Mrs Nabila') was discussing the case of a group member ('Azis') with the preacher:

Nabila: *Ustadz*, in group number 6 only Azis has not yet reported, but his *track record* [English in original] is good. Can I tolerate this?

Ustadz: It is a violation because he often forgets to report.

Nabila: But *ustadz*, as long as I have managed group number 6, he has always reported. But OK, I will follow what you say.

---

6 In February 2015, I attended a Kalqulus meeting in East Jakarta with my colleague Eva Nisa, who is researching OneDayOneJuz as part of our 'Islamic (inter)faces of the internet' project (see acknowledgment on page 146).

Ustadz: According to my records he has already violated the rules two times.

Under the rules introduced by the preacher, Azis had now reached the maximum number of violations (three) and was asked to leave the group, as Mrs Nabila did not succeed in changing the preacher's mind. He was nevertheless expected to continue reading the Qur'an on his own every day, and would be allowed to rejoin the group the following month, when a new round of Qur'an reading would begin. In the meantime, as a consequence of his lack of self-discipline, that is, of his failure to finish his chapters and to report, he would be deprived of the sociality of the group.

This example brings us to an important aspect of the new phenomenon of online Qur'an reading groups in Indonesia, one that evokes the classic work of Michel Foucault on prisons and disciplinary practices (Foucault 1995). Although I certainly do not intend to equate eighteenth-century prisons in Europe (the main subject of Foucault's book) with contemporary online Qur'an reading groups in Indonesia, (self-)disciplining 'systems of micro-power' (Foucault 1995: 222) can be observed in both. As we have seen, not reading one's assigned chapter of the Qur'an can have negative consequences. Moreover, given the strict rules on reporting at a designated time each day, the groups have a disciplining effect on their members. Thus, they represent a kind of online disciplinary institution (reminding us again of Foucault, who described not only prisons but a variety of modern institutions as 'disciplinary institutions'). Adhering to the daily deadline can be accomplished only through a form of self-discipline with which, as one can easily imagine, many people are struggling.

Indonesia's biggest Qur'an reading movement, OneDayOneJuz, is particularly concerned to ensure that its members manage to read one chapter of the Qur'an every day. On its Twitter account it publishes advice on how one can become a successful Qur'an reader despite having numerous other daily obligations. On 22 May 2014 it sent a particularly elaborate version of such advice in a tweet titled '*Solusi ODOJ agar disiplin untuk mengatur waktu*' [The ODOJ solution for being disciplined in organising one's time]. The tweet showed two pie charts, each dividing the day according to the five Islamic prayer times and the times of day during which ODOJ members could be expected to be busy (shown in red), moderately busy (orange) or not busy (green) carrying out their Qur'an-reading duties. In the left-hand chart, representing the most common, but undesirable, pattern of Qur'an reading, the red zone was between the afternoon prayer (Ashar) and the last prayer of the day (Isya) (around 3:00–7:00 pm). In the right-hand chart, representing the recommended pattern of Qur'an reading, the red zone was between the morning prayer (Shubuh) and noon (Lohor). This meant that the Qur'an reader could relax for the rest of the day, while the group coordinator would receive reports in a timely manner, not at the last minute in the evening.

The examples given here of online Qur'an reading groups indicate that Indonesian Muslims are not only finding new ways of expressing their piety, but also discovering how central time management has become to succeed in this endeavour. By voluntarily exposing themselves to pressure from the group to read and report, and by integrating regular Qur'an reading into their busy lives, participants in reading groups are forced both to accept discipline from others and to exercise self-discipline. In contrast, the example of digital piety I discuss next is far more contested, with many Muslims questioning the genuineness of those who participate in what I call 'posting Islam'.

POSTING ISLAM: CONTESTED VERSIONS OF *DAKWAH* AND ONLINE PIETY

As an extension of their daily religious activities, many Indonesian Muslims now like to express their piety not only on messaging apps and Twitter, but also on Facebook, which is immensely popular in Indonesia. Practising Islam goes hand in hand with 'posting Islam', that is, posting textual and visual material with a religious theme on social media. On Facebook, one can find both well-known preachers and ordinary Muslims engaging in what they call *dakwah* (proselytisation). To get an idea of how *dakwah* is related to Facebook status updates, let me quote one of my interviewees, a person I will call 'Mrs Kartika'. Mrs Kartika is a lecturer in computer science at a university in Yogyakarta. When I asked her about her religious activities on Facebook, she said:

> On Facebook anything that delivers Islamic content can be termed *dakwah*. And anyone can use Facebook, including myself when [for example] I communicate with people who have gone on the pilgrimage (*hajj*). When six family members of mine went on the pilgrimage, we asked them to send pictures. As a result, family members here could see what they were doing over there. This is one way of using Facebook for *dakwah*.[7]

At first glance, it might seem surprising that posting photos of a pilgrimage on Facebook can be regarded as *dakwah*, a term that is usually reserved for the more elaborate forms of proselytisation conducted by

---

7 Interview with 'Mrs Kartika', Yogyakarta, 6 August 2014. The interview was conducted by the author and Fatimah Husein.

learned scholars of Islam. This expansion of the definition of *dakwah* to online activities that do not require any particular theological expertise cannot be attributed solely to the popularity of social media among Indonesian Muslims, although this does seem to have reinforced the trend. I see it as an expression of a larger shift that is taking place in Indonesian Islam, in which new religious figures and their audiences are renegotiating the premises on which Islamic authority rests (Feillard 2010; Hoesterey 2016; Slama 2017). With this shift, it has become possible for ordinary Muslims like Mrs Kartika to regard themselves as performing *dakwah*. She gave me another example of this kind of proselytisation:

> Everybody likes soap operas. But even if they have an Islamic title, the content of many soap operas is negative. For example, the wife is angry with her husband and demands a divorce. Are there not many cases of divorce these days? In the soap operas people see this. So I tell people that watching soap operas is not good. On my Facebook page I write that soap operas exhaust your emotions, they give you a headache.

In addition to such moral exhortations, the necessity to be thankful to God is another common theme of social media posts. The people who post these messages sometimes address God directly, so that their status updates resemble prayers. On the Facebook pages of Mrs Kartika and other Indonesian Muslims, these spiritual expressions of religiosity are often found alongside more down-to-earth religious posts with a moralistic and demanding tone.

Thanks to digital photography, Indonesian Muslims are also using Facebook, Instagram and other platforms to portray their pious lifestyles in vivid detail. Images documenting people's travels to sites of religious significance within or outside Indonesia are particularly popular (Barendregt 2009). Although chiefly for religious purposes, such as visiting the tomb of an Islamic saint, these trips are often combined with secular activities such as visiting a (non-religious) local tourist attraction or enjoying the local cuisine. 'Consuming' religious sites and landscapes has become part of the Islamic middle-class lifestyle in Indonesia. To cater for this distinct market, the country's tourism industry offers religion-themed package tours, using slogans such as 'You can travel without leaving your Islamic practice behind' (Slama 2014: 117–18).

The ways in which some Indonesian Muslims—especially well-off Muslims living in urban areas—are expressing their piety in the real and digital worlds has attracted criticism on the grounds that it smacks of consumerism and violates the Islamic injunction against showing off one's piety (*riya*). On social networking and messaging sites, Indonesian Muslims and Islamic preachers are discussing which posts should be categorised as *riya*, that is, the point at which the laudable practice of wanting to please God is overtaken by the strongly discouraged practice of seeking admiration for one's pious deeds. As popular as it is to be digitally pious, it also generates ambivalence, since exemplary Islamic practice, when displayed by oneself on social media, can easily be regarded as the exact opposite. This applies in particular to Islamic charities, many of which use social media to publicise their activities, solicit funds and show they are making good use of donations. Like individual Indonesian Muslims, they must find a balance between, on the one hand, using the new opportunities social media provide to do good deeds, and, on the other, avoiding the social media pitfalls that put Muslims at risk of behaving in morally objectionable ways—that is, of committing *riya*.[8]

CONCLUDING REMARKS

When one looks at current Islamic developments through the lens of the digital in Indonesia, it immediately becomes obvious that one can find Islamic expressions and practices virtually everywhere online, that is, on every social medium that is currently popular. However, focusing on the online realm alone would risk missing a crucial point, namely the strong connections between digital and non-digital forms of being pious in Indonesia. Islamic study groups (*majelis taklim*) and Qur'an reading groups are not inventions of the digital era; rather, with the rise of social media they have experienced a reconfiguration, generating new forms of Islamic sociality that are located at the interface between the digital and non-digital realms. Similarly, the role of the Islamic preacher is experiencing a transformation as preacher–follower relationships are renegotiated and Indonesian Muslims become better equipped to engage in dialogue with, and make demands on, their preachers. Educated middle-class women in particular are taking the opportunity the new social media forums provide to intervene in the construction of Islamic authority. This is certainly not a consequence of digitalisation, as Muslim women have influenced the careers of Islamic preachers before (Millie 2011; Hoesterey 2016), but the way they engage with their preachers today—demanding quick, thoughtful and empathic responses—used to be uncommon and was perhaps even unthinkable at a time when these relationships were solely dependent on offline encounters. At the same time, this does not mean that the offline activities of preachers, such as giving sermons at prayer meetings, have become irrelevant, since these often serve as a prelude to private online exchanges.

---

8 My colleague Fatimah Husein has been researching the topic of *riya* and Islamic charities as part of our 'Islamic (inter)faces of the internet' project (see acknowledgment on page 146).

The entanglements between digital and non-digital ways of being pious, between online and offline forms of Islamic sociality, between change and continuity in Indonesia's religious life, are to a large extent informed by practices of (self-)discipline and (self-)empowerment. On Facebook, for example, proselytisation is clearly not the preserve of established Islamic scholars and professional preachers. Rather, *dakwah* has become an everyday activity conducted by ordinary Muslims, who provide status updates on Facebook referring to their religious activities as a reminder for their friends and families. The depth to which social media have already penetrated the everyday lives of Indonesian Muslims is perhaps best exemplified by online Qur'an reading groups. Members are expected to reorganise their daily schedules in order to be able to prove their piety to their fellow Muslims online. Being a member of a Qur'an reading group has a disciplining effect, and spurs Muslims to exercise self-discipline. Thus, with the introduction of social media, it is no longer only exemplary Muslims and Sufi mystics who engage in self-disciplining practices. Since Qur'an reading groups have become a mass phenomenon, online religious practices have become part of the Islamic middle-class lifestyle, with all the ambivalences (such as the risk of committing *riya*) that this implies.

As Indonesian ways of being pious have expanded to include being digitally pious, Islamic religiosity has spread into new spatial and temporal realms of Muslims' everyday lives. The growing interdependence of social media and Islamic practice has accelerated and intensified longstanding trends in Indonesian Islam, such as theological and socio-economic diversification, the pluralisation of authority and the growing influence of middle-class women. As members of Islamic study groups and Qur'an reading groups, as critical followers of preachers and as active social media users who regularly post Islamic messages, women in particular are informing the social formations and power relations of the contemporary Islamic community. This process is not without its tensions and contradictions, but it is hard to imagine that the online–offline dynamics at work in the field of Islam in Indonesia will wane. In religious affairs, as in society at large, there seems to be no turning back to a pre-digital era. For researchers of any aspect of Islam in Indonesia, this means that it will become increasingly difficult not to consider Indonesian ways of being digitally pious.

REFERENCES

Abaza, M. (2004) 'Markets of faith: Jakartan *da'wa* and Islamic gentrification', *Archipel*, 67: 173–202.

Alatas, I.F. (2016) 'The poetics of pilgrimage: assembling contemporary Indonesian pilgrimage to Ḥaḍramawt, Yemen', *Comparative Studies in Society and History* 58(3): 607–35.

Anderson, J.W. (1999) 'The internet and Islam's new interpreters', in D. Eikelman and J.W. Anderson (eds) *New Media in the Muslim World: The Emerging Public Sphere*, Indiana University Press, Bloomington: 41–55.

Anderson, J.W. (2005) 'Wiring up: the internet difference for Muslim networks', in M. Cooke and B.B. Lawrence (eds) *Muslim Networks from Hajj to Hip-Hop*, University of North Carolina Press, Chapel Hill: 252–63.

Barendregt, B. (2009) 'Mobile religiosity in Indonesia: mobilized Islam, Islamized mobility and the potential of Islamic techno nationalism', in E. Alampay (ed.) *Living the Information Society in Asia*, Institute of Southeast Asian Studies, Singapore: 73–92.

Barendregt, B. (2012) 'Diverse digital worlds', in H.A. Horst and D. Miller (eds) *Digital Anthropology*, Berg, London and New York: 203–24.

Barker, E. (2005) 'Crossing the boundary: new challenges to religious authority and control as a consequence of access to the internet', in M. Højsgaard and M. Warburg (eds) *Religion and Cyberspace*, Routledge, London and New York: 67–85.

Boellstorff, T. (2012) 'Rethinking digital anthropology', in H.H. Horst and D. Miller (eds) *Digital Anthropology*, Berg, London and New York: 39–60.

Bowen, J.R. (2013) 'Contours of sharia in Indonesia', in M. Künkler and A. Stepan (eds) *Democracy and Islam in Indonesia*, Columbia University Press, New York: 149–67.

Bush, R. (2008) 'Regional sharia regulations in Indonesia: anomaly or symptom?', in G. Fealy and S. White (eds) *Expressing Islam: Religious Life and Politics in Indonesia*, Institute of Southeast Asian Studies, Singapore: 174–91.

Chaplin, C. (2015) 'Islamic social movement in post-Soeharto Indonesia: life politics, religious authority and the Salafi Manhaj', in T. Petru (ed.) *Graffiti, Converts and Vigilantes: Islam outside the Mainstream in Maritime Southeast Asia*, Caesarpress, Vienna: 31–52.

Cheong, P.H. (2013) 'Authority', in H. Campbell (ed.) *Digital Religion: Understanding Religious Practice in New Media Worlds*, Routledge, London: 72–87.

Darmadi, D. (2013) '*Hak Angket Haji*: pilgrimage and the cultural politics of hajj organization in contemporary Indonesia', *Studia Islamika* 20(3): 443–66.

Fealy, G. (2008) 'Consuming Islam: commodified religion and aspirational pietism in contemporary Indonesia', in G. Fealy and S. White (eds) *Expressing Islam: Religious Life and Politics in Indonesia*, Institute of Southeast Asian Studies, Singapore: 15–39.

Feener, R.M. (2015) 'State shari'a and its limits', in R.M. Feener, D. Kloos and A. Samuels (eds) *Islam and the Limits of the State: Reconfigurations of Practice, Community and Authority in Contemporary Aceh*, Brill, Leiden and Boston: 1–23.

Feillard, A. (2010) 'From handling water in a glass to coping with an ocean: shifts in religious authority in Indonesia', in A. Azra, K. van Dijk and N.J.G. Kaptein (eds) *Varieties of Religious Authority: Changes and Challenges in 20th Century Indonesian Islam*, Institute of Southeast Asian Studies, Singapore: 157–76.

Foucault, M. (1995) *Discipline and Punish: The Birth of the Prison*, second edition, Vintage Books, New York.

Gade, A.M. (2004) *Perfection Makes Practice: Learning, Emotion, and the Recited Qur'an in Indonesia*, University of Hawai'i Press, Honolulu.

Hasan, N. (2009) 'The making of public Islam: piety, agency, and commodification on the landscape of the Indonesian public sphere', *Contemporary Islam*, 3(3): 229–250.

Hefner, R.W. (1996) 'Islamizing capitalism: on the founding of Indonesia's first Islamic bank', in M.R. Woodward (ed.) *Toward a New Paradigm: Recent Developments in Indonesian Islamic Thought*, Arizona State University, Tempe: 291–322.

Hefner, R.W. (2009) 'Islamic schools, social movements, and democracy in Indonesia', in R.W. Hefner (ed.) *Making Modern Muslims: The Politics of Islamic Education in Southeast Asia*, University of Hawai'i Press, Honolulu: 55–105.

Hoesterey, J.B. (2008) 'Marketing morality: the rise, fall and rebranding of Aa Gym', in G. Fealy and S. White (eds) *Expressing Islam: Religious Life and Politics in Indonesia*, Institute of Southeast Asian Studies, Singapore: 95–133.

Hoesterey, J.B. (2016) *Rebranding Islam: Piety, Prosperity, and a Self-help Guru*, Stanford University Press, Stanford.

Howell, J.D. (2015) 'Revitalised Sufism and the new piety movements in Islamic Southeast Asia', in B.S. Turner and O. Salemink (eds) *Routledge Handbook of Religions in Asia*, Routledge, London and New York: 276–92.

Jones, C. (2010) 'Materializing piety: gendered anxieties about faithful consumption in contemporary urban Indonesia', *American Ethnologist*, 37(4): 617–37.

Kersten, C. (2015) *Islam in Indonesia: The Contest for Society, Ideas and Values*, Hurst & Company, London.

Miller, D. (2011) *Tales from Facebook*, Polity Press, Cambridge.

Millie, J. (2011) 'Islamic preaching and women's spectatorship in West Java', *Australian Journal of Anthropology*, 22(2): 151–69.

Nisa, E.F. (2012) 'The voice of *syarifah* on Jakarta's *da'wa* stage', *RIMA: Review of Indonesian and Malaysian Affairs*, 46(1): 55–81.

Postill, J. (2011) *Localizing the Internet: An Anthropological Account*, Berghahn, New York and Oxford.

Rudnyckyj, D. (2010) *Spiritual Economies: Islam, Globalization and the Afterlife of Development*, Cornell University Press, Ithaca.

Sakai, M. (2008) 'Community development through Islamic microfinance: serving the financial needs of the poor in a viable way', in G. Fealy and S. White (eds) *Expressing Islam: Religious Life and Politics in Indonesia*, Institute of Southeast Asian Studies, Singapore: 267–86.

Slama, M. (2010) 'The agency of the heart: internet chatting as youth culture in Indonesia', *Social Anthropology/Anthropologie Sociale*, 18(3): 316–30.

Slama, M. (2014) 'From *wali songo* to *wali pitu*: the travelling of Islamic saint veneration to Bali', in B. Hauser-Schäublin and D. Harnish (eds) *Between Harmony and Discrimination: Negotiating Religious Identities within Majority/Minority Relationships in Bali and Lombok*, Brill, Leiden: 112–43.

Slama, M. (2017) 'A subtle economy of time: social media and the transformation of Indonesia's Islamic preacher economy', *Economic Anthropology*, 4(1): 94–106.

van Bruinessen, M. (2012) 'Indonesian Muslims and their place in the larger world of Islam', in A. Reid (ed.) *Indonesia Rising: The Repositioning of Asia's Third Giant*, Institute of Southeast Asian Studies, Singapore: 117–40.

van Doorn-Harder, P. (2006) *Women Shaping Islam: Reading the Qur'an in Indonesia*, University of Illinois Press, Champaign.

Watson, C.W. (2005) 'A popular Indonesian preacher: the significance of Aa Gymnastiar', *Journal of the Royal Anthropological Institute*, 11(4): 773–92.

Wildan, M. (2013) 'Mapping radical Islam: a study of the proliferation of radical Islam in Solo, Central Java', in M. van Bruinessen (ed.) *Contemporary Developments in Indonesian Islam: Explaining the 'Conservative Turn'*, Institute for Southeast Asian Studies, Singapore: 190–223.

Winn, P. (2012) 'Women's *majelis taklim* and gendered religious practice in northern Ambon', *Intersections: Gender and Sexuality in Asia and the Pacific*, 30. Available at http://intersections.anu.edu.au/issue30/winn.htm.

Woodward, M., I. Rohmaniyah, A. Amin, S. Ma'arij, D.M. Coleman and M.S. Umar (2012) 'Ordering what is right, forbidding what is wrong: two faces of Hadhrami *dakwah* in contemporary Indonesia', *RIMA: Review of Indonesian and Malaysian Affairs*, 46(2): 105–46.

Zamhari, A., and J.D. Howell (2012) 'Taking Sufism to the streets: *majelis zikir* and *majelis salawat* as new venues for popular Islamic piety in Indonesia', *RIMA: Review of Indonesian and Malaysian Affairs*, 46(2): 47–75.

10 Online extremism: the advent of encrypted private chat groups

Nava Nuraniyah

Although Indonesian extremist groups, like other political activists, have been using the internet to propagate their messages for years, the emergence of the so-called Islamic State in Iraq and Syria (ISIS) and its extensive use of social media have prompted fresh concerns about online terrorist recruitment and training. Social media platforms such as Facebook and Twitter have suspended the accounts of hundreds of thousands of extremists since 2014. For its part, the Indonesian government has banned dozens of jihadi websites. These crackdowns have contributed to an important trend in online extremism: the increasing use of encrypted mobile chat apps, in particular Telegram and WhatsApp. This chapter describes the shifting uses of digital technologies by extremist groups, and explains the importance of understanding how online social networks can be used to massage and mould extremist viewpoints.

Do the new digital technologies assist the causes of terrorists and their supporters? How do extremists interact in encrypted private chat groups? If repressive measures to restrict access to online platforms only lead to an exodus of extremists to encrypted chat applications, what other measures should be taken to address this trend? This chapter seeks to address these questions through a case study of pro-ISIS Telegram groups in Indonesia. I argue that the private chat groups function mainly as a space for social interaction and personal bonding, helping to broaden extremist networks, strengthen group cohesion and reinforce beliefs. In effect, the new social media, including private chat groups, are less about virtual training or plotting terrorist attacks, and more about sustaining and strengthening radical communities.

The Indonesian case study reveals that while social media has not replaced face-to-face contact as the main recruitment mode, it has allowed extremists to reach out to new audiences, including Indonesian migrant workers, and vice versa. The lone-wolf phenomenon (defined as an individual radicalised on his or her own without any interaction with other extremists, or through exposure to extremist materials and/or groups on the internet, without physical contact) remains very rare even in the age of social media. Indonesian extremists still rely heavily on study groups (*pengajian*) and other gatherings to maintain ideological conviction and group cohesiveness. However, private chat groups clearly facilitate the close interaction, frequent opportunities for conversation and relative anonymity that make people feel they can be more open about themselves. Long-lasting friendships, business partnerships and even marriages have sprung out of the internet's extremist private chat groups. The advent of encrypted private chat groups has made online surveillance more challenging, and comprehensive efforts to counter radicalisation will still need to include an offline component.

THE LITERATURE ON ONLINE EXTREMISM

Early research on online extremism was characterised by fear about how the internet might aid terrorist operations or make them more lethal. Arquilla and Ronfeldt (2001: 12) predicted that the biggest change brought about by the internet would be that leaderless groups would be quick to come together in 'swarming attacks' against computer systems; this would later be categorised as cyberterrorism, defined as attacks against information systems that result in physical damage to civilian targets (Bendrath 2003; Sieber 2006). Others argued that the cyberterrorist threat was exaggerated, and suggested that terrorists would use the internet mainly for fundraising, propaganda dissemination and 'cyber-planning' (Thomas 2003: 112; Weimann 2004, 2006).

A second wave of literature attempted to test earlier hypotheses by examining how, and how effectively, terrorists had actually used the internet. Rogan (2007) concluded that al-Qaeda's media strategy had been successful in rapidly expanding its online presence through e-magazines and web forums, but others suggested that the organisation had been less successful in its attempt to establish online bomb-making classes. The internet therefore served mainly as a 'resource bank' rather than as a 'virtual training camp' (Stenersen 2008: 215) because it was used chiefly to provide abstract knowledge, not practical skills (Kenney 2010).

The third wave of scholarship criticised earlier research as being underpinned by technological determinism, the view that technology changes human lives in negative ways as opposed to one in which technology both shapes and is shaped by social processes (Baym 2010; Benson 2014). Rather than seeing the internet merely as a tool, some recent studies view it as a social environment or 'milieu' in which ideas are generated, challenged and reaffirmed (Conway 2012). This is a direct result of scholars broadening the scope of their analysis from known terrorists to those who have engaged or sympathised with violent radicalism (Holbrook 2015: 122).

What role, then, does the internet play in radicalisation? Can someone be 'self-recruited', as Sageman (2008: 37) put it? Many scholars have tried to answer this question by examining the radicalisation pathways of individuals, including by highlighting the online–offline dynamic. Some conclude that the internet is a facilitating and reinforcing agent (Ramakrishna 2010; Behr et al. 2013), others that it is an accelerant (Pantucci 2011) and a few that it is a driver of violent extremism (Homeland Security Institute 2009). There is, though, an emerging consensus that self-radicalisation is very unlikely to happen: the majority of homegrown terrorists have at least a few virtual friends or mentors serving as enablers (Stevens and Neumann 2009; Jenkins 2011).

The current discussion tends to emphasise individual trajectories, especially in a Western context. This focus may obscure the broader environment from which radical individuals emerge in the first place. By focusing on interactions among Indonesian extremists in private chat groups, I attempt to shift the focus from the individual to the online community: how it is formed and maintained; how online interaction relates to participants' daily lives and their offline social relationships; and how such processes may or may not lead participants to engage in terrorism-related activities.

The focus on private chat groups is important, because existing research on extremism and social media predominantly looks at mainstream platforms such as Twitter (Prucha and Fisher 2013; Klausen 2015; Berger and Perez 2016), Facebook and YouTube (Sureka et al. 2010; Helfstein 2012; Klausen et al. 2012). People tend to talk more openly in private chat groups than they do on public platforms, so a study of these forums is likely to offer fresh insights. The private chat groups are also different from earlier web forums—such as the al-Qaeda-linked Global Islamic Media Front and Anshar al-Mujahidin—in that there is less control over discussion content (Zelin 2013). The administrators of a Telegram group can vet new members but they cannot filter or even categorise postings based on threads, resulting in much more natural, free-flowing conversation.

CONCEPTUAL FRAMEWORK

My analysis of extremist private chat groups is inspired by the concept of the online radical milieu. Malthaner and Waldmann (2014: 983) define a 'radical milieu' as 'the immediate social environment from which violent groups emerge and to which they remain socially and symbolically connected'. The online radical milieu is not just a passive socio-political context or an abstract ideology but rather represents a 'dynamic and evolving relational field that includes groups and individuals [...] interacting and to some extent collaborating with, but at times also criticizing, challenging, or even confronting the militant activists'. Some people in a radical milieu may eventually join a terrorist network, but they mostly provide logistical and moral support for the group. Malthaner (2010: 1) highlighted the centrality of face-to-face contact for the existence of a radical milieu, but Conway (2012: 12) argued that 'Web 2.0 in particular, has been shown to facilitate the virtual establishment of strong social and personal bonds in many different contexts [...] including amongst violent political extremists'.

During the early years of computer-mediated communication, scholars were sceptical that online relations could be as meaningful as face-to-face ones because of the reduced social cues in online settings (Sproul and Kiesler 1986). More recent research suggests, however, that the strength of social ties is determined less by the place where people meet and more by the level of intimacy with which they communicate, the duration of the friendship and the development of a group identity based on similar interests and worldviews (Mesch and Talmud 2006; Baym 2010). In the case of Indonesia's pro-ISIS extremists, information technology does facilitate the formation of strong social and personal bonds that go beyond the online realm, but direct involvement in the plotting or conduct of a terrorist act still usually requires some form of physical interaction.

FORMATION OF AN ONLINE RADICAL MILIEU IN INDONESIA

Radical milieus usually emerge in a context of escalating violence (Malthaner and Waldmann 2014: 984). In Indonesia, violent jihad and the recruitment of jihadi fighters bloomed following the outbreaks of Muslim–Christian conflict in Poso (Central Sulawesi) and Ambon (Maluku) in 1998–99. During this time Jemaah Islamiyah (JI)[1] and other

1 Jemaah Islamiyah was officially founded in 1992, with former Afghan fighters—or the 'Afghan alumni'—as its core members. It had links with al-Qaeda,

jihadi groups intensified their propaganda efforts, including on the web, to recruit fighters to send to those areas. Extremists have experimented with online platforms ever since, from LISTSERV and Internet Relay Chat (IRC) to password-protected forums and social media. Their activities have also expanded from indoctrination to fundraising, hacking and recruitment. The latest trend is characterised by a decline of extremist activity on Twitter and Facebook and a mushrooming of private groups on encrypted messaging services, in particular Telegram. As elsewhere, extremist social media recruitment is increasing in Indonesia, albeit with a distinctive pattern. Indonesian terrorist recruiters often invite people they already know in person to join the online forums, whereas in Europe and the United States it is more common for ISIS recruiters to identify potential targets on Twitter and Facebook.

A short history of online extremism in Indonesia

JI laid the ground for the formation of an online radical milieu by creating its first LISTSERV group, called Al-Bunyan, in 2000. At this time, 60–70 per cent of Indonesians still accessed the internet through public computers in internet cafes, schools and universities (Hill and Sen 2005; Yang Hui 2010). Al-Bunyan was mainly used to share news from the jihadi battlegrounds in Ambon and Poso. Most of its members were jihadi sympathisers, but non-jihadis were also allowed in, prompting occasional debate (IPAC 2015). One active participant in these debates was Imam Samudra, one of the perpetrators of the first Bali bombings in 2002 and a champion of online jihad. Samudra himself created some short-lived websites to claim responsibility for the Christmas Eve church bombings in 11 Indonesian cities in 2000, and to justify the Bali bombings (ICG 2002: appendix A; Fealy 2003).

Samudra was incarcerated in late 2002 but he nevertheless managed to inspire other JI members to create better websites and later managed to have a laptop smuggled into his prison cell. In 2004, he and the IT team he had put together before the Bali bombings established an online *pengajian* using the IRC-based mIRC chat utility. It was in the mIRC

---

although it operated independently. At its height, JI's network stretched across Indonesia, Malaysia, the Philippines, Singapore and Australia. The group has not committed any violent acts since 2007, when its last bastion in Poso was crushed by the Indonesian police. JI remains committed to the long-term struggle to establish an Islamic state in Indonesia, but for now is focused on rebuilding its capacity. Since late 2013, when ISIS split from the al-Qaeda-linked al-Nusra Front, many JI members and other Afghan alumni have been at the forefront of the anti-ISIS campaign because they remain loyal to al-Qaeda.

chat room that Samudra recruited new faces such as Agung Prabowo, a computer specialist (IPAC 2015). Agung helped Samudra create Anshar.net in 2005 to disseminate ideological content, military instructions and propaganda. Both men also worked with Noordin M. Top, the leader of the JI offshoot responsible for the Australian embassy bombing in 2004, the second Bali bombings in 2005 and the Jakarta hotel bombings in 2009.

After several JI-linked sites were banned in 2008, Samudra and his team created a password-protected site called Forum at-Tawbah, modelled on al-Qaeda's Global Islamic Media Front. Forum at-Tawbah was more exclusive than the mIRC group; only individuals approved by the administrator were allowed to join. The administrator also controlled the site's content, which was mostly taken from al-Qaeda media outlets (Yang Hui 2010). Another one of those involved in the development of at-Tawbah was Muhammad Jibril. A former JI operative like Samudra, he also created the popular jihadi news site, Arrahmah.com, in 2007.

Any online radical milieu is imbued with internal debate and criticism, and this has been the case in Indonesia as well. Around 2007–08, the followers of Aman Abdurrahman, then an up-and-coming jihadi ideologue, started to create blogs and websites featuring his writings and lectures. Aman, who went to jail in 2004 for running bomb-making classes, was highly critical of al-Qaeda-style jihad on the grounds that it focused on attacking the enemy without a clear long-term plan. He instead advocated a jihad aimed at establishing an Islamic state, a concept inspired by the Jordanian cleric Abu Muhammad al-Maqdisi (ICG 2010).

Yet another JI-linked site, Forum al-Busyro, emerged in 2010 after Forum at-Tawbah and a series of other extremist websites were shut down by the Indonesian government. At the time, the notion of individual jihad, including through online activism, was increasing in popularity following the mass arrests of extremists of all stripes in the aftermath of the break-up of a militant camp in Aceh (ICG 2010). Unlike its predecessor, Forum al-Busyro was run mainly by younger, less experienced activists and its membership was less exclusive, with membership drives announced periodically on jihadi websites. Non-vetted individuals were allowed to join from time to time, a risk that the group was willing to take in order to attract new recruits.

With the rapid uptake of smartphones from 2011, sympathisers without any formal links to established groups became even more active online. New websites, blogs and Facebook accounts sprang up, either tied to known jihadi publishers or run independently by individual sympathisers. As with other forms of media content in the digital era, the line between the producer and the consumer of extremist propaganda has become blurred. Indeed, Indonesia's vibrant jihadi community is characteristic of online radical milieus, which 'encompass a wide cross-section of producers and consumers, from [terrorist] organisations to the globally dispersed array of 'jihobbyists' [...] with no formal links to any violent jihadi organisation, all contributing to the everyday making and remaking of the violent jihadi narrative' (Conway 2012: 13).

As 'jihobbyists' became more involved in online forums—sometimes working with experienced terrorists—there were more crossovers from online to offline activism, and vice versa. A notable example was Arif Wicaksana, also known as Handolah al-Khurasani. Educated at a JI-linked school in Solo, Central Java, Handolah married into a blueblood jihadi family. In 2010 he founded Forum al-Busyro. After two years he decided that cyberactivism was no longer enough, so he joined Mujahidin Indonesia Timur (MIT), a Poso-based terrorist group led by Santoso. With Handolah's help, in late 2012 MIT hacked and defaced the websites of the military and the police, in addition to kidnapping and killing several police personnel in Poso.[2] Fortunately, a plot by another terrorist cell to bomb the US consulate general in Surabaya in 2012 was less successful. The members of the cell had met through Facebook, although they had also participated separately in extremist *pengajian* at various mosques and universities (IPAC 2015). In this case, Facebook helped already radicalised individuals meet like-minded friends.

When the Syria conflict erupted in 2012, turning the country into a jihadi battlefield, Indonesian extremist websites enthusiastically reported and promoted the jihad there. In 2013, Aman Abdurrahman's followers set up Almustaqbal.net, the leading pro-ISIS website in the Indonesian language until being banned in 2015. They also set up several ISIS fan pages on Facebook, where they promoted travel (*hijrah*) to ISIS-held territories by framing the war as the final battle prophesised by the Prophet Muhammad in the seventh century. For some, such narratives provided a strong motivation to join the fight. For others, it was the stories of daily life under a utopian caliphate that provided the motivation. Meanwhile, the ISIS love stories written by a Malaysian woman known as the Bird of Jannah inspired women to join the terrorist group (Shubert 2015). Similarly, Siti Khadijah, an Indonesian woman who travelled to Syria with her family in 2014, posted pictures and notes of her experiences on her Facebook page, and patiently answered hundreds of comments from interested followers.

---

2 In October 2012, MIT kidnapped two policemen, hacked a West Sumatra police website and posted a threat directed at the counterterrorism force Detachment 88. When the bodies of the policemen were found a few days later, MIT claimed responsibility for their deaths. In December 2012, MIT posted a threat on a military website, before killing three more police personnel.

By mid-2015, however, the Institute for Policy Analysis of Conflict was observing a decline in extremist activity on social media in Indonesia (IPAC 2015), consistent with the global trend (Berger and Perez 2016). In particular, this was due to the growing resistance to ISIS propaganda from both the mainstream Muslim community and pro-al-Qaeda jihadis, as well as stricter policing by social media services. Faced with repeated suspensions of their Facebook and Twitter accounts, some ISIS supporters persisted in creating new accounts in order to keep up with news updates, while others searched for more secure and reliable platforms where they could discuss issues more openly and safely.

The switch to Telegram

The mobile application Telegram made international headlines when it was revealed that terrorists had used it to plot the Paris attacks of November 2015, which killed 130 people. Launched in 2013, Telegram claims to be the fastest and most secure messaging app. It allows users to quickly upload and share videos, text and audio messages. It also has end-to-end encryption, which other popular apps such as WhatsApp did not have when Telegram was launched. Telegram enjoys an image of independence from government because its founder, Paul Durov—formerly the owner of VKontakte, the Russian Facebook—has famously defied the Russian government on multiple occasions.[3] One pro-ISIS Telegram user said that she trusted the app because:

> The owner of Telegram is unwilling to share data with the intelligent [sic]. They are not like WhatsApp, Twitter, Facebook and Kik, which are paid to collect the data of Islamic State supporters (private Telegram group conversation, 15 August 2015).

Telegram has become a favourite platform for pro-ISIS groups in Indonesia since 2014 because of its perceived security and independence from government, all at zero cost. As of October 2016, ISIS supporters in Indonesia had established over a hundred public channels and dozens of private groups based on the Telegram app.

Telegram offers three layers of communication: public channels (used for broadcasting messages to large groups); private chat groups; and secret chats. Extremist groups use public channels to broadcast ISIS propaganda to as many people as possible. A channel can have an unlim-

---

3 In 2011, Durov refused to comply with a Russian government order to close the VKontakte account of Russian opposition leader Alexei Navalny. Following the Russia–Ukraine war in 2014, he again defied the government by refusing to release the personal details of Ukrainian opposition leaders (Walt 2016).

ited number of members; the biggest pro-ISIS channel has over 4,000 members.

In general, Telegram restricts the size of private chat groups to 200 members, although 'supergroups' can have up to 5,000 members. Pro-ISIS groups usually restrict membership to people recommended by the administrator or an existing member, but supergroups are less selective about who can join. The degree of selectiveness is best described as a spectrum: at one end are the semi-open groups meant for new sympathisers; in the middle are the groups created for more committed sympathisers; and at the other end are the very exclusive groups whose members are selected personally by terrorist leaders. The latter groups aim to groom the most committed and skilled members for terrorist operations. Sensitive matters are usually discussed through two-way secret chats that use a more secure level of encryption (client-to-client instead of client-server-client).

As shown in Figure 10.1, online recruitment of jihadis in Indonesia can be either top-down or peer-to-peer. There is an offline element in both cases; purely online recruitment is still very rare. In top-down recruitment, terrorist leaders or recruiters deliberately identify potential targets from among their social media and offline acquaintances. The recruiter then forms a very small group on Telegram where the new recruits are given detailed instructions on how to make explosives or plan an operation. Most Telegram groups, though, are formed through peer-to-peer recruitment. Most of the members would have been exposed to radical ideas before joining the group, either through *pengajian*, family or friends, including online friends.

Recruitment into a Telegram group usually starts with the members or teacher (*ustadz*) of an ISIS *pengajian* creating an informal online chat group to keep in touch with one another; over time, the group expands to include *pengajian* members from other mosques, other cities and even other countries (Nuraniyah 2015). The stories of three women (identified here as 'A', 'B' and 'C') represent the different ways in which people may become attracted to ISIS.

- 'A' was a member of an Islamist political party, the Prosperous Justice Party (Partai Keadilan Sejahtera, or PKS), but she left because she thought the female members acted like socialites. She then joined a Salafi *pengajian* because the theological teaching (*aqidah*) fitted her beliefs better. But she was still unsatisfied because the group 'lacked a sense of community (*ukhuwwah*)'. In late 2014, she became interested in the idea of a caliphate as propagated by ISIS and started attending a pro-ISIS *pengajian* in Jakarta. There, she met like-minded friends and joined a Telegram group set up by the members. She was so convinced that she had at last found the true Islamic community she had

Figure 10.1 Jihadi recruitment models in Indonesia, Europe and the United States

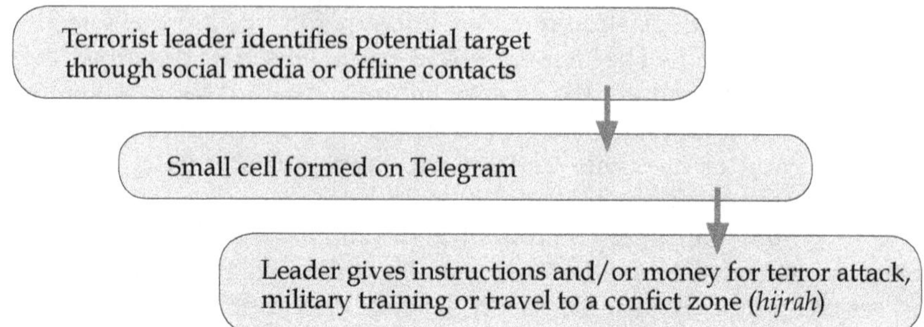

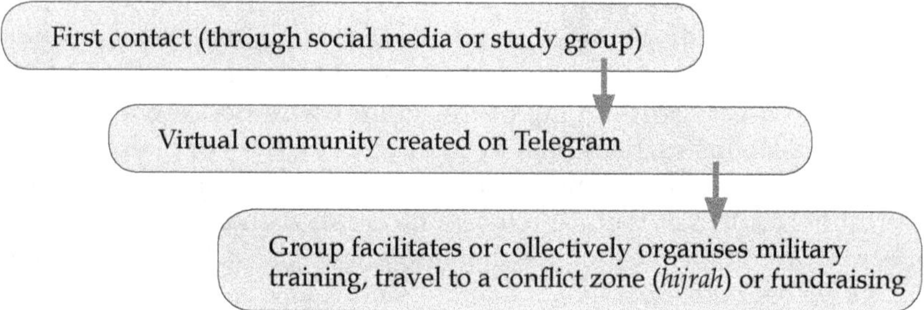

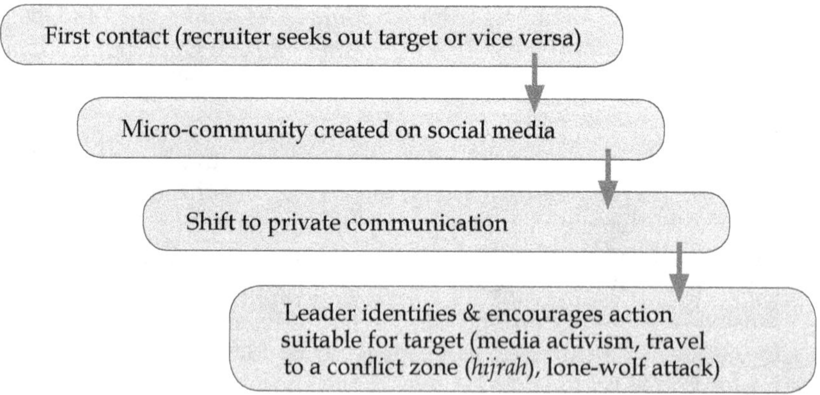

Source: Indonesian models: author; European/US recruitment model: Berger (2015: 19).

been longing for that she divorced her husband, who had refused to join (interview with ISIS sympathiser, Jakarta, 27 June 2015).

- 'B' came from a JI family in Solo. Although many JI members sided with the al-Qaeda-linked al-Nusra Front when ISIS split from al-Qaeda in late 2013, she and her husband chose to join ISIS. She quickly joined a pro-ISIS *pengajian* in Solo, and was invited to join several Telegram groups (private Telegram group conversation, 24 July 2016).
- 'C' was a newcomer to Salafi jihadism. Her family was not devout, but she was eager to learn more about Islam after divorcing her husband. During her religious studies, she became curious about ISIS because she wanted to discover the truth behind its grotesque media image. She then came across an international ISIS fan page on Facebook, befriended the Pakistani administrator and asked him to tell her about ISIS. After a series of online discussions, she became convinced that the media were wrong and that ISIS had indeed established a true caliphate. She searched for ISIS *pengajian* in Jakarta and decided to join. She also became active in several Telegram groups, both local and international. The *ustadz* at the *pengajian* introduced 'C' to an ISIS sympathiser, and they got married. Her husband was arrested in December 2015 for planning terrorist attacks in Jakarta and West Java (interview with ISIS sympathiser, Jakarta, 27 June 2015).

The Indonesian patterns of recruitment described above differ from the Western recruitment model, where the first contact usually takes place on social media (Figure 10.1). One reason for the difference is that it is easier for extremist groups to congregate in Indonesia than it is in the United States, Europe or even Malaysia (IPAC 2015). But there is only so much people can discuss during a typical *pengajian* session, as the *ustadz* usually dominates the conversation. Much of the personal bonding and networking happens afterwards, with chat groups playing an important role.

ENCRYPTED CHAT GROUPS: MORE BONDING, LESS PLOTTING

In this section I describe my findings from a study of two groups of ISIS sympathisers – one all-male and the other all-female – that I observed for over a year (June 2015 to August 2016). The two groups were selected based on the quantity and quality of their chats; the members of both tended to engage actively in conversation on a daily basis rather than just sharing information. They may not have been the most important ISIS groups, but because I was able to gain prolonged access to them, and interview some of their members, I was able to combine a quantitative with a qualitative analysis.

The quantitative content analysis is based on 3,163 messages produced by the groups during a two-week period. Despite having over 600 members, the men's group generated only 848 messages (an average of 60 messages per day) during the period, whereas the women's group, with only 109 members, exchanged 2,315 messages (around 165 messages per day). The content of the chats could be categorised under 15 broad headings (Figure 10.2). Two of the three most-discussed items for both groups were personal issues and recruitment; making up the top three for the men was discussion about which groups of Muslims could be classed as infidels (*takfir*), and for the women, discussion of religion. Planning a terrorist attack came near the bottom of the list for the men, and wasn't discussed at all by the women.

In addition to my study of these two Telegram groups, I will discuss the case of a Telegram group led by Bahrun Naim in order to illustrate the unabated role of direct personal contact in establishing trust and carrying out a terrorist attack.

Content analysis

A common concern about encrypted chat is that it may increase the number of terror attacks by making cyberplotting more difficult to intercept. In the groups I studied, however, both female and male members mainly talked about mundane personal matters such as their pasts and their daily activities (swapping, for example, recipes or parenting tips); gossiped about fellow ISIS sympathisers; or discussed deeper personal issues such as problems with their spouses and families. Even the women's religious discussions, which made up 8.5 per cent of the content of their chats, had a personal element: they mostly discussed Islamic rulings on polygamy (for example, whether Islam allowed a man to take a second wife without the permission of the first), focusing on their personal experiences.[4] The fact that both men and women often referred to the group as 'family' indicates how close their relationships had become.

Part of the in-group bonding process involves setting clear definitions of the 'other'. This may be why discussion of which groups of Muslims were 'real Muslims' and which were infidels (*takfir*) was the main topic of conversation among the men and the fifth most popular among the women. When group members talked about attacking the enemy, it was often just incitement rather than detailed plotting, although it is possible that they discussed such matters further in a one-on-one secret chat or in

4 Among the men, the main topic of religious discussion was the imminent end of the world as prophesised by Prophet Muhammad, and their desire to fight together in the final battle.

Figure 10.2 Content of chat group discussions (% of messages)

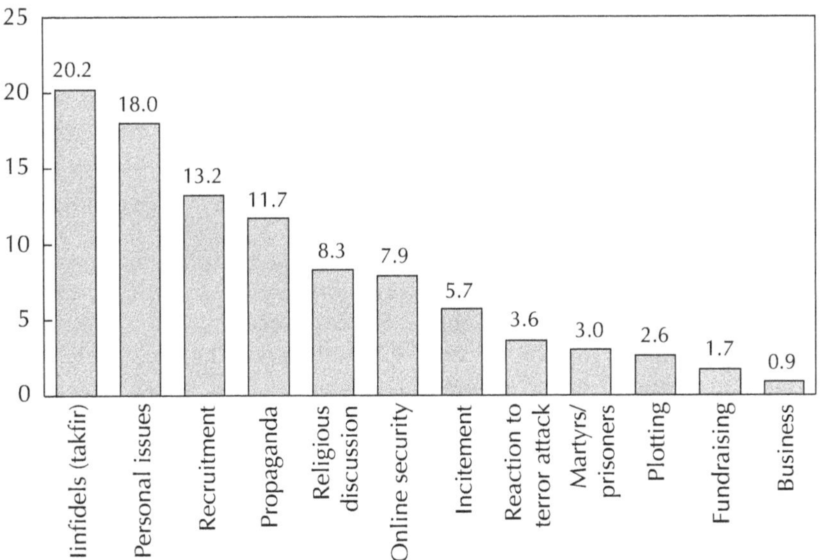

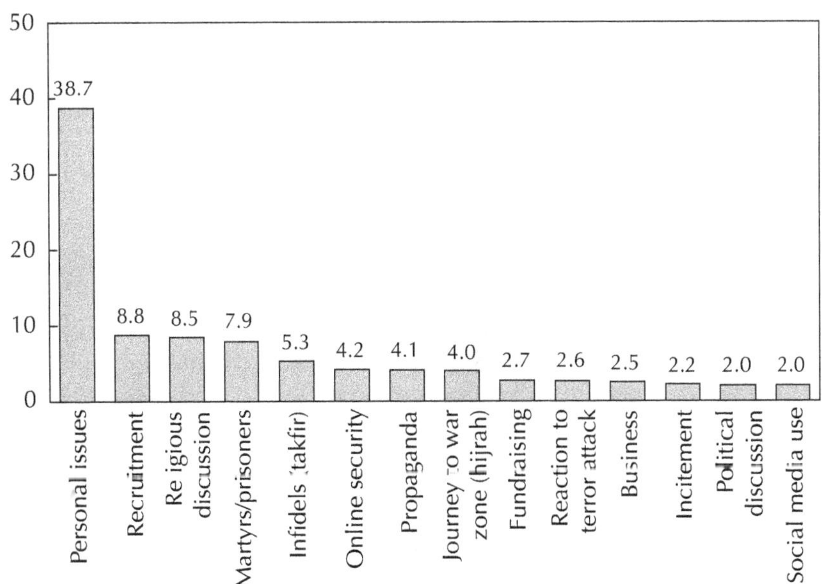

Source: Author.

a more exclusive chat group. Incitement to violence made up 5.7 per cent of the content of the men's conversations, whereas plotting—defined loosely as identifying a specific target and/or terror weapon—made up only 2.6 per cent.

While the topics of conversation generally seemed harmless, many of the members engaged in low-risk activities that aided terrorism, such as fundraising and providing logistical support (as would occur also in a traditional radical milieu). What the women lacked in interest for incitement and plotting, they made up for in enthusiasm for fundraising and helping to arrange *hijrah*. Thus, the women conversed more often than the men about collecting donations for the families of convicted and 'martyred' terrorists, and were more likely than the men to boast of facilitating *hijrah* either by providing contacts in Syria or by arranging itineraries for would-be fighters. Indeed, social media has empowered female jihadis to become more active than ever before. While these women mainly play a supportive role, it is one that is crucial to the overall operations of extremist groups.

My study confirmed that social media groups excel at broadening and strengthening extremist networks. Thus, recruitment was the second most-discussed topic for the women's group and the third most-discussed topic for the men's group. It includes introducing members to one another, arranging offline meetings or *pengajian*, and connecting different groups. This has made it easier for extremists in Indonesia to contact pro-ISIS Indonesian migrant workers in East Asia and the Gulf states as well as fellow sympathisers in Southeast Asia, the Middle East and Europe; these connections in turn have increased extremists' access to resources and *hijrah* routes.[5] Such social media connections often lead to long-lasting personal relationships that further strengthen global terrorist networks.

Telegram as a virtual support group

The chief reason that personal issues dominate group discussion is that the Telegram community has turned into a support group for individuals who have become estranged from their families and communities owing to their commitment to ISIS. These online friendships often facilitate the formation of new relationships in the real world. Like other jihadi forums (Hegghammer 2014), however, Telegram groups experience problems with online fraud, spying and infiltration. That partly explains why plotting almost always involves face-to-face meetings.

5 The new recruits also include Indonesian students studying in the Middle East, some of whom have joined ISIS in Syria (Bubalo et al. 2016).

The path to becoming part of a violent extremist group is not easy. Many members of the groups I studied claimed they had become alienated from their families, teachers and neighbours because of their outspoken support for ISIS. Some had been disowned by their families, and some talked about escaping from home, leading other members to offer shelter (private Telegram group conversation, 5 November 2015, 17 October 2016).

A common problem discussed by both male and female members was whether they should obey parents who disapproved of their religious beliefs (*aqidah*), as exemplified by the following conversation.

> A: Brother, I have a question. If I quit my job as a security guard and upset my parents, is that OK? I don't want to become idolatrous (*thaghut*) by becoming a security guard. The company [I work for] belongs to some infidels. [...] They make me delay performing prayers because of my duties. [...] It doesn't make sense. [...] If it weren't for my parents I'd rather become a trader.
>
> B: Brother, it is only a sin if you commit an immoral act (*maksiat*) and make your parents cry.
>
> A: Can anybody give me a job? Please help me brothers. [...] My parents don't want to listen to me anymore. [...] They still like visiting and praying in the graveyard [which is comparable to idolatry according to Salafi jihadi ideology] [...] but I still live with them (private Telegram group conversation, 8 August 2016).

One male user said that he would be more willing to conduct a suicide operation if he could be sure that his family would be taken care of after he died (private Telegram group conversation, 10 August 2016).

For some, a virtual friendship could be as good as or even better than a friendship in the offline world. Some members admitted to not having any like-minded friends (*teman seaqidah*) in the real world because there was no pro-ISIS *pengajian* in their hometown; the online community therefore meant a lot to them. One member said that she felt closer to her online Telegram group than to her own family:

> How happy I am to have friends like you guys. [...] Even though we only know each other in the cyberworld [we are] closer than those living under the same roof. [...] Honestly, I'm crying now (private Telegram group conversation, 17 September 2016).

The online community, with the 24-hour access it provides to like-minded friends, helps convince members that they are not alone, and that their beliefs are right while those of the rest of the world are wrong. Members seek advice as well as moral and material support from one another. They regularly donate to the families of convicted and killed terrorists through jihadi charity groups such as the Azzam Dakwah Centre and Gerakan Sehari Seribu (Gashibu). This type of material support has helped build some sort of social security system for the jihadi community. Some members meet their future spouses online, and some, including jailed terrorists, have even married by phone or video call. In fact, there is an online dating site for ISIS supporters called Channel Ta'aruf.

While friendships are nurtured online, offline activities remain an important part of the relationship-building process. After sharing many discussions and intimate chats online, members and sometimes the whole group decide to meet up. One male group of Telegram users held a gathering in early 2016 at a camping ground in West Java, with members encouraged to bring their families along. Hundreds of people attended the event, and pictures of the gathering were shared with the Telegram group afterwards.

The rise of a network of radicalised Indonesian maids in Hong Kong illustrates how relationships forged online can help to internationalise local extremist networks. The Hong Kong group initially consisted of 20 women, including at least one Filipina, who had met at a Salafi *pengajian* in Hong Kong around 2013.[6] They developed ties to jihadi groups and clerics in Indonesia, some of whom came to Hong Kong to give sermons and collect donations, seeing the maids as cash cows for the jihadi cause. Other Indonesian jihadis began to contact the group through Telegram, asking for money for *hijrah*. Some of the migrant workers wired monthly stipends to their jailed terrorist husbands, whom they adored as heroes of jihad. One radicalised migrant worker transferred $575 to her husband in Tangerang (near Jakarta) to fund a bomb attack that was foiled in December 2015 (Jakarta Globe 2015).

With their good English skills and regular internet access, the migrant workers found it easy to contact foreign terrorist fighters on social media. These international contacts could be very helpful. In March 2015, for example, they were used to help Syahputra, a former policeman from Sumatra, to travel to Syria. When the person who was supposed to pick Syahputra up at the Turkish border did not show up, he turned to a particular Telegram group for assistance. The male members refused to help as they suspected him of being a government spy, but one of the maids in the group contacted an Afghan friend in Syria, who arranged for someone to smuggle Syahputra into ISIS territory. The maids also provided a transit route for would-be foreign fighters and their families. To avoid suspicion, fighters usually transited through a third country when travelling to a conflict zone. Many chose Hong Kong, where the Indonesian maids could help them find cheap accommodation and pose as tourists.

---

6 In mid-2014 these women were expelled from the Salafi *pengajian* when it became clear that they were ISIS supporters.

Over time, the members of extremist Telegram groups develop mutual trust, to the extent that they do not hesitate to give money to online friends in need, or even to form business partnerships. They nevertheless remain wary of new members because there have been several instances of online fraud. The most infamous of these was the case of Susan Ermawati (alias Susan Lubis), who allegedly made over $10,000 by posing as a *hijrah* agent for ISIS extremists. She offered to provide fake passports and tickets for would-be fighters from Java, Medan and Makassar, but ran away with their money. In July 2015, a message was posted on all pro-ISIS social media warning the online community that Susan was a con artist. Group members have since developed ways to avoid online fraud: by conducting background checks, by setting up video calls and in-person meetings, and by sending friends who live near a suspected infiltrator to investigate. It is apparent that even violent extremist groups are not protected from the wave of cybercrime that has hit Indonesia.

The members of the groups I studied were aware of the risk of surveillance and infiltration, and online security was the sixth most-discussed topic for both groups. Tech-savvy members taught others how to conceal their Internet Protocol (IP) addresses and increase the security of their communications using free apps such as CyberGhost. If a member started talking about a terror plot, other members would quickly advise him to talk about it in a private online chat or in person. A typical response would be:

> Sorry, don't talk about the operation (*amaliyah*) here [...] Look after your safety (*amniyah*) [...] or you will get caught before you even start (private Telegram group conversation, 18 March 2016).

Surveillance concerns have made cyberplotting more problematic for extremists. In August 2016, a Telegram group lost 70 per cent of its members after some were arrested while conducting training exercises on a mountain in Central Java (Sohuturon 2016). It turned out that the plan had been posted online, although the exact location was not disclosed. Despite the risks, however, individuals in some groups, especially those that have developed a higher level of trust, continue to use Telegram to plan attacks.

Bahrun Naim's Telegram group

A Telegram group led by Bahrun Naim, an Indonesian who joined ISIS in Syria in late 2014, provides an example of Telegram-based recruitment and plotting. A social media celebrity in the jihadi community, Naim actively interacts with hundreds of followers on Facebook and Twitter and runs a website where he regularly posts bomb-making instructions, praises successful terror attacks in Indonesia and encourages do-it-yourself jihad.

In June 2015, Naim and an old friend from Solo, Ibadurrahman (alias Ibad), formed a new Telegram group called the Explosives and Electrochemistry Division. Its eight members were selected from an existing Telegram group (called Junud Daulah Khilafah, or JDK) that had been handpicked from people Ibad and Naim knew personally. Naim gave Ibad the money to train the group in bomb-making (trial dossier of Ibad, 18 August 2015).

The son of a former JI activist, Ibad had learned how to make explosives in 2012 while still in junior secondary school. He attended the bomb-making classes run by Badri Hartono, the leader of the Solo-based group al-Qaidah Indonesia, and subsequently joined Tim Hisbah, an anti-vice vigilante group. Ibad and Naim had known each other since they were children, as both had grown up in the same neighbourhood. After Naim left for Syria, they kept in touch through Facebook and Telegram. Among the people Ibad recruited for Naim's Telegram group were Arif Hidayatullah, a high-school mate of Naim's and a member of JDK, and Nur Rohman, a member of JDK and Tim Hisbah whom Naim had met in 2014 at a terrorist training class in Solo.

Among other things, Naim taught his Telegram disciples how to make car bombs and how to hack credit cards. The Telegram cell members were responsible for at least five failed plots and a suicide bombing that succeeded only in killing the perpetrator. The first plot, a bombing operation targeting a church, a Buddhist temple and a police post in Solo, was thwarted by the police in August 2015. In September 2015, Naim instructed Arif, Nur Rohman and another cell member to make more bombs. The plan was to kill Jakarta's Christian governor, bomb a Jewish and a Shi'a gathering in Bogor, murder the Indonesian police chief and attack random Westerners (testimony of Arif Hidayatullah, 24 December 2015). None of this happened because Arif was arrested in December 2015. Nur Rohman managed to escape and eventually used the explosives to conduct a suicide bombing operation at a Solo police station in July 2016, which killed no one but himself. A police investigation revealed that he was linked to another of Naim's Telegram cells in Batam, which had allegedly discussed a plan to fire a rocket into Singapore (IPAC 2016). In fact, however, the cell members had no rockets.

As the above cases show, the plotting of a terrorist attack is rarely instigated solely by individual online learning. In fact, Indonesia has seen only two lone-wolf attacks,[7] and there is little reason to believe

---

7 These were the bombing of an A&W restaurant in Jakarta in November 2006 and the Bekasi bicycle bombing in September 2010.

that the number will increase significantly in the near future. The general assumption is that in a country with a strong communal culture such as Indonesia, jihad is very much a social activity: people become radicalised through mosques and schools, and the fervour for jihad is inherited from the family. Moreover, it appears that for an individual to commit a socially unacceptable, violent act, a complex psychological mechanism is required in which most individuals would need to block out alternative perspectives and embed themselves in a support group that confirms their own views and normalises what is otherwise abnormal behaviour (Behr et al. 2013). The online community provides such social support and, in some cases, a 'surrogate command and control network' (Pantucci 2011: 36). The case studies presented above demonstrate the importance of social interaction with like-minded individuals in the radicalisation process, a process that is increasingly incorporating digital media platforms.

CONCLUSION

Private chat groups have not necessarily turned into virtual training grounds for terrorists, nor have they produced an army of radicalised lone wolves. For a start, terrorist leaders are aware that they cannot trust anyone they have only met online to carry out high-risk activities. Indonesia has not seen a major bombing attack since 2009 because the most skilled terrorists have been arrested or killed. The sheer number of terrorist manuals online has not done much to improve the capabilities of would-be terrorists; they also need training in the real world to translate that abstract knowledge into practical skills. It remains rare for individuals to become radicalised solely by reading materials online, although this may have less to do with the limited power of communication technology than with the fact that it is relatively easy to join extremist study groups at mosques.

The bad news is that social media does enable extremists to expand their networks and resources more cheaply and faster than in the past. Once, JI recruitment relied heavily on kinship and blood ties. With the rise of social media, however, extremist groups are able not only to maintain or reactivate old networks, but also to reach out to people outside their traditional recruitment pools, such as diaspora communities of students and migrant workers whose relatively higher incomes provide welcome financial resources. Better-educated, tech-savvy individuals from non-jihadi backgrounds who develop an interest in extremist ideas can find a safe space to meet like-minded friends on the internet, which may serve as a bridge to more active involvement in violence.

Social media has also allowed women to progress from being 'mujahidin baby factories' to becoming propagandists and public relations officers responsible for ensuring international cooperation. After seeing videos of ISIS women's brigades and female suicide bombers in Palestine, some Indonesian women have even discussed the possibility of becoming active combatants.

This flourishing online radical milieu cannot be eradicated simply through censorship or online counternarratives. Online forums are a goldmine of information, so it is in the interests of counterterrorism agencies to monitor rather than ban them. Infiltration, if conducted effectively, can wreak havoc in a group by instilling doubts and prompting debate among online activists. One of the most valuable insights from the Telegram groups I studied is that many members turn to the online community for a sense of belonging and acceptance. More research is needed on why young, alienated youths turn to online extremist communities, and what can be done to counter this, beyond simply cutting off online communications. Offline efforts remain crucial to prevent individuals from deepening their involvement in a radical online community. Too often families and communities turn away from these troubled individuals when they need their support the most. The government needs to work with grassroots leaders and civil society organisations to help parents and family members recognise early signs of radicalisation, so that they can engage with and support those vulnerable to radicalisation rather than treating them as outcasts.

REFERENCES

Arquilla, J., and D. Ronfeldt (2001) *Networks and Netwars: The Future of Terror, Crime, and Militancy*, RAND, Santa Monica. Available at http://www.rand.org/pubs/monograph_reports/MR1382/index.html.

Baym, N.K. (2010) *Personal Connections in the Digital Age*, Polity, Cambridge.

Behr, I., A. Reding, C. Edwards and L. Gribbon (2013) 'Radicalization in the digital era', RAND Europe, Brussels and Cambridge. Available at http://www.rand.org/content/dam/rand/pubs/research_reports/RR400/RR453/RAND_RR453.pdf.

Bendrath, R. (2003) 'The American cyberangst and the real world—any link?', in R. Latham (ed.) *Bombs and Bandwidth: The Emerging Relationship between IT and Security*, New Press, New York: 49–73.

Benson, D.C. (2014) 'Why the internet is not increasing terrorism', *Security Studies*, 23(2): 293–328.

Berger, J.M. (2015) 'Tailored online interventions: the Islamic State's recruitment strategy', *CTC Sentinel*, 8(10): 19–23.

Berger, J.M., and H. Perez (2016) 'The Islamic State's diminishing returns on Twitter: how suspensions are limiting the social networks of English-speaking ISIS supporters', George Washington Program on Extremism Occasional

Paper, February. Available at https://cchs.gwu.edu/sites/cchs.gwu.edu/files/downloads/Berger_Occasional%20Paper.pdf.

Bubalo, A., S. Jones and N. Nuraniyah (2016) 'Indonesian students in Egypt and Turkey', Lowy Institute Report, April. Available at https://www.lowyinstitute.org/publications/indonesian-students-egypt-and-turkey.

Conway, M. (2012) 'From al-Zarqawi to al-Awlaki: the emergence and development of an online radical milieu', *CTX: Combating Terrorism Exchange*, 2(4): 12–22.

Fealy, G. (2003) 'Hating Americans: Jemaah Islamiyah and the Bali bombings', *International Institute for Asian Studies (IIAS) Newsletter*, 31: 3–4, July. Available at iias.asia/sites/default/files/IIAS_NL31_0304.pdf.

Hegghammer, T. (2014) 'Interpersonal trust on jihadi internet forums', unpublished paper, Norwegian Defence Research Establishment (FFI), Kjeller, 19 February. Available at hegghammer.com/_files/interpersonal_trust.pdf.

Helfstein, S. (2012) 'Edges of radicalization: ideas, individuals and networks in violent extremism', Combatting Terrorism Centre (CTC), Westpoint, February. Available at https://www.ctc.usma.edu/v2/wp-content/uploads/2012/06/CTC_EdgesofRadicalization.pdf.

Hill, D., and K. Sen (2005) *The Internet in Indonesia's New Democracy*, Routledge, London and New York.

Holbrook, D. (2015) 'A critical analysis of the role of the internet in the preparation and planning of acts of terrorism', *Dynamics of Asymmetric Conflict*, 8(2): 121–33.

Homeland Security Institute (2009) 'The internet as a terrorist tool for recruitment and radicalization of youth', Arlington, 24 April. Available at http://www.homelandsecurity.org/docs/reports/Internet_Radicalization.pdf.

ICG (International Crisis Group) (2002) 'Indonesia backgrounder: how the Jemaah Islamiyah terrorist network operates', Asia Report No. 43, 11 December. Available at https://d2071andvip0wj.cloudfront.net/43-indonesia-backgrounder-how-the-jemaah-islamiyah-terrorist-network-operates.pdf.

ICG (International Crisis Group) (2010) 'Indonesia: jihadi surprise in Aceh', Asia Report No. 189, 20 April. Available at http://old.crisisgroup.org/_/media/Files/asia/south-east-asia/indonesia/189%20Indonesia%20-%20Jihadi%20Surprise%20in%20Aceh.pdf.

IPAC (Institute for Policy Analysis of Conflict) (2015) 'Online activism and social media usage among Indonesian extremists', IPAC Report No. 24, 30 October. Available at http://file.understandingconflict.org/file/2015/10/IPAC_24_Online_Activism_Social_Media.pdf.

IPAC (Institute for Policy Analysis of Conflict) (2016) 'The failed Solo suicide bombing and Bahrun Naim's network', IPAC Report No. 30, 29 July. Available at http://file.understandingconflict.org/file/2016/08/The_Failed_Solo_Suicide_Bombing_and_Bahrun_Naim%E2%80%99s_Network.pdf.

Jakarta Globe (2015) 'Suspects in terror raids planned to bomb Shiites, Densus says', *Jakarta Globe*, 20 December. Available at http://jakartaglobe.beritasatu.com/news/suspects-terror-raids-planned-bomb-shiites-densus-says/.

Jenkins, B. (2011) 'Stray dogs and virtual armies: radicalization and recruitment to jihadist terrorism in the United States since 9/11', Occasional Paper, RAND, Santa Monica. Available at http://www.rand.org/content/dam/rand/pubs/occasional_papers/2011/RAND_OP343.pdf.

Kenney (2010) 'Beyond the internet: *mētis*, *techne*, and the limitations of online artifacts for Islamist terrorists', *Terrorism and Political Violence*, 22(2): 177–97.

Klausen, J. (2015) 'Tweeting the jihad: social media networks of Western foreign fighters in Syria and Iraq', *Studies in Conflict & Terrorism*, 38(1): 1–22.

Klausen, J., E. Barbieri, A. Zelin and A. Reichlin-Melnick (2012) 'The YouTube jihadists: a social network analysis of Al-Muhajiroun's YouTube propaganda campaign', *Perspectives on Terrorism*, 6(1). Available at http://www.terrorismanalysts.com/pt/index.php/pot/article/view/klausen-et-al-youtube-jihadists/html.

Malthaner, S. (2010) 'The radical milieu: conceptualizing the social environment of radicalization and terrorist violence', unpublished paper, University of Bielefeld, Bielefeld, November.

Malthaner, S., and P. Waldmann (2014) 'The radical milieu: conceptualizing the supportive social environment of terrorist groups', *Studies in Conflict & Terrorism*, 37(12): 979–98.

Mesch, G.S., and I. Talmud (2006) 'Online friendship formation, communication channels, and social closeness', *International Journal of Internet Science*, 1(1): 29–44.

Nuraniyah N. (2015) 'More than a fanclub', *Inside Indonesia*, 3 December. Available at http://www.insideindonesia.org/more-than-a-fanclub.

Pantucci, R. (2011) 'A typology of lone wolves: preliminary analysis of lone Islamist terrorists', Developments in Radicalisation and Political Violence, International Centre for the Study of Radicalisation and Political Violence, London, March. Available at http://icsr.info/wp-content/uploads/2012/10/1302002992ICSRPaper_ATypologyofLoneWolves_Pantucci.pdf.

Prucha, N., and A. Fisher (2013) 'Tweeting for the caliphate: Twitter as the new frontier for jihadist propaganda', *CTC Sentinel*, 6(6): 19–22.

Ramakrishna, K. (2010) 'Self-radicalisation and the Awlaki connection', RSIS Commentaries No. 075, S. Rajaratnam School of International Studies (RSIS), Nanyang Technological University, Singapore. Available at http://dr.ntu.edu.sg/bitstream/handle/10220/6622/RSIS0752010.pdf?sequence=1.

Rogan, H. (2007) 'Al-Qaeda's online media strategies: from Abu Reuter to Irhabi 007', FFI-rapport 2007/02729, Norwegian Defence Research Establishment (FFI), Kjeller, 1 December. Available at https://www.ffi.no/no/Rapporter/07-02729.pdf.

Sageman, M. (2008) 'The next generation of terror', *Foreign Policy*, 8 October. Available at http://foreignpolicy.com/2009/10/08/the-next-generation-of-terror/.

Shubert, A. (2015) 'The women of ISIS: who are they?', *CNN*, 29 May. Available at http://edition.cnn.com/2015/05/29/middleeast/who-are-the-women-of-isis/.

Sieber (2006) 'International cooperation against terrorist use of the internet', *Revue Internationale de Droit Pénal*, 77: 395–449. Available at www.cairn.info/revue-internationale-de-droit-penal-2006-3-page-395.htm.

Sohuturon M. (2016) 'Polisi gagalkan upaya pengibaran bendera ISIS di Sindoro' [Police thwart ISIS flag-raising attempt in Sindoro], *CNN Indonesia*, 17 August. Available at http://www.cnnindonesia.com/nasional/20160817182542-12-152044/polisi-gagalkan-upaya-pengibaran-bendera-isis-di-sindoro/.

Sproul, L., and S. Kiesler (1986) 'Reducing social context cues: electronic mail in organizational communication', *Management Science*, 32(11): 1,492–512.

Stenersen, A. (2008) 'The internet: a virtual training camp?', *Terrorism and Political Violence*, 20(2): 215–33.

Stevens, T., and P.R. Neumann (2009) *Countering Online Radicalisation: A Strategy for Action*, International Centre for the Study of Radicalisation and Political Violence (ICSR), London.

Sureka, A., P. Kumaraguru, A. Goyal and S. Chhabra (2010) 'Mining YouTube to discover extremist videos, users and hidden communities', paper presented at the 6th Asia Information Retrieval Societies Conference (AIRS 2010), Taipei, 1–3 December. Available at http://precog.iiitd.edu.in/Publications_files/AS_PK_AG_SC_AIRS-2010.pdf.

Thomas, T.L. (2003) 'Al Qaeda and the internet: the danger of "cyberplanning"', *Parameters: US Army War College*, 33(1): 112–23.

Walt, V. (2016) 'With Telegram, a reclusive social media star rises again', *Fortune*, 23 February. Available at http://fortune.com/telegram-pavel-durov-mobile-world-congress/.

Weimann, G. (2004) 'Cyberterrorism: how real is the threat?', United States Institute of Peace Special Report 119, Washington DC, December. Available at http://www.usip.org/sites/default/files/sr119.pdf.

Weimann, G. (2006) *Terror on the Internet: The New Arena, the New Challenges*, United States Institute of Peace Press, Washington DC.

Yang Hui, J. (2010) 'The internet in Indonesia: development and impact of radical websites', *Studies in Conflict & Terrorism*, 33(2): 171–91.

Zelin, A. (2013) 'The state of global jihad online: a qualitative, quantitative and cross-lingual analysis', New America Foundation, Washington DC.

PART 4

Knowledge

11 Digitalising knowledge: education, libraries, archives

Kathleen Azali

This chapter presents an overview of the digitalisation of knowledge, specifically in relation to education, libraries and archives in Indonesia. After providing background on the broader academic field to which this study relates, I demonstrate how the tropical, humid climatic conditions of the archipelago, and the historical contexts of colonial and autocratic regimes, have affected libraries and archives in Indonesia. My main theoretical and empirical focus is on the digitalising of knowledge, which started around the turn of the twenty-first century. I analyse not only the library and information science (LIS) profession in the higher education and government sectors, but also initiatives involving open-source materials, the visual arts and music, among others. I conclude by highlighting various historical precedents and arguing for more socio-political analysis of the construction of knowledge in both conventional and digitalised libraries and archives.

I also have to mention my own position and limitations: while I have a longstanding interest in the field, I have never undergone any formal training in LIS. My encounters, instead, have been facilitated by my position as the founder of an independent library in 2008, which put me in contact with various interlocutors involved in archiving processes both within and outside the LIS profession. LIS, and technical systems in general, requires very careful attention to mechanisms and precise detail. In Indonesia, the 'great divide' (Bowker et al. 1997) between social sciences and cultural studies on the one hand, and LIS and the analysis of technical systems on the other, remains wide. Readers interested in more in-depth discussions of education, libraries and archives in Indonesia are therefore encouraged to follow up on the relevant references included in this article.

BACKGROUND

Over the past two decades, the ways in which we acquire, access, exchange and interact with information have changed dramatically. All over the world, the ubiquitous growth of digital technologies has brought massive changes to the ways information is collected, stored and accessed. The new technologies have had a significant impact on the traditional gatekeepers of information storage and access, such as educational institutions, libraries and archives. The rise of digital technology has also triggered numerous academic and popular publications on the future of learning (Davidson and Goldberg 2009), the changing functions of libraries (Lankes 2012: Palfrey 2015) and the role of archiving in the digital age (Herr-Stephenson et al. 2011; Xing et al. 2011). Discussions have tended to focus on technological advancement, the falling costs of consumer technology, the World Wide Web, and multifunctional mobile phones, digital cameras and other portable devices. However, the enthusiasm about the ease of digital recording frequently lulls people into archival complacency. Whereas digital recording may have become easier and cheaper, preservation and archiving are subject to rapid technical obsolescence and physical decay, making the process of ensuring interoperability and longevity more difficult and costly.

The increased use of and reliance on digital resources have also blurred the boundaries between traditionally distinct information organisations, leading to what some have called a digital convergence of libraries, archives and museums (LAMs). This digital convergence is a strong argument for a break with 'the silos of the LAMs' and for greater collaboration between the various organisations (Zorich, Waibel and Erway 2008). Pointing to various historical precedents, some argue that the recent developments should be considered a *re*convergence rather than a convergence of LAMs (Given and McTavish 2010). Common topics of discussion on both sides are the increasingly porous boundaries between libraries, archives, museums and other institutions, and their overlapping functions.

Scholars from a diverse range of disciplines—anthropology, literary and cultural studies, history, sociology, political science and law, among others—have started studying archives and libraries as sites of knowledge production (Manoff 2004). There is increased awareness of the relations between information, knowledge, ideological construction and power, particularly through high-profile legal cases as well as postmodern and post-structural scholarship (Foucault 1972; Derrida 2009). Post-colonial and cultural studies scholars have also highlighted the relations between knowledge structures and colonial or imperial state power (Said 1994), as keenly felt in post-colonial Southeast Asia (Anderson 2013), including Indonesia. Stoler (2002, 2009), for instance, has demonstrated the significant implications of archives for acts of governance. The seemingly neutral, value-free forms, taxonomies and classification systems of archives define and codify connections between secrecy, law and power. In line with the growing recognition that the personal and the political are intertwined, the scope of archival works has also widened. More intimate, personal documents such as family photographs, recipes, medical guides and folksongs now share a space with government documents, court proceedings and classified state papers.

These developments have contributed to a broader notion of how records can be used (their functions and practices) and what they represent (their authenticity, reliability, authority). The use, storage, classification and circulation of information through archives and libraries therefore have very significant social, legal, political, economic and cultural consequences, as each standard or category brings visibility and advantages to some points of view, and silences others. As Indonesia prepares to join the global, transnational circuit of information and digital technologies, there is a strong urgency to consider critically the foundations of knowledge construction in education, libraries and archives.

THE GEOGRAPHICAL AND HISTORICAL CONTEXTS

Libraries and archives in Indonesia, as in many places around the world, are deeply intertwined with the geographical and historical conditions of the nation. The country's tropical, humid climate and the geopolitical conditions of thousands of islands at different stages of infrastructural development make preservation a demanding task. The diverse cultures and hundreds of languages of more than 300 ethnic groups bring further complications and challenges to the tasks of archiving and building interoperability and classification standards.

Statistics on the number of libraries in Indonesia are highly divergent. An online map produced by the National Library (Perpustakaan Nasional) indicated that the country had 1,105 public libraries and 499 special libraries in July 2016.[1] Citing the National Library as his source, Ismail Fahmi, a consultant for Indonesia OneSearch, stated that Indonesia had a total of 25,728 libraries in December 2015, composed of 22,375

---

1 See http://pemetaan.perpusnas.go.id. At the time of my visit to the National Library on 19 July 2016, the website still seemed to be a work in progress, with many incorrect legends; for example, libraries belonging to hospitals and schools were mistakenly identified as subdistrict libraries (*perpustakaan kecamatan*). Ensuring and maintaining the integrity of the data down to the village (*kelurahan*) level will be a long, arduous process indeed.

school libraries, 845 libraries in higher education institutions, 1,506 public libraries and 1,002 special libraries.[2] In July 2016, Fahmi revised the total to 66,267 libraries, consisting of 61,621 school libraries, 1,106 higher education institution libraries, 2,354 public libraries and 1,186 special libraries (email communication, 19 July 2016).[3] The number of certified librarians has been estimated at around 2,500–3,500.[4]

It is not surprising that the figures differ, but we can discern a number of patterns. First, the number of certified librarians is much smaller than the stated number of libraries.[5] Second, schools have the highest, but also the most volatile, number of libraries (ranging from 22,000 to 62,000)—again, this is not surprising considering the lack of clarity on what constitutes a 'library' in a school.[6] Third, there are only around 1,500–2,400 public libraries. Lastly, mirroring the differences in the level of development across Indonesia, the libraries are concentrated in Java and have a highly uneven spread outside Java.

Indonesians frequently lambast themselves for a supposed lack of interest in reading (*minat baca*), bemoan the country's underdeveloped archive culture (*budaya arsip*) and point to the need to educate the nation (*mencerdaskan bangsa*) in response to their country's low Programme for International Student Assessment (PISA) scores. Nevertheless, libraries and archives in Indonesia continue to suffer from persistent, deep-seated problems, including a lack of funds, material resources, staff, and professional knowledge and skills. The small number of higher education institutions that offer LIS programs lack trained teaching staff and funding.[7]

---

2 See Fahmi's presentations at http://www.slideshare.net/IsmailFahmi3/indonesia-onesearch-latar-belakang-road-map-dan-progress.

3 The report of the 2016 Coordinating Meeting of Public Libraries (Rapat Koordinasi Perpustakaan Umum), published in the National Library's official magazine, *Warta*, stated that Indonesia had 1,495,238 libraries, of which only 149,132 (10.0 per cent) received government support.

4 Statistics on librarians certified by the National Library are available at http://pustakawan.perpusnas.go.id/.

5 The certification of competence process has long been decried as problematic, and the number of certified staff does not necessarily reflect the number of those working in an LIS profession. See Priyanto (n.d.) for discussion of the LIS professions and the effect of continuing education.

6 While the situation seems to be improving, decades of highly uneven development and poor education policy have caused a lack of libraries throughout most of Indonesia.

7 Currently, the supporting institutions for LIS in Indonesia comprise 15 universities offering diploma, bachelor and master degrees in LIS; libraries and other institutions staffed by library practitioners; the government through its support for the National Library, the National Archives, ministerial libraries and so on; and the Indonesian library associations, consisting of the

The library and information sector also suffers from low self-esteem and a poor public image. The sector offers poor remuneration and ill-defined career paths, and the jobs it provides are often viewed as mere administrative or clerical work. Many schools and academic institutions do not offer reference services or interlibrary loan services, and some do not even have a library (Liauw 2008; Maesaroh and Genoni 2013).

In Indonesia, as in many other countries around the world, the history of libraries and archives has become deeply intertwined with the practical day-to-day needs of the government administration and bureaucracy, and has served to legitimise authority through the construction of history and identity. However, the resources on the history of libraries and archives in Indonesia are limited. Although the National Library was inaugurated only in 1980, its precursor dated back to the library of the colonial National Museum, which itself originated in the Batavian Society of Arts and Sciences (1778).[8] The National Archives (Arsip Nasional), meanwhile, originated in the State Archives (Landsarchief) established by the Dutch colonial government in 1892, a decade before the establishment of the General State Archives (Algemeen Rijksarchief) in the Netherlands (Basuki et al. 1996).

This colonial dimension needs to be taken into account when discussing the stunted, painful growth of LIS in Indonesia. Anderson (2013: 15) observes that during colonial times many archives were 'sequestered by a basic change in the language of state and of the citizenry', and describes how huge numbers of documents in the Dutch language—unintelligible to many—were leaked in bundles, peddled in flea markets and used to light stoves, insulate windows or wrap peanuts.[9] He goes on to say that

---

Indonesian Librarian Association (Ikatan Pustakawan Indonesia, or IPI) and the Indonesian Association of Library and Information Science Scholars (Ikatan Sarjana Ilmu Perpustakaan dan Informasi Indonesia, or ISIPII) (Basuki 2004b, 2013; Laksmi and Wijayanti 2015). See Priyanto (2016) for an overview of LIS education in Indonesia.

8 The National Library was founded through the integration of four institutions: the library of the National Museum; the libraries of two departments in the Library Development Centre—the Department of Political and Social History and the Department of Bibliography and Deposits; and the library of the territorial office of the Ministry of Education and Culture in Jakarta (Massil 1989: 476). Arguably, before the colonial period, the precursors of the government-run libraries could be found in the courts and kingdoms in Java, Sumatra, Bali and Sulawesi, which provided very limited access to collections of manuscripts for a select few (Håklev 2008: Ch. 3).

9 During the Dutch period, the Dutch language was not taught widely, and was spoken by only a small minority of educated elites. Nevertheless, the language became the basis of the legal system. During the Japanese period, many Dutch documents and speakers of Dutch were purged. Subsequent

'the rise of autocratic regimes, military or communist, during the height of the Cold War in Asia made for much more state secrecy than hitherto'. In Indonesia and elsewhere, the politicisation of information in various forms not only made source documents inaccessible, but also created public distrust of national archives together with the institutions (colonial government or autocratic regime) and the 'fact' production they served (see also Stoler 2002).

An outcome of this distrust of the state has been the growth of (quasi-)public collections initiated by individuals and funded privately or collectively (through families, friends, membership systems or a mix of grants). Notable examples include the HB Jassin Literature Documentation Centre (Pusat Dokumentasi Sastra HB Jassin, or PDS HB Jassin), Sinematek Indonesia, the Bung Hatta Library (Perpustakaan Bung Hatta) and the Idayu Library (Perpustakaan Idayu) in Jakarta, and the Medayu Agung Library (Perpustakaan Medayu Agung) in Surabaya. Typically, these collections have their own filing and classification systems, subjectively—even if meticulously—developed by their founders, most of whom did not have any formal training in LIS. Typically, too, the collections develop some sort of dependency on the founder: they decline with age, and rarely last beyond the founder's lifetime. There is still considerable reluctance to hand over private collections to the National Library or the National Archives. The people in charge of these collections commonly fear that documents will be damaged or neglected for ideological reasons or for lack of professional, technological or financial resources. They also fear that handing over certain types of documents may damage reputations and bring reprisals.

Indonesia has experienced many decades of political and military control over information and historiography, including the physical and symbolic presence of the military in libraries and archives.[10] As a consequence, future researchers will need to consider seriously the politics and history of archives and libraries, and to approach archives and libraries not only as sources but also as subjects of knowledge construction.[11]

---

generations have become further alienated from Dutch, which—in contrast to the colonial languages in, for example, Singapore, Malaysia or the Philippines—never took deep root in Indonesia.

10 See Jaquet (1979), Basuki et al. (1996), Liu and Tagliacozzo (2008), Minarchek (2015) and Zhou (2015) for historical and other overviews of the National Archives. An example of the relationship between archives and politics was the installation of a multimedia diorama on national history at the National Archives in 2008.

11 See Basuki's (2004b) criticism of the lack of academic rigour and consistency of existing accounts of the history of the National Library.

DEVELOPMENTS IN DIGITALISATION SINCE 1998

Early developments

The turn of the century coincided with the fall of the New Order authoritarian regime and the growth of the internet (Hill and Sen 2005). Since the start of the millennium, there have been sporadic attempts to build digital networks in Indonesia. In 1998, the Computer Network Research Group, the Knowledge Management Research Group and the Central Library of the Bandung Institute of Technology began to develop the Ganesha Digital Library (GDL), now known as the Indonesian Digital Libraries Network (IDLN, later IndonesiaDLN) (Basuki 2004a). By 2003 it had 87 partners, consisting of 73 institutions, 11 individuals and three internet cafes (*warung internet*, or *warnet*) (see also Fahmi 2002, 2005). In 1999, Petra Christian University in Surabaya established the Indonesian Christian University Virtual Library (InCU-VL), which later evolved into the SPEKTRA Virtual Library. The Ministry of Research, Technology and Higher Education purchased Docushare, software produced by Xerox for digital library development, and distributed it to various universities in 2002. The University of Indonesia in Jakarta, Gajah Mada University in Yogyakarta, Brawijaya University in Malang and various Islamic state universities also started digitising research documents and theses. In 2006, the Ministry of Research, Technology and Higher Education released the Indonesia Higher Education Network (InherentDL) as part of a long-term plan to improve communication among Indonesia's higher education institutions. However, most of the above portals have become inaccessible or have changed their address. This confirms that links and sources evaporate very quickly online (Zittrain, Albert and Lessig 2014), and that the 'inventors of the internet' are still struggling to devise a decentralised, permanent web (Finley 2016).

In December 2009 the Ministry of Research, Technology and Higher Education, in collaboration with the Indonesian Institute of Sciences (Lembaga Ilmu Pengetahuan Indonesia, or LIPI), launched Garba Rujukan Digital (Garuda), a portal specifically for academic and scientific references (http://garuda.dikti.go.id). Garuda provides an online union catalogue, based on metadata collected from various higher education institutions. It also provides server space and internet bandwidth, which the majority of higher education institutions in Indonesia would normally not be able to afford or maintain. In 2010, the ministry promised to 'upload electronically all scholarly works by students/lecturers/researchers/staff of any higher education institution' (Government Regulation No. 17/2010, article 7(2)). In 2011, the ministry issued a policy on the uploading of scholarly works and journals that strengthened the role of Garuda (Liauw and Genoni 2017). A similarly named but separate site called Portal Garuda, set up by the Indonesian branch of the Institute of Advanced Engineering and Science, acts as an Indonesian publication index, specifically indexing scientific journals in Indonesia (http://portalgaruda.org). By 1 August 2016 it had indexed 3,677 journals and 350,086 articles. LIPI also has its own Indonesian Scientific Journal Database (http://isjd.pdii.lipi.go.id/).

Indonesia OneSearch

Indonesia OneSearch was launched in March 2016 at the National Library.[12] Developed by Ismail Fahmi with the support of the library, Indonesia OneSearch can be considered a continuation of GDL and IndonesiaDLN, which Fahmi had maintained until starting postgraduate studies in information science at the University of Groningen in the Netherlands.[13] Indonesia OneSearch is the only portal that uses the Open Archives Initiative Protocol for Metadata Harvesting (OAI–PMH), a low-barrier mechanism for repository interoperability that allows users to harvest catalogue information from different kinds of repositories. Some of the library and archiving software packages that support OAI–PMH include INLISLite; Senayan Library Management Systems (SLiMS); Koha (an open-source library automation package originating in New Zealand); Dspace (open-source repository software, typically used for publishing scholarly and/or published digital content); EPrints; Open Journal Systems (OJS); and Open Monograph Press (OMP). Many of these software packages are used in Indonesia, albeit in an ad hoc, scattered fashion.

Indonesia OneSearch attempts to address three main problems: disjointed and insufficiently integrated information repositories; the high cost and time of accessing fragmented and rarely used documents; and unequal access to information. It harvests and indexes catalogues and makes them accessible from its own platform. Fahmi claims that the system has considerable advantages over portals such as Garuda, Portal Garuda and the Indonesian Scientific Journal Database, namely:

1 it indexes all sorts of collections (journals, records of existing library management systems, catalogues of institutional repositories);

---

12 The National Archives seems to be much slower in moving towards the digital; on my last visit to the archives on 20 May 2016, staff were still processing search requests manually. For a useful overview of the holdings at the National Archives, and an explanation of how to obtain access and materials, see Minarchek (2015).

13 See the presentation by Ismail Fahmi at https://www.youtube.com/watch?v=rkdzZCrFuTM.

2 it is mobile friendly—crucial in Indonesia where most people access the internet through their mobile phones;
3 it is interoperable and easy to update;
4 it has an attractive user interface and user-friendly features;
5 it is optimised for search engines—many results from Indonesia One-Search appear on Google, something that most journal and library catalogues in Indonesia fail to do;
6 it is rich in authors' data and metadata; and
7 it is supported by a system that allows the portal to be scaled up in future.

Registering a repository with Indonesia OneSearch is relatively simple in technical terms, especially if the library already has a library management system installed, but the library also needs to be legally registered.

Diffusion across the silos of the LAMs

Jogja Library for All, a collaborative network of libraries, was established in 2005 based on an agreement between the regional government and a number of universities in Yogyakarta. After a shaky start and many changes of address, it now seems to have settled on the address jogjalib.com.

In 2010, a community of SLiMS users based in Yogyakarta set up an alternative site called JogjaLib.Net, whose coverage extended beyond formal higher education institutions. According to Surachman (2011), 15 higher education institution libraries, 14 school libraries, six community or NGO libraries, three research institution libraries and two private libraries are participating in JogjaLib.Net, giving them access to 83,880 records. The site seems to function as an online community (*paguyuban*) for SLiMS users in Yogyakarta and as a testing ground for building a digital information network.

Open-source library management systems

SLiMS is a free, open-source library management system that automates many library functions, including bibliographic database, circulation and membership. It is built on free, open-source technology such as PHP and MySQL.[14] According to its history page, SLiMS was developed for the library of the Ministry of Education and Culture, which could not afford the cost of extending the licence of its existing library management

14 INLISLite is another open-source library management system, released by the National Library; see http://inlislite.perpusnas.go.id/. However, SLiMS seems to have a more active community base of developers.

system, Alice (developed by Softlink). The licence for the Alice software had been donated to the library by the British Council. Because it was proprietary software, it could not be distributed freely even within the ministry, and the library's staff had trouble mastering and modifying the program. Other existing open-source library management systems, such as PhpMyLibrary, OpenBiblio or Koha, had their own limitations, including the challenging computing languages of Perl and C++, and a lack of active user bases or updates. A team coordinated by Hendro Wicaksono and Arie Nugraha then suggested creating a new program under the free and open General Public Licence, so that the software would be free for anyone to use, modify and distribute. After some beta testing with a limited set of users, the first 'stable' version of the new software was launched in November 2007 to coincide with the third anniversary of the establishment of the library of the Ministry of Education and Culture.

In 2016, SLiMS reached its eighth version. It is now able to accommodate electronic files, photos and videos, and it has developed a union catalogue server. Since the software is free, the exact number of SLiMS downloads and installations is unclear; however, the SLiMS website claims at least 250,000 downloads and lists 379 Indonesian and 11 overseas libraries as users. Its free, open-source licence has contributed to wider use and expanded the community base. In addition to JogjaLib.Net, many other local SLiMS communities, such as SLiMS Banten, SLiMS Kudus, SLiMS Makassar, AmbonLib.Net and so on, are using the system. There is also an annual SLiMS community meeting (SLiMS Commeet) for users, developers and enthusiasts from across Indonesia. The lack of female participation at these gatherings is conspicuous. While there are no statistics on the gender of SLiMS users, the gender gap is highly visible just from browsing the photos and discussion forums on the internet. The massive gender gap in the information and communication technology (ICT) and teaching professions has received ample theoretical and empirical attention in the West, but the point still needs to be raised and addressed more seriously in Indonesia, where a high proportion of those working in libraries, children's 'reading gardens' (*taman bacaan*) and early childhood education are female.

Visual arts and culture

The Indonesian Visual Art Archive (IVAA) had its origins in Yogyakarta's Cemeti Art Foundation. Cemeti was founded in 1995 in response to the lack of libraries and accessible documentation on the arts, despite the growing contemporary arts scene. Merdikaningtyas (2007) has identified three stages during its first 10 years of development. The first stage involved hunting for documentary materials, building trust with partners, artists and users, and conceptualising the collection (1995–2000). The second stage consisted of collection development, system formation and network expansion (2000–02). The third stage concerned utilisation and optimisation of the collection (2003–05). Since 2008, IVAA has focused on digitising its archives and publishing them on its website (ivaa-online.org). It has continued to build partnerships with various arts and cultural organisations with a view to preserving their archives. It also publishes a bilingual volume called *Arsipelago* in which diverse archiving concepts and practices are discussed (Mariana et al. 2014). *Arsipelago* focuses on analysis of arts clippings and dance, music, film and action-poster archives, which may defy standard archiving methods and classifications.

Under a program funded by the Ford Foundation, the Indonesian Cultural Archive Network (Jaringan Arsip Budaya Nusantara, or JABN) was established in 2011 to expand Indonesia's digital archiving capacity and networks. In addition to IVAA, its members include the Jakarta Arts Council (Dewan Kesenian Jakarta), the Bandung-based Tikar Media Budaya Nusantara, Yogyakarta's Studio Audio Visual Puskat, the Dayak Studies Institute (Institut Dayakologi) and the Museum of East Nusa Tenggara.

Other organisations involved in the digitalising of knowledge are self-funded, depend on small grants or survive by selling publications and other items. For example, publishing company Indonesia Boekoe (I:boekoe) has established a subsidiary, Warung Arsip, to digitise clippings, books, newspapers and videos, and sell them online (http://warungarsip.co/). This relatively small enterprise economises by using digital cameras rather than scanners, although this affects scan quality and causes difficulties for optical character recognition.

Music

A more recent trend is the growth of music archives.[15] Irama Nusantara is a digital archive of Indonesian popular music, established in 2013 by David Tarigan, Christoforus Priyonugroho, Toma Avianda, Alvin Yunata, Norman Illyas, Dian Wulandari and friends. It grew out of their hobby of collecting Indonesian music on vinyl, cassette and CD. David Tarigan had bought Indonesian music records since secondary school, but had

---

15 This subsection is based on information from the websites of Irama Nusantara (http://iramanusantara.org/), Lokananta (http://lokanantamusik.com/), Rolling Stone Indonesia (http://www.rollingstone.co.id/article/read/2016/01/28/140506035/1093/lokananta-luncurkan-perpustakaan-digital-arsip-musik) and Tirto.id (https://tirto.id/20160723-41/jalan-sunyi-para-pengarsip-musik-279779).

found it difficult to collect further information on past Indonesian music and musicians. He and his friends started digitising music in 2008 as a way to document the 'raw data' of the release, including audio, textual and visual information. They began with their own private collections before moving on to those of other private collectors. They also obtained material second-hand from markets and explored radio archives. In particular, a recent collaboration with the president's Creative Economy Agency (Badan Ekonomi Kreatif) has helped them obtain access to the archives of public radio station Radio Republik Indonesia (RRI).

Lokananta, founded in 1956, initially produced and distributed vinyl records for RRI. It then expanded from a record label specialising in regional songs (*lagu daerah*) into arts performances, book and magazine publishing, and audio record archiving. It reached its golden age in the 1970s and 1980s and stopped production in 1999. After being liquidated in 2004, it became part of the Indonesian Government Printing Office (Perum Percetakan Negara Republik Indonesia, or Perum PNRI), which provides multimedia, recording, remastering, printing and graphics services. Under the Lokananta Project, supported by the Djarum Foundation, photographers, writers, designers and curators are attempting to evaluate the music archive of Lokananta and make it accessible to the public. According to its website (lokanantamusik.com), 5,000 reel masters have been transferred to digital formats.

The websites of both Irama Nusantara and Lokananta give a taste of the richness of Indonesian music. In tackling the tricky issue of copyright, Lokananta uploads only samples of songs onto its website, while Irama Nusantara uses the lowest bit rate. Lokananta is also exploring the possibility of streaming music from its record catalogues, using services such as iTunes, Deezer and Spotify.

The popularity and searchability of social media such as Instagram and Facebook have made them ideal platforms for exhibiting and archiving artists' work. Rather than systematic archiving based on strict classification and metadata, social media produces 'archives' that are fluid, transient, fragmented and highly subjective. The platforms simultaneously exhibit social, archival and performative dimensions. The Indonesian Street Art Database (ISAD), self-described as 'a guerrilla initiative of street art archiving in Indonesia', uses Instagram, Facebook and Tumblr to document street art in Indonesia, calling for submissions with hashtags.[16] Not surprisingly, the move to social media has raised critical questions about the desirability of relinquishing control and privacy to

16 ISAD also attempted to build a website as part of a 2012 project funded by Cipta Media Bersama and Wikimedia Indonesia (http://indonesianstreetart-database.org/). At the time of writing, this website appeared to be defunct.

an external 'archivist' or 'curator' who, by changing algorithms or servers, can unexpectedly or unintentionally modify, reconfigure or delete the submitted data (Hogan 2010). To a certain extent this may reflect the ephemeral real-life conditions of street art, which is subject to unexpected erasure and modification at any time. At the same time, the growing use of social media suggests that street artists want to use this platform to document and raise awareness of this form of art.

OTHER CHALLENGES FOR ARCHIVING AND CLASSIFICATION SYSTEMS

The diverse formats and growing 'intangibility' of material to be archived pose difficulties for developing archiving and classification systems. The challenges of digitising collections in academic libraries in Indonesia (Basuki 2004a) are generally also faced by libraries and archives in other sectors.

The first challenge is a lack of funding. The Directorate General of Higher Education stated in 1998 that universities should allocate at least 5 per cent of their budgets to their libraries. It is doubtful, however, that many institutions are abiding by this rule.

The second challenge is technical. As many universities are not equipped with stable internet or telephone connections, they lack the ICT facilities and infrastructure to support document digitisation projects.

The third challenge is human resources. Because of the problems in the LIS education and professional sectors described above, many library staff in Indonesia lack training in ICT use (Laksmi and Wijayanti 2015).

The fourth challenge concerns publishing policies. At universities, the publishing policies for the digitisation of documents have been arbitrarily implemented. This may change now that universities are taking a greater interest in digital repositories in order to increase their 'web presence and impact' and to improve their ratings on websites that rank institutions on their repositories, such as the Ranking Web of Repositories (Liauw and Genoni 2017).

The fifth challenge is cultural. Not every school or university department has access to ICT, is media savvy or is aware of copyright and plagiarism issues.

The sixth challenge is the digital divide. Although Indonesia has seen a rapid uptake of mobile internet, it still has very limited landline, broadband, electricity and other basic infrastructure. Again, the country's historical and geographical conditions need to be considered. The annotated bibliography by Teygeler et al. (2001) brings valuable insights to the preservation of archives in tropical climates. More attention needs to be paid to the value of and work involved in maintaining and caring for an archive, considering the rapid decay of both offline and online material.

CONCLUSION: BACK TO THE FUTURE?

On top of these technical and institutional challenges, I would like to address issues of a more socio-political nature. In Indonesia, the 'great divide' between the social sciences and computer science continues to affect the way information technology systems are conceptualised and developed. In addition, the common discourse for discussing problems related to libraries and archives tends to be apolitical. Rarely are 'errors', 'incompetence' or 'lack of resources' discussed as political issues burdened by the past and intertwined with changing power dynamics. Here, it is worth quoting at length Hill's (1990: 113) overview of the PDS HB Jassin collection more than a quarter of a century ago:

> Like any public repository in Indonesia the PDS operates within certain fluid and ill-defined political constraints. The collection initially reflected Jassin's own interests and position within Indonesian literature and literary criticism. The amount of leftist material is limited and no banned material is available (to public users). It appears, too, that certain unproscribed documents, such as newspaper clippings on the leftist cultural organisation Lekra (many of which were in fact highly critical of the organisation), which had been accessible in the early 1980s are now not publicly available. There is always the danger that, although a collection may have incorporated a range of ideological positions, changing circumstances may result in limited access to material deemed politically sensitive.

At the time, PDS HB Jassin was 'the only such (semi-)autonomous public access collection' (Hill 1990: 113). The state, as discussed briefly above, has intentionally ensured that 'politically sensitive' materials remain inaccessible and fragmented. At the same time, private collections that might have rivalled Jassin's, such as the manuscripts and other documents collected by Pramoedya Ananta Toer and Bakrie Siregar, were destroyed or broken up, on the premise that unexpected risks would be involved in keeping them.[17]

---

17 Ironically, PDS HB Jassin also experienced chronic underfunding and underwent a similar decline. In 2011, news of the dismal condition of the collection created a spontaneous crowd-funding movement, although it did not seem to generate significant funds. In 2013, the Jakarta city government gave the repository Rp 1.5 billion, the highest amount it had ever received, after Joko Widodo, then the governor of Jakarta, visited the centre. Nevertheless, legacy structures and issues of (dis)trust continued to pose challenges in subsequent plans to integrate the centre within the structures of the regional government.

The same logic still applies, even after the period of democratic reform (*reformasi*). In May 2016, the then acting head of the National Library, Dedi Junaedi, made a controversial statement in support of a crackdown on leftist books, although he backed down following a public outcry. It is easy to shrug off the incident now that the raids have slowed down and a new head of the National Library has been installed. However, the incident demonstrates the socio-political and legal constraints curbing the actions of archives and libraries in Indonesia. These constraints have to be considered carefully, especially amidst increasing efforts within Indonesia to bring visibility to materials that were seen as controversial and therefore left 'in the dark'.

Digital technology, file sharing and the external servers provided by sites such as Facebook, Instagram, Google, WordPress.com and archive.org may offer alternative platforms to bypass state surveillance and interference. Considering the turbulent state of the digital world, however, such a view may be naive. In 2015, Freedom House reported that internet freedom had been declining globally for the previous five years, with 'more governments censoring information of public interest and placing greater demands on the private sector to take down offending content' (Freedom House 2015). Indonesia's internet freedom status was downgraded to 'partly free' on the grounds that the Supreme Court had upheld a ministerial regulation on 'negative content' that gave officials the power to block websites; Vimeo had been blocked for allegedly hosting pornographic content; and five people had been jailed under Indonesia's notorious Information and Electronic Transactions Law (Law No. 11/2008). The more Indonesia moves into 'digitalising knowledge', the more it needs to take seriously the socio-political and legal issues affecting libraries and archives.

Given the importance of socio-political issues, I argue that the process of digitalising knowledge in education, libraries and archives should be seen as a form of infrastructure building. First, although infrastructure has long been associated with physical buildings and material procurement, the growing body of work in the information and social sciences focusing on information and knowledge deserves to be recognised as an equally valid form of infrastructure.[18] Second, the weak institutional capacity and low budgets of the LIS education and professional sectors, and Indonesians' supposed lack of interest in reading, are often blamed for the poor quality of education, libraries and archives in Indonesia. Now is the time to analyse how education, libraries and archives have been deeply affected, or intentionally stunted, by politics.

---

18 Examples are the work of Susan Leigh Star, Geoffrey Bowker, Steve Jackson and Paul Edwards.

REFERENCES

Anderson, B. (2013) 'Letters, secrecy, and the information age: the trajectory of historiography in Southeast Asia', *Southeast Asia Program Fall Bulletin 2013*, Cornell University, Ithaca: 13–17. Available at https://seap.einaudi.cornell.edu/publication/2013-fall-bulletin.

Basuki, S. (2004a) 'Digitisation of collections in Indonesian academic libraries', *Program: Electronic Library and Information Systems*, 38(3): 194–200. Available at http://www.emeraldinsight.com/10.1108/00330330410547241.

Basuki, S. (2004b) 'Perpustakaan Nasional dan Asosiasi Pustakawan di Indonesia: dilihat dari segi sejarah' [The National Library and the Indonesian Librarian Association: a historical overview], in *Temu Ilmiah Berdirinya Perpustakaan Nasional RI dan Peran Organisasi Profesi* [Meeting Commemorating the Establishment of the National Library of Indonesia and the Role of Professional Organisations], National Library, Jakarta. Available at http://eprints.rclis.org/8730/.

Basuki, S. (2013) 'A study of the curriculum of Indonesia's existing five graduate LIS programs', Sulistyo-Basuki's Blog: Library and Information Science. Available at https://sulistyobasuki.wordpress.com/2013/05/05/a-study-of-the-curriculum-of-indonesias-existing-five-graduate-lis-programs/. Accessed 25 June 2016.

Basuki, S., et al. (1996) *ANRI: Dalam Gerak Langkah 50 Tahun Indonesia Merdeka* [ANRI: In the Footsteps of 50 Years of Indonesian Independence], Arsip Nasional Republik Indonesia (ANRI), Jakarta.

Bowker, G.C., et al. (1997) *Social Science, Technical Systems, and Cooperative Work: Beyond the Great Divide*, Psychology Press, New York.

Davidson, C.N., and D.T. Goldberg (2009) *The Future of Learning Institutions in a Digital Age*, MIT Press, Cambridge and London. Available at https://mitpress.mit.edu/books/future-learning-institutions-digital-age.

Derrida, J. (2009) 'Archive fever: a Freudian impression', *Diacritics*, 25(2): 9–63.

Fahmi, I. (2002) 'The Indonesian Digital Library Network is born to struggle with the digital divide', *International Information and Library Review*, 34(2): 153–74.

Fahmi, I. (2005) 'Development of Indonesia's National Digital Library Network', in Y.-L. Theng and S. Foo (eds) *Design and Usability of Digital Libraries: Case Studies in the Asia Pacific*, Idea Group Publishing, Hershey: 38–54. Available at http://hdl.handle.net/10760/9323.

Finley, K. (2016) 'The inventors of the internet are trying to build a truly permanent web', *Wired*, 20 June. Available at http://www.wired.com/2016/06/inventors-internet-trying-build-truly-permanent-web/.

Foucault, M. (1972) *The Archaeology of Knowledge*, Pantheon, New York.

Freedom House (2015) 'Freedom on the Net 2015: privatizing censorship, eroding privacy'. Available at https://freedomhouse.org/report/freedom-net/freedom-net-2015.

Given, L.M., and L. McTavish (2010) 'What's old is new again: the reconvergence of libraries, archives, and museums in the digital age', *Library Quarterly*, 80(1): 251–69.

Håklev, S. (2008) *Mencerdaskan Bangsa: An Inquiry into the Phenomenon of Taman Bacaan in Indonesia*, University of Toronto at Scarborough, Toronto. Available at http://eprints.rclis.org/12294/.

Herr-Stephenson, B., et al. (2011) *Digital Media and Technology in Afterschool Programs, Libraries, and Museums*, MIT Press, Cambridge and London.

Available at http://dmlhub.net/publications/digital-media-and-technology-afterschool-programs-libraries-and-museums.
Hill, D. (1990) 'The H.B. Jassin Literary Documentation Centre', *Asian Studies Review*, 14(2): 109–14.
Hill, D., and K. Sen (2005) *The Internet in Indonesia's New Democracy*, Routledge, London and New York.
Hogan, B. (2010) 'The presentation of self in the age of social media: distinguishing performances and exhibitions online', *Bulletin of Science, Technology and Society*, 30(6): 377–86.
Jaquet, F.G.P. (1979) '1200 meters of colonial past', *Itinerario*, 3(1): 47–56. Available at http://www.journals.cambridge.org/abstract_S0165115300017265.
Laksmi, and L. Wijayanti (2015) 'Indonesian library and information science research as the social construction process', in A. Spink and D. Singh (eds) *Library and Information Science Trends and Research: Asia-Oceania*, Emerald Group Publishing Ltd, Bingley: 271–90.
Lankes, D. (2012) *The Atlas of New Librarianship*, MIT Press, New Haven and London.
Liauw, T.T. (2008) 'Glancing at the rearview mirror, focusing on the road ahead', *Bulletin of the American Society for Information Science and Technology*, 34(3): 43–6.
Liauw, T.T., and P. Genoni (2017) 'A different shade of green: a survey of Indonesian higher education institutional repositories', *Journal of Librarianship and Scholarly Communication*, 4: 1–26. Available at http://jlsc-pub.org/articles/abstract/10.7710/2162-3309.2136/.
Liu, O., and E. Tagliacozzo (2008) 'The National Archives (Jakarta) and the writing of transnational histories of Indonesia', *Itinerario*, 32(1): 81–94.
Maesaroh, I., and P. Genoni (2013) 'Future directions for Indonesian academic library education', *New Library World*, 114(5/6): 228–41. Available at http://www.emeraldinsight.com/doi/abs/10.1108/03074801311326858.
Manoff, M. (2004) 'Theories of the archive from across the disciplines', *Libraries and the Academy*, 4(1): 9–25. Available at http://muse.jhu.edu/content/crossref/journals/portal_libraries_and_the_academy/v004/4.1manoff.html.
Mariana, A., et al. (2014) *Arsipelago: Archival Work and Archiving Art and Culture in Indonesia*, Indonesian Visual Art Archive (IVAA) and Komunitas Bambu, Yogyakarta and Jakarta.
Massil, S.W. (1989) 'The history of the National Library of Indonesia: the bibliographical Borobudur', *Libraries and Culture*, 24(4): 475–88.
Merdikaningtyas, Y.A. (2007) 'Oase dokumentasi seni rupa dari Yogyakarta' [An oasis of art documentation in Yogyakarta], in F. Wardani et al. (eds) *Folders: 10 Tahun Dokumentasi Yayasan Seni Cemeti* [Folders: 10 Years of Cemeti Art Foundation Documentation], Indonesian Visual Art Archive (IVAA), Yogyakarta: 16–71.
Minarchek, M. (2015) 'The National Archives of the Republic of Indonesia (ANRI)', *Dissertation Reviews*, 26 May. Available at http://dissertationreviews.org/archives/12299. Accessed 1 February 2016.
Palfrey, J. (2015) *BiblioTech: Why Libraries Matter More Than Ever in the Age of Google*, Basic Books, New York.
Priyanto, I.F. (2016) 'The development, challenges, and opportunities of library and information science education in Indonesia', in M. Seadle et al. (eds) *Educating the Profession: 40 years of the IFLA Section on Education and Training*, De Gruyter, Berlin: 258–77.

Priyanto, I.F. (n.d.) 'LIS and tracer study: a case study on GMU LIS graduates', Gadjah Mada University, Yogyakarta. Available at https://www.academia.edu/4095622/LIS_tracer_Study.

Said, E. (1994) *Culture and Imperialism*, Vintage Books, New York.

Stoler, A.L. (2002) 'Colonial archives and the arts of governance', *Archival Science*, 2(1–2): 87–109. Available at http://link.springer.com/10.1007/BF02435632.

Stoler, A.L. (2009) *Along the Archival Grain: Epistemic Anxieties and Colonial Common Sense*, Princeton University Press, Princeton and Oxford.

Surachman, A. (2011) 'Jaringan perpustakaan digital di Indonesia: pembelajaran dari IndonesiaDLN, InherentDL, Jogjalib for All, Garuda dan Jogjalib.Net' [Digital library networks in Indonesia: lessons learned from IndonesiaDLN, InherentDL, Jogjalib for All, Garuda and JogjaLib.Net], in *Konferensi Perpustakaan Digital Indonesia IV, 8–10 November 2011* [Fourth Indonesian Digital Library Conference, 8–10 November 2011], Samarinda: 1–27. Available at http://eprints.rclis.org/17555/.

Teygeler, R., et al. (2001) *Preservation of Archives in Tropical Climates: An Annotated Bibliography*, International Council of Archives, National Archives of the Netherlands and National Archives of the Republic of Indonesia, Paris, The Hague and Jakarta. Available at https://www.researchgate.net/publication/270273714_Preservation_of_Archives_in_Tropical_Climates_An_annotated_bibliography.

Xing, C., F. Crestani and A. Rauber (eds) (2011) *Digital Libraries: For Cultural Heritage, Knowledge Dissemination, and Future Creation*, Springer-Verlag, Berlin and Heidelberg. Available at http://link.springer.com/book/10.1007/978-3-642-24826-9.

Zhou, T. (2015) 'The National Archives of the Republic of Indonesia', *Dissertation Reviews*, 10 February. Available at http://dissertationreviews.org/archives/10930. Accessed 10 May 2015.

Zittrain, J., K. Albert and L. Lessig (2014) 'Perma: scoping and addressing the problem of link and reference rot in legal citations', *Harvard Law Review*, 127(4): 176–99. Available at http://harvardlawreview.org/2014/03/perma-scoping-and-addressing-the-problem-of-link-and-reference-rot-in-legal-citations/.

Zorich, D., G. Waibel and R. Erway (2008) *Beyond the Silos of the LAMs: Collaboration among Libraries, Archives and Museums*, OCLC Research, Dublin.

12 Digital art: hacktivism and social engagement

Edwin Jurriëns

A remarkable development in Indonesian art since the early 1990s has been the experimentation with unconventional new media such as video, the internet, the mobile phone and biotechnology. This is a product of global trends in art and the media, the enhanced accessibility of consumer technology in Indonesia and the increased freedom of speech since the fall of Suharto's totalitarian New Order regime (1965–98). Digitalisation here is not merely about new electronic communication strategies and financial transactions surrounding art, but affects art at the very core of its production, circulation and appreciation. Thus, contemporary art and the broader creative economy to which it belongs constitutes an important form of expression and area of social life—on a par with electronic finance, governance, health care and education—for analysing and putting into critical perspective the idea of a digital revolution in Indonesia.

This chapter is meant as an early inquiry into the much flagged idea of a digital revolution, by putting both the 'digital' and the 'revolution' into critical perspective. I discuss how the contemporary art market, as an essential part of Indonesia's creative economy, has been shifting interest from traditional media such as painting and sculpture to new media such as digital art. Some artists and art collectives have remained under the commercial radar, however, due to the nature of their work, ideas and interests. They frequently engage in collaborative projects with local communities to creatively and critically address urgent social issues such as health care and food security. I argue that their ideas and practices are not the product of a digital revolution only, but build on a longer history of social engagement in Indonesian creative practice.

I specifically focus on the idea of 'hacking' in the context of Indonesian digital art. Hacking in this instance does not mean sabotaging information and communication networks, but rather creating open laboratories for exploring and executing alternative scenarios for more sustainable, socially inclusive and environmentally friendly futures. Some digital artists use new, techno-cultural hacking strategies to go beyond the market, and establish creative connections with various groups in society that are ignored or underrepresented by mainstream politics and business. By describing part of the history of the Yogyakarta biennale, I seek to demonstrate that hacking culture is not only the result of recent technological developments, but also part of a cultural evolution over an extended period of time, steered by innovative and socially engaged artists using a variety of creative strategies.

INDONESIAN ART AND THE MARKET

The paintings by aristocrat Raden Saleh (1807–80) are commonly referred to as the first Javanese engagements with modern art. In the 1930s and 1940s, the paintings of Sindudarsono Sudjojono (1913–86), Hendra Gunawan (1918–83), Affandi (1907–90) and Sudjana Kerton (1922–94), among others (Turner 2005), reflected a strong engagement with daily life, ordinary Indonesians, the struggle for independence and nationalism. Since then, Indonesian artists have experimented with a rich diversity of themes, genres and mediums. The best-selling artists today include both the pioneers of Indonesian contemporary art and a rapidly expanding group of talented living artists.

In the mid-1990s, the work of contemporary artists such as Dadang Christanto (b. 1957), Heri Dono (b. 1960), Franciscus Xaverius Harsono (b. 1949) and Agus Suwage (b. 1959) began to be exhibited in international biennales, museums and galleries (Genocchio 2013). Around the same time, reputed international auction houses such as Sotheby's and Christie's moved into the Asian art market (Zineng 2011: 461–3). In the late 1990s, the growth of Indonesian contemporary art slowed due to a lack of local gallery and auction infrastructure, the Asian financial crisis, the economic and socio-political chaos following the fall of Suharto, and the international focus on the Chinese economic and cultural booms at the expense of attention to artistic developments in Southeast Asia (Genocchio 2013).

In the 2000s the market regained strength, with a steady increase in the number of art communities, spaces and galleries, greater representation of Indonesian art at notable international art fairs and exhibitions, and spectacular sales at auction houses. In April 2014, the 1979 oil painting *Pasukan Kita Yang Dipimpin oleh Pangeran Diponegoro* [Our Soldiers Led by Prince Diponegoro] by Sudjojono sold for HK$58.36 million ($7.53 million)—a record for Southeast Asian art—at an auction at Sotheby's in Hong Kong. At other Sotheby's Hong Kong auctions, Gunawan's 1971 oil painting *Pandawa Dadu* [The Dice Game from the Mahabharata Epic] fetched HK$26.4 million ($3.39 million) in April 2015 (Li 2015), while his 1979 oil painting *Mandi di Pancuran* [Bathing in the Shower] sold for HK$9.7 million ($1.3 million) in October 2015. The price of the last painting was five times that of the most expensive Southeast Asian painting sold at Sotheby's first auction of regional artwork in Singapore in 1996 (Ungku 2015). *Man from Bantul* [The Final Round], the 2000 triptych of one of the most commercially successful younger artists, I Nyoman Masriadi, sold at Sotheby's Hong Kong in 2008 for HK$7.8 million ($1 million), then an auction record for a living Southeast Asian artist (Genocchio 2013).

Some of the major international Indonesia-themed exhibitions in recent years include 'The grass looks greener where you water it' at the French art fair, Art Paris, in 2010 and the 2011 exhibitions 'Trans-figurations: mythologies Indonésiennes' at the Espace Culturel Louis Vuitton in Paris, 'Indonesian eye: fantasies and realities' at the Saatchi Gallery in London and 'Beyond the East' at the Museum of Contemporary Art in Rome. Indonesian galleries and artists were represented at Art Dubai in 2012, and Indonesia had its own pavilions at the Venice Biennale and at Art Stage Singapore in 2013 (Genocchio 2013). Noted art historian Benjamin Genocchio (2013) believes Jakarta itself may become 'the next art market capital'.

Reflecting the global emergence of Indonesian contemporary art, in 2014 art critic and curator Carla Bianpoen compiled a list of the most influential living Indonesian art collectors (Bianpoen 2014). The locally best-known figure on the list was Dr Oei Hong Djien, who had made his private art collection accessible to the public by opening the Oei Hong Djien (OHD) Museum in Magelang in 1997. The list did not include Indonesian art collectors based abroad, such as Budi Tek in Shanghai and Konfir Kabo in Melbourne. Budi Tek, also known under his Chinese name Yu Deyao, was the only Indonesian art collector ranked in the *ARTnews* list of the 'World's Top 200 Collectors' of 2012. He was also ranked 76 in the *ArtReview* list of the 'Power 100' art world figures of 2012, and was even included on the *Art&Auction* list of the 10 most influential people in the art world in 2011 (Kolesnikov-Jessop 2012). Tek is the founder of the Yuz Foundation, which opened the (now temporarily closed) Yuz Art Museum in Jakarta in 2008 and a museum of the same name in Shanghai in 2014.

For people like Djien and Tek, collecting art is not merely a business investment, but also a product of personal motivations and broader socio-cultural factors. They have established their own art museums and galleries, positioned themselves as art curators and critics and become superstars in their own right (Zineng 2011: 464–6). Their multitasking is partly explained by the mutual rivalry between the members of a small, wealthy elite who use their financial capital to buy into creative capital, and to gain socio-cultural prestige beyond their economic power. They also see themselves as filling a gap in the material and immaterial art infrastructure in Indonesia, which has been suffering from a lack of art museums, galleries, libraries, and academic research and educational resources.

'NO PAINTING TODAY': THE ZEITGEIST OF CONTEMPORARY ART COLLECTING

Mirroring a type of rivalry and rebellion that is common among junior artists in response to their predecessors, some of the younger Indonesian collectors try to distinguish themselves from their seniors by focusing on digital art and art installations, two relatively underexplored areas of the art market. Because their wealth does not equal the financial capital of a Tek or a Djien, they are unable to buy Indonesian, Chinese or Western masters, and therefore feel encouraged to be innovative and selective in building their collections (Wahono, personal communication, Jakarta, 18 December 2014). Prominent members of this group of collectors are Arif Suherman, Indra Leonardi, Nicholas Tan, Tom Tandio and Wiyu Wahono, all of whom, like Tek and Djien, are of Chinese-Indonesian ethnic background, and some of whom were included in Bianpoen's 2014 list.

Dr Wahono is one of the most outspoken and knowledgeable of the younger art collectors. Since 1999, he has focused specifically on collecting art installations and digital art. He attempts to build and share his expertise by organising exhibitions and monthly 'art lover dinners'. At the dinners, invited artists and art experts give presentations on designated topics to Wahono and his fellow collectors (Wahono, personal communication, Jakarta, 18 December 2014). Wahono himself has been invited to give talks about art on various occasions, including international events such as the 'Suspended histories' contemporary Asian art exhibition at Museum Van Loon in Amsterdam on 13 October 2013 (Museum Van Loon 2013). His standing in the art world has also been confirmed by his role as a jury member for the Bandung Contemporary Art Awards (Firmansah 2010).

In May 2012, Wahono and fellow collector Leonardi demonstrated their interest in the relationship between contemporary art and society in a co-curated exhibition called 'Zeitgeist' held at Gallery Kunstkring in Jakarta (Bianpoen 2012). The German title of the exhibition reflected Wahono's personal background, as he lived, studied and worked in Berlin for more than 20 years before returning to Jakarta in 1998 (Wirajuda 2014). As well as being a collector of art, Wahono is a mechanical engineer specialising in the production and sale of plastic containers, while Leonardi is a professional photographer.

The exhibition's location had symbolic value as the place where in the mid-1930s one of the early private collectors, the Dutch paint manufacturer Pierre Alexandre Regnault (1868–1954), put his art collection on display, including paintings by Picasso, Gauguin and Van Gogh. Wahono and Leonardi attempted to express the spirit of their own times by exhibiting video installations by Amalia Kartika Sari (b. 1987), Davi Linggar (b. 1974), Tintin Wulia (b. 1972) and Yusuf Ismail (b. 1982); stop-motion animation by new media art collective Tromarama (established in 2006); a sound and video installation by Agustinus ('Jompet') Kuswidananto (b. 1976); digital prints by Agan Harahap (b. 1980), Jim Allen Abel (b. 1975) and Wimo Ambala Bayang (b. 1976); scanography prints by Angki Purbandono (b. 1971); and video-recorded performance art by Melati Suryodarmo (b. 1969) (Bianpoen 2012).

In May 2013, Wahono and fellow collectors Suherman and Paula Dewiyanti curated the exhibition 'Beyond boundaries' at the commercial gallery Umahseni in Jakarta (Hamdani 2013; Umahseni 2013). The title referred to the organisation of an exhibition without the interference of an outside curator. The concept encouraged the collectors to entertain personal connections with their favourite artists, and to deepen their knowledge of contemporary art. The collectors also wrote their own curatorial texts. Yet another exhibition focusing on digital art and installations was 'No painting today', held in July 2014 at the Pacific Place Mall in Jakarta. According to Wahono, who was one of the organisers, this event was 'a form of protest against the excessively major standing of painting among Indonesian art collectors, and how a fixation on the art form, as well as sculptures, has kept the true message of contemporary art from being disseminated' (Wirajuda 2014).

Wahono's favourite artist, Agan Harahap, produces digital prints that are often manipulations or simulations of historical events. For instance, his photo montage *Sejarah X 6* [History X 6] shows Indonesia's first president, Sukarno, with Marilyn Monroe, Elizabeth Taylor and Jackie Kennedy. Although art lover and womaniser Sukarno was acquainted with each of these celebrities, he never met all three of them together. According to Wahono, Harahap's artwork is

> touching on our collective memory and challenging our notions of reality, as well as the idea that photographs can't lie. The work shows how this perception still persists, despite advances in technology that saw the development of Photoshop and other photo editing applications (Wirajuda 2014).

For Wahono, Harahap's work confirms that contemporary art is 'all about context, especially with the times or zeitgeist, which runs counter to [the traditional] notion of using aesthetics in art to move emotions' (Wirajuda 2014).

While the younger art collectors rightly appreciate the different, more context- and process-based aesthetics used in art based on digital and other new media, they are still, like other collectors, interested in owning the artworks and treating them as objects. The objects represent and tell part of the story of the creative processes from which they originated but receive new meaning and become decontextualised from their original socio-political settings once they end up in a private home or gallery. Upon entering Wahono's private art space at his business premises in North Jakarta, guests are asked to leave an electronic signature in the form of a portrait taken and digitally modified by the Yogyakarta-based new media art collective House of Natural Fiber (HONF, established in 1999). HONF itself illustrates that Indonesian new media art cannot be reduced to objects and conventional art categories, venues and markets, but embodies and responds to much broader socio-cultural dimensions, as will be explained in the following sections.

DIGITAL ART AND HACKTIVISM: MICRONATION/ MACRONATION

HONF is one of the drivers of an Indonesian, post-authoritarian avant-garde of the digital age, together with other art collectives such as ruangrupa and Forum Lenteng in Jakarta, Ruang MES 56 in Yogyakarta, Common Room in Bandung, Jatiwangi Art Factory in Jatiwangi (West Java) and WAFT in Surabaya (Jurriëns 2013). The members of HONF have created their own communities, which, often in interaction with local society, produce collaborative project- or process-based art, to be displayed in galleries as well as public outdoor spaces (Kera 2012).

One of HONF's recent projects is *Micronation/Macronation: Democratizing the Energy*. The project was inspired by the public outrage at the government's plans to cut fuel subsidies in March 2012, and has been responding ever since in ways that are in line with HONF's mission to bridge art, science and free technology (Jurriëns 2013). The intent is to explore alternative, cheaper and renewable energy sources, which would ideally secure energy independence for Indonesia (Supriyanto 2012). The project includes collaborations with farming communities and on-site experiments in the Cangkringan (Merapi) and Kalibawang (Kulonprogo) areas in the Yogyakarta Special Region. Its three basic components are fermentation/distillation machines to transform hay into ethanol; satellite receivers to obtain data related to agricultural production, such as data on weather, climate and seasonal conditions; and supercomputers to process data on agricultural conditions, ethanol production, and food and energy sustainability. Aspects of the project were presented at an exhibition and workshops held at the Langgeng Art Foundation gallery in Yogyakarta in April–May 2012.

Apart from devices that can turn waste (hay) into fuel (ethanol) and can be displayed as art installations in their own right, a key aspect of *Micronation/Macronation* is the use of hacking strategies to enhance public access to restricted data. HONF calls its self-designed satellite receivers 'satellite data grabbers' (Supriyanto 2012). One of HONF's subdivisions, called v.u.f.o.c., or 'velocity UFO centre', is instrumental in collecting, processing and presenting the data. The art collective describes v.u.f.o.c. as 'a "dark" or "ghost" artistic bioresearch and extra-terrestrial data hacklab created for outdoor and field investigation activities' (v.u.f.o.c. 2012). The mobile lab consists of a 1970s VW Transporter van, repainted in black, with a satellite dish on top and multiple computers and monitors inside. Its name and shape are meant to make an artistic, performative statement, and reflect the background of HONF founder Vincensius ('Venzha') Christiawan (b. 1975) in interior design as well as his obsession with UFOs and extra-terrestrial life (Jurriëns 2013). The dramatic exterior of the lab simultaneously promotes and conceals its more down-to-earth, pragmatic and socio-political purpose of hacking and sharing data that are beneficial to the agricultural practices and food and fuel needs of local farming communities. That is, rather than trying to get in touch with aliens, the purpose of the project is to protect life on our planet. For HONF, the advantage of having a mobile lab—in addition to its stationary lab for creative fabrication using open-source hardware (the so-called HonFab Lab)—is the ability it provides to tour the Yogyakarta region and engage local communities in on-the-spot collaborative projects and workshops.

The HONF project provides a completely different picture of hacking compared to the use of cyberstrategies for the violent disruption of information and communication networks. During East Timor's struggle for independence in the late 1990s, for instance, hackers based in Portugal attacked Indonesian domains, including the website of the Ministry of Defence, while Indonesian hackers (the so-called 'electronic cockroaches' or *kecoak elektronik*) took down pro-independence sites associated with East Timor's top-level '.tp' domain (Hill and Sen 2005: 108). While these hacking strategies come close to cyberterrorism or cyberwarfare, in general hacking activism ('hacktivism') may cause temporary disorder or infringe intellectual property rights or security systems, but it is not meant to create permanent damage (Hill and Sen 2005: 107–10).

In line with the HONF example, Kera (2012) describes how, since around the turn of the century, hacktivism has moved from 'entrepreneurial individuals (Steve Jobs, Bill Gates), technological revolutions (PC, WWW), and anarchism (Cyberpunk SF)' to the formation of alternative networks and collectives for producing and sharing knowledge. The HONF collective and its activities can be seen as part of the global emergence of hackerspaces aimed at integrating 'community building with prototype testing' and translating between 'scientific knowledge produced in the labs (official academic and research institutions) and the everyday interests, practices and problems of ordinary people'. Based on case studies of hackerspaces in Indonesia, Japan and Singapore, Kera (2012) identifies the social impact of these spaces in terms of offering innovative, hybridised and multidirectional models 'for policy and decision-making different from the traditional division of powers between people doing the research and people representing the interests of the citizens'.

The *Micronation/Macronation* project also shows that hacking is not only about hijacking, jamming, rewriting, remixing or reappropriating information, but also about interfering with the codes and systems in which data are embedded. This includes analysing and where necessary changing the complex, intertwined ecologies of technological, sociocultural and natural environments (Guattari 1989). Singapore-based art curator and critic David Teh (2012) sees the HONF project, and hacking culture more broadly, as a response to 'the age of the code' as 'the codes governing social and political life have become increasingly digital ones'. Following the emergence of genetic engineering in the 1970s, 'all other codes are being rendered in this electronic form [including] the fate of life itself'. This would explain 'why biotechnology and media art are increasingly hard to separate, and why hacking has a certain bond with environmentalism'. The hacking of scientific information has enabled HONF to change 'the code' of hay, and turn it into ethanol. Subsequently, it has the potential to radically alter the structures of and interrelated ways of doing agriculture, business, politics and art.

ONGOING HACKING: XXLAB AND LIFEPATCH

The acceptance of digitalisation and hacking culture as two distinctive features of Indonesian contemporary art is demonstrated by the resilience and popularity of the new media art collectives. The increased accessibility of consumer technology in Indonesia, particularly laptops, mobile phones and handycams, and the increased freedom of expression in the post-Suharto era, fostered the establishment of these collectives. While the emergence of digital art in the art market could be described as a 'revolution', the creation of this form of art has been part of a longer, ongoing creative struggle responding to all sorts of socio-political factors. Some of the collectives have been able to survive for close to two decades now, and have also contributed to the sustainability of Indonesian digital art by inspiring a second generation of spin-off communities.

Two of HONF's own spin-off communities in Yogyakarta are XXLab and Lifepatch. XXLab, founded in 2013, is an all-female collective whose members include HONF co-founder Irene Agrivina (b. 1976). Its concepts and projects relate to gender, hacking strategies, open-source hardware and software, and the reappropriation of daily practices and objects. Like HONF, XXLab explores previously undetected or understudied links between waste management, food and fuel shortage or unaffordability, and poverty reduction, and seeks artistic and innovative solutions.

One of its projects is titled *WATI: The Domestic Hacking Project*. 'Wati' was once a popular name for girls, often used in school textbooks to refer to the 'quintessential Indonesian woman' (Piksel 14 2014). While Indonesian women have traditionally been associated with domestic chores such as cooking, the *WATI* project attempts to expand the space and activities of women by using the kitchen as a laboratory for turning food into fashion. It has experimented with using spices, food waste and other micro-organisms to make fabric dye, and fermented soy bean (*tempeh*) and other types of fungi to create fabric dye patterns and jewellery (Piksel 14 2014).

In a related project, *SOYA C(O)U(L)TURE* (2015), XXLab uses digital and biological hacking methods to design 'haute couture' dresses and other items. The clothes are made from a leather-look biofabric, which is based on the liquid waste of *tempeh* and other soy industries that pollute Indonesian rivers and soils (Rap 2015). Other products made by the collective are soy waste-based edible cellulose, biofuel and fertiliser (XXLab 2015). The development of businesses using these techniques could potentially alleviate some of the economic problems in Indonesia's low-income areas (Basari 2015). *SOYA C(O)U(L)TURE* was one of the winners of a prestigious European Commission-supported competition accompanying the annual international Ars Electronica Festival for cyberarts in Linz, Austria.

Lifepatch, founded in 2012, describes itself as a 'citizen initiative in art, science and technology'. Some of its members, such as Andreas Siagian (b. 1981), were previously involved in HONF. In 2013, the community created its own Lifepatch Bio-electronics Laboratory, a 'citizen laboratory' (*laboratorium warga*) using do-it-yourself (DIY) and do-it-with-others (DIWO) methods to explore and develop the potential of local technologies and human and natural resources (Biennale Jogja 2015; Lifepatch 2015a). In close collaboration with the Microbiology Laboratory of the Faculty of Agriculture at Gadjah Mada University in Yogyakarta, Lifepatch developed the *Jogja River Project*. Established in 2011 (before the formal establishment of Lifepatch), this project is still helping local citizens to investigate the water quality of the rivers in the Yogyakarta urban area. It has also trained participants to document the social activities of the communities that live along the riverbanks (Lifepatch 2015b).

For the Jakarta Biennale in 2015, Lifepatch created a project and installation called *Banyu Mili* [Flowing Water]. Like the *Jogja River Project*, it deals with the problem of water pollution. For the *Banyu Mili* project, Lifepatch worked with the Surabaya Strenkali Citizens Organisation (Paguyuban Warga Strenkali Surabaya), an association of local riverside communities in Surabaya. Water pollution is one among many serious problems faced by these communities, including settlement disputes, forced eviction, lack of water and electricity, and prostitution. Apart from conducting research on the quality of the river water, Lifepatch and the Strenkali Citizens Organisation worked on the development of a water-filtering and cleaning device and the planting of Moringa (*Kelor*) trees, known for their water-cleaning capacity. The art installation at the 2015 Jakarta Biennale exhibited various aspects of the project, including two ponds—one containing dirty water and the other clean water—grass patches, a Moringa tree, the water purification prototype and video footage of the activities of the Strenkali communities (Lifepatch 2015c).

These and other types of new media art encompass more than the objects bought and sold at the Indonesian and international art markets. One of the movement's achievements has been to move aesthetics beyond the formal characterisation of a work of art to include what the French curator and art critic Nicolas Bourriaud (2002) calls 'relational aesthetics'. While every form of art is relational with regard to the social setting of its reception, in relational aesthetics intersubjectivity and interactivity form the very basis of creative concepts and production practices (Bourriaud 2002: 22). In Indonesian new media art, this relational aesthetics is reflected in a strong interest in creative processes through or in the form of the organisation of communities, festivals, performances, discussions and laboratory-like experiments rather than a concern with the creation of tangible artworks as such.

This type of relationality has been strongly supported by the growth of the internet and social media. At the same time, it has been inspired by forms of social engagement that have a much longer history in Indonesian art and society. Elsewhere (Jurriëns 2013) I have argued that the contemporary digital art communities can be seen as a modern interpretation of the *sanggar*, or the Indonesian art communities of the 1940s and 1950s, in which a senior artist lived and worked with groups of aspiring artists in a spirit of communality (Holt 1967: 218; Wright 1994: 21; Harsono 2009: 129–31). In the 1950s and early 1960s, social commitment in a broader sense was also promoted by the Institute of People's Culture (Lembaga Kebudayaan Rakyat, or LEKRA), which was affiliated with the Indonesian Communist Party (Partai Komunis Indonesia, or PKI) and supported by President Sukarno.

In the aftermath of the 1965 'coup', and the shift in power from Sukarno to Suharto, LEKRA was abolished and many of its followers imprisoned or murdered in acts of mass violence. Suharto's New Order regime encouraged art dominated by individual expression and by internationalist and decorative styles such as abstract modernism, post-impressionism and classical realism. In the mid-1970s, the New Art Movement (Gerakan Seni Rupa Baru, or GSRB) took a stand against these politically and academically accepted, and socially distanced or 'universal', styles. The current new media art communities build on GSRB's pioneering of new artistic forms in Indonesia, such as installation and performance art. At the same time, they go beyond GSRB's discussion of social commitment in relatively distanced and narrow artistic terms by also developing concrete art projects with and for society (Jurriëns 2013).

THE EVOLUTION OF SOCIAL ENGAGEMENT: FROM 'WILD HORSE' TO 'HACKING CONFLICT' IN THE YOGYAKARTA BIENNALE

The historical development of the Yogyakarta biennale, in which the work of both HONF and Lifepatch has been exhibited, is also instructive in identifying the evolutionary as opposed to revolutionary or purely technological character of contemporary digital art and hacking strategies. It shows that the 2015 biennale theme of 'hacking conflict' is the outcome of artistic struggles and hacking-like strategies within the Yogyakarta art world that go back at least to the early 1990s.

The curator of the 2015 Jogja Biennale, FX Woto Wibowo (also known as Wok the Rock or Wowok), observed that in the biennale, and in Indonesia more generally, the idea of 'hacking' goes beyond the use of technology, and refers to a broader field of social practices:

> The term 'Hacking' is not referring to computing/technology practice. It's more into social hacking. My curatorial direction is not only to use the theme as a narration but also for a working method. That's why the exhibition is

> project-based. I invite participants from various backgrounds (visual art, dance, theatre, journalist, design, music) to work collaboratively. Collaboration practice is an exact way to implement conflict naturally (Artling Team 2015).

The collaborative art projects at the Jogja Biennale could be seen as interventions in, or simulations of, social practices that, by creating or recreating conflicts, may be able to generate alternative solutions or scenarios for a better future. According to Wibowo, the 'conflict' reflected or created in hacking practices constitutes an essential aspect of new democracies such as Indonesia and 2015 biennale partner-country Nigeria, and can be exploited as a 'positive resource' for creating 'unpredictable harmony' (Artling Team 2015).

The 2015 curatorial concept builds on and responds to the developments in Indonesian art and society discussed in the previous section, but also, and more specifically, to the history of the Yogyakarta biennale itself. The popular, global exhibition format of the biennale (Gardner and Green 2014) was introduced in Yogyakarta in 1988 with the Yogyakarta Painting Biennale (Biennale Seni Lukis Yogyakarta), which replaced the Yogyakarta Painting Exhibition (Pameran Seni Lukis Yogyakarta) that had taken place between 1983 and 1987 (Samboh 2013). Until 1992, the painting biennale took the form of a competition judged by an expert jury (Nugroho 2014: 145–6).

One day before the start of the third biennale in 1992, a remarkable protest took place. A counterbiennale, titled 'Binal experimental art', was organised by the young artists Dadang Christanto (the 'coordinator', b. 1957), Eddie Hara (b. 1957), Ong Harry Wahyu (b. 1958) and Heri Dono (b. 1960). 'Binal' was a play on the word 'biennale', and means 'rebellious', 'uncontrollable', 'disobedient' or 'wild' in Indonesian. The group of artists, all in their early thirties, protested against various aspects of the official biennale, especially the limitation of participation to artists aged 35 years and older, and the restriction to the medium of painting only (Nugroho 2014: 147).

The most discussed and characteristic work of the protest event was Dono's *Kuda Binal* [Wild Horse]. Unlike the paintings displayed at the official biennale, Dono's work was exhibited in an open public space, crossed a range of art genres and media and involved multiple participants, including craftspeople and ordinary Indonesians (Antoinette 2007; Posyananda 2011). This collaborative art project could be considered an example of 'hacking culture' *avant la lettre*, as it was not merely an act of resistance but also a reappropriation of the very code or system of the official biennale. This and other works in the counterbiennale dramatically influenced the format and management of the following official biennales. For instance, the 1994 biennale, called 'Pameran rupa-rupa seni rupa' [Exhibition of various forms of fine art], was no longer restricted to painting, but consisted of a painting biennale, an outdoor sculpture exhibition and a contemporary art exhibition. There were no longer any age restrictions, although participation was still for 'professionals' only, and not for 'students'. The biennale no longer included a competition, and the jury had been replaced by a team of curators (Nugroho 2014: 151–2).

In the early 2000s, the event received its current brand name, Biennale Jogja, and further widened its scope by focusing on socio-political issues beyond developments within the world of art as such. In 2003 the theme was 'Countrybution' (about the responsibility of artists towards their own countries), in 2005 'Di sini dan kini' [Here and now] (about art reflecting on and contributing to local socio-political issues) and in 2007 'Neo nation' (about art on issues of national and international importance). The main breakthrough that set the parameters for the current series of biennales came in 2009, when Biennale Jogja X adopted the theme 'Jogja jamming: art archives movement'.

The 2009 biennale was the first comprehensive attempt to not only represent social issues but also encourage large-scale social engagement and direct audience interaction. More than 300 artists and community groups took part, including 'contemporary artists whose works fetch billions of rupiah, such as Entang Wiharso, Nyoman Masriadi, Putu Sutawijaya, Ivan Sagita, and traditional artists who work behind the scenes at Wayang Orang performances, such as Mbah Ledjar Subroto and Mbah Sucipto' (Sudiarno 2010). The diversity of participants was also reflected in the organising committee, which had 'both culture expert Dr Sindunata SJ and Gandung, a becak driver who also gives massages' (Sudiarno 2010). The venues ranged from the Taman Budaya culture park in Yogyakarta, the Bank Indonesia Building, the Jogja National Museum and Sangkring Art Space, to bus terminals, train stations, airports, major intersections, sidewalks, the Alun-Alun central town square, billboards and red-light districts. According to the director, well-known theatre and television actor Butet Kartaredjasa (b. 1961), 'jamming, as in a musical jam session, means working together to create a more interesting outcome, while the parties involved feel content and not pressured to work together' (Sahana 2009). This idea is closely related to the 2015 Biennale Jogja theme of hacking, although the focus in 2009 was stronger on the potential for, rather than the possible conflicts involved in, collaboration.

Another important step in the development of the biennale was taken on 23 August 2010 with the launch of the Yogyakarta Biennale Foundation (Yayasan Biennale Yogyakarta, or YBY) as the official host of the biennale (Biennial Foundation 2016). The foundation presented a new, long-term vision for a 10-year series of biennales focusing on the theme of 'The Equator'. It has encouraged collaborations between Indonesian artists, curators and communities and their counterparts in other tropical countries. The 2011 biennale (titled 'Shadowlines') focused on India, the 2013 biennale ('Not a dead end') on the Arab-speaking region (Egypt, Oman, Saudi Arabia, United Arab Emirates and Yemen) and the 2015 biennale ('Hacking conflict') on Nigeria. The 2017, 2019 and 2021 biennales will concentrate on countries from South America, the Pacific region (including Australia) and Southeast Asia, respectively. The 10-year project will conclude with an Equator Conference in 2022 (Anshari 2015: 8).

According to the organisers, the Equator series can be seen as an artistic intervention in, or hacking of, the Western-dominated global art world:

> Amidst the dynamics of the global art domain that is very dynamic—as if it is inclusive and egalitarian—the hierarchy between centre and periphery is in fact still very real. Therefore the need to conduct interventions becomes very urgent. The YBY imagines a common tool (platform) that is able to oppose, interrupt or at least provoke the dominance of the centre, and to present alternatives through a diversity of contemporary art practices from an Indonesian perspective. [...] The Equator/Khatulistiwa will become a common platform to 're-read' the world (Anshari 2015: 7–8).

The 2015 biennale therefore engaged with hacking practices on various levels. First, it included digital artworks that used techno-cultural hacking strategies to provide alternative aesthetic and social scenarios. Second, by focusing on collaborative projects between artists and ordinary citizens, and between artists from different parts of the world, the event attempted to hack the conventional 'white cube' format of international exhibitions focusing on the individual and relatively autonomous works of global superstar artists (Budhyarto 2015). Third, the biennale continued, if it did not complete, the hacking of the Yogyakarta biennale itself, which had started as early as 1992 with the 'Binal' counterevent. What was apparent across all levels was an ongoing attempt to make Indonesian contemporary art accessible to both local and international practitioners and audiences, and to relink artistic production and reception to a broad variety of urgent socio-political questions, beyond issues of formal aesthetics.

The history of the Yogyakarta biennale can be seen as succinctly summarising the evolution of the broader field of Indonesian contemporary art, which provides the context for the emergence of digital art and hacking culture in the early 2000s, and which itself has been shaped by myriad internal and external socio-political factors. The development of digital technology has been influential, but does not constitute the first or final element among these factors. It also took the fall of an Indonesian president, revisions to the Indonesian academic art system, reorientations in global exhibition formats and the courageous ideas and actions of individual artists and collectives, among others.

CONCLUSION

Since approximately 2010, following the boom in Asian painting, Indonesian multimedia art, including digital videos and installations, has been attracting the attention of national and international festival organisers and art collectors. The younger generation of Indonesian collectors believes new media gives meaningful expression to important issues of our times. The objects they collect allow them to distinguish themselves from their seniors, but often tell only part of the bigger story and context surrounding the artworks. Some of the works are not in the form of static artefacts, but designed as time- and process-based collaborative projects with local communities.

One of the recurring strategies in the art projects is the use of hacking methods to access, share and where necessary modify information on pressing issues such as food and fuel security and environmental sustainability. This alternative type of interpersonal communication and networking has been encouraged and facilitated by the digital technologies of video camera, mobile phone and internet. At the same time, it builds on other, older, creative traditions and media that have used durational, interactive and collaborative methods to express social commitment, to break with artistic and socio-political conventions and to present alternative scenarios or solutions for the future.

The historical perspective reminds us that hacking culture is not merely a transient phenomenon or ephemeral trend based on contemporary digital gadgets, but is rooted in an ongoing creative struggle. This struggle is led by artists who are attempting to have their own and their societies' voices and interests heard amidst the complex and sometimes overwhelming ideological, geopolitical and commercial threats and challenges of the digital age.

REFERENCES

Anshari, I.N. (2015) 'Biennale Jogja: visi Khatulistiwa/vision of Equator', in I.N. Anshari (ed.) *Hacking Conflict: Guide Book*, Yayasan Biennale Yogyakarta, Yogyakarta: 7–8.

Antoinette, M. (2007) 'Deterritorializing aesthetics: international art and its new cosmopolitanisms, from an Indonesian perspective', in E. Jurriëns and J. de Kloet (eds) *Cosmopatriots: On Distant Belongings and Close Encounters*, Rodopi, Amsterdam and New York: 205–33.

Artling Team (2015) 'Interview with "Wok the Rock"', *Artling*, 22 October. Available at http://theartling.com/blog/2015/10/22/interview-wok-the-rock/. Accessed 21 March 2016.

Basari, T.M. (2015) 'Olah limbah tahu, 5 perempuan Indonesia menangi Prix Ars Electronica 2015' [By processing tofu waste, 5 Indonesian women win the

Prix Ars Electronica 2015], *Bisnis.com*, 26 May. Available at http://entrepreneur.bisnis.com/read/20150526/263/437384/olah-limbah-tahu-5-perempuan-indonesia-menangi-prix-ars-electronica-2015. Accessed 13 January 2016.

Bianpoen, C. (2012) 'Art on display at Gallery Kunstkring', *Jakarta Post*, 10 May. Available at http://www.thejakartapost.com/news/2012/05/10/art-display-gallery-kunstkring.html. Accessed 27 January 2016.

Bianpoen, C. (2014) 'The league of extraordinary collectors', *Art Republik*, 3: 80–85.

Biennial Foundation (2016) 'Biennial Foundation'. Available at http://www.biennialfoundation.org/biennials/biennale-jogja/. Accessed 25 November 2016.

Biennale Jogja (2015) 'Lifepatch: "SKS—sistem kebut sekolah"' [Lifepatch—'school racing system'], Yogyakarta. Available at http://www.biennalejogja.org/2015/program/pameran/seniman/lifepatch/. Accessed 21 March 2016.

Bourriaud, N. (2002) *Relational Aesthetics*, translated by S. Pleasance and F. Woods, with the participation of M. Copeland, Les presses du réel, Dijon.

Budhyarto, M. (2015) 'Unik, seperti yang lain' [Unique, like the others], *Equator*, 3(2): 27–31. Available at http://www.biennalejogja.org/2015/artikel/unik-seperti-yang-lain/. Accessed 1 November 2016.

Firmansah, A. (2010) 'Modus operandi seni rupa kontemporer: "pasar banget"' [The modus operandi of contemporary art: 'very market oriented'], *Indonesia Art News*, 30 June. Available at http://indonesiaartnews.or.id/artikeldetil.php?id=57. Accessed 10 April 2014.

Gardner, A., and C. Green (2014) 'Mega-exhibitions, new publics, and Asian art biennials', in L. Hjorth, N. King and M. Kataoka (eds) *Art in the Asia-Pacific: Intimate Publics*, Routledge, London and New York: 23–36.

Genocchio, B. (2013) 'Is Jakarta the next art market capital? Inside Indonesia's contemporary boom', *Blouinartinfo International*, 4 May. Available at http://www.blouinartinfo.com/news/story/897976/is-jakarta-the-next-art-market-capital-inside-indonesias. Accessed 27 January 2016.

Guattari, F. (1989) 'The three ecologies', translated by C. Turner, *New Formations*, 8(Summer): 131–47.

Hamdani, S. (2013) '"Beyond boundaries" a winner', *Jakarta Globe*, 11 May. Available at http://jakartaglobe.beritasatu.com/features/beyond-boundaries-a-winner/. Accessed 27 January 2016.

Harsono, F.X. (2009) 'Meraba peta komunitas seni rupa Indonesia' [Towards a map of the Indonesian fine arts], in F.X. Harsono, *Seni Rupa, Perubahan, Politik* [Art, Change, Politics], Langgeng Gallery, Magelang: 129–37.

Hill, D., and K. Sen (2005) *The Internet in Indonesia's New Democracy*, Routledge, London and New York.

Holt, C. (1967) *Art in Indonesia: Continuities and Change*, Cornell University Press, Ithaca.

Jurriëns, E. (2013) 'Between utopia and real world: Indonesia's avant-garde new media art', *Indonesia and the Malay World*, 41(119): 48–75.

Kera, D. (2012) 'Hackerspaces and DIYbio in Asia: connecting science and community with open data, kits and protocols', *Journal of Peer Production*, 2: 1–8. Available at http://peerproduction.net/issues/issue-2/peer-reviewed-papers/diybio-in-asia/. Accessed 14 July 2016.

Kolesnikov-Jessop, S. (2012) 'Chinese-Indonesian collector makes up for lost time', *New York Times*, 15 March. Available at http://www.nytimes.com/2012/03/16/arts/16iht-rartjessop16.html?_r=1. Accessed 10 April 2014.

Li, Z. (2015) 'Sotheby's Hong Kong rakes in $110 million from modern and contemporary Asian art', *artnet News*, 7 April. Available at https://news.artnet.

com/market/sothebys-hong-kong-modern-and-contemporary-asian-art-sales-report-285652. Accessed 2 March 2017.

Lifepatch (2015a) 'Lifepatch', Yogyakarta. Available at http://lifepatch.org/Lifepatch. Accessed 21 March 2016.

Lifepatch (2015b) 'JRP—Jogja River Project', Yogyakarta. Available at http://lifepatch.org/JRP_-_Jogja_River_Project. Accessed 21 March 2016.

Lifepatch (2015c) 'Jakarta Biennale 2015', Yogyakarta. Available at http://lifepatch.org/Jakarta_Biennale_2015. Accessed 13 January 2016.

Museum Van Loon (2013) 'Presentaties door Aziatische hedendaagse kunstverzamelaars' [Presentations by Asian contemporary art collectors]. Available at http://www.museumvanloon.nl/agenda/29. Accessed 27 January 2016.

Nugroho, G.P.S. (2014) 'Membuka katalog, mengungkap ideologi' [Opening catalogues, expressing ideology], in F. Wardani and Y.F. Kresno Murti (eds) *Arsipelago: Kerja Arsip dan Pengarsipan Seni Budaya di Indonesia* [Archipelago: Archival Work and the Archiving of Art and Culture in Indonesia], Indonesian Visual Art Archive (IVAA), Yogyakarta: 143–67.

Piksel 14 (2014) 'XXLab—WATI: the domestic hacking project', *Piksel 14*, 10 October. Available at http://14.piksel.no/2014/10/10/honflab-new-works. Accessed 21 March 2016.

Posyananda, A. (2011) 'Playing with shadows', *Contemporary Aesthetics*, 17 November. Available at http://www.contempaesthetics.org/newvolume/pages/article.php?articleID=627&searchstr=apinan. Accessed 21 March 2016.

Rap (2015) 'XXLab bawa Indonesia menangkan Prix Ars Electronica 2015' [XXLab lets Indonesia win Prix Ars Electronica 2015], *Tribun Jogja*, 21 June. Available at http://jogja.tribunnews.com/2015/06/21/xxlab-bawa-indonesia-menangkan-prix-ars-electronica-2015. Accessed 21 March 2016.

Sahana, M. (2009) 'Jamming the Jogja way', *Jakarta Post*, 17 December. Available at http://www.thejakartapost.com/news/2009/12/17/jamming-jogja-way.html. Accessed 21 March 2016.

Samboh, G. (2013) 'Biennale Jogja dari masa ke masa: mengumpulkan dokumen dan dokumentasi Biennale Jogja' [The Jogja Biennale from time to time: collecting Jogja Biennale documents and documentation], Yayasan Biennale Yogyakarta, 15 January. Available at http://www.biennalejogja.org/yayasan-biennale/biennale-jogja-dari-masa-ke-masa/. Accessed 21 March 2016.

Sudiarno, T. (2010) 'Biennale Jogja X 2009 art for the people', *Garuda: The Magazine of Garuda Indonesia*, January. Available at http://v2.garudamagazine.com/features.php?id=159. Accessed 21 March 2016.

Supriyanto, E. (2012) 'Micronation/macronation curatorial'. Available at http://www.natural-fiber.com/index.php?option=com_content&view=article&id=282:micronationmacronation-curatorial&catid=63:latest-projects&Itemid=65. Accessed 21 March 2016.

Teh, D. (2012) 'Project realization phase A', Singapore, April. Available at http://www.natural-fiber.com/index.php?option=com_content&view=article&id=300&Itemid=107. Accessed 21 March 2016.

Turner, C. (2005) 'Indonesia: art, freedom, human rights and engagement with the West', in C. Turner (ed.) *Art and Social Change: Contemporary Art in Asia and the Pacific*, Pandanus Books, Canberra: 196–217.

Umahseni (2013) 'Beyond boundaries: when collector curates a show', *Newsletter*, 1. Available at http://umahseni.com/main/index.php?option=com_content&view=article&id=152&Itemid=69. Accessed 27 January 2016.

Ungku, F. (2015) 'Interest, prices for Southeast Asian art soar: Sotheby's', *Reuters*, 3 December. Available at http://www.reuters.com/article/us-art-southeastasia-sotheby-s-idUSKBN0TM0AU20151203. Accessed 27 January 2016.

v.u.f.o.c. (2012) 'v.u.f.o.c', House of Natural Fiber, Yogyakarta. Available at http://www.natural-fiber.com/index.php?option=com_content&view=article&id=295&catid=77. Accessed 21 March 2016.

Wirajuda, T. (2014) 'Modern art takes center stage in new exhibition', *Jakarta Globe*, 23 July. Available at http://jakartaglobe.beritasatu.com/features/modern-art-takes-center-stage-new-exhibition/. Accessed 14 January 2016.

Wright, A. (1994) *Soul, Spirit, and Mountain: Preoccupations of Contemporary Indonesian Painters*, Oxford University Press, Kuala Lumpur.

XXLab (2015) 'Soya c(o)u(l)ture', Yogyakarta. Available at http://xxlab.honfablab.org/soya-coulture/. Accessed 21 March 2016.

Zineng, W. (2011) 'Market watch: notes on the contemporary Southeast Asian art market', *Third Text*, 25(4): 459–66.

PART 5

Commerce

13 Indonesia and the digital economy: creative destruction, opportunities and challenges

Mari Pangestu and Grace Dewi

The digital economy has multifaceted, sweeping yet wildly unpredictable effects on society (Eisenmann 2016). In addition to its economic impact, digitalisation can have cascading and transformative impacts on environment, education, health and governance. The digital economy can be defined as 'the economic activity that results from billions of everyday online connections among people, businesses, devices, data, and processes'; the smooth functioning of the digital economy depends on hyperconnectivity, referring to the 'growing interconnectedness of people, organisations, and machines that results from the Internet, mobile technology and the internet of things' (Deloitte n.d.). Inextricably intertwined with any definition of the digital economy is the notion of the sharing economy, that is, the use of the internet to facilitate peer-to-peer, rather than firm-centred, commercial exchanges (Belk 2014; Hamari, Sjöklint and Ukkonen 2015; Sundararajan 2016).

The introduction of new technologies has affected economies and societies many times during the course of human history. What is different about digitalisation is the unprecedented speed of the changes in digital technologies and their widespread impact. To be as well prepared as they can be, countries like Indonesia need to understand what the digital economy is and what the impacts are likely to be. This can help them make informed policy and business decisions that prepare the way

* The authors would like to acknowledge the excellent research assistance of Novia Xu.

for the adoption of technological innovations while safeguarding against the risks.

This chapter discusses the potential for the digital economy to generate 'creative destruction'. First coined by Schumpeter (1934, 1950), this term describes how innovations can revolutionise economic structures by increasing productivity and efficiency, but in the process destroy traditional industries and business models. Creative destruction can be disruptive but it is considered an essential part of economic growth.

First, we provide a conceptual framework for the digital economy and look at how digitalisation fundamentally affects economic activity by reducing market frictions and inefficiencies in ways that are not available in the non-digital environment. Second, we review the available data to identify trends in the digital economy in Indonesia. Third, we provide some preliminary estimates of the impact of the digital economy on the overall economy and on productivity, efficiency, inclusiveness and innovation. We also provide examples of how business models are changing, including some that highlight the potential of the digital economy to promote inclusion. We conclude by looking at the current policy framework for the digital economy, and offer some policy recommendations in light of global developments in policy and technology.

DIGITALISATION AND THE TRANSFORMATION OF THE ECONOMY

The digital economy converts 'things' that interact in the physical world to a piece of information or a digital representation in the virtual world. This entails processes to digitally represent buyers, sellers and physical assets.[1] The conversion of things to digital information transforms the economy in three ways: it transforms the market; it transforms the transaction; and it shifts corporate-centric capitalism to crowd-centric capitalism (Figure 13.1). The easier it is to establish an accurate digital representation of the asset and those involved in the transaction, the faster it is for a marketplace to emerge.

Digitalisation can diminish the market frictions faced by buyers and sellers in order to transact, such as the need to travel, meet and gather information. Frictions that have their origins in severe information asymmetry and frictions that have their origins in opportunistic behaviour

---

1 We use the word 'asset' here as a general umbrella term for anything that can be bought and sold: goods and services, whether tangible or intangible, from books (Amazon), ride sharing (Uber, Lyft, Didi, Go-Jek) and housing (Airbnb) to legal services (LawDingo) and many more.

Figure 13.1 *Three ways digitalisation transforms the economy*

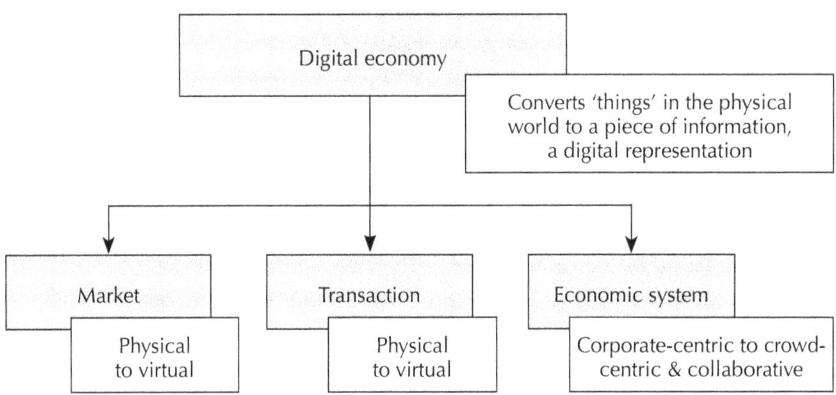

Source: Authors, based on literature review.

that reduces overall welfare can impede trade. To understand the sweeping impacts of digitalisation, we need to understand first how it affects markets and transactions—two elements that are the bedrock of the modern economy today.

We use Alvin Roth's (2008) elements of market design to explain how digitalisation reduces market frictions. First, digitalisation enhances market *thickness* by increasing the number of parties that can transact. The presence of a trading platform in which every possible buyer and seller is digitally represented gives both the buyer and the seller a wide choice of potential transactors. Second, digitalisation helps create a balanced condition in the market that allows the transaction to be fast enough to clear, yet slow enough to allow the buyer or the seller to seek and consider alternative transactors. Third, digitalisation promotes market safety—a condition in which it is safe for a buyer and a seller to transact, as opposed to transacting outside the market.

Digitalisation also reduces transaction costs. A transaction happens in a market when the cost of transacting is not prohibitive. Ronald Coase describes the various elements of a transaction as follows:

> In order to carry out a market transaction it is necessary to discover who it is that one wishes to deal with, to inform people that one wishes to deal and on what terms, to conduct negotiations leading up to a bargain, to draw up the contract, to undertake the inspection needed to make sure that the terms of the contract are being observed, and so on (Coase 1960: 15).

The digital economy reduces the costs associated with a transaction in three ways. First, it modifies the costs associated with searching for information and discovering potential buyers or sellers by making it easier to match suitable buyers and sellers. Ride-sharing apps, for example, make it simpler and quicker for consumers to locate, and drivers to provide, cabs. Second, the digital economy modifies the costs associated with bargaining by streamlining price discovery. For example, sellers on online shopping sites such as Amazon are asked to provide estimates on the price range at which they are willing to sell. This can save buyers from the need to haggle with sellers or to seek financing. However, the savings from a reduction in bargaining costs may be lost without adequate monitoring to ensure that sellers do not collude to collectively increase prices. Third, the digital economy modifies the transaction costs associated with drafting, monitoring and enforcing contracts between transactors. Often the goods or services being traded leave space for either the buyer or the seller to behave opportunistically. Digitalisation, to some extent, can reduce the likelihood that this will occur. For example, companies that employ freelancers can use a platform called Elance to take screenshots of a freelancer's work at pre-determined intervals to ensure that the freelancer does not artificially inflate the number of billed hours.

The results of a survey conducted in 2014–15 suggest that in Indonesia digitalisation is already enabling people to search for (and to some extent verify the quality and features of) the goods and services they are planning to purchase (Figure 13.2). The presence of the internet and digitalised information can minimise or even eliminate some transaction costs that would have been present in the absence of digitalisation.

As well as reducing market frictions and making it easier and cheaper to transact, the third way in which digitalisation transforms the economy is through the shift from corporate-centric to crowd-centric capitalism. The theory of the firm aims to explain why a firm emerges and what its boundaries are. The firm emerges as the organisational form of choice in many business models because it is the most economical way to minimise transaction costs, including search, regulatory, bargaining, negotiating and enforcement costs (Coase 1937; Ouchi 1980; Williamson 1991). Depending on which strategy offers the lowest transaction cost, a firm may choose to form a strategic alliance, to engage in horizontal or vertical integration (acquire a buyer or a supplier) or to develop and secure unique strategic assets that allow it to maintain a competitive advantage (Dyer 1989; Mahoney 1992; Brouthers and Brouthers 2000; Reuer and Koza 2000; McCann, Reuer and Lahiri 2016).

Digitalisation can redefine all of these 'traditional' aspects of the firm. The transaction costs that are minimised through the formation of a firm under corporate-centric capitalism may be reduced further in the sharing economy. For example, the costs associated with price discovery, coordination, buyer/supplier contract enforcement and the creation of

Figure 13.2 *How the internet is being used to minimise transaction costs (% of responses)*

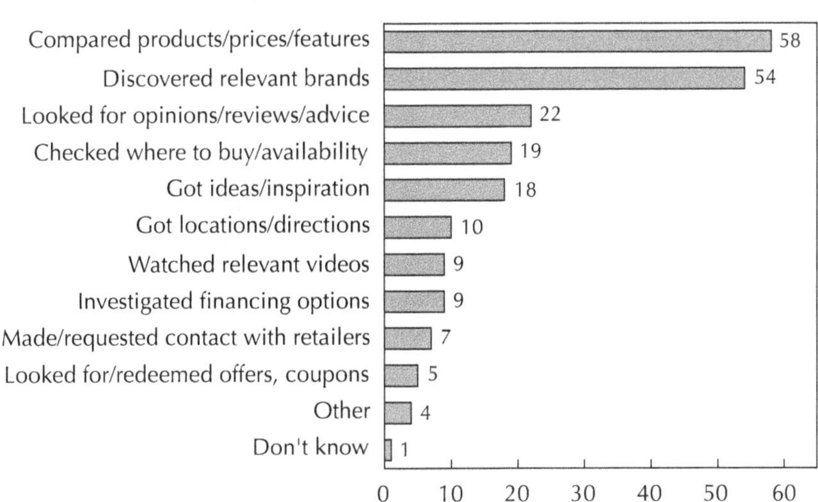

Note: The question asked was 'Which of these did you do on the internet/using apps in relation to your recent purchase decision?'

Source: Consumer Barometer Survey 2014/15, https://www.consumerbarometer.com/en/graph-builder/?question=S28&filter=country:indonesia, accessed 10 September 2016.

contracts with workers may become trivial enough that the existence of a corporation, the boundary of the firm and even the boundary between employer and employee become imprecise (Davis 2016). Airbnb does not own the apartments it rents out to consumers, for example, and Uber does not own the cars or employ the drivers providing its ride-sharing service.[2] While having as many as 160,000 driver 'partners' (MacMillan 2015), Uber only has about 6,700 employees (Loizos 2016). In other words, the unit—the transaction cost—that defines a firm and its strategic behaviour in non-digital, corporate-centric capitalism is gradually being eliminated.

Crowd-centric capitalism relies on a different way of organising economic activity (Sundararajan 2016). In the Airbnb example, with internet facilitation, the parties to a transaction share otherwise excess or idle assets, while in the Zipcar or Go-Jek business model, a car or motorcycle that would otherwise be unused can be put to use transporting consumers. These crowd-centric ways of organising economic activity create

2 A court ruling in the United Kingdom in October 2016 may put this in question: the court ruled that Uber drivers were employees of the company, not self-employed, and therefore entitled to the minimum wage and holiday pay.

value within an ecosystem (Belk 2014; Williamson and De Meyer 2012) and, compared with the corporate-centric model, rely on a wider range of parties that are external to the firm. Consequently, the boundary of the firm is increasingly imprecise and the organisation of the firm is increasingly evolving towards virtual organisation (Davis 2016).[3]

The widely held perception that the digital economy will contribute to economic growth is not without challenges. Robert Solow said that 'You can see the computer age everywhere but in the productivity statistics' (Solow 1987: 36). This has become known as the Solow paradox. Why did US output not grow faster as investment in computer use increased? Why, after 1973, did labour productivity and total factor productivity (TFP) remain low in the United States, with a similar situation in other OECD countries? More than 25 years later, the jury is still out on resolving the Solow paradox (Acemoglu et al. 2014).

Scholars have come up with several possible explanations for Solow's paradox.[4] First, technical bottlenecks, such as a reliance on humans to input data (Triplett 1999) or a lack of access to the latest computing equipment (Katz and Koutroumpis 2012), may mean that digital technology is underutilised. Hence, while we see extensive progress in the capability of machines, that progress may not immediately become visible in the economic statistics because humans are slow at processing data and because the more capable machines may be inaccessible or unaffordable.

Second, it is likely that the impact of digital technologies on productivity and growth is visible only after a sufficiently long lag. Paul David (1989, 1990) used the example of the long lag between electrification and improvements in productivity in the United States to argue that the impact of computers on US productivity might become apparent only after a similarly long lag. He observed that it took decades for the impact of the breakthroughs in electrification to become visible in the productivity statistics. It was only when electrification crossed the critical 50 per cent diffusion threshold in the 1920s and the price of electricity dropped substantially that it made sense for factory owners to start relying on electric motors rather than non-electrified mechanical processes.

Third, it is possible that the contribution of digital technology to growth and productivity has been overhyped (Wolf 2015). Perhaps increases in digitalisation do not greatly increase aggregate output, or perhaps the increases in aggregate output due to digitalisation are not

---

3 John Byrne (1993) defines a virtual organisation as an organisation that consists of a temporary network of independent parties—suppliers, customers, sometime rivals—which are linked by information technology to share skills, costs and access to one another's markets.

4 For an overview, see Triplett (1999).

well measured (Triplett 1999). It could also be that 'the sectors with really fast falling prices because of rapid growth in productivity are less demand exposed [and] shrink as a share of GDP' (Wolf 2015). Finally, the impact of digitalisation may be less than generally assumed because the sectors with large workforces that cannot easily be replaced by computers (such as health care) tend to be the largest in the economy, whereas the sectors that make the largest productivity gains due to digitalisation (such as manufacturing) typically experience declining shares of employment and GDP (Wolf 2015).

Although digital technology should have an impact on productivity, to date the empirical evidence is not conclusive. It is therefore important to start approaching this question on a case-by-case basis. In the next section, we focus on the case of Indonesia.

DYNAMICS OF DIGITALISATION IN INDONESIA

In this section we examine the dynamics of digitalisation in Indonesia along three dimensions: the extent of digitalisation and the main uses that Indonesians are making of the internet; the potential for digitalisation to contribute to growth and development; and the capacity or readiness of Indonesian society to derive benefits from the digital economy.

Extent of digitalisation and how Indonesians are using the internet

The extent of digitalisation can be proxied by the share of the population accessing the internet over time.[5] Globally, the number of internet users has grown exponentially, tripling from 1 billion in 2005 to 3.2 billion in 2015. In Indonesia, the number of people using the internet has followed this upward global trend, increasing sevenfold from 8.1 million in 2005 to 56.6 million in 2015 (Figure 13.3). As a share of the population, the internet penetration rate rose from 3.6 per cent in 2005 to 22.0 per cent in 2015. The increase was particularly marked in the five years from 2010 to 2015, when the number of users grew by 15.3 per cent per year—slower than in India and Myanmar but on a par with the growth rates in China and Thailand.

At the same time, there has been a steep rise in mobile penetration rates as the cost of mobile phones and smartphones has declined. As Figure 13.4 shows, growth in the number of mobile subscriptions has outpaced growth in other important indicators of human development

5 Unless stated otherwise, the data in this subsection are sourced from the International Telecommunication Union (ITU).

Figure 13.3 Internet penetration in Southeast Asia, 2005–15

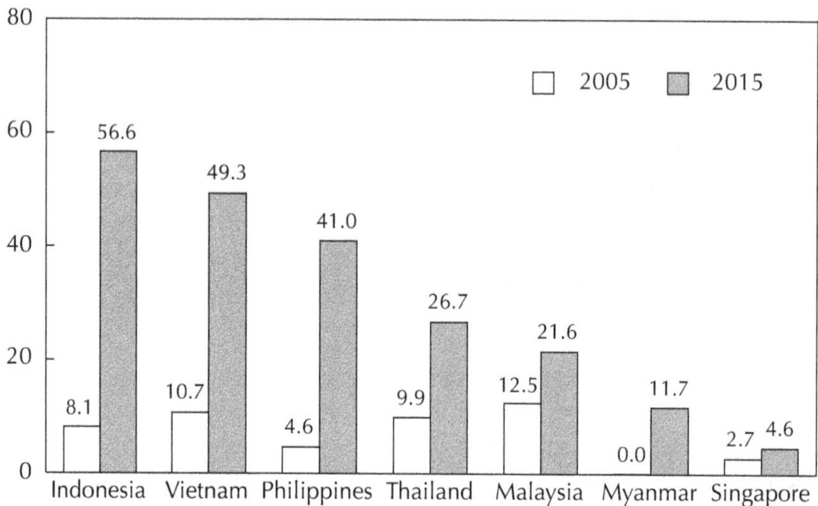

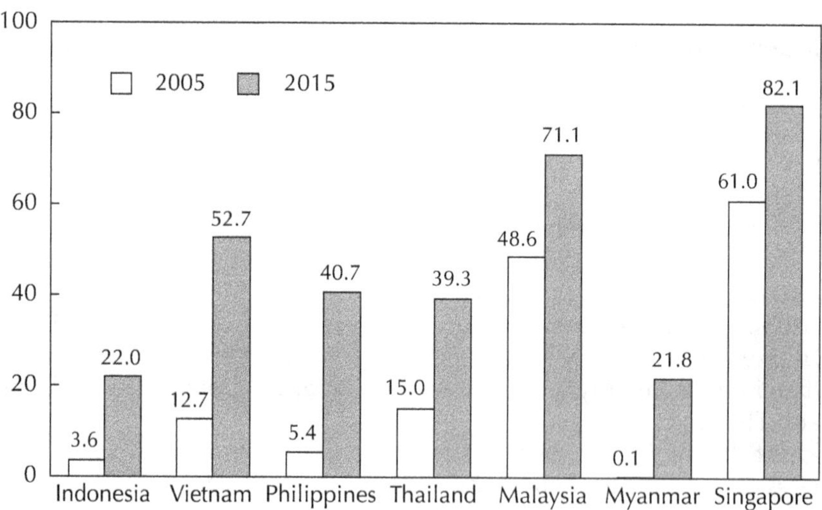

Source: International Telecommunication Union (ITU), Statistics, http://www.itu.int/en/ITU-D/Statistics/Pages/stat/default.aspx.

Figure 13.4 *Mobile and internet penetration rates compared with other development indicators, 2000–15*

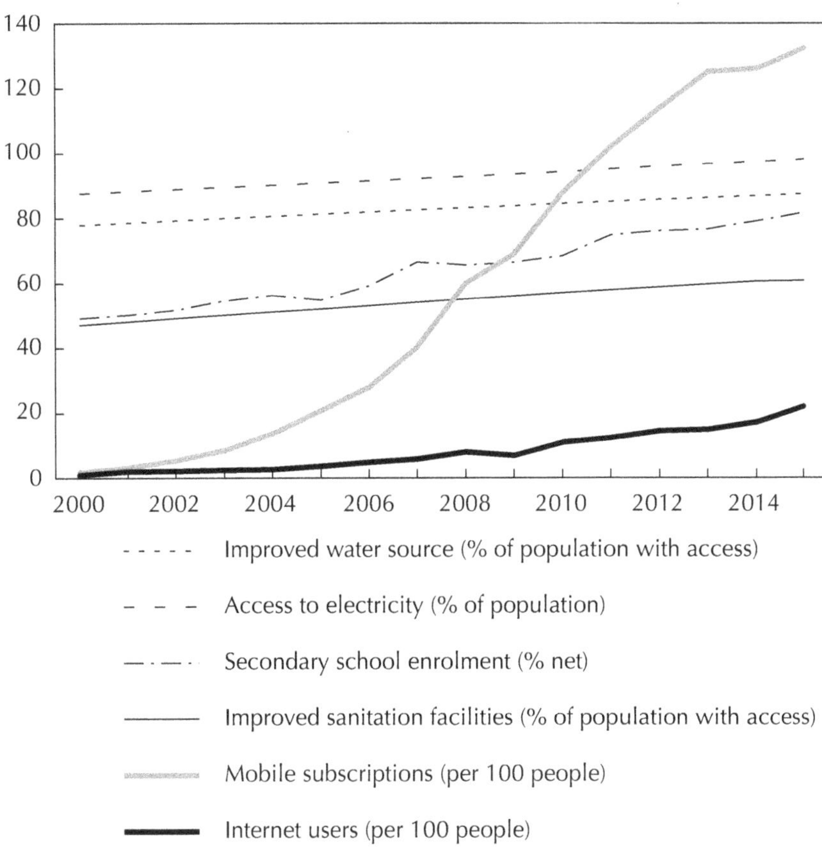

Source: World Bank, World Development Indicators, http://data.worldbank.org/data-catalog/world-development-indicators.

such as electrification and secondary schooling. The Indonesian Internet Service Providers Association (Asosiasi Penyelenggara Jasa Internet Indonesia, or APJII) estimates that 85 per cent of Indonesians access the internet through their mobile phones (APJII 2014: 24).

Data from the annual household surveys conducted by the national statistics agency (Badan Pusat Statistik, or BPS) show that Indonesians mainly use the internet to connect to social media sites (82.0 per cent), to search for information and news (73.5 per cent) and for recreational purposes (entertainment and games) (45.1 per cent) (Figure 13.5). The popularity of social media has risen rapidly over the last few years, leading to Indonesia being listed as the fourth-largest user of Facebook in the

Figure 13.5 Main uses of the internet, 2014

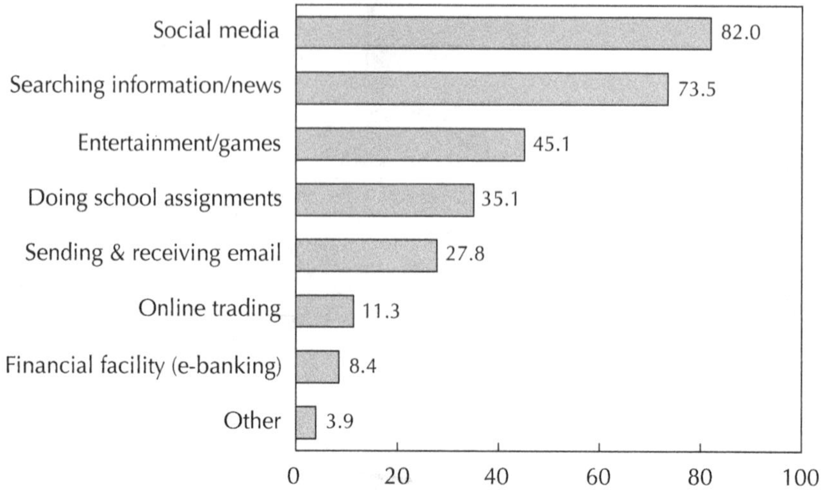

Source: BPS, National Socio-economic Survey (Susenas), 2014.

world and Jakarta being named the world's Twitter capital based on the number of tweets and trending topics. As in other countries, this has had an impact on the marketing of goods and services, the way news is presented and disseminated, the conduct of political campaigns and so on. However, the use of the internet to extract value from business activities remains low in Indonesia, with only 11.3 per cent of Indonesians using online trading platforms and a mere 8.4 per cent using e-banking.

Despite the rapid growth in internet and mobile penetration rates, the transformation of the economy due to digitalisation is still at a nascent stage in Indonesia. There are several reasons for this. First, the capacity of digitalisation to transform markets, transactions and forms of economic organisation depends on a level of hyperconnectivity among transactors. With 78 per cent of the population still not connected to the internet, Indonesia has not yet reached the point of hyperconnectivity (Figure 13.3). Second, the Indonesians who do connect to the internet mainly do so through their mobile devices and use it chiefly to access social media and search for information. In contrast, internet users in developed nations such as Australia, South Korea and Japan use a far wider range of devices to access the internet—desktop computers, laptops and notebooks in addition to mobile phones. These observations imply that Indonesia needs to broaden the population's access to the internet. Given that mobile phones are the technology of choice for many Indonesians, this will mean encouraging greater use of smartphones and other 'smart' devices that are suitable for purposes beyond social and informational activities. At the same time, it will mean improving the broadband network so that Indonesians are not restricted to activities that can be delivered on the mobile phone.

The digital economy and development

The digital economy enhances development by promoting efficiency, innovation and inclusion (World Bank 2016). We have already discussed its role in improving efficiency through increased productivity and innovation and how this can lead to creative destruction. For emerging and developing countries, the role of the digital economy in promoting inclusion is equally important. By reducing the cost and increasing the accessibility of open and transparent information, the internet makes it possible for farmers, micro-enterprises and small enterprises to engage more fully in economic and financial activities. For farmers, the advantages might include better and quicker access to weather and price information and more opportunities to participate in micro-financing schemes. For micro-enterprises and small enterprises, they would include being able to sell goods and services through e-commerce platforms, check customers' credit histories and use e-banking services. In essence, the digital economy has the potential to contribute to development and inclusiveness by expanding trade opportunities, encouraging financial inclusion, creating jobs and increasing access to public services.

For the digital economy to contribute to inclusive growth and development, all citizens need to have access to and know how to make best use of the internet. This is not yet the case in Indonesia, where levels of internet use fracture along income, locational, gender, age and educational lines (Figure 13.6). In Indonesia, most internet users are in the upper income group, live in urban areas and are better educated. There is also a demographic dimension to the digital divide, with more younger than older people and more men than women using the internet. Rather than viewing the problem solely as an access issue, policy-makers need to be mindful of the need to reduce the particular constraints that are causing each of the country's digital divides. For instance, the urban/rural divide could be narrowed by improving telecommunications infrastructure in rural areas; the income divide could be addressed by making access more affordable; and the educational divide could be overcome by providing training and capacity building.

The only data that we have been able to find on firms' use of information and communication technology (ICT) come from the World Bank's Enterprise Surveys. The data for 2015 reveal differences across industries and provinces in how firms are using email and websites to con-

Figure 13.6 Share of individuals using the internet by income, location, gender, age and education, 2014 (%)

		%
Income distribution	Bottom 40%	21.4
Income distribution	Top 60%	76.6
Location	Rural	26.3
Location	Urban	73.7
Gender	Men	54.1
Gender	Women	45.9
Age	Young (16-30)	53.6
Age	Mature (45+)	6.5
Education level	Primary school	9.3
Education level	High school	42.7

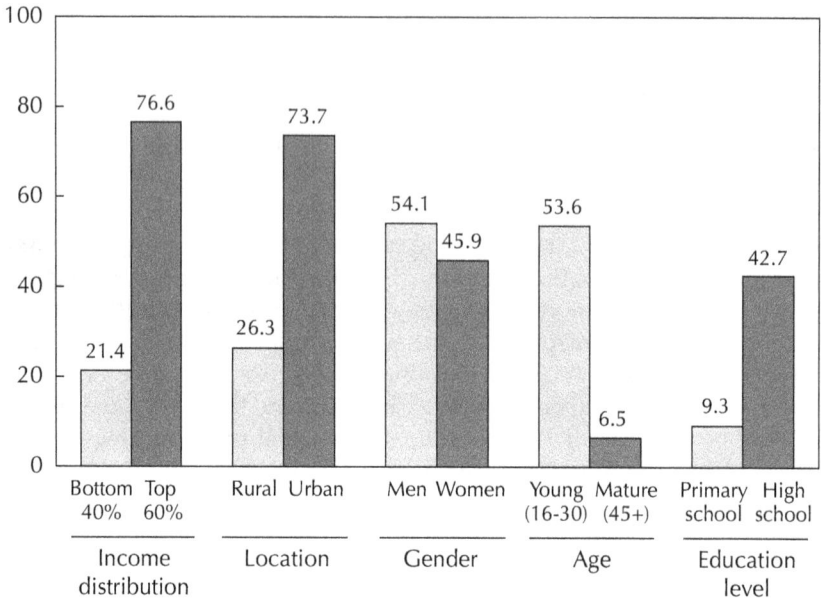

Source: BPS, National Socio-economic Survey (Susenas), 2014.

duct business (World Bank 2015). From the data, we can infer that about half of all Indonesian firms neither use email nor have a website, and that only 33 per cent use both to communicate with their customers. As one might expect, firms located in the capital, Jakarta, are the most likely to use email, have a website or both. Large firms with more than 1,000 workers and firms in the services sector also make more use of ICT than other firms.

More studies are needed to understand which industries and provinces would benefit the most from an improvement in internet utilisation; perhaps the firm-level surveys undertaken by BPS can begin to capture this. In the next section, we attempt to estimate the general impact of internet use on firms' productivity and exports, controlling for provincial and industrial differences and for firms' unobservable differences (see below).

Readiness

As a World Bank report on 'digital dividends' makes clear, internet access is a necessary but not sufficient condition for a country to maximise the benefits from the digital economy; it must also have the capacity to take advantage of that access (World Bank 2016). Here, we discuss Indonesia's readiness to derive benefits from the digital economy using two proxies: infrastructure and skills.

First, we use the level of infrastructure development to indicate the extent to which ICT-related innovation and economic activity is able to occur. Indonesia ranked fourth among ASEAN countries with respect to electricity production in 2015, producing 748 kWh per capita. The mobile phone network covers nearly 100 per cent of the population, although, as discussed, the people who access the internet on their mobile phones mainly use it to access social media or search for information. To create an environment in which the ICT sector can thrive, the internet needs to become faster, more accessible, more affordable and more secure. As Figures 13.7 and 13.8 show, Indonesia lags behind its Southeast Asian peers in the capacity per person of its international internet links and in the security of its internet servers.[6]

Second, we use ability or skills to assess the capacity of the population to derive benefits from digitalisation. Indonesia ranks sixth among ASEAN countries with respect to literacy, with a literacy rate among adults of 93.9 per cent. Indonesia's secondary enrolment ratio is higher than the average for Asia-Pacific countries, but both its secondary and tertiary enrolment rates are lower than those of Singapore, Malaysia and Thailand (Figure 13.9). These figures suggest that Indonesia has some way to go to improve the population's ICT skills and advance the country's preparedness to participate in the digital economy.

THE IMPACT OF DIGITALISATION ON THE ECONOMY

Macroeconomic impact

The impact of the digital economy on the overall Indonesian economy can be assessed, first, by looking at the growth of the ICT sector and its share of GDP (Figure 13.10). The sector has grown at double-digit or high single-digit rates for at least 15 years, recording growth well above the national average of 5–6 per cent. As a result, its share of GDP increased from 2.5 per cent in 2005 to 7.2 per cent in 2015. These high growth rates reflect the openness and competitiveness of the Indonesian telecommunications sector—especially the mobile telephony sector—and the huge

6 Singapore is not shown in the graphs because of its outlier status. Singapore had an international internet bandwidth of 580.8 kb/s per user, and had 609.3 secure servers per million people, in 2015.

Figure 13.7 *International internet bandwidth in Asia, 2012–15 (kb/s per user)*

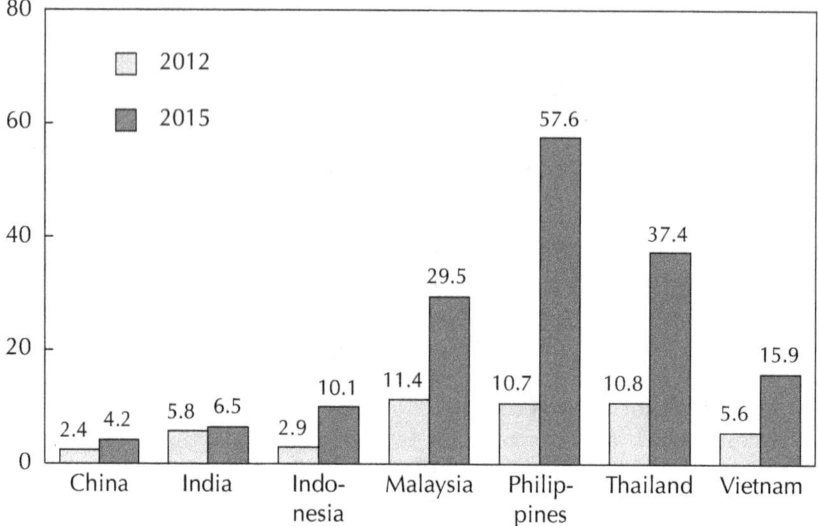

Source: International Telecommunication Union (ITU), ICT Development Index, http://www.itu.int/net4/ITU-D/idi/2016/#idi2016rank-tab.

Figure 13.8 *Secure internet servers in Asia, 2012–15 (no. per million people)*

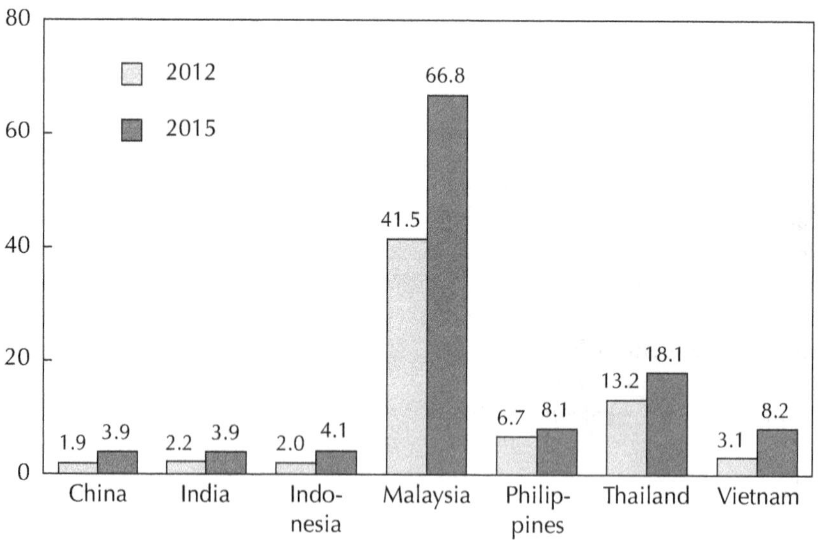

Source: International Telecommunication Union (ITU), ICT Development Index, http://www.itu.int/net4/ITU-D/idi/2016/#idi2016rank-tab.

Figure 13.9 *Secondary and tertiary enrolment ratios in the Asia-Pacific region, 2014*

	Secondary	Tertiary
Asia-Pacific	81	33
Singapore	97	44
Malaysia	87	37
Thailand	86	51
Indonesia	85	32
Philippines	82	28
China	77	27
India	71	25
Vietnam	68	25
Myanmar	50	13

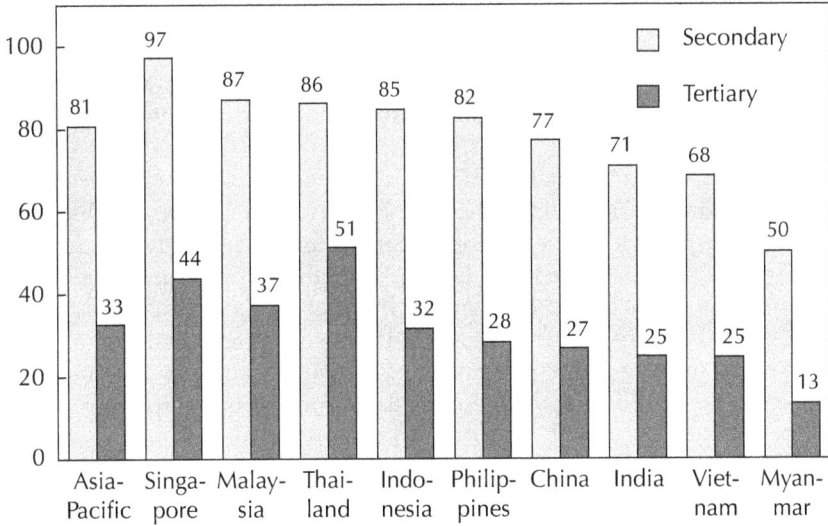

Source: International Telecommunication Union (ITU), ICT Development Index, http://www.itu.int/net4/ITU-D/idi/2016/#idi2016rank-tab.

Figure 13.10 *Share of GDP and growth rate of ICT sector, 2001–15*

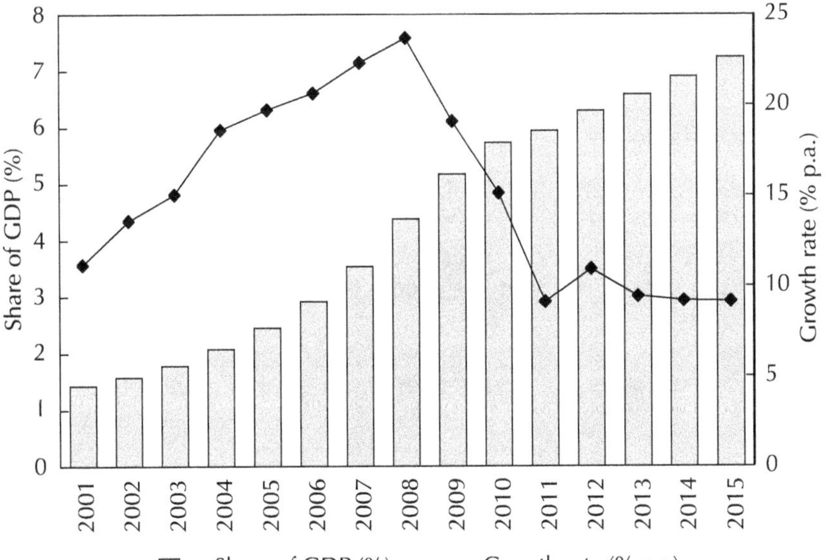

Source: BPS, National Income Accounts.

advancements in telecommunications infrastructure and services over the last few years.

The impact of the digital economy can also be seen in the growth of the computer services and software industry relative to other sections of the creative economy (Figure 13.11). While still making a relatively small contribution to GDP (Rp 10 trillion), computer services and software recorded the fastest growth of all sectors within the creative economy in 2013 (8.2 per cent).

Third, the impact of digitalisation is evident in the growth of the mobile phone market. Oxford Economics (2016: 21–2) estimates that each percentage point increase in mobile penetration over the five years from 2015 to 2020 will add $640 million to GDP and support an extra 10,700 formal jobs in 2020, and that mobile internet will sustain around 8 per cent of the country's total forecast GDP growth in that year.

Finally, we can judge the impact of the digital economy on the overall economy by looking at the contribution of labour, capital and TFP growth to GDP growth. Figure 13.12 shows that during the period 2000–14, the main contributor to GDP growth was capital accumulation, including ICT capital accumulation, rather than TFP growth. In other words, growth was generated more from increased capital accumulation, rather than productivity growth from existing factors. The figure also shows that the contribution of ICT capital accumulation has been increasing since 2004, and especially since 2011. This reflects the decline in the cost of ICT capital and (as indicated earlier), the growth of the ICT sector due to a more open telecommunications regime and rapid rates of mobile and internet penetration. However, the impact of increased ICT capital on productivity is not yet evident in these statistics.

Firm-level impact

Using data from the World Bank Enterprise Surveys for the years 2009 and 2015, in this subsection we estimate the impact of digitalisation on firm productivity and firm exports. Using basic econometric regression, we test the hypotheses that the productivity of firms and the value of firm exports are positively related to email use and having a website. There are many ways of approximating firm productivity but in this chapter we use sales per worker (Cirera, Sabetti and Lage 2016).[7]

7 The impact of digitalisation on productivity is modelled as:

$$Ln\,Productivity_{it} = \beta_0 + \beta_1 Email\ use_{it} + \beta_2 Website\ use_{it} + \mathbf{X}_{it} + I_p + I_s + I_t + \varepsilon_{ist}$$

The impact of the digital economy on exports is estimated as:

Figure 13.11 *Growth rate and contribution to GDP of creative industries, 2013*

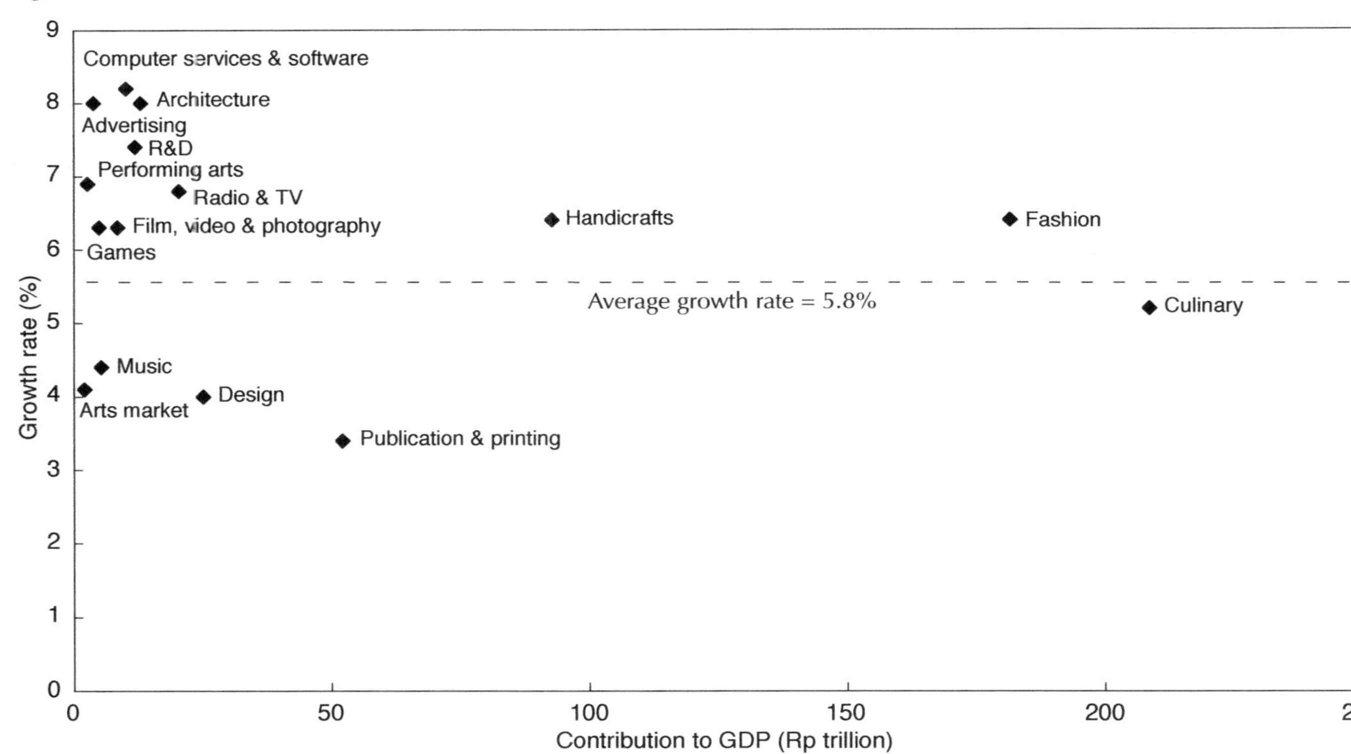

Source: BPS, estimates conducted for the Ministry of Tourism and Creative Economy.

Figure 13.12 *Contribution of labour, capital and total factor productivity (TFP) growth to GDP growth, 2000–14 (%)*

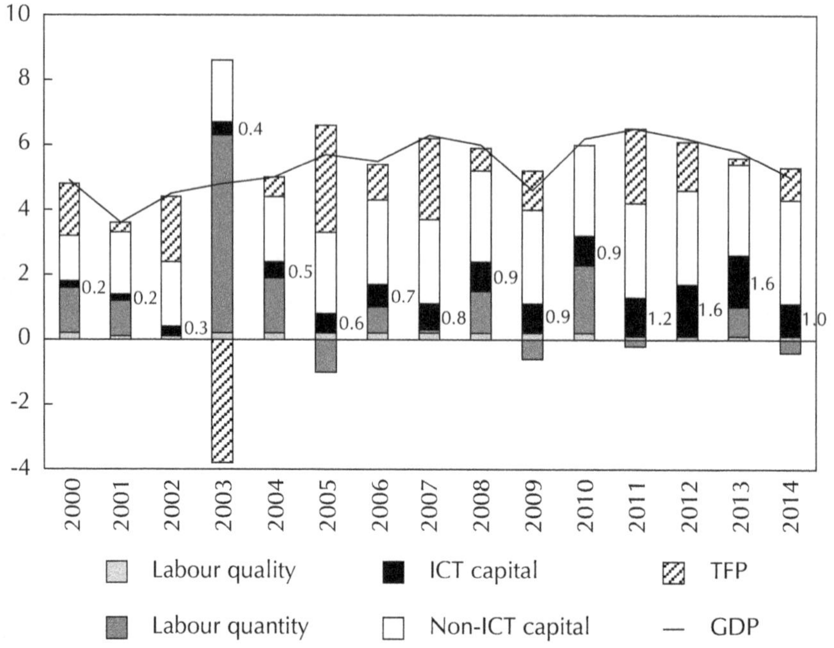

Source: Conference Board, Total Economy Database, May 2015, http://www.conference-board.org/data/economydatabase/.

The results for the productivity regression show that firms that use email have 1.8 times higher productivity than those that do not and that firms that have a website have 1.6 times higher productivity than those that do not (Table A13.1). The results for the export regression show that the export value of firms that use email is 7.4 times higher than that of firms that do not use email, and that the export value of firms that have a website is 8.6 times higher than that of firms that do not have a website

---

$$Export\ value_{it} = \beta_0 + \beta_1 Email\ use_{it} + \beta_2 Website\ use_{it} + \mathbf{X}_{it} + I_p + I_s + I_t + \varepsilon_{ist}$$

Export values are in rupiah. Email use and having a website are both dummy variables that take a value of 1 if a firm uses email or has a website. The control variables are the firm's age and export status. I_p, I_s and I_t are, respectively, province, industry and year fixed effects, while ε is an independent and identically distributed error. We use a fixed effects estimator to control for time-invariant unobservable variables associated with email use and having a website. The results of the regressions can be seen in Tables A13.1 and A13.2 in the appendix.

(Table A13.2). Our data do not allow us to impose more controls or to identify the direction of causality. However, they do allow us to infer that there is a strong likelihood that digitalisation has a positive association with firm performance.

Disruption of traditional business models

The explosion of digital technologies has reshaped corporate and community behaviour by providing new avenues for sharing and community-based exchange (Sundararajan 2016). This has created commercial opportunities for many businesses while undermining the business models of many others. In other words, digitalisation is changing the ways in which firms create value and deal with their external constituents in factor and product markets (Amit and Zott 2001; Zott and Amit 2008; Kathan, Matzler and Veider 2016). In Indonesia, the disruptive effects of digitalisation are already apparent in the traditional media, retail, film, music and transportation industries, and are beginning to be felt in the financial industry.

Digitalisation increases the productivity and efficiency of firms by allowing them to provide highly customised or modular products and services at a cheaper cost. In the sharing economy model, it is entirely possible for firms—even if they are competitors—to share resources so that there is an optimal use of available resources and infrastructure (Davis 2016). For instance, Netflix has shifted all its data onto the servers of Amazon, its prime competitor, and Uber and Lyft, as well as Go-Ride and GrabBike, sometimes use the same drivers and vehicles.

Digitalisation also gives successful online companies a pathway to expand their consumer bases—and therefore their valuations—by adding to their original goods and services. For instance, Go-Jek now provides not only transport services but also food and goods delivery, beauty, cleaning and massage services. As this example suggests, the success of the online business model depends on a great deal of collaboration between the producers of different types of goods and services, in particular those providing infrastructure (especially telecommunications infrastructure), payment and delivery services.

At the same time as it has created numerous commercial opportunities, digitalisation has also disrupted the traditional business models of many Indonesian companies. The first to be affected were media, film and music businesses due to the advent of online media. In the media industry, detikcom (established in 1998) was the first company to take up the challenge of making a profit in the online news space; it was acquired by a major Indonesian media company in 2011 for a rumoured price of $60 million (Septiadi 2011). In the film industry, the shift towards the digital production and distribution of movies has reduced costs, allowing cinemas to invest in expanding the number of screens. At the same time, the widespread availability of free downloads has disrupted the physical markets for film and music distribution, such as DVDs and CDs, and the royalty-based business model for artists. Artists have had to invent new ways of profiting from their work, such as bundling sales with sales of other products and earning revenue from advertising on free live-streaming sites, while also lobbying government to enforce copyright infringement and royalty payment provisions more strictly.

In recent years, the sectors most affected by digitalisation have been the retail sales and transportation industries, with e-commerce and ride-sharing start-ups successfully raising capital domestically and abroad. The e-commerce sector has grown rapidly but still accounted for only 1.5 per cent of total retail sales in 2015 (Statista n.d.), compared with 7.9 per cent in China (eMarketer 2015). There is thus a lot of potential for this sector to grow as small enterprises realise the opportunities to sell goods and services online. Despite not having a local presence, Amazon was the most popular business-to-consumer site in Indonesia in 2013. It has since been overtaken by Lazada (founded by Rocket Internet), which quickly expanded its share of the local market by providing an Indonesian-language website and offering services such as same-day delivery and customised payment schemes.[8] In the consumer-to-consumer marketplace, online retailers Tokopedia and Bukalapak, both local players, have been growing exponentially. Venture capital firm SoftBank invested $100 million in Tokopedia in 2014 and major media company Emtek took a stake in Bukalapak in 2015. Indonesia's bricks-and-mortar retailers are responding to the threat of digital disruption by introducing their own e-commerce platforms, such as Matahari Mall and MAP EMALL.

In the transportation sector, the entry of Go-Jek, then Grab and Uber and their offshoots GrabBike and uberMOTOR, has disrupted the business models of the traditional motorcycle taxi and taxicab industries. In response to violent protests by traditional motorcycle taxi and taxicab drivers in 2015, the government introduced regulations on vehicle roadworthiness and employment conditions for the ride-sharing companies (Faisal 2016). In fact, however, the pace of change in Indonesia's digital economy is faster than government regulation can hope to keep up with. In 2016, Go-Jek became the first 'unicorn' start-up in Indonesia to be valued at more than $1 billion, after receiving $1.3 billion in venture capital

---

8 In 2016, Alibaba acquired a controlling stake in Lazada for $1 billion. Other successful e-retailers currently operating in Indonesia include Zalora (Rocket Internet's fashion platform) and Rakuten Belanja Online (a subsidiary of Japanese giant Rakuten).

funds from various sources, including Sequoia Capital and KKR (Russell 2016).

In the travel sector, the growing popularity of cheap airline tickets sold online by budget airlines has pressured full-service airlines such as Garuda to substantially improve their online booking systems. Similarly, the success of online aggregation platforms for booking hotels and tours, such as Traveloka and tiket.com, has forced traditional travel agents to rethink their business models.

Digitalisation of the financial sector is just beginning, starting with online banking and some more recent innovations in fintech products and services. The ability of the digital economy to support financial inclusion is one of its biggest potential benefits. In 2015, for example, the Financial Services Authority (Otoritas Jasa Keuangan, or OJK) issued a circular letter (No. 6/SEOJK.03/2015) allowing branchless banking, which should make it easier for people living in remote areas to access basic financial services through their mobile phones. Given that only 36 per cent of Indonesian adults currently have a bank account,[9] there is huge scope for growth in the fintech sector, with commensurate opportunities for financial inclusion.

It is clear that digitalisation is affecting business models in Indonesia. Traditional products and services are being delivered in original and collaborative ways, creating new pathways for consumers and producers to profit from the digital economy. One concrete example is the case of the Indonesian villagers who work as farmers by day and design logos for the web-based graphic design company 99designs by night. The company outsources logo design through a competitive process, then monitors, manages and pays for the service through the internet. In February 2015, 130,000 Indonesian designers spread across many villages were registered on the company's platform.

CONCLUSIONS AND RECOMMENDATIONS

The data and other information presented in this chapter indicate that there is a positive association between the digital economy and economic growth, both at the firm level and at the macro level. The data are far from comprehensive and the digital economy is still at an early stage of development in Indonesia, so our evaluation is necessarily preliminary. Better data and more research will be needed, at the individual level and at the firm level, to better understand the trends.

---

9 This information is sourced from http://datatopics.worldbank.org/financial-inclusion/country/indonesia.

The 14th Economic Policy Package announced by the government on 10 November 2016 included, for the first time, an e-commerce roadmap.[10] The package aims to make Indonesia the biggest digital economy in Southeast Asia by 2020, with 1,000 technopreneurs valued at $10 billion and an e-commerce market of $130 billion. The e-commerce roadmap provides policies in eight areas to accelerate the development of the digital economy: funding programs for digital businesses; tax incentives for local investors; consumer protection mechanisms; education and human capital development; telecommunications infrastructure; e-commerce logistics; cybersecurity; and the formation of a taskforce to ensure implementation of the roadmap. We refer to some of these policies in our recommendations, below.

First, we conclude that there has been rapid growth of digitalisation in Indonesia, as reflected in the growth in mobile and internet penetration rates and the large number of Indonesians who access the internet through their mobile phones. The macroeconomic impact of digitalisation is evident in the rapid growth of the ICT sector and its expanding share of GDP; moreover, preliminary estimates show that firms that use the internet and have a website are more productive and export more than those that do not. Nevertheless, 78 per cent of Indonesians still do not use the internet and there is a digital divide by region, income and educational level between those who access the internet and those who do not. The implication for policy is that the government needs to improve telecommunications infrastructure and make access to the internet more affordable in order to create a more conducive environment for the digital economy. In the Indonesia Broadband Plan announced in 2014, the government stated that it would increase the speed and accessibility of broadband by April 2019. In addition, it needs to upgrade physical transport infrastructure so that the delivery of goods can keep pace with the digitalisation of trade.

Second, it is clear that connectivity alone is not sufficient to allow producers and consumers to benefit from the digital economy. At present, Indonesians are using the internet mainly to access social media and search for information. This suggests that the country is not extracting full economic value from the digital economy, including its potential to contribute to development and inclusion. Moreover, measures of infrastructure and education show that the country does not have the capacity to capitalise on digitalisation and is lagging behind its ASEAN peers. The government therefore needs not only to provide the hard infrastruc-

---

10 See the website of the Coordinating Ministry for Economic Affairs (https://ekon.go.id/) for full information on the roadmap; see also the summary in Indonesia Services Dialogue Council (2016: 2–3).

ture needed to improve connectivity but also to increase the population's readiness to benefit from technological change.

One of the major constraints voiced by digital businesses is a lack of skilled human resources, especially engineers, coders and platform developers. Beset by bugs in its software that its domestic staff were unable to fix, even Go-Jek eventually had to outsource its software development to tech companies in India (Velayanikal 2016). At the same time, there is a gap in the ability of many small enterprises to transition their businesses to e-commerce platforms. The 14th Economic Policy Package announced in late 2016 proposes an e-commerce curriculum that includes training in coding; education and training for small enterprises; an incubator program for start-ups; and a campaign to increase digital awareness among the wider population. The national government, local governments, educational institutions and the private sector will all need to work together to train the ICT-ready workforce that Indonesia so urgently needs.

An ecosystem that fosters the development of start-ups also depends on funding sources that are suited to digital economy business models. Typically this would mean angel investment and venture capital rather than traditional bank loans, as well as fiscal and other incentives. To make it easier for digital businesses to obtain funding, the 14th Economic Policy Package proposes establishing credit, grant and subsidy programs; facilitating angel investment and crowd funding; and allowing 100 per cent foreign ownership in e-commerce. To be effective, any government programs should of course be designed in such a way that grants or subsidies go only to projects with a high degree of commercial and economic viability.

A mature venture capital system should provide mechanisms not only to encourage people to invest in start-ups but also to allow them to exit their investments without too much difficulty, whether through the capital market or through mergers and acquisitions. In Indonesia, however, uncertainty about the role of financial capital in investments and the tax treatment of investors' capital gains is considered to be a major obstacle to the sustainable financing of start-ups in the digital economy. As a result, many Indonesian entrepreneurs choose to establish their businesses in Singapore to take advantage of its friendlier tax regime.[11]

Third, the government needs to actively manage the impact of creative destruction on traditional business models. Like other countries facing the problem of digital disruption, Indonesia must make room for creative innovations in the delivery of both new and traditional goods and services while at the same time ensuring a level playing field in

---

11 This observation is based on interviews with start-ups and venture capital players in the digital economy in Indonesia.

terms of tax and regulatory compliance. This also means finding ways to protect consumers from identity theft and fraud, to address privacy concerns and to ensure cybersecurity, without stifling innovation.

The government is trying to find the right balance between all these competing concerns, but some issues—such as taxation—are proving particularly challenging. Local e-commerce companies complain that they pay a larger share of value-added and corporate taxes than internet giants like Google and Facebook, which can repatriate their advertising and other revenue to low-tax countries such as Singapore. The government is struggling with how to resolve this issue without driving away large foreign tech companies and the competition and innovation they inject into the economy.

Regulators are also only just beginning to come to terms with the issues related to cybersecurity, consumer protection and privacy. Given that other countries are ahead of it on the digital development curve, Indonesia should be able to learn lessons and adopt best practices from those countries. For instance, one current policy problem facing Indonesia is how to implement the requirement for government agencies' servers to be located in Indonesia by October 2017 and whether a 'server' means a physical server or, in addition, data stored in the cloud. To resolve these issues before the impending deadline, Indonesia should study not only how data storage technology has evolved, but also how other countries are handling similar issues of data storage and security.

Digitalisation has as much potential to contribute to development as the industrial revolution once did (Sundararajan 2016). For developing countries, it also offers opportunities for social and economic inclusion and the chance to leapfrog less efficient, more expensive technologies and move directly to more advanced ones. Still at the beginning of this technological revolution, Indonesia has the opportunity to use digital technology to promote equitable and inclusive economic growth. The role of government in this process is twofold. First, it needs to provide hard infrastructure such as telecommunications, broadband and transport infrastructure, and soft infrastructure such as education and training. Second, it needs to create the right balance between regulation and incentives, while also addressing consumer protection and cybersecurity issues. For the digital economy to thrive, the government should be careful not to intervene or direct development too much.

REFERENCES

Acemoglu, D., D. Autor, D. Dorn, G.H. Hanson and B. Price (2014) 'Return of the Solow paradox? IT, productivity, and employment in US manufacturing', *American Economic Review*, 104(5): 394–9.

Amit, R., and C. Zott (2001) 'Value creation in e-business', *Strategic Management Journal*, 22(6–7): 493–520.

APJII (Asosiasi Penyelenggara Jasa Internet Indonesia) (2014) 'Profil pengguna internet Indonesia 2014' [Profile of Indonesian internet users 2014], Jakarta. Available at https://apjii.or.id/downfile/file/PROFILPENGGUNAINTERNETINDONESIA2014.pdf.

Belk, R. (2014) 'You are what you can access: sharing and collaborative consumption online', *Journal of Business Research*, 67(8): 1,595–600.

Brouthers, K.D., and L.E. Brouthers (2000) 'Acquisition or greenfield start-up? Institutional, cultural and transaction cost influences', *Strategic Management Journal*, 21(1): 89–97.

Byrne, J. (1993) 'The virtual corporation', *Bloomberg.com*, 8 February. Available at http://www.bloomberg.com/news/articles/1993-02-07/the-virtual-corporation.

Cirera, X., L. Sabetti and F. Lage (2016) 'ICT use, innovation, and productivity: evidence from Sub-Saharan Africa', Policy Research Working Paper No. 7868, World Bank Washington, DC. Available at http://documents.worldbank.org/curated/en/997211476897844312/ICT-use-innovation-and-productivity-evidence-from-Sub-Saharan-Africa.

Coase, R.H. (1937) 'The nature of the firm', *Economica*, 4(16): 386–405.

Coase, R.H. (1960) 'The problem of social cost', *Journal of Law and Economics*, 3: 1–44.

David, P.A. (1989) 'Computer and dynamo: the modern productivity paradox in a not-too-distant mirror', Warwick Economics Research Paper No. 339, University of Warwick, Warwick, July.

David, P.A. (1990) 'The dynamo and the computer: an historical perspective on the modern productivity paradox', *American Economic Review*, 80(2): 355–61.

Davis, G.F. (2016) *The Vanishing American Corporation: Navigating the Hazards of a New Economy*, Berrett-Koehler Publishers, Oakland.

Deloitte (n.d.) 'What is digital economy? Unicorns, transformation and the internet of things'. Available at https://www2.deloitte.com/mt/en/pages/technology/articles/mt-what-is-digital-economy.html.

Dyer, W.G. (1989) 'Integrating professional management into a family owned business', *Family Business Review*, 2(3): 221–35.

Eisenmann, T. (2016) 'Black swans and big trends can ruin anyone's internet prediction', *Forbes*, 18 August. Available at http://www.forbes.com/sites/hbsworkingknowledge/2016/08/18/black-swans-and-big-trends-can-tuin-anyones-internet-prediction/. Accessed 11 September 2016.

eMarketer (2015) 'Mobile accounts for almost half of China's retail ecommerce sales', *eMarketer*, 30 July. Available at https://www.emarketer.com/Article/Mobile-Accounts-Almost-Half-of-Chinas-Retail-Ecommerce-Sales/1012793. Accessed 10 March 2017.

Faisal, F. (2016) 'Indonesia sets new rules for ride-sharing companies', *The Conversation*, 10 May. Available at http://theconversation.com/indonesia-sets-new-rules-for-ride-sharing-companies-57187.

Hamari, J., M. Sjöklint and A. Ukkonen (2015) 'The sharing economy: why people participate in collaborative consumption', *Journal of the Association for Information Science and Technology*, 67(9): 2,047–59.

Indonesia Services Dialogue Council (2016) *Indonesia Service Sectors Update & News (Issues)*, 3 November – 2 December. Available at http://isd-indonesia.org/issues-indonesia-services-sectors-update-news-2/.

Kathan, W., K. Matzler and V. Veider (2016) 'The sharing economy: your business model's friend or foe?', *Business Horizons*, 59(6): 663–72.

Katz, R.L., and P. Koutroumpis (2012) 'Measuring socio-economic digitization: a paradigm shift', SSRN Scholarly Paper No. ID 2070035, Social Science Research Network (SSRN), Rochester, 29 May. Available at http://papers.ssrn.com/abstract=2070035.

Loizos, C. (2016) 'Handcuffed to Uber', *TechCrunch*, 29 April. Available at http://social.techcrunch.com/2016/04/29/handcuffed-to-uber/.

MacMillan, D. (2015) 'Uber touts its employment opportunities', *Wall Street Journal*, 25 January. Available at http://www.wsj.com/articles/uber-touts-its-employment-opportunities-1422229862.

Mahoney, J.T. (1992) 'The choice of organizational form: vertical financial ownership versus other methods of vertical integration', *Strategic Management Journal*, 13(8), 559–84.

McCann, B.T., J.J. Reuer and N. Lahiri (2016) 'Agglomeration and the choice between acquisitions and alliances: an information economics perspective', *Strategic Management Journal*, 37(6): 1,085–106.

Ouchi, W.G. (1980) 'Markets, bureaucracies, and clans', *Administrative Science Quarterly*, 25(1): 129–41.

Oxford Economics (2016) 'One million opportunities: the impact of mobile internet on the economy of Southeast Asia', June. Available at https://www.oxfordeconomics.com/recent-releases/one-million-opportunities-the-impact-of-mobile-internet-on-the-economy-of-south-east-asia.

Reuer, J.J., and M.P. Koza (2000) 'On lemons and indigestibility: resource assembly through joint ventures', *Strategic Management Journal*, 21(2): 195–7.

Roth, A. (2008) 'What have we learned from market design?', *Economic Journal*, 118(527): 285–310.

Russell, J. (2016) 'Indonesia's Go-Jek raises $550 million to battle Uber and Grab', *TechCrunch*, 4 August. Available at https://techcrunch.com/2016/08/04/indonesias-go-jek-raises-550-million-to-battle-uber-and-grab/.

Schumpeter, J.A. (1934) *The Theory of Economic Development*, Harvard University Press, Cambridge, MA.

Schumpeter, J.A. (1950) *Capitalism, Socialism, and Democracy*, third edition, HarperCollins, New York.

Septiadi, E. (2011) 'Detik.com, Indonesia online portal news, is acquired with US$60 million value?', *Tech in Asia*, 4 August. Available at https://www.techinasia.com/detik-com-indonesia-online-portal-news-is-acquired-with-us-60-millions-value.

Solow, R.M. (1987) 'We'd better watch out', *New York Times Book Review*, 12 July: 36.

Statista (n.d.) 'E-commerce share of total retail sales in Indonesia from 2014 to 2019'. Available at https://www.statista.com/statistics/379170/e-commerce-share-of-retail-sales-in-indonesia/. Accessed 13 March 2017.

Sundararajan, A. (2016) *The Sharing Economy: The End of Employment and the Rise of Crowd-based Capitalism*, MIT Press, Cambridge, MA.

Triplett, J.E. (1999) 'The Solow productivity paradox: what do computers do to productivity?', *Canadian Journal of Economics*, 32(2): 309–34.
Velayanikal, M. (2016) 'Sequoia plays matchmaker: Go-Jek acquires 2 Indian startups for tech muscle', *Tech in Asia*, 19 February. Available at https://www.techinasia.com/sequoia-plays-matchmaker-go-jek-acquires-2-indian-startups.
Williamson, J.P., and A. De Meyer (2012) 'Ecosystem advantage: how to successfully harness the power of partners', *California Management Review*, 55(1): 24–46.
Williamson, O.E. (1991) 'Comparative economic organization: the analysis of discrete structural alternatives', *Administrative Science Quarterly*, 36(2): 269–96.
Wolf, M. (2015) 'The long goodbye: why the global financial crisis has cast such a long shadow', video, 9 September. Available at http://livestream.com/sipa/events/4331521/videos/98675999. Accessed 23 August 2016.
World Bank (2015) 'World Bank Enterprise Surveys: Indonesia'. Available at http://www.enterprisesurveys.org/data/exploreeconomies/2015/indonesia. Accessed 10 September 2016.
World Bank (2016) 'World development report 2016: digital dividends', Washington DC. Available at http://documents.worldbank.org/curated/en/961621467994698644/pdf/102724-WDR-WDR2016Overview-ENGLISH-WebResBox-394840B-OUO-9.pdf. Accessed 10 September 2016.
Zott, C., and R. Amit (2008) 'The fit between product market strategy and business model: implications for firm performance', *Strategic Management Journal*, 29(1): 1–26.

Table A13.1 Estimated impact of email use and having a website on productivity at firm level

Variable	*Ln (Productivity)*
Digitalisation proxies	
Email use	0.605***
	(–0.173)
Own website	0.409*
	(–0.188)
Control variables	
Age	0.00403
	(–0.00566)
Export status	
Indirect exports	0.0022
	(–0.00554)
Direct exports	0.0114***
	(–0.00276)
Constant	16.46***
	(–1.855)
Number of observations	898
Number of firms	491
Year fixed effects	Yes
Industry fixed effects	Yes

*** $p < 0.001$; ** $p < 0.01$; * $p < 0.05$; + $p < 0.1$.
Robust standard errors are in parentheses.

Table A13.2 Estimated impact of email use and having a website on exports at firm level

Variable	Direct exports
Digitalisation proxies	
Email use	7.353***
	(2.040)
Own website	8.557***
	(2.230)
Control variables	
Age	–0.0460
	(0.0704)
Constant	–0.876
	(22.880)
Number of observations	962
Number of firms	491
Year fixed effects	Yes
Province fixed effects	Yes
Industry fixed effects	Yes

*** $p < 0.001$; ** $p < 0.01$; * $p < 0.05$; + $p < 0.1$.
Standard errors are in parentheses.

14 A recent history of the Indonesian e-commerce industry: an insider's account

Bede Moore

This chapter presents an insider's account of the Indonesian e-commerce industry from 2011 to 2016. Despite several years of impressive growth, the Indonesian digital economy remains in the relatively early stages of inception. This chapter traces the origins of the tech industry from its beginnings in pioneer companies such as KASKUS, Rocket and Go-Jek, through to the now diverse array of start-ups and tech initiatives that are sprouting across the country.

It is hard to believe that only a few years ago, few people in Indonesia believed in the prospects of a domestic e-commerce industry. At that time, newly formed technology companies were struggling with the same problems that beset many other industries, causing many in the market to doubt that a robust industry could ever emerge. The ecosystem yearned for the sustenance of stronger physical infrastructure. Ageing, pre-digital logistics companies groaned under the pressure of parcel delivery growth. Powerful banks and a thicket of financial regulations had failed to nourish a simple, user-friendly online payments provider. Slow, labyrinthine bureaucracy complicated the process of establishing companies and of meeting corporate obligations. Financiers looking at these conditions wondered why they should invest in Indonesia. Most struggled to find an affirming answer.

Over the period from 2011 to 2016, Indonesia's technology industry blossomed despite these many headwinds. A small number of predominantly non-transactional, information-sharing internet companies were overtaken by a vast ecosystem of operators providing physical and digital wares as diverse as food delivery and bridal services. These new companies navigated and exploited the conditions they found in the archipelago—the ebb and flow of industry regulation, the weaknesses of ancillary industries to support their growth and the shortage of people with the experience to help them chart a successful course through these challenges—and were able to build large, well-financed technology companies that attracted the attention and investments of global financiers.

Today, Indonesia's growing digital economy is often touted by economists, entrepreneurs and even President Joko Widodo (Jokowi) as a flagship industry for Indonesia's future economic success. At a stretch, some would even argue that the country has built an internationally relevant technology industry. Several factors provide evidence for this claim. First, Indonesia has its own 'unicorn' (a company with a valuation in excess of $1 billion), as confirmed when private equity firm KKR invested $550 million in ride-sharing company Go-Jek in August 2016. Second, an Indonesian firm has achieved an internationally recognised 'exit' (the industry term for a sale or IPO), which took place when global internet giant Alibaba put in $1 billion to acquire a controlling stake in e-commerce site Lazada in 2016 (Chen and Wang 2016; Lee 2016). Finally, the number of venture-funded deals is climbing fast, with the number deals most likely doubling between 2014 and 2015 and the valuations of tech companies also rising (Wijaya 2016). 'People come here with fresh money because they see Indonesia as a second India', Steven Ghoos, chief executive of online real estate group Lamudi, told the *Financial Times* in March 2016 (Chilkoti 2016).

Alongside the appealing fundamentals of the Indonesian market—an enormous population, stable economic growth and rising smartphone adoption—the successes of Lazada, Go-Jek and a smattering of other companies have whetted the appetites of investors and focused attention on the enormous potential for Indonesia in the e-commerce industry. But the fanfare over some successful deals and strong macroeconomic fundamentals obscures the deeper question of whether Indonesia's political economy can successfully handle and support the growth of this new industry, or whether the commercial and policy-making environments will, rather, act as a brake on its development.

This chapter gives some insights into what it has been like on the ground for someone in the e-commerce industry, managing a digital economy business in Jakarta on a daily basis. It does so from the perspective of a foreigner, although most of the difficulties I mention would affect Indonesian entrepreneurs and their start-ups as well. By tracing the early stages of the Indonesian e-commerce industry, this chapter elucidates many of the challenges and opportunities of the emerging technology industry in Indonesia.

GETTING STARTED: THE VIEW BEFORE 2011

Like most developing countries, Indonesia largely missed the first phase of the internet industry. The advent of consumer internet prior to the dotcom crash in 2001 brought the internet, search engines and e-commerce to the world through now-household brands such as Google and Amazon. Suddenly consumers were connected with a previously unimaginable world of information and products. But there was one formidable barrier: accessing the spoils of the internet required a reliable terrestrial internet connection, and this was hard to find in Indonesia, even in Jakarta. Internet penetration remained the preserve of the fortunate. While even die-hard computer fans in the West found accessing the net over ratty phone lines unappealing, the situation was far worse in Indonesia, which had only an estimated 200,000 internet users in 1998 (Gunaratne and Idris 2000: 283).

A dearth of internet users meant there was no market online for companies looking to sell their wares digitally. Without any obvious 'opportunity', few Indonesian companies sought to build an internet presence, although there were some important exceptions. In 1999, with internet penetration still miniscule (Sen 2011), a group of Indonesian students based in Washington founded an online forum called KASKUS. At the time, KASKUS was not directly involved in e-commerce because the platform could not facilitate financial transactions, but the site's earliest iterations were still a 'proto' form of e-commerce, presenting Indonesians with a novel mechanism for trade beyond the traditional *pasar*. More formal attempts to create e-commerce sites—that is, where the entire transaction was undertaken on the website—were not financially successful, as epitomised by Lippo's optimistic Rp 100 billion foray into online shopping through its Lippo Shop (Kuswandini 2009). Nevertheless, the idea of online shopping remained afloat, and the growth of forums like KASKUS meant that the internet continued to function as a locus for trade, even if the transactions still took place offline.

In the mid-2000s, a second phase took off as the internet's momentum at home and abroad began to inspire a new set of Indonesian entrepreneurs to diversify the types of online businesses. Indonesia's first household technology names emerged during this era: Tokobagus (now OLX), DOKU and Tokopedia. These companies laid the groundwork for the local industry by expanding fundamental services (classifieds, payments, marketplaces) to new internet users, and they helped transform internet usage from interactions based predominantly on information sharing (government and company webpages, community engagement, searching) to interactions based on financial transactions. A fledgling e-commerce ecosystem was emerging in Indonesia, but it was still incomplete and a long way behind those in the developed markets.

In the late 2000s, two enormous upheavals led to a revision of Indonesia's status in the global technology landscape. Although companies such as KASKUS and DOKU had been quietly building an e-commerce ecosystem in Indonesia, the archipelago was little more than an 'other' column in the back of a banker's spreadsheet. Instead, Western tech firms and venture capital had been looking towards China and then India as emerging giants, and the collapse of Lehman Brothers in September 2008, which led to the global financial crisis (GFC), sharpened their interest. Collapsing banks and profits in the West sent skittish investors in search of safe assets, often abroad. Gold was the first safe haven, as it is in most crises. Then other asset classes found favour, including technology companies. Tech start-ups weathered the storm better than other companies, and new technologies, such as applications designed for the iPhone, proliferated in spite of the wider woes in the economy (Economist 2009). A similar trend could be seen across the Pacific, where China's e-commerce industry had been growing at 120 per cent on an annual basis since 2003, and only looked like accelerating further (Economist 2013). The resilience of technology companies both at home and abroad seemed to offer one solution for stranded investors.

As confidence in Western investments eroded, successive rounds of quantitative easing by the US Federal Reserve provided cheap money and lowered the risk of investing in developing markets. Bitten by the Asian financial crisis, Indonesia was now relatively well placed to profit from the malaise haunting Western markets. Its government and financial institutions had responded wisely to the 1997–98 crisis with a range of reforms that left Indonesia better prepared for the GFC than many of its ASEAN or developing nation peers. Owing in part to tighter bank regulation and low levels of government debt, the country navigated the GFC while still maintaining 4 per cent GDP growth—only its two larger northern neighbours, China and India, enjoyed better times (Thee n.d.). Indonesia's perceived resilience helped it gain the attention of international investors, and the country's rate of foreign direct investment climbed from $9.32 billion in 2008 to $15.29 billion in 2010.[1]

While this surfeit of cheap money washed around the globe, another great developmental stimulus was finally rolling across Indonesia: smartphone technology. Apple released its first iPhone worldwide in 2007. After a decade of sluggish page loads and emailing on feature phones,

1 The data are sourced from http://data.worldbank.org/indicator/BX.KLT.DINV.CD.WD?locations=ID, accessed 4 January 2017.

it suddenly became bearable to browse on a mobile device. Despite the dotcom bubble, technology companies had continued to make advances, which were rapidly adapted to suit new mobile platforms, leading to extensive application ecosystems and on-demand content. In developing countries, telecommunications companies played a crucial role in facilitating mobile adoption by rolling out mobile networks that would finally bring the internet to those who had never been able to connect through the terrestrial network. And Google did much of the rest, releasing a free, high-quality operating system, Android, which was readily adopted by low-cost smartphone makers in Korea, Taiwan and China. Now, the owners of cheap smartphones could enjoy access to the wide variety of applications and other services offered by Google at a fraction of the price paid by Apple users.

In the meantime, Indonesians were resisting the early rush to get involved in smartphone technology. Old habits die hard, and for Indonesian phone users this meant a long, slow break-up with BlackBerry Messenger (BBM) and the easy functionality of Canadian firm Research In Motion's BlackBerry mobile phone. Even while BlackBerry sales were dwindling globally, Indonesian consumers maintained their fervent loyalty to the brand—when the BlackBerry Bold 9790 was released in Jakarta in 2011, dozens of people were injured when a stampede erupted as customers pushed to get in line (CBC News 2011). The previous year, Android-driven smartphones had dropped below the $200 price mark in Jakarta and it had become trendy to use WhatsApp rather than the ailing BBM. Over the following three years, smartphone penetration climbed from just 15 per cent to 40 per cent of all phones in the country.[2]

The transition away from feature phones improved the quality and quantity of users' online interactions. Feature phones offered some internet browsing, and some of the cheaper ones even allowed some app use, although this was often limited to systemic applications such as Facebook and Twitter. As a result, there were still well over 100 million active feature phones in use in 2015. But the smartphone presented a formidable rival. These phones usually connected to the 3G network (instead of 2.5G, where most feature phones languished), and they boasted access to a cornucopia of applications through app stores. The lure of these applications—which would become the basis for everyday interactions with Go-Jek, Waze and Instagram—gradually enticed users away from the feature phone, and at the same time provided a launching pad for the nascent technology industry.

---

2 The estimates of smartphone and feature phone use in this section are sourced from Redwing Asia; see http://redwing-asia.com/market-data/market-data-telecoms/.

ROCKET

Seeing new opportunities abroad, Western technology firms began to invest more heavily and more diversely in developing countries. The information-sharing products of these firms were already wildly popular in Indonesia: the archipelago boasted two of the top five cities globally for Twitter activity in 2012, Jakarta and Bandung (Lipman 2012); Facebook use was widespread; and the use of messaging apps such as WhatsApp and its tenacious forerunner, BBM, was ubiquitous among urban middle-class youth. But now a new era was dawning with the physical entry of foreign players into the market who were prepared to make large investments to establish a foothold in the industry. Into this environment came the lead search party for e-commerce, Rocket Internet, which touched down in late 2011. Its arrival marked the beginning of a third phase in the history of the Indonesian technology scene, one characterised by the entry of foreign start-ups, with a physical presence in Indonesia, whose growth was propelled to a large extent by mobile-driven commerce.

At the helm of Rocket Internet stood a trio of German brothers, the Samwers. They had spent their youth copying successful American business models and replicating them in Europe. In 1999, while still in their twenties, they launched a German-language version of eBay, after their attempts to open a local office with the Californian company's blessing had been rebuffed. They were promptly bought out by the Silicon Valley giant for £35 million, within 100 days of starting operations (Sharma 2012). Their meteoric rise didn't stop there. Rocket expanded its horizons to gain experience in the developing world through the successful deployment of a fashion e-commerce site, Dafiti, in Brazil, and later by taking operational responsibility for the roll-out of Groupon in China. At the head of the family stood Oliver Samwer, the media-averse middle brother, who provided the operational smarts and drive behind the company's Asian deployments. Samwer intended to open a slew of e-commerce sites across the developing world, including several in Indonesia.

What seemed so obvious to the Samwers was frequently viewed as irrational by commercial operators in developing markets, including many in Indonesia. Instead of trusting in the macro trends (which Western entrepreneurs like the Samwers believed would result in the transference of technology and rapid growth in less developed parts of the globe), many domestic companies in Indonesia continued to believe that the barriers that had prevented the uptake of technology in the past would remain insurmountable. When Rocket's merchandise buyers went into their first meetings with major Indonesian distributors, they noticed that the most common response from their Indonesian counterparts was to question the plausibility of the e-commerce model for the archipelago.

Rather than seeing the opportunity, sceptics focused on the entrenched weaknesses in the Indonesian ecosystem—poor infrastructure, lack of trust in the safety and veracity of e-commerce sites, and shifting government regulation—which they worried would prevent the spread of e-commerce in the country, in spite of the successes of sites like KASKUS, the growth of local players such as BliBli and the accelerating penetration of smartphones.

Personally, I agreed with the Samwers' vision. I believed in the growth story, and I had moved to Indonesia to be part of it. I was intrigued by the history of the country and its transition to a modern economy. At university I had studied Indonesian history, and after several years in Australia with a global management consultancy, I asked to be transferred to its Jakarta office, where I assisted blue-chip companies to modernise their activities. The opportunity for e-commerce in Indonesia was obvious to me. I had lived through the birth and growth of e-commerce business models in the West and remembered the time when the same arguments about trust and reliability had been used in the United States (where I had studied) and in Australia. The opportunity to be part of the development of Indonesia's technology industry seemed a lucky and fortunate one. When I was approached by Rocket, I quit my job and signed up with them to launch Lazada.

Although most people inside the company believed in the story, many foreign companies and foreign investors shared the misgivings about the industry. They found it difficult to see past a set of commonly known facts that prejudiced their view of Indonesia: it was a victim of locally born terrorists; it was a majority-Muslim country; and it had been spectacularly bankrupted during the Asian financial crisis, precipitating the fall of a longstanding and stable (if corrupt and despotic) government and the wild depreciation of the country's currency. Could the recent growth story really be relied upon to continue in light of Indonesia's dubious and chequered past? Little evidence in the technology sphere existed to disprove their fears. Even in 2012, no company had yet managed to secure an exit of meaningful proportions. The general sentiment among many foreign and domestic digital entrepreneurs was that Indonesia promised so much, but had actually delivered so little.

Still, Rocket was not (completely) alone in its buoyant view of the Indonesian technology scene, nor was it the only conspicuous entrant into the market. Renowned American internet giant eBay entered the Indonesian market in 2012 through a partnership with Indonesian telecommunications company Telkom. Together they rebranded Plasa.com and converted it into Blanja, at a cost (to eBay) of $9.2 million, an enormous sum for the industry at the time (Cosseboom 2014b). Even more conspicuously, the world's leading internet company, Google, announced that it would establish a local office in early 2012. Aspects of the technology giant's offering had already been adapted to the Indonesian market, such as Google Maps, Voice Search, Google Translate and the Chrome Web Store, but the physical presence was intended to expand the number of local businesses online—in other words, to stoke the furnace of local e-commerce (Kevin 2012).

If the actions of global giants such as eBay and Google were not enough to disprove the doubters, by late 2012 another global player, McKinsey and Company, was adding its voice to the chorus of international companies singing the praises of Indonesia's digital future. The global consultancy firm released a report suggesting that Indonesia could become the world's seventh-largest economy by 2030 (Oberman et al. 2012: 1) and told of 90 million new consumers, as yet untapped, who would soon come online amidst continuing economic growth. The food and beverages, leisure, apparel and transport sectors were all projected to double in size by 2030, growing at or above 5 per cent on a compounded annual rate. According to McKinsey, the country was on the precipice of a seismic transformation.

By the time of the McKinsey report's release in September 2012, Rocket had been operating in the country for almost 12 months, and the early indications from inside Rocket's two largest e-commerce sites, Zalora and Lazada, were indeed looking very positive. The two sites had been live since February and March respectively, and over the course of the ensuing months, most market insiders could already see the impact on the local industry. Rocket's aggressive hiring tactics were the first signal of the companies' likely impact on the market. Its heavy reliance on recruiters to find strong local candidates meant that the size and scale of Rocket's investment were visible through the big bills it was generating with its head-hunters. Hundreds of young Indonesian graduates, many of them pulled from elite universities in the United States and Australia, began what would become lasting careers in the technology sector, even though very few of them had previous experience in the industry. As Lazada and Zalora grew during the first half of 2012, they quickly overtook their competitors in terms of traffic and almost certainly in terms of orders.[3] Their growth caught the attention of logistics companies, which fought to capture the new business by introducing services such as cash-on-delivery and shortened timeframes for urban deliveries.

---

3 At present, Indonesia's internet companies are privately owned and, like most retailers, do not release their sales data, which makes it difficult to determine the exact comparative sizes of companies. Nevertheless, other indicators, such as data on search traffic and conversations with service providers, allow companies to understand their relative sizes in the market.

But ultimately what overcame doubts in the local industry was the sheer growth in the number of active customers that occurred throughout 2012. On a daily basis, order volumes in Rocket companies were already well beyond anything seen previously in Indonesia. And the inception of the '12.12' shopping day at the end of the year was a symbolic achievement of the company's first year of operations. Teaming up to make best use of the combined market power of the company's several ventures, Rocket executives created 12.12.12, a jointly run day of discounts on 12 December 2012 modelled on the world's largest online shopping day, China's Singles Day (BBC News 2015). Rocket's leadership convinced other leading sites, such as BerryBenka, Plasa and Fimela, to participate in the campaign, leading to the largest day of sales for Rocket companies of the year, and starting what would become an annual event on the country's e-commerce calendar. The customer response was so strong that it proved to insiders how far the industry had advanced in a single year. It was a resounding note on which to complete a year of successful gains in Rocket's—and the industry's—fortunes.

In 2012, the very public success of several foreign companies was the Indonesian industry's most conspicuous development. In 2013, what became conspicuous was not just the performance of foreign companies, but the dramatic increase in the flow of entrants and funds. With mounting urgency companies and investors pursued new niches (fashion, toys, baby products) that were either 'empty' or open to competition. East Asian corporations and venture capital firms led the way. In January 2013, Japanese corporate giant Sumitomo set up Sukamart, the nation's first online grocery store (Sumitomo Corporation 2013). In the same month, Gree Ventures, a Japanese venture capital firm, led a significant investment round in successful online fashion retailer BerryBenka (Lukman 2013b). Other deals soon followed: the first investment by Japan's SoftBank in Tokopedia; Japanese venture capital firm Rebright Partners' stake in Adskom; and South Korean online firm SK Planet's $18.3 million founding investment in Elevenia, a joint venture with Indonesian telco XL Axiata (Lukman 2013a). By the end of 2013, the industry had recorded twice the number of investment deals as in the preceding year (Freischlad 2016a). The development of a robust local industry now seemed fully under way.

REGULATORY BARRIERS

Amidst the flurry of deals towards the end of 2013 came unsettling word of an impending set of new government regulations. Rumours emerged of an elaborate game unfolding at the government's foreign investment regulator, the Investment Coordinating Board (Badan Koordinasi Penanaman Modal, or BKPM), where some regulators seemed more willing than others to process the requisite e-commerce approvals. Representatives of foreign companies would often wait days for the chance to meet with a sympathetic official. The numbers of such bureaucrats gradually dwindled, and in 2014 what had become the de facto state of affairs at BKPM became law: the government officially placed e-commerce on the negative investment list, halting the flow of foreign capital into the fledgling industry (Emerhub 2016; Widyawan and Linklaters 2016).

The regulations were a sobering reminder of the fickleness of Indonesia's regulatory regime, but they did not entirely spoil the party. The need—and desire—for international capital remained a feature of the industry and funds continued to flow in 2014, with the total value of technology investment probably rising within most investment classes.[4] Tokopedia broke all previous industry records by raising $100 million from SoftBank and the famed American venture capital firm, Sequoia Capital (Cosseboom 2014a). Most of these investments were probably structured through a web of off-shore investment vehicles in order to mitigate risks for investors and bypass the government's new regulations. Nevertheless, big-ticket investments such as the Tokopedia deal were enough to allow foreign companies and investors to make sanguine remarks in public about the state of the market, although in reality the regulations made it more difficult for them to access foreign capital and dramatically increased the compliance and corporate costs for start-ups.

The new regulations also gave local conglomerates a significant advantage. Long used to operating within the uncertainties of the Indonesian legal system, they had both the appetite and the willingness to invest. By the final months of 2014, venture capital firms representing many of the leading business families in Indonesia were springing up across Jakarta. These firms undoubtedly saw an appealing opportunity in the rapid rise of companies such as Lazada, but it seems likely that their engagement with the industry was also encouraged and aided by the abrupt changes in the regulatory environment unleashed by the government.

---

4 A number of factors complicate efforts to assess the value of investments in the technology industry. Most importantly, almost all companies are privately owned and hence not required to disclose how much they raise in financing deals. It has been a feature of Indonesian e-commerce that the value of most deals is not disclosed to the market. Nevertheless, basic analysis of disclosures by tech companies suggests that the value of seed, series A and series B investments probably rose in 2014, even if outlier deals such as SoftBank's $100 million investment in Tokopedia are removed (Freischlad 2016a).

A total of four venture capital firms representing powerful families were launched between the end of 2014 and mid-2015, adding to the existing three, and thereby ensuring that the largest pool of capital deployed towards technology in Indonesia was effectively family money.[5] By the end of 2015, these powerful families held a significant stake in almost every large tech company in the country: Rocket Internet, GrabTaxi, Bukalapak, BliBli, KASKUS, Path, DailySocial, HappyFresh, aCommerce, Bridestory, Female Daily, Qraved, Munchery, YesBoss, MBDC Media, PropertyGuru, Kudo, Hijup, BoboBobo, Merah Puti and Adskom.[6]

THE UNICORN AND THE PRESIDENT

No company in the history of the Indonesian tech industry has enjoyed as much fanfare as Go-Jek, which started out providing a phone-based motorcycle transport service before developing an app to mimic the ride-sharing service developed by Uber. Finally the crown of home-grown king had passed from an ageing KASKUS to a new prince. Go-Jek deservedly assumed the mantle, not just because it was a wholly Indonesian success story (Tokopedia had been that), but because for the first time an Indonesian tech company had reached a mass audience by providing an everyday service that changed people's lives. Along with Go-Jek's affordable appeal came significant amounts of money from abroad, and a highly recognisable uniform that cloaked the streets of the capital as the company signed up new riders at lightning speed.

With Go-Jek firmly in the public imagination, the company's value extended beyond the commercial and into the political realm. Throughout 2015, as Go-Jek asserted its dominance over the domestic technology industry, Indonesia's new president, Joko Widodo, was attempting

---

5 The four new venture capital funds were Venturra Capital (with extensive involvement by the Riady family), Sinar Mas Digital Ventures (Widjaja family), Convergence Ventures (Bakrie family) and Emtek (Sariaatmadja family). The three existing funds were held by the Salim, Hartono and Soeryadjaya families. It is worth noting that large, successful business families have invested in e-commerce globally. The feature that sets the Indonesian market apart is that, in Indonesia, these family offices exert more influence over the industry as a whole.

6 Two obvious omissions from this list are Go-Jek and Tokopedia, both of which have almost certainly received some level of investment from leading Indonesian families as a result of Northstar Capital's investment in Go-Jek and East Ventures' investment in Tokopedia. However, as these two funds are not publicly associated with a specific family, they have not been included in the list.

to change the unfavourable political situation he had inherited upon his ascension. Jokowi was a harbinger of the 'new'; many Indonesians saw him as a people's president who would ride into the presidential palace and weed out years of entrenched corruption and venal rule. Indonesians elected him in the hope of a better and fairer future. What better represented a 'new' Indonesia than the ubiquitous green jackets of Go-Jek drivers and the modern service those drivers rendered in Jakarta?

A visit to Silicon Valley in October 2015 gave Jokowi the opportunity he was seeking to take political ownership of the technology industry. The president put together a delegation to accompany him to meetings in Silicon Valley to tout Indonesia's tech credibility. His entourage included Go-Jek founder and CEO Nadiem Makarim, plus the leaders of three other large home-grown tech companies, William Tanuwidjaya (Tokopedia), Ferry Unardi (Traveloka) and Andrew Darwis (KASKUS). Makarim neatly summarised the purpose of the trip to a *Kompas* journalist, stating:

> This is in the state's interests. I will meet with people in Washington DC and Silicon Valley to explain about start-ups in Indonesia. We want to tell them that Indonesia is a potential market for startup investment, not just India or China. [...] These small startups need assistance, both from local and foreign investment. They have not received injections from capital ventures and our role is to help them achieve that (Jakarta Post 2015).

The president's embrace of the technology industry continues to the present day and has led to some important changes in the way the industry is perceived and regulated. Aligning himself with Go-Jek's Nadiem Makarim and other tech idols like Mark Zuckerberg presented Jokowi with an obvious political opportunity—as countless other world leaders have found over recent years—but at the same time created a very public dissonance between the president's calls for foreign capital and the various regulations that were inhibiting it from entering the country. This tension between rhetoric and policy, together with the pressure on the president to make wider economic reforms and sustain the country's growth, led to a more mature government discourse on industry regulation. New e-commerce regulations released in May 2016 went some way to redressing earlier mistakes. Instead of lumping all technology businesses into a single monolithic category, the new regulations identified four different types of business model and provided distinct rules for each. Significantly, the businesses in all four categories would be open to some form of foreign investment (Freischlad 2016c).

Indonesia still has a long way to go before it lives up to the lofty name given to the president's latest policy to encourage start-ups, the National Movement for 1,000 Digital Start-ups (Gerakan Nasional 1000 Startup Digital). Jokowi says he wants the total valuation of the tech industry to reach $10 billion by 2020, a lofty aim that his 1,000 start-ups policy is designed to support. But for an industry that has delivered a worrying paucity of exits, profits or anything other than very large rounds of funding being distributed to consumers with low levels of disbursable income, there is good cause to be sceptical. That said, similar arguments were peddled in 2011 before the tech sector had a foothold and when nobody could imagine Indonesians being so indulgent as to trust a website with their credit card details. After a swift five years, nobody talks of trust any more, and even the country's ageing industrial dinosaurs all view an internet presence as a contemporary necessity. In five years' time, maybe we will all be hailing Jokowi as tech's political visionary.

FUTURE PROSPECTS AND CHALLENGES

The tech industry is particularly sensitive to political and economic stewardship, which will mean that the e-commerce industry will likely act as a leading indicator of whether the country is undertaking sufficient reform to support continuing growth. Many pundits and politicians neglected to read the fine print in McKinsey's 'Unleashing Indonesia's huge potential' report (Oberman et al. 2012). The 115 pages that followed the executive summary highlighted a raft of serious challenges that could prevent Indonesia from attaining a place as a leading global economy. While a large number of these challenges are applicable to the technology industry, four in particular are worth mentioning here: the lack of effective regulation, capital, talented staff and infrastructure. To solve these problems, there needs to be more effective regulation of the industry, including clarification of the role of foreign ownership; attraction of capital to support both early- and growth-stage companies; investment in resolving critical infrastructure constraints; and development of the capacity to nurture and attract appropriate talent to drive technological innovation. None of these issues are peculiar to Indonesia, and if they are addressed effectively, the outcome will contribute to a robust technology industry.

Stable, thoughtful industry policy, including a reasonable approach to foreign ownership regulation, is vital if the objectives of Jokowi's 1,000 start-ups policy are to be reached. Given the role foreign funds play in providing risk capital to developing markets, the issues involved in technology industry policy and foreign regulation are often intertwined and should be considered together. It is worth noting at the outset that debate over foreign involvement in the national economy rages in many countries, not just in Indonesia. Recent events in the West perfectly demonstrate the appeal of protectionist trade policies and the fear of foreigners that often underlies them. Britain's exit from the European Union is one example, while in the United States around a third of citizens have consistently told pollsters over the last 25 years that they view foreign trade as a threat, and many made clear how fervently they hold these views by electing Donald Trump (Newport 2016). Even in Australia, 80 per cent of Australians say they support tighter restrictions on foreign ownership of agricultural land (Jasper, Felton-Taylor and Vidot 2016).

It is also worth noting that restrictions on foreign trade are not entirely unreasonable in developing countries. Local industries often need time to develop before they can flourish, and the presence of large multinationals with economies of scale, access to capital and technological advantages can hamper or preclude the growth of local competitors. The example of China provides an enduring counterpoint to the arguments of the proponents of free trade. Protected by the Great Firewall and a swathe of other useful restrictions for the last 20 years, China has created an enviable local technology industry that includes some of the world's mightiest technology companies. By restricting the activities of companies such as Facebook, Google and most recently Uber, Beijing gave indigenous internet companies time to develop and to capitalise on the country's large internal market (Mozur 2016). China's protectionism was not without some downsides, not the least being that its technology companies have so far proven unable to replicate their success in Western markets. But to anyone seeking an alternative growth model to free markets, China's strategy is appealing.

The policy problem facing Indonesia's leaders is that the country's commercial and political leadership did not develop a clearly articulated policy to guide how the nation would approach the rapid uptake of digital technology and e-commerce until the last few years, by which time it was probably too late to replicate China's approach. Nor was there an attitude of urgency, possibly because substantive adoption of digital technology and commerce in Indonesia occurred only relatively recently. But the consequence of this failure to develop a clearly articulated policy was that the framework of the Indonesian technology industry was laid before policy-makers had decided on the level of integration they desired with the global industry. By 2013, when the first evidence of tighter regulations appeared, Indonesia had long since hewed to the Western technology backbone—Microsoft, Google, Facebook (including Instagram and WhatsApp), Twitter and other smaller players—meaning that for technology companies to be successful in Indonesia, they needed to master the use of these platforms. Simulating China's closed environment was therefore impossible in the short term because the country had not developed its own technology backbone and instead the core functions of the industry were being performed by Western companies. This necessitated continued interaction with foreign platforms and recommended an open attitude towards foreign skills and expertise.

Foreign involvement is also critical for most start-ups and Indonesia's policy settings must be sufficiently welcoming to ensure that foreign funds flow into the archipelago. Typically, foreign involvement in a company simply means that money has been invested by an overseas fund and, as a result, that a certain percentage of the shareholding of the start-up will be 'foreign owned'. Although there may be patriotic appeal to the idea of 100 per cent Indonesian ownership, in reality foreign ownership restrictions simply reduce the number of available investors and thereby the level of competition among those holding the capital. Lack of competition means that fewer ideas are tested in the marketplace, that companies may struggle to get the funds they need to succeed and that entrepreneurs have less leverage in negotiating fair terms for their companies. Foreign funds fill the shortfall in Indonesian capital and they add to the competition for deals that are in the best interests of entrepreneurs and their companies. Naturally the government will need to consider exemptions, such as start-ups within the defence sector, but for most companies, access to foreign capital is an essential component of their financing activities.

Investment in addressing critical infrastructure constraints will also play a substantial role in the technology industry's long-term fortunes. Physical infrastructure remains a thorn in the side of most e-commerce operators, not to mention the broader economy. As *The Economist* correctly summarised, there are 'too few roads, berths and systems; too many ships, cars and grasping hands, leading to high costs and lost time' (Economist 2016). Start-ups have been forced to find creative ways to solve these problems, and they have frequently succeeded, but at a heavy financial cost. The proliferation of package delivery services is one such example. Companies such as Lazada, Zalora and aCommerce have all built distribution centres in major cities outside Jakarta in an attempt to control delivery costs and improve reliability. They have succeeded, but at a cost to investors and their customers. According to *The Economist*, Indonesia's logistics costs are twice those of neighbouring Malaysia and three times those of the regional front-runner, Singapore.

In the same vein, the absence of an effective online payments system also hampers growth, although the causes are, unusually, the result of (mostly) good regulation gone bad. Indonesia's successful overhaul of its banking and financial system after the Asian financial crisis led to greater financial stability and institutional independence, but it also created a rigid system that has failed to adapt to new mechanisms of payment or to support the introduction of suitable systems from abroad (Busch 2016). Evidence of the system's failure can be seen at almost any Indonesian store that accepts credit card payments. Instead of having a single machine to process all cards, as in most countries, an Indonesian point-of-sale is cluttered with machines from most of the major banks. The same is true online: customers are offered an unwieldy array of payment mechanisms, one to suit the payment system of each individual bank. For the e-retailers, this diffusion of payment techniques creates a management headache (cost), wasting tech-team time on integrations and finance-team time on accounts. One of the country's largest e-commerce players maintains a team of over 40 individuals with the sole responsibility of reconciling bank transfers with online purchases. These glaring inefficiencies have not yet yielded an adequate response from the industry. Stefan Jung, a long-time player in the local industry and a partner at Venturra Capital, acknowledged the problem at a recent industry event when he asked rhetorically: 'Should I wait until the regulation in this space becomes more clear?' So far, the industry has answered in the affirmative (Freischlad 2016b).

Attracting and developing globally competitive human resources is the final big hurdle Indonesia needs to overcome to support a vibrant industry. For companies seeking to operate in such complex conditions, access to talented, well-trained staff is a must. Here again the industry is facing headwinds. At the heart of the issue lies a chronic shortfall in skilled graduates. For example, the Boston Consulting Group estimates that Indonesia currently produces 20,000 fewer engineers than the economy requires, and that only one or two universities produce graduates of sufficient quality (Tong and Waltermann 2013). Within the technology sector, this shortfall is compounded by the relative novelty of the industry, with heavy demand for sophisticated technical positions appearing only in the last few years.

Some of the country's leading tech companies have attempted to solve the problem by handling it offshore. Go-Jek signalled its intention to create a research and development centre in India in February 2016, and acquired two Indian technology companies to smooth the process (Chanchani 2016). The e-commerce services firm aCommerce, founded in Thailand, has also kept its R&D offshore in the absence of high-quality engineers to support the company's operations in Indonesia. Smaller companies are faced with the less appealing prospect of waiting for extended periods to fill positions – it took online retailer Bilna two years to fill the role of chief technology officer. According to the CEO of Ardent Capital, Adrian Vanzyl, a dearth of talent is the primary drag on growth: 'Why are things growing less fast than they can? The answer is talent shortage. That is the number one factor' (Aravindan and Nangoy 2016). If Indonesia's political economy cannot resolve the skills shortage, the country as a whole, and the technology industry more specifically, will suffer.

CONCLUSION

Will Indonesia weather the various challenges and emerge as a global titan of technology? The answer is not yet clear. Indonesia's fickle approach to foreign investment and (with some important exceptions) its ill-developed institutions meant that the country was late to develop an indigenous technology industry and that the current swathe of large companies are largely copies of similar Western organisations. Today, it is hard to imagine that the country will make the sort of enduring changes to its political economy that would substantially alter the technology industry's growth trajectory, despite the government's stated intentions of reform. The regulatory regime is likely to remain unpredictable; construction of adequate infrastructure and reform of the education system are likely to be slow. Overcoming the enormous challenges that exist in these areas will require a strong vision, extensive planning and careful implementation.

Nevertheless, the gilded optimism of McKinsey and others is not entirely misplaced. Indonesia has the world's fourth-largest population, and it has already managed to nurture several of Southeast Asia's most impressive technology companies. To bet against Indonesia would therefore be an error. It will continue to create large and important technology companies. With sound political and economic stewardship, it may even create world-beating ones.

REFERENCES

Aravindan, A., and F. Nangoy (2016) 'Talent shortage stymies Indonesia's tech scene', *Reuters*, 7 June. Available at http://www.reuters.com/article/us-indonesia-startups-idUSKCN0YT2SM.

BBC News (2015) 'China's Alibaba breaks Singles Day record as sales surge', *BBC News*, 11 November. Available at http://www.bbc.com/news/business-34773940.

Busch, M. (2016) 'Don't expect a rerun of the Asian financial crisis', *The Conversation*, 2 December. Available at http://theconversation.com/dont-expect-a-rerun-of-the-asian-financial-crisis-69474.

CBC News (2011) 'RIM Indonesia chief suspect in BlackBerry stampede', *CBC News*, 5 December. Available at http://www.cbc.ca/news/world/rim-indonesia-chief-suspect-in-blackberry-stampede-1.1089365.

Chanchani, M. (2016) 'Go-Jek to set up development centre in India with acquisition of C42 Engineering, CodeIgnition', *Economic Times*, 19 February. Available at http://economictimes.indiatimes.com/small-biz/startups/go-jek-to-set-up-development-centre-in-india-with-acquisition-of-c42-engineering-codeignition/articleshow/51048406.cms.

Chen, L.Y., and S. Wang (2016) 'Alibaba expands in Southeast Asia with $1 billion Lazada deal', *Bloomberg Technology*, 12 April. Available at

https://www.bloomberg.com/news/articles/2016-04-12/alibaba-to-pay-1-billion-for-control-of-lazada-e-commerce-site.
Chilkoti (2016) 'Fight to become Indonesia's Alibaba begins', *Financial Times*, 30 March. Available at https://www.ft.com/content/a20aecca-f55a-11e5-803c-d27c7117d132.
Cosseboom, L. (2014a) 'Indonesian online marketplace Tokopedia raises $100M from SoftBank and Sequoia', *Tech in Asia*, 22 October. Available at https://www.techinasia.com/tokopedia-softbank-sequoia-capital-funding-news.
Cosseboom, L. (2014b) 'Ebay wants to buy into Indonesia's ecommerce race, set to increase shares in Blanja', *Tech in Asia*, 10 December. Available at https://www.techinasia.com/ecommerce-indonesia-blanja-telkom-metraplasa-ebay.
Economist (2009) 'Technology firms in the recession: here we go again', *The Economist*, 15 January. Available at http://www.economist.com/node/12936523#footnote1.
Economist (2013) 'Alibaba: the world's greatest bazaar', *The Economist*, 21 March. Available at http://www.economist.com/news/briefing/21573980-alibaba-trailblazing-chinese-internet-giant-will-soon-go-public-worlds-greatest-bazaar.
Economist (2016) 'The 13,466-island problem', *The Economist*, 27 February. Available at http://www.economist.com/news/special-report/21693404-after-decades-underinvestment-infrastructure-spending-picking-up-last.
Emerhub (2016) 'Establishing e-commerce company in Indonesia', blog, *Emerhub*, 29 November. Available at http://www.indosight.com/blog/establishing-e-commerce-company-indonesia/.0.
Freischlad, N. (2016a) '5 years in review: Indonesia's growth in startup funding since 2011', *Tech in Asia*, 5 January. Available at https://www.techinasia.com/ndonesia-startup-funding-up-to-2015.
Freischlad, N. (2016b) 'Everything you need to know about payments, ecommerce, and venture capital in Indonesia', *Tech in Asia*, 24 March. Available at https://www.techinasia.com/payments-ecommerce-venture-capital-indonesia.
Freischlad, N. (2016c) 'More ecommerce opportunity in Indonesia as foreign investment bans are lifted', *Tech in Asia*, 1 June. Available at https://www.techinasia.com/indonesia-lifts-ban-on-ecommerce-investments.
Gunaratne, S., and N. Idris (2000) 'Indonesia', in S. Gunaratne (ed.) *Handbook of the Media in Asia*, Sage, Thousand Oaks: 263–95.
Jakarta Post (2015) 'Jokowi invites Indonesia's top startups on US visit', *Jakarta Post*, 22 October. Available at http://www.thejakartapost.com/news/2015/10/22/jokowi-invites-indonesias-top-startups-us-visit.html.
Jasper, C., A. Felton-Taylor and A. Vidot (2016) 'Vote Compass: most Australians want greater restrictions on foreign ownership of farm land', *ABC News*, 25 May. Available at http://www.abc.net.au/news/2016-05-25/vote-compass-foreign-investment/7432598.
Kevin, J. (2012) 'Google Indonesia launched, Rudy Ramawy chosen as country head', *Tech in Asia*, 31 March. Available at https://www.techinasia.com/google-indonesia-office-2.
Kuswandini, D. (2009) 'Shop till you log off: online shopping addiction takes hold', *Jakarta Post*, 14 February. Available at http://www.thejakartapost.com/news/2009/02/14/shop-till-you-log-online-shopping-addiction-takes-hold.html.
Lee, Y. (2016) 'Go-Jek raises over $550 million in KKR, Warburg-led round', *Bloomberg Markets*, 4 August. Available at http://www.bloomberg.com/

news/articles/2016-08-04/go-jek-said-to-raise-over-550-million-in-kkr-warburg-led-round.

Lipman, V. (2012) 'The world's most active Twitter city? You won't guess it', *Forbes*, 30 December. Available at http://www.forbes.com/sites/victorlipman/2012/12/30/the-worlds-most-active-twitter-city-you-wont-guess-it/#14a2eb986343.

Lukman, E. (2013a) 'Elevenia, a joint venture marketplace between XL Axiata and SK Planet opens in Indonesia', *Tech in Asia*, 13 November. Available at https://www.techinasia.com/elevenia-joint-venture-marketplace-xl-axiata-sk-planet-opens-indonesia.

Lukman, E. (2013b) 'Show me the money! Here are 30 funding rounds and acquisitions from Indonesia this year', *Tech in Asia*, 31 December. Available at https://www.techinasia.com/30-fundings-acquisitions-indonesias-tech-scene-2013.

Mozur, P. (2016) 'Chinese tech firms forced to choose between playing home or away', *Australian Financial Review*, 10 August. Available at http://www.afr.com/news/world/asia/chinese-tech-firms-forced-to-choose-between-playing-home-or-away-20160809-gqow5i.

Newport, F. (2016) 'American public opinion on foreign trade', *Polling Matters*, Gallup, 1 April. Available at http://www.gallup.com/opinion/polling-matters/190427/american-public-opinion-foreign-trade.aspx.

Oberman, R., R. Dobbs, A. Budiman, F. Thompson and M. Rossé (2012) 'The archipelago economy: unleashing Indonesia's potential', McKinsey Global Institute, September. Available at http://www.mckinsey.com/global-themes/asia-pacific/the-archipelago-economy.

Sen, K. (2011) 'Introduction: re-forming media in Indonesia's transition to democracy', in K. Sen and D. Hill (eds) *Politics and the Media in Twenty-first Century Indonesia*, Routledge, London: 1–12.

Sharma, M. (2012) 'Internet clone's Australian blitzkrieg', *Sydney Morning Herald*, 28 June. Available at http://www.smh.com.au/it-pro/business-it/internet-clones-australian-blitzkrieg-20120628-2143a.html.

Sumitomo Corporation (2013) 'Daily shopping e-commerce site Sukamart.com launches in Indonesia', news release, 9 January. Available at http://www.sumitomocorp.co.jp/english/news/detail/id=25497.

Thee K.W. (n.d.) 'The Indonesian economy after the global financial crisis', Indonesian Institute of Sciences (Lembaga Ilmu Pengetahuan Indonesia, LIPI), Jakarta. Available at https://crawford.anu.edu.au/acde/ip/pdf/lpem/2012/2012_10_24_-_SEADI_Thee_Kian_Wie.pdf.

Tong, D., and B. Waltermann (2013) 'Tackling Indonesia's talent challenges: growing pains, lasting advantage', *bcg perspectives*, Boston Consulting Group, 28 May. Available at https://www.bcgperspectives.com/content/articles/people_organization_leadership_talent_tackling_indonesias_talent_challenges_growing_pains_lasting_advantage/.

Widyawan and Linklaters (2016) 'Revision of Indonesia's negative investment list', Widyawan & Partners and Linklaters, February. Available at https://www.allens.com.au/pubs/pdf/asia/indonesia-negative-list-of-investment.pdf.

Wijaya, K.K. (2016) 'Indonesia's startup funding exploded in 2015 (infographic)', *Tech in Asia*, 11 January. Available at https://www.techinasia.com/indonesias-startup-funding-exploded-2015-infographic.

15 The Go-Jek effect

Michele Ford and Vivian Honan

Worldwide, debate is raging over the growth of app-based transport services as companies like Uber transform the way transport is provided and how consumers access it (Isaac 2014; Aloisi 2015). Often referred to as 'ride-sharing' or 'peer-to-peer' services, these companies connect passengers with drivers typically not formally registered for taxi work or car hire services through a smartphone app. Passengers pay a set rate, determined by the company, from which a percentage is deducted before the driver receives the rest.

Like other large countries in Southeast Asia, Indonesia has enthusiastically embraced app-based transport services. Indeed, Indonesian consumers have adopted app-based transport services with alacrity, hailing cars, motorcycle taxis (*ojek*) or even the noisy three-wheel vehicles known as *bajaj* with just a few taps on their phones. The proliferation of what is known locally as 'online transport' (*transportasi online*) has benefited from commuters' increasing frustration with traffic congestion and poor public transport, as well as the growing use of smartphones.

One of the most popular app-based transport services operating in Indonesia is Go-Jek, a locally owned venture whose drivers' signature green helmets and jackets can be seen on the streets of most major cities across the archipelago.[1] Such has been the rise of Go-Jek that it is not so much a form of transport as a phenomenon. As one journalist observed, 'school children, university students, office workers, even the governor of Jakarta ... everyone is talking about Go-Jek' (*Kompas*, 18 June 2015).

1 While Greater Jakarta remains Go-Jek's geographic heartland, the company has rapidly developed a presence in Bali, Bandung, Surabaya, Makassar, Yogyakarta, Medan, Semarang, Balikpapan and Palembang, and has announced plans for further expansion (Go-Jek 2016).

Even President Joko Widodo (Jokowi) is on record as a strong supporter of Go-Jek, having invited its chief executive officer to accompany him to the United States to sell Indonesia's digital potential (*Tribun News*, 22 October 2015). Jokowi's confidence proved to be justified, with Go-Jek raising $550 million in new capital in 2016 (*Digital News Asia*, 5 August 2016).

The introduction of this 'disruptive technology' by Go-Jek and others has not, however, been without its challenges.[2] Indonesian consumers may have embraced it, but there has been fierce resistance to Go-Jek and other app-based transport services from conventional transport providers, who have pressured authorities to rein in online providers. Pressure from the transport lobby has prompted transport authorities to assess the legality of the app-based companies, leading to attempts to ban them, the impounding of vehicles and the introduction of new regulatory measures. A second important element of the controversy around app-based platforms has been their impact on the welfare of motorcycle taxi drivers who have shifted to them and on those left behind.

What, in fact, has been the impact of the platform on this group of workers? Has it brought better wages and conditions, or simply increased levels of exploitation? Internationally, scholars have pointed to the erosion of 'traditional' labour markets, and subsequently of workers' rights, as a consequence of the introduction of demand-driven, app-based employment (see, for example, Aloisi 2015). What this assessment fails to consider, however, is the potential impact of this disruptive technology on workers in the part of the 'traditional labour market' known as the informal sector.

Formal sector employment varies in its reliability and conditions. However, in theory at least, workers in the formal sector are protected by laws regulating their relationship with the entity that employs them. While informal sector employment may be waged, it is not based on a formal legal relationship, so workers in this sector do not have access to institutionalised protection of their labour rights. The vast majority of Go-Jek drivers we interviewed had previously worked as conventional motorcycle taxi drivers or in other informal sector jobs.[3] As Go-Jek drivers, they continued to lack the job security or employment standards of

---

2 For a discussion of the literature on the origins of the term 'disruptive technology', see Christiansen (1997) and Danneels (2004).

3 We conducted interviews with 25 Go-Jek drivers, five Uber drivers, seven Grab drivers (car and motorcycle), nine traditional taxicab and motorcycle taxi drivers, and 33 consumers in Jakarta, Denpasar and Makassar between January and March 2016. We also interviewed four representatives of the Bali Legal Aid Institute (Lembaga Bantuan Hukum Bali). Unless noted otherwise, information is sourced from these interviews or from fieldwork observations.

workers in most formal sector occupations, but made the switch because they saw the opportunity for a higher income and more reliable access to customers. A less obvious (and unintended) effect of the rapid growth of app-based transport companies has been the emergence of greater opportunities for collective action. These companies refer to their drivers as 'partners' rather than 'employees'. But they nevertheless provide a focal point for drivers seeking to act collectively to demand better working conditions, which is not available to conventional motorcycle taxi drivers.

GO-JEK AND ITS COMPETITORS

Go-Jek was established in 2010 by Nadiem Makarim, an Indonesian graduate from Harvard working for McKinsey in Jakarta.[4] Makarim found himself resorting to motorcycle taxis to avoid the city's notorious traffic jams. Having spoken to many motorcycle taxi drivers, he pieced together a picture of their working lives, concluding that the majority spent much of their time waiting for fares. His solution: if drivers and clients could be connected, customers would have a better experience and the time of the drivers would be much better utilised, leading to an increase in their income and general welfare.

When it began operations in 2011, Go-Jek received orders for motorcycle taxis by telephone before progressing first to BlackBerry Messenger (BBM). It was not until its app was launched in January 2015, however, that Go-Jek truly took off. Within just a year, the app had been installed 10 million times and driver numbers had reportedly risen to 200,000. Having successfully made the transition from a phone-based service to the online environment, it occurred to the company's founder that drivers could also run errands, such as picking up chargers or buying cigarettes. By 2016, the company had developed 12 separate services, all offered through the app. Go-Ride, the new name for Go-Jek's motorcycle taxi service, is now complemented by two other transport services in Go-Busway's live-time schedules for Jakarta's busway system, and Go-Car. Go-Send and Go-Box offer courier and removal services. The popular Go-Food and Go-Mart apps have been joined by Go-Clean, Go-Massage and a mobile beauty service called Go-Glam. Go-Jek has also ventured into entertainment services with Go-Tix. The final element in the system is Go-Pay, a virtual wallet that allows users to pay for the services Go-Jek provides by topping up their balances using an ATM, or through mobile or internet banking (Go-Jek 2016).

---

4 For a personal profile of Nadiem Makarim, see Cosseboom (2015).

While Go-Jek was the first app-based transport service operating in Indonesia, it has since been joined by several other local and international players. Its multinational competitors include Uber, which arrived in Indonesia in August 2014, and the Malaysian company Grab, which entered the Indonesian market in June 2015 (Faisal 2015; Freischlad 2015).[5] Local competitors include a woman-only motorcycle taxi service in Surabaya; the Jakarta branch of the Organization of Land Transportation Owners (Organda); a nationwide, government-sponsored association of land-based transport companies whose members includes the Blue Bird Group (DPP Organda 2016); and a Jakarta-based company called Blu-Jek, which claims that 90 per cent of its drivers were previously conventional motorcycle taxi drivers. Go-Jek executives acknowledge that the entry of new players has increased pressure in the market. But despite stiff competition from Grab, in particular, Go-Jek remains a major player, with the greatest geographic scope in its operations and the most varied provision of services.

REGULATORY CHALLENGES

Attempts to regulate and even outlaw app-based transport services have presented a serious challenge to Uber and Grab, and to a lesser extent Go-Jek. The debate over regulation has focused on the failure of app-based transport services to comply with conditions associated with public transport licensing. As is the case in other jurisdictions (Isaac 2014), the fact that these companies do not pay taxes or for licence permits means that they are able to undercut the price of regulated public transport, making them cheaper and more attractive to consumers. Established transport providers subject to government regulation see app-based transport companies' ability to avoid the normal costs of doing business as an unfair advantage. Uber and Grab have been the primary focus of opprobrium because their car services directly challenge those offered by conventional taxis. They have also attracted criticism because of their status as foreign companies with no local links or offices. While still controversial, Go-Jek has benefited from its primary focus on motorcycle taxis, which, unlike taxicabs, are not regulated in Indonesia. Its indigenous roots also set it apart from its major competitors.

The transport lobby's calls for greater regulation of the app-based providers have been supported by the transport authorities. Matters first came to a head in June 2015, when Organda reported Uber for fraud, infor-

5 Grab's founder, Anthony Tan, and Makarim met each other at Harvard, and founded parallel businesses in Indonesia and Malaysia around the same time (*Bloomberg Technology*, 23 March 2016).

mation and electronic transaction crimes and money laundering, but also for violations of Law No. 22/2009 on Road Traffic and Transportation,[6] a 2014 government regulation on transport and a 1991 gubernatorial regulation on taxi operations (*Jakarta Post*, 21 June 2015). The Jakarta police confiscated five Uber cars following the complaint. Although these were later returned, a further 10 Uber cars were impounded in August 2015 (*Jakarta Globe*, 5 September 2015). In the following month, an official taskforce was created under the Jakarta Transport Agency to monitor and seize cars operating primarily through Uber, but also Grab, on the basis that they were privately owned and did not have the permits required to provide transport services (*Digital News Asia*, 17 September 2015). The taskforce announced that drivers would be charged under the 2009 law for operating an unlicensed public transport vehicle (*Berita Jakarta*, 17 September 2015).

The fact that Uber and Grab did not have Jakarta offices and did not pay Indonesian taxes was also a consideration for the taskforce. Following a meeting involving the Jakarta Transport Agency, the Jakarta metropolitan police and the Jakarta Transportation Council in August 2015, Uber and Grab were instructed to fulfil a number of legal requirements, namely to establish an Indonesia-registered legal entity; obtain an operating licence; demonstrate the possession of a minimum of five cars and a carpool for service and maintenance; and present evidence that their vehicles had passed the required inspections (*Kompas*, 7 August 2015, 12 August 2015). In September 2015, Mayor Ridwan Kamil declared Uber to be illegal in Bandung on the basis that it did not meet the requirements, including the requirements to establish a legal entity in Indonesia and to use the yellow licence plates mandated for public transport on its drivers' cars (*Nikkei Asian Review*, 10 September 2015).

Controversy again emerged on 7 December 2015, when the app-based companies appeared to gain a reprieve. Claims were made that the Jakarta governor, Basuki Tjahaha Purnama (known as Ahok), had granted permission for Uber and Grab to operate in the city. Organda responded by accusing Uber of lying, saying that in fact Ahok had merely stated that Uber could operate if it complied with registration requirements (*Jakarta Post*, 10 December, 2015). This exchange led to a further tightening in the regulators' stance. On 17 December 2015, the Ministry of Transport announced a ban on all app-based transport services on the basis that they did not meet the requirements of Law No. 22/2009 on Road Traffic and Transportation or Presidential Regulation No. 74/2014 on Road Transport (*Jakarta Post*, 18 December 2015). According to Go-Jek's vice

6 Motorcycle taxis are not mentioned in Law No. 22/2009. The text of this law is available at http://www.hukumonline.com/pusatdata/detail/lt4a604fcfd406d/nprt/1060/uu-no-22-tahun-2009-lalu-lintas-dan-angkutan-jalan.

president for marketing, management was very concerned when the ban was announced (interview, Jakarta, 18 January 2016). However, the mood quickly changed when the announcement was met with a mass public outcry and the hashtag #savegojek quickly became the top-trending topic on Twitter in Indonesia. Such was the public pressure that Jokowi intervened within a matter of hours to reverse the decision.

Following widespread demonstrations by taxi drivers on 14 March 2016, Ahok made statements urging Uber and other app-based transport services to follow the regulations (*Detik News*, 14 March 2016). At the same time, however, he stressed his support for the app-based transport companies, emphasising that 'they're a reflection of the times' (*Okezone*, 14 March 2016). Pressure nevertheless continued to build, with further demonstrations on 22 March. Two days later, a meeting was called involving the minister of transport, officials from several other government ministries and representatives from Uber and Grab, at which the government told the companies to comply with the legal requirements by 31 May (*Tempo*, 24 March 2016). As part of the guidelines set out at the meeting, drivers working with app-based platforms were required to join a cooperative or company and to obtain a public transport driver's licence. To meet these requirements, Grab established a cooperative called the Indonesian Car Rental Entrepreneurs Association (Persatuan Pengusaha Rental Indonesia, or PPRI), while Uber formed the Transport Service Cooperative (Jasa Trans Usaha Bersama, or JTUB). Go-Jek's car service, Go-Car, quickly followed suit, establishing a company called Panorama Mitra Sarana. However, just 419 of the 3,309 registered cars operating under these cooperatives and companies had passed the required road test by the deadline. The minister of transport responded by threatening to implement a 'three strikes and you're out' rule, under which if three cars from the same company were found operating without meeting the requirements, the company's public transport licence would be suspended (*Jakarta Globe*, 2 June 2016).

In the meantime, the Ministry of Transport announced a new regulation, originally meant to come into effect on 1 October 2016, to further address the conflict between conventional and app-based transport providers.[7] In addition to requiring the companies to hold a permit to operate and to pay tax, Ministerial Regulation No. 32/2016 on Non-route-based Motorised Public Transport places several restrictions on

---

7 A few days before the regulation was due to come into force, the ministry announced that it would delay its implementation in response to criticisms of the regulation. These included claims that the regulation violated the principles of the people's economy, and that there had been no process of public hearings or consultation with other ministries (*Beritasatu.com*, 27 September 2016).

app-based companies, including requiring them to work with registered public transport companies and to disclose data on cars and drivers to the Ministry of Transport.[8] It also prohibits companies from setting tariffs or driver incomes, and makes it illegal for information technology companies to directly recruit drivers. Importantly, however, the ministerial decision failed to regulate motorcycle taxi services, despite pressure from Ahok and others for Law No. 22/2009 to be revised to recognise motorcycles as a mode of public transport (*Jakarta Post*, 19 August 2015).

It is not clear if Go-Jek and other app-based transport companies will continue to be able to operate unhindered in the face of the growing regulatory pressures. What is clear, however, is that ride-sharing apps have generated a great deal of support from their customer base. Even while leading the crackdown, the chief inspector general of the Jakarta metropolitan police acknowledged that banning the apps would come at a social cost because people were dependent on their services (*Jakarta Globe*, 3 September 2015). In addition to the Twitter backlash, as many as 17,000 people signed a change.org petition calling for an alternative solution.[9] Uber has also benefited from strong public backing. Within just four days of the establishment of a government taskforce, 24,000 customers had signed a petition on the company's behalf (*Digital News Asia*, 17 September 2015). Support for the app-based providers was underlined by the backlash from consumers when Blue Bird encouraged its drivers to strike on 22 March 2016, with netizens again taking to Twitter to express their anger and uploading videos of taxi drivers breaking the road rules during the demonstration (*Metro TV News*, 22 March 2016).

IMPLICATIONS FOR MOTORCYCLE TAXI DRIVERS

Consumer pressure has bought Go-Jek, Grab and Uber time to find alternative solutions, such as establishing cooperatives and forming partnerships with official transport companies. But while the debate has focused on the impact of the apps on conventional taxi services, its effect on the nature of employment is equally, if not more, important. Many taxi driv-

8 The text of this regulation is available at http://jdih.dephub.go.id/assets/uudocs/permen/2016/PM_32_Tahun_2016.pdf. The regulation complements Circular No. 3/2016 on the Delivery of Application and/or Content Services through the Internet, issued by the Ministry of Communications and Informatics, which states that foreign app providers in all sectors must establish an entity in Indonesia and comply with local tax laws.

9 See https://www.change.org/p/menhub-tinjau-ulang-larangan-ojek-dan-taksi-online-kemenhub151?recruiter=30830812&utm_source=share_petition&utm_medium=whatsapp.

ers and informal workers have made the switch to online transport providers because of benefits such as higher incomes, as well as access to insurance and other forms of support. We found that a significant proportion of drivers at all four Jakarta motorcycle taxi ranks (*pangkalan ojek*) we visited had signed up to a ride-sharing platform. Those who had moved to Go-Jek said that their association with the company had brought benefits in terms of higher wages and better working conditions. Despite the obvious allure of these benefits, however, many drivers noted the continuing risks of this form of employment in terms of their diminished control over ride pricing and the absence of job security. These concerns have compelled drivers to act collectively in protest against unilateral changes to income-splitting arrangements and attempts to discipline their relationship with the company, in ways that are not available to conventional motorcycle taxi drivers.

Working conditions

Concern about drivers' incomes and working conditions is very much part of Go-Jek's foundational narrative, as reflected in its mission statement. According to the company website:

> Go-Jek is a socially motivated technology company that aims to improve the welfare of workers in a number of informal sectors in Indonesia. We partner with around 200,000 of the most experienced and trusted motorcycle taxi drivers in Indonesia [...] Go-Jek drivers say that their income has increased since becoming a Go-Jek partner. They also benefit from health and accident benefits, and get access to more customers through our application (Go-Jek 2016).

Go-Jek hires motorcycle taxi drivers of up to 50 years of age. They must have their own motorcycles, but are given basic training and are issued with two helmets, a jacket and an Android phone to be paid off in instalments. They are also covered by the company's medical and accident insurance, as are commuters; Allianz provides coverage of up to Rp 10 million for accidents, Rp 5 million for hospital expenses and up to Rp 10 million for lost items sent by courier.

Medical and accident insurance is of clear benefit for the drivers who choose to work for Go-Jek. At the core of the company's offering, however, is the technology that connects drivers to middle-class commuters, and thus increases the number of fares a driver can accept during the working day. Go-Jek's motorcycle taxi service, Go-Ride, allocates passengers to a driver using a global positioning system (GPS) tracker to determine which drivers are in the passenger's vicinity. Passengers are given a price before ordering, based on the distance of the trip and the time of day. Once at their destination, passengers can pay with cash or through the internal Go-Pay service on the app. Eighty per cent of the fare is allocated to the driver, while the remaining 20 per cent is retained by the company. Under 2016 tariffs, Go-Jek drivers earn far less per trip then regular motorcycle taxi drivers. For example, the standard price for the 13-kilometre trip between the gated community of Kalibata City in South Jakarta and Tanah Abang in Central Jakarta was Rp 50,000 in 2016, but Go-Jek charged only Rp 15,000. However, Go-Jek drivers have the potential to earn more than regular motorcycle taxi drivers because they accept more fares per day than the regular drivers and receive bonuses for completing a certain number of trips.

Over time, though, Go-Jek drivers' ability to accrue a large number of trips has declined. One Jakarta-based driver claimed he had made up to Rp 7 million per month upon first signing with Go-Jek in October 2015, but could make only Rp 1–3 million per month in January 2016. Another had recently decided to quit because of the increase in competition. Go-Jek drivers in Makassar had similar responses, with one driver saying he had experienced a more than 50 per cent drop in income between October 2015, when he joined the company, and February 2016. One factor in this development is the rapid increase in the number of motorcycle taxi drivers associated with Go-Jek. A second is the decision by the company to drop the tariff by 25 per cent from November 2015. When drivers complained to Go-Jek about this unilateral decision, the company told them to leave if they did not like it. Third, the company made changes to its points-based bonus system. Whereas previously drivers had received a bonus of Rp 50,000 for amassing eight points, they now had to amass 10 points to qualify for the bonus.

Go-Jek drivers continued to earn more than their peers even after these changes were introduced. The conventional motorcycle taxi drivers we interviewed reported earning Rp 50,000–100,000 per day, while Go-Jek drivers reported making a minimum of Rp 150,000 per day. There was nevertheless widespread dissatisfaction with the company's actions, prompting Go-Jek drivers to organise themselves. To some extent, their efforts have mirrored the informal associations of conventional motorcycle taxi drivers, which generally operate in a particular territory and coalesce around a particular rank; tend to self-regulate, for example by charging a standard fare; and may provide members with uniforms, access to repair equipment and sometimes an emergency fund (CDIA 2011; Energy and Resources Institute 2013). In other ways, however, they mirror the operation of a trade union in a formal sector workplace, as one would expect given Go-Jek's status as a pseudo-employer.[10]

---

10 For an overview of Indonesia's trade union movement in the post-Suharto period, see Caraway and Ford (2014).

Taking collective action

While the associations that have sprung up among Go-Jek drivers focus predominantly on creating a community, in Jakarta they have also begun to focus on shared demands that target Go-Jek's management. This tendency was clearly evident in a demonstration organised on 3 November 2015 in response to the reduction in the payment to drivers from Rp 4,000 to Rp 3,000 per kilometre, which had been announced the previous day. According to management, the company could no longer bear the cost of subsidising trips. It did not want to risk increasing prices, so instead chose to reduce the payment to drivers. Drivers reported that hundreds participated in a demonstration held outside the Go-Jek office. Some described the event as a strike, during which Go-Jek drivers across the Greater Jakarta region refused to take orders on their phones. Go-Jek management threatened to sack the striking drivers (*Jakarta Post*, 4 November 2015), but drivers confirmed that no attempt was made to follow through on this threat.

In December 2015, further protests broke out in Jakarta, Bandung, Denpasar and Makassar when Go-Jek ordered a mass suspension of drivers accused of creating 'fictive orders', a practice by which drivers maximise their access to subsidies and bonuses by using a second phone to make orders that they then accept on their Go-Jek accounts.[11] The largest demonstrations took place in Denpasar, where 1,400 drivers were suspended without notice and subjected to heavy fines, in some cases experiencing confiscation of their motorcycles for not paying the fines (*Kabar24*, 2 December 2015). Seventy of the suspended drivers approached the Bali Legal Aid Institute, which organised a meeting between representatives from the Ministry of Transport, the Ministry of Manpower, Go-Jek management and the suspended drivers; no agreement was reached, however.[12] When management offered suspended drivers in Makassar a choice between resigning or paying a fine, members of the Makassar Go-Jek Drivers Union (Serikat Driver Go-Jek Makassar) threatened to shut down the Go-Jek office and resign *en masse* (*Kompas*, 2 December 2015). The demonstration continued for a second day in front of the Makassar city government offices, where the drivers demanded that the gov-

11 One driver reported that he received up to 10 orders a day, but a 'cheating' driver could claim up to 30.

12 The Bali Legal Aid Institute is a regional affiliate of the Indonesian Legal Aid Foundation (Yayasan Lembaga Bantuan Hukum Indonesia, or YLBHI). This network of legal institutes was strongly involved in labour issues under the New Order from the 1970s. For a detailed scholarly account of YLBHI, see Aspinall (2005). For a discussion of its involvement in labour issues, see Ford (2009).

ernment meet with Go-Jek management to resolve this and other issues (*Kompas*, 3 December 2015). Several months later, the problem had still not been resolved, and drivers continued to communicate and organise through social media applications such as WhatsApp.

Ironically, one explanation for the high level of organisation among Go-Jek drivers is that many of them had previously belonged to a conventional motorcycle taxi service. Some had even previously organised resistance to app-based services. In August 2015, for example, the drivers belonging to the motorcycle taxi ranks located outside each of the gates to Kalibata City collaborated in a picket designed to stop Go-Jek and other app-based motorcycle taxi drivers from entering the complex, with support from taxi drivers and public minibus drivers who had also been affected by the rise of app-based services. This very effective action came unstuck when residents mounted an online petition calling on the motorcycle taxi drivers to allow drivers using the ride-sharing platforms to enter the grounds (*Merdeka*, 10 August 2015). By September 2015, the motorcycle taxi drivers were ready to admit defeat, and the majority have since signed up to Go-Jek or Grab. Indeed, the only drivers not to do so were those who did not have the correct documents or could not meet one of the schemes' other requirements (interviews with conventional motorcycle taxi drivers, Kalibata City, 25 January 2016). In the long term, however, the presence of a pseudo-employer means that the campaigns of the Go-Jek 'partners' have a better chance of success than those of the truly self-employed.

Impact on conventional motorcycle taxi drivers

Despite drivers' increasing disillusionment with app-based transport platforms, they recognise that those who have not signed up are worse off than those who have signed up, and in absolute terms. This belief is shared by conventional motorcycle taxi drivers and borne out by anecdotal evidence. For example, the income of one driver, who felt he was too old to join a ride-sharing platform, had dropped from Rp 100,000 to just Rp 60,000 per day.

Conventional motorcycle taxi drivers are also frustrated that the online transport companies are undercutting them and saturating the market. On a number of occasions, this frustration has boiled over into physical confrontation. On 1 September 2015, thousands of workers rallied outside the presidential palace, protesting against job losses and demanding better health insurance. Following clashes between Go-Jek drivers and conventional motorcycle taxi drivers, Jokowi invited representatives from both sides to the presidential palace in an attempt to mediate between them (*Jakarta Post*, 1 September 2015). A few months later, a brawl broke out between Go-Jek drivers and conventional motorcycle taxi drivers on the campus of the University of Indonesia in Depok (*Coconuts Jakarta*, 19 January 2016). Similar incidents have occurred in many other places. Such was the severity and frequency of conflict at the FX Sudirman shopping mall in Central Jakarta, for example, that Go-Jek set up a shelter for its drivers to protect them from intimidation (*Jakarta Globe*, 8 September 2015).

Conflict reached a new level on 22 March 2016, when Blue Bird taxicab drivers went on strike against the app-based platforms, including Go-Jek. As a convoy of taxicab drivers passed by Sudirman station they were chased by Go-Jek motorcycle taxi drivers throwing rocks and sticks, but the fight was broken up by police as the taxicab drivers began to respond (*Viva*, 22 March 2016). Elsewhere, a brawl broke out between the protesters and passing Go-Jek drivers, who were subsequently rescued by police. Shortly after, several waves of Go-Jek drivers approached protesters in front of the national parliament but were stopped by the police before physical contact could occur (*Antara News*, 22 March 2016).

Similar tensions have followed the path of the app-based transport services as they have expanded to other cities. Drivers interviewed in Bali recounted their experiences of intimidation and threats from drivers in the conventional transport sector. Several Go-Jek drivers in Makassar admitted that they chose not to wear their uniforms for fear of being targeted by regular motorcycle taxi drivers. In Yogyakarta, Go-Jek drivers avoided areas in which conventional motorcycle taxi drivers waited for passengers for fear that a fight could break out. Similar instances of conflict between Go-Jek drivers and other transport providers have been reported in Bandung, Medan and Surabaya. In short, while some have benefited from the rise of app-based transport services, these services have had a detrimental effect on the incomes of conventional motorcycle taxi and taxicab drivers.

CONCLUSION

As this discussion suggests, the rise of Go-Jek and other app-based transport providers in Indonesia has had a polarising effect. On the one hand, consumers have not only embraced the convenience and economy of app-based transport services but have also demonstrated their willingness to come to the defence of Go-Jek, Uber and Grab. On the other hand, transport authorities and taxicab drivers have vigorously opposed the unregulated growth of disruptive technologies that threaten the viability of conventional transport providers. App-based transport services have also proved divisive among motorcycle taxi drivers. Those who have decided to join an app-based platform have profited from greater demand, higher incomes and other benefits such as insurance. As these companies increasingly absorb market share, however, the working lives of drivers who do not join their ranks have become even more vulnerable than they already were.

In the long term, the initial benefits accorded to early adopters may be eroded by the platforms' ability to drive down costs as they achieve increasing dominance in the market; for now, however, predictions of the long-term effects of app-based transport services on drivers' working conditions remain speculative. What is clear is that rather than contributing to the informalisation of work—as has been the case in many other countries—the presence of app-based transport services has actually increased the level of formalisation in Indonesia's motorcycle taxi industry. App-based motorcycle taxi drivers are considered independent contractors and so are not covered by Law No. 13/2003 on Manpower.[13] This means that they do not have access to the job security and working conditions that are at least nominally guaranteed in the formal sector. It must be remembered, however, that—in contrast to taxicab drivers—conventional motorcycle taxi drivers are fully self-employed. Although they have long-established cooperatives, the absence of a shared employer limits their activities to fare setting and the provision of mutual benefits, akin to the activities of the guilds established by craftsmen in pre-industrial times. In short, app-based motorcycle taxi drivers now have a more structured employment relationship than Indonesia's conventional motorcycle taxi drivers, rather than the converse.

Go-Jek and its competitors claim that they are not employers. However, they are employer-like organisations in the sense that they not only set fees and regulate driver behaviour, but also have the power to discipline drivers by depriving them of access to customers and therefore to a viable income. As demonstrated here, an important element of this semi-formalisation has been the potential for collective action against one or more of these companies, and ultimately possibly for collective bargaining. The app-based motorcycle taxi drivers have already shown their capacity to act collectively. Although their protests and mass actions have thus far been unsuccessful, the potential for collective action to improve working conditions and income shows the benefit of this increased formalisation in an economy where informal sector employment remains the norm.

---

13 The text of this law is available at http://www.ilo.org/dyn/travail/docs/760/Indonesian%20Labour%20Law%20-%20Act%2013%20of%202003.pdf.

REFERENCES

Aloisi, A. (2015) 'Commoditized workers: the rising of on-demand work, a case study research on a set of online platforms and apps', Bocconi University, Milan.

Aspinall, E. (2005) *Opposing Suharto: Compromise, Resistance, and Regime Change in Indonesia,* Stanford University Press, Stanford CA.

Caraway, T., and M. Ford (2014) 'Labor and politics under oligarchy', in M. Ford and T.B. Pepinsky (eds) *Beyond Oligarchy? Critical Exchanges on Political Power and Material Inequality in Indonesia,* Cornell University Southeast Asia Program, Ithaca.

CDIA (Cities Development Initiative for Asia) (2011) 'Informal public transportation networks in three Indonesian cities', Manila. Available at http://cdia.asia/publication/informal-public-transportation-networks-in-three-indonesian-cities/. Accessed 9 March 2016.

Christiansen, C. (1997) *The Innovator's Dilemma: When New Technologies Cause Great Firms to Fail,* Harvard Business School Press, Boston.

Cosseboom, L. (2015) 'This guy turned Go-Jek from a zombie into Indonesia's hottest startup', *Tech in Asia,* 27 August. Available at https://www.techinasia.com/indonesia-go-jek-nadiem-makarim-profile. Accessed 9 March 2016.

Danneels, E. (2004) 'Disruptive technology reconsidered: a critique and research agenda', *Journal of Productive Innovation Management,* 21(4): 246–58.

DPP Organda (Dewan Pimpinan Pusat Organda) (2016) 'Tentang kami' [About the author], Jakarta. Available at http://organda.or.id/tentang-kami/. Accessed 9 June 2016.

Energy and Resources Institute (2013) 'Improving informal transport: case studies from Asia, Africa and Latin America'. Available at http://mirror.unhabitat.org/downloads/docs/11804_1_594697.pdf.

Faisal, F. (2015) 'Uber and Gojek just the start of disruptive innovation in Indonesia', *The Conversation,* 8 July. Available at https://theconversation.com/uber-and-gojek-just-the-start-of-disruptive-innovation-in-indonesia-43644. Accessed 18 August 2015.

Ford, M. (2009) *Workers and Intellectuals: NGOs, Trade Unions and the Indonesian Labour Movement,* NUS Press, Singapore.

Freischlad, N. (2015) 'Indonesian motorcycle taxi startup Go-Jek is hiring 16,000 new drivers at a sports stadium', *Tech in Asia,* 13 August. Available at https://www.techinasia.com/go-jek-recruiting-16000-new-drivers/. Accessed 18 August 2015.

Go-Jek (2016) 'Apa itu Go-Jek' [What is Go-Jek]. Available at http://www.go-jek.com/. Accessed 9 June 2016.

Isaac, E. (2014) 'Disruptive innovation: risk-shifting and precarity in the age of Uber', BRIE Working Paper 2014-7, Berkeley Roundtable on the International Economy, 7 December.

Index

Z

INDONESIA UPDATE SERIES

1989
Indonesia Assessment 1988 (Regional Development)
Edited by Hal Hill and Jamie Mackie

1990
Indonesia Assessment 1990 (Ownership)
Edited by Hal Hill and Terry Hull

1991
Indonesia Assessment 1991 (Education)
Edited by Hal Hill

1992
Indonesia Assessment 1992: Political Perspectives on the 1990s
Edited by Harold A. Crouch and Hal Hill

1993
Indonesia Assessment 1993: Labour: Sharing in the Benefits of Growth?
Edited by Chris Manning and Joan Hardjono

1994
Indonesia Assessment 1994: Finance as a Key Sector in Indonesia's Development
Edited by Ross McLeod

1996
Indonesia Assessment 1995: Development in Eastern Indonesia
Edited by Colin Barlow and Joan Hardjono

1997
Indonesia Assessment: Population and Human Resources
Edited by Gavin W. Jones and Terence H. Hull

1998
Indonesia's Technological Challenge
Edited by Hal Hill and Thee Kian Wie

1999
Post-Soeharto Indonesia: Renewal or Chaos?
Edited by Geoff Forrester

2000
Indonesia in Transition: Social Aspects of Reformasi and Crisis
Edited by Chris Manning and Peter van Diermen

2001
Indonesia Today: Challenges of History
Edited by Grayson J. Lloyd and Shannon L. Smith

2002
Women in Indonesia: Gender, Equity and Development
Edited by Kathryn Robinson and Sharon Bessell

2003
Local Power and Politics in Indonesia: Decentralisation and Democratisation
Edited by Edward Aspinall and Greg Fealy

2004
Business in Indonesia: New Challenges, Old Problems
Edited by M. Chatib Basri and Pierre van der Eng

2005
The Politics and Economics of Indonesia's Natural Resources
Edited by Budy P. Resosudarmo

2006
Different Societies, Shared Futures: Australia, Indonesia and the Region
Edited by John Monfries

2007
Indonesia: Democracy and the Promise of Good Governance
Edited by Ross H. McLeod and Andrew MacIntyre

2008
Expressing Islam: Religious Life and Politics in Indonesia
Edited by Greg Fealy and Sally White

2009
Indonesia beyond the Water's Edge: Managing an Archipelagic State
Edited by Robert Cribb and Michele Ford

2010
Problems of Democratisation in Indonesia: Elections, Institutions and Society
Edited by Edward Aspinall and Marcus Mietzner

2011
Employment, Living Standards and Poverty in Contemporary Indonesia
Edited by Chris Manning and Sudarno Sumarto

2012
Indonesia Rising: The Repositioning of Asia's Third Giant
Edited by Anthony Reid

2013
Education in Indonesia
Edited by Daniel Suryadarma and Gavin W. Jones

2014
Regional Dynamics in a Decentralized Indonesia
Edited by Hal Hill

2015
The Yudhoyono Presidency: Indonesia's Decade of Stability and Stagnation
Edited by Edward Aspinall, Marcus Mietzner and Dirk Tomsa

2016
Land and Development in Indonesia: Searching for the People's Sovereignty
Edited by John F. McCarthy and Kathryn Robinson

2017
Digital Indonesia: Connectivity and Divergence
Edited by Edwin Jurriëns and Ross Tapsell

www.ingramcontent.com/pod-product-compliance
Lightning Source LLC
Chambersburg PA
CBHW050224270326
41914CB00003BA/566

* 9 7 8 9 8 1 4 7 6 2 9 9 1 *